This is the first rural and cultural study of the great English country-man William Cobbett (1763–1835). It binds Cobbett's radical career to his rural heritage and to the experiences and politics of agricultural workers during the early nineteenth century.

As a Radical, Cobbett's first quest was to represent the hardships of the labouring poor, and he adopted the labourers' cultural experiences and class consciousness as the basis of his political platform. He revolutionized press history by joining the 'pedlar's pack', from where he dispensed his two-penny broadsheets along with other varieties of popular literature. The rural labourers understood Cobbett because he articulated their beliefs and values as expressed in their own folksongs and broadside ballads. They embraced Cobbett as a radical leader and as an educator, heeding his moral instruction, his treatises on cottage economy, and his prescriptions on the recovery of old England. Cobbett lived and moved among the labourers, and knew their political or economic grievances; thus long before the 'Captain Swing' rising he forecast the date and patterns of the revolt. His predictions came to pass and he became the single most important leader of the insurrection. His position of authority in the villages carried him forward in the cause of the Great Reform Bill and the Old Poor Law, so that by the end of his eventful career he was the sole public exponent of the cottage charter.

This is a major and original work on Cobbett, and represents a breakthrough in the study of rural popular culture and in Cobbett scholarship. It will appeal strongly to a wide range of social and political historians, and have much of value for all those interested in the language of class, the evolution of the English language and the history of journalism.

WILLIAM COBBETT AND RURAL POPULAR CULTURE

1 Cobbett in 1800. Reproduced by permission of Lady Lathbury.

Born at Farnham in 1763, Cobbett spent most of his boyhood and ado-
lescent years as an agricultural worker and gardener. In 1784 he enlisted in a
marching regiment, and after a year of military training at Chatham was sent
to a garrison in New Brunswick where he assisted to guard the Canadian
border from American incursion. After six years of duty the regiment was
sent home to England, where Cobbett requested and received his discharge
in 1791. Following a brief stay in revolutionary France he removed to
America, where under the pen name of Peter Porcupine he rose to fame as an
anti-Jacobin journalist. A steady flow of libel suits prompted him to return to
England in 1800.

WILLIAM COBBETT
AND RURAL
POPULAR CULTURE

IAN DYCK

*Assistant Professor of History, Simon Fraser University,
British Columbia*

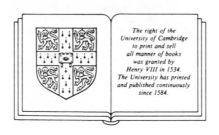

The right of the
University of Cambridge
to print and sell
all manner of books
was granted by
Henry VIII in 1534.
The University has printed
and published continuously
since 1584.

CAMBRIDGE UNIVERSITY PRESS

CAMBRIDGE

NEW YORK   PORT CHESTER   MELBOURNE   SYDNEY

Published by the Press Syndicate of the University of Cambridge
The Pitt Building, Trumpington Street, Cambridge CB2 1RP
40 West 20th Street, New York, NY 10011–4211, USA
10 Stamford Road, Oakleigh, Melbourne 3166, Australia

© Cambridge University Press 1992

First published 1992

Photoset, printed and bound in Great Britain by
Redwood Press Limited, Melksham, Wiltshire

A catalogue record for this book is available from the British Library

Library of Congress cataloguing in publication data
Dyck, Ian.
William Cobbett and rural popular culture / Ian Dyck.
p.   cm.
Includes bibliographical references and index.
ISBN 0 521 41394 X
1. Cobbett, William, 1763–1835 – Contributions in popular culture.
2. Great Britain – History – 1800–1837 – Historiography.   3. Great
Britain – History – 1789–1820 – Historiography.   4. Great Britain –
Rural conditions – Historiography.   5. Great Britain – Popular
culture – Historiography.   6. Agricultural laborers – Great Britain –
Historiography.   I. Title.
DA522.C5D93   1992
941.07′3′092–dc20   91–17636   CIP

ISBN 0 521 41394 X hardback

For my parents,
Clifford and Agnes Dyck,
farmers both

CONTENTS

List of illustrations   *page* x
Preface   xii
List of abbreviations   xiv

1 'Common cause': Cobbett and the village worker   1

2 The making of a Radical   14

3 Discovering class: countrymen, labourers and
   new-fashioned farmers   45

4 The battle for the pedlar's pack   76

5 Cottage economy   107

6 Old England: nostalgia and experience   125

7 'Rural war': Cobbett and Captain Swing   152

8 Towards revolution: the Reform Bill, the Poor Law and
   the cottage charter   190

   Epilogue   Ploughing the home field   213

   Appendix I   Popular rural song   219

   Appendix II   The petition of the hard parishes   222

Notes   228
Bibliography   273
Index   303

ILLUSTRATIONS

1	Cobbett in 1800	*frontispiece*
2	Cobbett in 1810–12	*page* 16
3	*Important Considerations for the People of this Kingdom*	26
4	Cobbett's house at Botley	34
5	Cobbett with the bones of Thomas Paine	43
6	'God Speed the *Plow*, and bless the *Corn-mow*'	54
7	'The Nobleman's Generous Kindness: or, the Country Man's Unexpected Happiness'	55
8	'The New-Fashioned Farmer'	57
9	'Times are Altered'	59
10	'The Poor Labourers'	61
11	'The Jolly Ploughboys'	63
12	'The Laboring Man'	80
13	'The Riot'	93
14	'The Methodist Parson or the Flitch of Bacon'	99
15	Cobbett on Long Island	117
16	Cobbett's house at Normandy near Ash, Surrey	118
17	*Mr. Cobbett's Petition to Parliament*	129
18	'The Roast Beef of Old England'	133
19	'A New Song. On the Loss of the Beef of Old England'	134
20	*Cobbett's Oppression!*	141
21	'Boys Wanted'	142
22	Roster of labour at Botley farm	144
23	Schedule of wages at Botley farm	146
24	'Honest Ploughman'	148
25	'My Old Hat'	149
26	*To the Rate-Payers of Kensington*	154
27	Cobbett in 1830	155
28	*Petition to the Honourable the Commons of Great Britain and Ireland*	158

29 'What will Old England Come to?'   163
30 *Arouse, People of England*!   167
31 Cobbett's *Two-Penny Trash*   170
32 *A True Account of the Life & Death of Swing,*
    the Rick-Burner   172
33 Confession of Thomas Goodman   173
34 'A True Englishman', *Imposture Unmasked*   174
35 Deposition of David Lovell   179
36 Cobbett's notes on the Hampshire Special Commission   180
37 Documents for Cobbett's 1831 trial   186
38 Cobbett in 1831   188
39 Cobbett in the House of Commons   203
40 'The Fatal English Poor Law Bill'   207

PREFACE

Several years ago at the University of Saskatchewan I was introduced to William Cobbett by Christopher Kent, and to the study of rural popular culture by Michael Hayden. As I began to observe a relationship between these two subjects I was interrupted by an encounter with the journalist in Dickens's *Pickwick Papers* who created an essay on Chinese metaphysics by joining the *Encylopaedia Britannica*'s information on 'China' with its entry on 'metaphysics'. But as I moved from *Rural Rides* to the depths of the eighty-nine volumes of the *Political Register* I became convinced that I was not on the path of Dickens's journalist: 'Cobbett' and 'rural England', it seemed to me, were so integrally related as to warrant their mutual study. Their appearance in tandem here, I hope, yields viable and refreshing new perspectives on Cobbett, Regency radicalism and rural popular culture.

Most of the research for this study was carried out at the University of Sussex where I had the good fortune to work with an English countryman in the person of Alun Howkins, who encouraged me from the start to pursue a rural and cultural approach to Cobbett. Eileen Yeo and Stephen Yeo taught me to attend to Cobbett's language and political context, while my fellow students in the History Graduate Division, especially Malcolm Chase, Rohan McWilliam, Mick Reed and Ruth Richardson, shared with me their understandings of popular radicalism and agrarianism in nineteenth-century England. I am also indebted to Edward Royle, Joanna Innes, Roger Wells and the anonymous readers of Cambridge University Press for providing helpful comments and suggestions on various parts of the text. Edward Thompson and Dorothy Thompson kindly offered their opinions on an early version of the opening chapter. Keith Snell did the same with the second chapter. I also owe much to Keith's steady encouragement and to his manifest conviction that culture and lore can legitimately be incorporated into the 'new' rural history.

Helpful in the early stages of the project was the late George Spater, who as a senior research fellow at Sussex often shared with me his unrivalled knowledge of Cobbett's private life. Without his masterful two-volume life of Cobbett, published in 1982, the present study would not have liberty to venture beyond matters biographical. A very special note of gratitude must go to my supervisor, John Harrison, whose intellectual generosity, together with his insistence that this Canadian farm lad be well-walked in rural England before writing about it, kept me happily to the task. I thank John for his counsel and for his friendship.

I am grateful for the generous assistance that I have received at the Bodleian and Nuffield College libraries at Oxford; the University Library and the Fitzwilliam Museum at Cambridge; the British Library and Museum; the Public Record Office at Kew; the county record offices of Hampshire, Kent and both halves of Sussex; the Goldsmiths' Library of the University of London; the London Library; the Vaughan Williams Memorial Library of the English Folk Dance and Song Society; and the libraries of Sussex and Simon Fraser Universities. For financial support I thank the Social Sciences and Humanities Research Council of Canada, the Canadian chapter of the Imperial Order of the Daughters of the Empire, the Committee of the Vice-Chancellors and Principals of the Universities of the United Kingdom and my own institution of Simon Fraser University. My appreciation is also extended to Linda Randall for her careful attention to the script, and to Michael Moore for permission to reprint some portions of an early version of chapter 2 which appeared in the pages of *Albion*.

Far from least I thank Karen Chappell for her patience and varied means of support. Over the last few years she has heard much talk about Cobbett's recipes for bread and beer, rather less about his advice that men and women take an equal hand in the preparations.

Port Coquitlam,   C.I.D
British Columbia
March 1991

ABBREVIATIONS

Adelphi	Adelphi University
BL	British Library
BL Colindale	British Library Newspaper Library, Colindale
BM	British Museum
BM Add. MSS	British Museum Additional Manuscripts
Bodleian	Bodleian Library, Oxford
BPL	Boston Public Library
Cornell	Cornell University
EFDSS	English Folk Dance and Song Society, London
Faithfull	Faithfull MSS, Nuffield College, Oxford
Firth	C. H. Firth collection of ballads, Bodleian Library, Oxford
Fitzwilliam	Fitzwilliam Museum, Cambridge
Goldsmiths'	Goldsmiths' Library, University of London
GVAC	*General View of the Agriculture of the County of...*
HO	Home Office Papers, Public Record Office, Kew
HRO	Hampshire County Record Office
Illinois	University of Illinois
JJ	John Johnson collection of printed ephemera, Bodleian Library, Oxford
LUCB	London University collection of broadsides
Madden	Madden collection of ballads, Cambridge University Library
NALU	National Agricultural Labourers' Union
Nuffield	Nuffield College Library, Oxford
NUWC	National Union of the Working Classes

NYPL	New York Public Library
Rutgers	Rutgers University
SC	Select Committee
SDUK	Society for the Diffusion of Useful Knowledge
Yale	Yale University

COBBETT'S WORKS

Advice	*Advice to Young Men and (Incidentally) to Young Women* (London, 1830)
Cottage Economy	*Cottage Economy: Containing Information Relating to the Brewing of Beer, Making of Bread, Keeping of Cows* ... (London, 1822)
Emigrant's Guide	*The Emigrant's Guide; in Ten Letters* ... (London, 1829)
George the Fourth	*History of the Regency and Reign of King George the Fourth* ... (London, 1830–4)
Horse-Hoeing Husbandry	Cobbett's edition of Jethro Tull, *The Horse-Hoeing Husbandry* ... (1731, London, 1822)
Hundred Days	*A History of the Last Hundred Days of English Freedom*, ed. J. L. Hammond (London, 1921)
Legacy to Labourers	*Legacy to Labourers; Or, What is the Right which Lords, Baronets and Squires have to the Lands of England?* (London, 1834)
Legacy to Parsons	*Legacy to Parsons; Or, Have the Clergy of the Established Church an Equitable Right to the Tithes...?* (London, 1835)
Life and Adventures	*The Life and Adventures of Peter Porcupine*, ed. G. D. H. Cole (1796, London, 1927)
Paper Against Gold	*Paper Against Gold and Glory Against Prosperity* ... (1815, London, 1828)
Poor Man's Friend	*Poor Man's Friend, Or, A Defence of The Rights of Those Who Do the Work* ... (London, 1826–7)

Porcupine's Works	*Porcupine's Works; Containing Various Writings and Selections . . .*, 12 vols. (London, 1801)
PR	*Political Register*, 89 vols. (London, 1802–35)
Protestant 'Reformation'	*A History of the Protestant 'Reformation' in England and Ireland . . .* (London, 1824–7)
Rural Rides	*Rural Rides in the Counties of Surrey, Kent, Sussex, Hampshire . . .*, ed. G. Woodcock (1830, Harmondsworth, 1967). Unless otherwise mentioned, references are to this edition.
Sermons	*Cobbett's Sermons . . .* (London, 1821–2)
Trash	*Two-Penny Trash; Or, Politics for the Poor* (London, 1830–2)
Treatise on Corn	*A Treatise on Cobbett's Corn . . .* (London, 1828)
Woodlands	*The Woodlands; Or, A Treatise on the Preparation of the Ground for Planting . . .* (London, 1828)
Year's Residence	*A Year's Residence in the United States of America . . .* (New York, 1818–19)

CHAPTER I

'COMMON CAUSE': COBBETT AND THE VILLAGE WORKER

I, as far as I am convinced, am quite willing to trust to the talent, the justice and the loyalty of the great mass of the people . . . I am quite willing to make *common cause* with them, *to be one of them*.

> PR, 24 April 1819, p. 980.

Nobody tells the tale of the labourer.

> PR, 22 February 1823, p. 482.

THE name William Cobbett inspires a variety of associations and meanings. For many readers he is the author of the delightful and often reprinted works *Rural Rides*, *Cottage Economy* and *Advice to Young Men*, where among other things, he offered instruction in how to court the opposite sex, plant a garden and fatten hogs. At the same time, and often in the same works, he turned his hand to economic and political commentary. His earliest writings, which alone constitute the twelve substantial volumes of *Porcupine's Works*, can be counted among the most influential pro-British propaganda during the second decade of the new American Republic. Upon returning home to his native England in 1800, he founded the *Political Register*, a leading periodical first in anti-Jacobin and then in radical politics, while on the side he originated the systematic collection and printing of parliamentary debates, better known today as *Hansard*. As a journalist he addressed open letters to the aristocracy, the middle class and the working class, as well as to individuals from kings, to prime ministers to country labourers. He socialized with the rich and the poor, dining in 1800 with William Pitt to celebrate the new measures against treason and sedition, and in 1832 with the farm workers to celebrate the Great Reform Act. Twice the government prosecuted him for fomenting popular disturbances; twice it circulated his writings to quell them. And among his several stage-credits are his performances as the soldier's friend, the king's advocate and the spokesman for the entire working class as a member of Parliament for Oldham.

Cobbett's diversity as a commentator on politics, society and culture is implicit in the cultural and ideological diversity among his admirers of past and present – a notable company which includes Karl Marx, Matthew Arnold, G. K. Chesterton, A. J. P. Taylor, Raymond Williams, Michael Foot, Asa Briggs, Edward Thompson and the ex-editor of *Private Eye*, Richard Ingrams.[1] Each of these writers, together with the numerous other essayists and the dozen biographers who have written on Cobbett over the past 150 years, has advanced our knowledge of this great Englishman; the problem is that the collective portrait has become polarized and fragmented to the point of reducing Cobbett studies to an exercise in free association. During the past two decades alone, he has been diagnosed as 'the consummate Utopian reactionary', 'the original patriarch', a 'most untypical Englishman' and 'the most English of Englishmen'.[2] He has been called 'the greatest Radical of his day' by one writer; 'incompetent as a popular leader' by another.[3] Some commentators even doubt whether he warrants the title 'Radical'; others prefer to characterize him as a 'father of reform', a founder of 'a new form of Tory-Radicalism', a popularizer of 'old-style Whiggish radicalism' or simply 'a maverick without party'.[4] The ironic thing is that each of these captions bears application to some moment of Cobbett's ideological evolution, but they have collectively reduced him to an ideological chameleon while leaving unposed and unanswered the question of whether there exists a dominant Cobbett or only a series of Cobbetts who waxed and waned according to opportunity and fortune.[5]

It is the neglect of Cobbett's rural and cultural associations that accounts for much of the current indiscipline in Cobbett studies, and in particular for the oft-heard lamentation that he is 'so difficult to classify'.[6] So preoccupied are we with industrialization and town-based politics that Cobbett has more often been denounced for his shortcomings as an urban and industrial witness than acclaimed for his service as a rural and agrarian one. It is certainly a sound historical method to enquire into what a given person or ideology is not, but this approach becomes a liability if we insist that contemporaries answer our questions ahead of their own. Industrialization and urbanization, furthermore, do not represent the full extent of historical process in the nineteenth century; indeed, we too readily forget that farm workers comprised the single largest occupational group in Regency England. Their subsequent decline in relative and absolute numbers was perhaps predictable from Cobbett's own day, but this does nothing to reduce their importance as historical actors and agents.

Miners, handloom weavers and domestic servants have experienced similar numerical declines, yet their stories, quite rightly, continue to be told and re-told without apology. Village workers, it is true, did not leave us an abundance of autobiographies; nor did they have many friends and supporters to articulate their experiences and aspirations. Yet it is precisely this archival disadvantage that should encourage us to delve more deeply into their past, and at the same time to take seriously a prolific contemporary who claimed to orient his culture and politics around their interests and experiences.

Cobbett's social and political commentary underwent dramatic evolution, but for too long his credibility has been crippled by an assumption that he was adrift in paradox and self-contradiction. Yet paradox can be no one's essence, and there is no more contradiction in his writings than one would expect of someone who composed for publication some thirty million words over the course of forty years. Thus in the manner of Edward Thompson's approach to the concept of class, we should not freeze or codify Cobbett at any one point in his career; much of his significance inheres in his very evolution from an anti-Jacobin to a Radical and from a countryman to a class commentator. Rubrics such as 'Whig' or 'Tory' are sometimes necessary to explain this evolution, but they have only a transient relevance for understanding Cobbett's long-term thought. For three-quarters of his public life he qualifies as a Radical in the full sense of the word, yet in order to understand the motivations and character of his radicalism we must appreciate the rural cultural mortar that gave shape and consistency to his discourse and ideology. It was rural popular culture, it will be suggested, that nurtured Cobbett's idiom, directed his reform programme and made of him a cultural as well as a political commentator. In turn, Cobbett volunteered as the rural labourer's leader in politics, economic protest and cottage technology. He believed this to be 'a rational ground for action'; and so ingested this 'sacred duty' as to assure one of his sons that he would 'think it no disgrace to be a labourer again'.[7]

Although this latter conviction was never put to the test, Cobbett was unable to separate himself and the condition of England from its country workers. 'I say WE,' he once informed Coke of Norfolk, 'because I never can separate myself from the Labouring Classes', and in particular from the agricultural labourers, whom he represented as 'the very best and most virtuous of all mankind'.[8] Shortly after returning to England in 1800, he made it his object to liberate the village workers, or 'chopsticks'[9] as he preferred to call them, from the condescension of the Whigs and Evangelicals, but by the 1810s he began to claim more for his rural studies, identifying himself as a member of the 'Order of Chopsticks' and boasting that 'I know more of their toils and sufferings than any other man.'[10] Had he never left his native Farnham, he mused before an audience of farmers in 1822, 'in all probability I should have been a labourer to this day'.[11] Cobbett's association with rural workers was in part an autobiographical mission, but he pursued that mission with a sense of responsibility and cultural sympathy that was unique in the English radical movement of the early nineteenth century. Of leading Regency Radicals, only Henry Hunt shared Cobbett's sympathy for the village worker, and then only intermittently. Richard Carlile would join Cobbett in falling afoul of the Whigs during the Captain Swing disturbances, but he was otherwise silent on rural subjects. Francis Place understood the rural worker as 'ignorant' and confused;[12] John Cartwright and Francis Burdett implied as much.

Sixty-five years ago G. D. H. Cole described Cobbett as a spokesman for the first generation of industrial workers who were 'torn from the land and flung into the factory'.[13] Cole's presentation of Cobbett as an industrial commentator with rural memories is not invalid, but efforts to locate Cobbett's significance in his industrial commentary have reduced his meaning to a series of negative caricatures: anti-urban, anti-industrial, anti-modern. At the same time the industrial focus has distorted Cobbett's competence by emphasizing his urban constituency at the expense of his rural following. By his own admission, Cobbett knew very little about industrial conditions; he was ill at ease with most manifestations of industrial protest (his advice to the Luddites to return to the plough, for example, was culturally significant but economically impertinent), and not until late in his career did he develop an appreciation of industrial trade unionism. Even Cole, the founder of the industrial approach to Cobbett's career, confessed that the town worker rejected much of the *Register*'s advice on political and economic matters. It was Cobbett's strength (and sometimes one of his weaknesses) to require direct experience of the conditions of labour, though not until his last years did he as much as enter a factory; and even then his experience was limited to the unrepresentative mills of Robert Owen and John Fielden. As Gertrude Himmelfarb has remarked, 'Cobbett did not "understand", or want to understand, a world of factories and factory towns.'[14]

This is not to say that Cobbett was without relevance to his industrial and urban audience. The fact that his writings appealed to industrial workers who aspired to return to the land meant that he articulated an agrarian ideal for industrial Radicals as well as a radical ideal for agrarians. In much of his political writing, as Edward Thompson and Olivia

Smith have shown, he articulated a political vernacular that brought the weaver, schoolmaster and shipwright into a common discourse.[15] Yet it must also be recognized that Cobbett was never comfortable with the culture of the workshop and factory, especially the secularist, republican and cosmopolitan creeds of London artisans. Nor was he averse to rebuking artisans and industrial workers who ignored agrarian protests or who assumed rural workers to be 'ignorant on public matters'.[16] When in 1821 Thomas Attwood accused him of ignoring the town worker, he defended himself without denying the charge: 'Born amongst husbandmen, bred to husbandry . . . it is natural that I should have a strong partiality for country life, and that I should enter more in detail into the feelings of labourers of husbandry than into those of other labourers. But, in my wishes and endeavours, I have the welfare of *all* in view.'[17] This emphasis on the rural worker might seem at first glance a divisive strategy in the popular radical movement. John Belchem has argued that during the 1820s, especially after the popular agitations on behalf of Queen Caroline, Cobbett 'deserted his popular audience' and his erstwhile ally Henry Hunt.[18] But Cobbett's apparent desertion of the radical platform of the town was to enable him to create a corresponding radical platform in the countryside. The creation of a countryman political union was the great object of his rural rides and of his attendance at county agricultural meetings throughout the late 1810s and 1820s. Just as many urban popular Radicals sought a working alliance with middle-class Utilitarian reformers during the 1820s, Cobbett sought to ensure the presence of rural interests in the reform movement by uniting rural labourers and employers on a country platform.

This is to say, of course, that Cobbett did not play a direct part in the events at Spa Fields or Cato Street or Peterloo, but to expect of him equal devotion to the platform of town and of country is to underestimate (and by implication, to undervalue) his contributions to political radicalism among farm workers. As James Obelkevich and Howard Newby have shown,[19] rural workers did not always come easily to radical politics or to class consciousness. Although they might not have needed a leader to the extent that Marx argued for the Continental peasantry, they were only loosely bound by common economic experience, for by the 'chopsticks' Cobbett meant not merely day-labouring men and women, but also farm servants, the piece-worker, the village craftsman who toiled part time on the land, and even the small farmer who worked his own land with his own hands and those of his family. Yet Cobbett did not feel that his task was in any way impaired by the so-called 'idiocy of rural life'. Face to face relations with employers, relatively low rates of literacy, as well as the labourer's much-maligned veneration for old England were not seen by Cobbett as liabilities upon the development of a political consciousness; indeed he turned these characteristics of village culture to radical advantage by arguing that they facilitated popular protest and class consciousness. Country people, he argued, are more difficult to 'deceive and cajole on political matters than townspeople'.[20]

In order to approach Cobbett and the Country political platform we must maintain the shift away from the old labour history conventions of divorcing politics from culture, of emphasizing town over country, and of assuming that the ideal Radical must almost volunteer for dispossession. We must also rethink the Regency and Victorian stereotype of Hodge that continues to afflict some species of English rural history in our own day, even if it now takes the rather muted form of statements to the effect that farm workers shared 'a sense of identity with the interests of their employers'.[21] The way ahead in rural history, as exemplified in the new journal by that title and in the work of historians such as Keith Snell, Malcolm Chase, Alun Howkins, David Jones, Barry Reay, John Archer, Mick Reed and Roger Wells, is to permit the village workers to inform us of their own experiences, complaints and pleasures – the 'cottage charter' as it will be called here.[22] Similarly, the starting point for our understanding of Cobbett should be his understanding of himself: a 'South-of-England' person, the son of a Surrey smallholder, whose most valued constituency was the rural workers of that region.[23]

Cobbett's relationship with the land and its workers has yet to be studied in a detailed way, though it has long been the subject of passing comment.[24] In 1874, as the start of the Great Depression renewed public interest in rural poverty, Richard Heath entitled an essay on Cobbett 'A Peasant Politician'.[25] Matthew Arnold, in 1880, remarked that Cobbett's politics were governed by 'the master-thought ... of the evil condition of the English labourer'.[26] For Leslie Stephen, J. B. Morton and G. K. Chesterton, Cobbett was the 'voice' or 'tribune' of the labourer or peasant; the Hammonds went further and declared his association with the village workers to be 'the key to his career'.[27] Not until the appearance of Raymond Williams's *The Country and the City*, however, were we provided with a sophisticated search for Cobbett's rural meanings. Williams rightly argued that Cobbett was radical in his 'class viewpoint' and 'persistent social questioning',[28] but the dominant context of Williams's interpretation was the 'structure of feeling' that Cobbett shared with other rural writers of past and present. Similarities there certainly were, but these should not cause us to ignore the immediacy of Cobbett's association with the rural society of his day. As George Sturt once remarked, 'Cobbett did not use his brains as his peasant and folk ancestors used theirs. Yet really he was nearer to them than to me.'[29] It is this extraordinary proximity to Regency rural experience that sets Cobbett apart from other rural writers; and it is important that we leave him oriented towards that society rather than steer him in the direction of 'eternal truths'. There are indeed, as H. J. Massingham discovered,[30] many 'Sons of Cobbett' in twentieth-century England, but to liberate Cobbett from his Regency context is to obscure the empirical causes behind his ideological incarnations, especially his transition to radicalism (chapter 2) and his subsequent evolution from a countryman to a class commentator (chapter 3).

The obscuring of the Regency context is an unfortunate side-effect of some of Professor Williams's work and of the assimilation of Cobbett's writings into anthologies of romantic prose. Many literary scholars have identified passages in Cobbett's texts which harmonize with the finest prose of Hazlitt or Wordsworth, but sometimes they have missed the implications of Cobbett's mastering grammar, not at Christ's Hospital like Coleridge, or Westminster School like Southey, but in an army barrack in the company of other ex-ploughboys; and when the time came to compose his own grammar of the English language (it sold 100,000 copies in its first fifteen years), he subtitled it 'especially for the Use of Soldiers, Apprentices, and Plough-Boys'.[31] In way of poetic inspiration, Cobbett was too suspicious of idealism and metaphysics to seek subject matter in Shelley's heavens or in the urns and nightingales of Keats. Even his well-known reflections about a disused farm-table derive from careful and sustained study of proletarian experience:

> Squire Charington's father used, I dare say, to sit at the head of the oak table along with his men, say grace to them, and cut up the meat and the pudding. He might take a cup of *strong beer* to himself, when they had none; but, that was pretty nearly all the difference in their manner of living. So that all lived well. But, the *Squire* had many *wine-decanters* and *wine-glasses* and 'a *dinner-set*', and 'a *breakfast-set*', and '*desert-knives*'; and these evidently imply carvings on and a consumption that must of necessity have greatly robbed the long oak table if it had remained fully tenanted ... Therefore, it became almost untenanted; the labourers retreated to hovels, called cottages; and, instead of board and lodging, they got money.[32]

Similarly, in chatting with a labourer near the beautiful hill of rotten Old Sarum, Cobbett's allegorical discourse on political corruption has its primary and functional truth, not in the dialogue's *internal* referents (the usual means by which literary scholars, especially structuralists, measure truth), but in its *external* referents – namely its empirical allusions to the labourer's experience of dispossession and hunger:

> I asked how he *got on*. He said, very badly. I asked him what was the cause of it. He said the *hard times*. 'What times', said I; 'was there ever a finer summer, a finer harvest, and is there not an *old* wheat-rick in every farm-yard?' 'Ah!' said he, 'they make it bad for poor people, for all that.' '*They?*' said I, 'who is *they?*' He was silent. 'Oh, no, no! my friend,' said I, 'it is not *they*'; it is that Accursed Hill that has robbed you of the supper that you ought to find smoking on the table when you get home.' I gave him the price of a pot of beer, and on I went.[33]

Cobbett's purpose in this dialogue was less to stimulate an emotional response in the reader than to offer political instruction to the rural workers. The dominant meaning of the passage therefore lies in its political prescriptions, which incline towards radicalism at the point where Cobbett directs the labourer beyond an ill-defined 'them' to the specific oppressions of 'that Accursed Hill', or the unreformed House of Commons.

Cobbett's uniqueness as a rural writer lies in his celebration of both the microcosm of popular culture and the macrocosm of radical politics. Rural popular culture was primarily the creation of the community or microcosm, or of the 'parish pump' as Eric Hobsbawm calls it.[34] It was Cobbett's quest to leave culture within the orbit of the village community, while at the same time providing workers with new and wider premises for their political thought. Thus one minute we find him directing the labourers into conflict with the ideologies of the ruling class, and the next defending the local sense of place of a labouring woman in a village near Andover:

> I got, at one time, a little out of my road, in, or near, a place called Tangley. I rode up to the garden-wicket of a cottage, and asked the woman, who had two children, and who seemed to be about thirty years old, which was the way to Ludgarshall, which I knew could not be more than about *four miles* off. She did *not know*! ... 'Well, my dear good woman,' said I, 'but you *have been* at Ludgarshall?' 'No.' 'Nor at Andover?' (six miles another way) 'No.' 'Nor at Marlborough?' (nine miles another way) 'No.' 'Pray, were you born in this house?' 'Yes.' 'And, how far have you ever been from this house?' 'Oh! I have been *up in the parish*, and over *to Chute*.' That is to say, the utmost extent of her voyages had been about *two and a half miles*!' Let no one laugh at her ... It is a great error to suppose, that people are rendered stupid by remaining always in the same place. This was a very acute woman, and as well behaved as need to be.[35]

By the 1830s, as we will see, radicalism was rife in this very district, including among persons whose geographic horizons were little wider than this woman's. A similar example emerges from Cobbett's acquaintance with a Preston man who broadened his physical sense of place (although hitherto never more than 8 or 9 miles from home) by taking a walking-tour of northern France, 'and that, too, without being able to speak, or to understand, a word of French!'[36] Here was an opportunity for an advertisement of Cobbett's *French Grammar* or of *A Year's Residence in the United States*, but nothing of the sort follows. Despite his notorious egotism, Cobbett represented the Andover woman and the Preston man as the cultural and intellectual equals of their rulers, and of himself. It was not in jest that he declared a carter or a hedger to be 'a more edifying companion than a *politician*'.[37]

The fact that Cobbett does not properly belong to high literature does not necessarily assign him a place in popular culture.[38] Yet this is his rightful home. Not only did he articulate political and economic problems in a language familiar to the traditions and experiences of rural folk, he disseminated many of his writings in the traditional manner of the marketers of chapbooks and broadside ballads.[39] Although himself the author of a best-selling *Grammar*, he also wrote popular sermons, theatrical plays, alehouse songs and broadside petitions – all of which he intended for oral dissemination and consumption. His expressed contempt for book-learning (a subject on which he remains misunderstood) was moved in part by his understanding that written cultural productions were too easily infiltrated by the dominant culture, and that these texts sought to isolate popular politics from common sense, oral traditions and from what he called 'the great teacher, experience' (chapters 4 and 5). Thus it was the language and politics of rural oral culture, especially of popular rural song, that Cobbett emulated when he represented the cottage charter (see Appendix I). Indeed, as will be seen in the following chapters, we can witness in both Cobbett's writings and in popular rural song a mutual shift towards radical politics and class consciousness.

The term most frequently invoked to identify Cobbett's reform programme is 'populism'. Cobbett's ideologies, as they unfolded after 1800, bore much in common with the Country Party platform of the eighteenth century, especially his animosity towards stock-jobbers, public credit, placemen and sinecurists.[40] Part of the ideological dynamic of the Country Party platform, according to Isaac Kramnick, qualifies as populist, 'even though an early and most aristocratic populist manifestation'. Inherent in populism, Professor Kramnick suggests, 'is a force at once intensely radical and revolutionary. It is always "the people", be they yeoman farmers, urban small traders, and failing gentry who are being victimized by the small conspiratorial financial interests.'[41] As we will see, Cobbett derived some of his reforming ideology from the Country platform as articulated by Swift, Pope and the early Dr Johnson, but even if the younger Pitt was to Cobbett what Walpole was to the Country Tory, the eighteenth-century Country critique was not the great moving force behind Cobbett's entry into radical politics. Country Tories (or for that matter, most Common-wealth Whigs) were neither democrats nor agrarians; the Country was for them an anti-bourgeois symbol designed to elevate the status and influence of the country gentleman, not that of his workers. Between 1800 and 1805 Cobbett shared the Country Party aspirations of placing the independent country gentleman in Parliament, but he subsequently shifted to distinctly radical terrain when he realized that the economic betterment of the English rural worker required actual rather than virtual parliamentary representation.

But even if Cobbett can be shown to have democratized the Country platform, and to have identified the Country with its proletarian workers, this does not deliver him from all constructions of populism. J. G. A. Pocock, for example, identifies Cobbett as both a radical and an 'authen-tically populist' critic of commercial society.[42] For the sociologist Donald Macrae, Cobbett is 'a very complete case' of English populism; while the economist Peter Wiles observes that except for his opposition to paper money, Cobbett is 'an otherwise perfect populist'.[43] A populist is understood by these scholars as someone who is anti-élitist and anti-cosmopolitan, as one who subscribes to a golden age theory, 'romantic primitivism', and physiocratic economics; the 'populist' is sometimes anti-urban, racialist, usually self-righteous and often anti-intellectual.[44] All of these symptoms apply in some measure to Cobbett, and nowhere more vividly than in the violent anti-Semitism that Professor Rubinstein has shown to be characteristic of too much nineteenth-century radical-ism.[45] But the conventional depiction of Cobbett as the ideologue of the smallholder ignores the fact that his mentor was the 'half a labourer', or peasant proletarian, of the southern woodlands and weald.[46] The problem with framing Cobbett as a populist (according to most definitions and examples of the term) is that it obscures the subtleties of his political evolution while leading us inexorably to the riddle of his affiliation with Juan Peron, Enoch Powell, Jimmy Carter and David Lloyd George. Would Cobbett have supported the Tichborne Claimant with as much enthusiasm as he supported Queen Caroline? And so on.

Isaiah Berlin has rightly stated that 'there exists a shoe – the word "populism" – for which somewhere there exists a foot'.[47] Even if Cobbett does not shatter the glass slipper, the explanatory utility of such cobbling is at best questionable. Populism has been called a 'mood', an 'ethos', 'a syndrome, not a doctrine', and even an ideology.[48] It is said by one scholar to have an agrarian focus or 'a more political focus'[49] (what does this mean: is the 'agrarian focus' something less than political?); others see it as an urban phenomenon, a democratic impulse or a style of dictatorship. Even if we follow the advice of many political theorists and arbitrarily reduce populism to popular rural radicalism, we are confronted with a catalogue of obscurities and contradictions. Some so-called populist movements (if I might invoke examples from my own agrarian heritage), such as the Co-operative Commonwealth Federation in the western Canadian province of Saskatchewan, have pursued left-wing ideologies, combining Owenite co-operation with Fabian gradualism and assorted schemes for the nationalization of farm land. In the neighbouring provinces of Alberta and British Columbia, on the other hand, populism has partaken of right-wing ideologies by giving a free hand to the agrarian capitalist and the urban entrepreneur, while cloaking it in the rhetoric of a Chestertonian distributism that goes by the party political name of Social Credit. The ideological differences between the CCF and the Social Credit parties are profound and important, yet for their mutual antagonism towards eastern Canadian bankers and financiers, they have become subsumed in the populist flock, with Cobbett holding the crook.[50]

In his important essay on Cobbett in *The Making of the English Working Class* Edward Thompson avoids the term 'populist', and therefore does not elicit the cacophony of symptoms that we have just reviewed.[51] Yet Thompson does observe that Cobbett blended radicalism and traditionalism, which is a key ingredient in most plenary definitions of populism. Thompson is not unaware that class consciousness and populist consciousness are usually seen as antithetical, especially when abstracted into categories or structures. He does not deny in Cobbett the existence of symptoms that others see as characteristic of populism, yet it is his deliberate reluctance to discuss these symptoms independent of cultural process that has come in for such staunch criticism in Craig Calhoun's *The Question of Class Struggle*. Populism, according to Calhoun, is the ideology of Cobbett and 'the most widespread body of public opinion in early nineteenth-century England', especially among village craftsmen and labourers. Populists can qualify as 'radical', he argues, inasmuch as they might reject capitalism and embrace democratic principles, yet they are 'fundamentally conservative' and 'reactionary' in that their primary object is the preservation of a traditional way of life. Yet despite the assurances of Professor Calhoun that 'class' and 'populism' are 'not diametrically opposed' and that they can be 'mixed with little sense of contradiction', he unwittingly treats them as conceptually exclusive ideological structures.[52]

Among Calhoun's major points is that the transfer from a populist consciousness to class consciousness requires two passports: there is needed 'an argument of exploitation based on the labour theory of value', and a 'new organizational infrastructure' (i.e. trade unions) to loosen the cultural and economic bonds of community and to provide the basis for 'collective action' that will affix the 'attention of men and women as workers, rather than as consumers'.[53] First, Cobbett developed a theory of exploitation and a labour theory of value. Second, he identified the working class as producers, representing the urban middle class and the aristocracy as consumers. Third, even though he did not formally charter trade unions, he sought to organize village workers for collective thought and action, performing himself the function of a responsible, and accountable, trade union leader.

In this study 'populism' will be understood, not as an ideology, but as Cobbett's method for studying rural society: 'hearing what gentlemen, farmers, tradesmen, journeymen, labourers, women, girls, boys, and all have to say; reasoning with some, laughing with others, and observing all that passes'.[54] If the populist does not always clearly define the 'people', Cobbett's method is populist; but when we move from his method to his discourse and activism, we find him prompted by his witness of the labourers' consciousness of class, which he sought to incorporate into his mission to make 'common cause' with the village worker. This is all to say that Cobbett's methodological populism did not corrupt his recognition of class society, and that his writings contain few of the demagogic devices that have been attached to modern understandings of populism. He sensed as much himself by taking issue with Dr Johnson's definition of a demagogue as 'a ringleader of the rabble', suggesting that it refers instead to one who comes forward in the name of the people: thus 'in the proper sense of the word, I am the greatest of all English demagogues'.[55] In sales money from his readers, Cobbett sought little more than his production costs, and as a practising farmer he went bankrupt before cutting back on his workers' pay. Even his gravitation towards radicalism originated in a set of experiences, accidentally obtained, which he interpreted with reference to common sense, cultural tradition and political innovation. Expressed another way, Cobbett was not psychologically propelled into sympathy with any one class in English society, which means that his alliance with rural workers commands us to attend to the cultural and economic experiences that induced him to devote thirty years to the representation of the cottage charter.

To some of us, perhaps most of all to historians of the metropolitan radical platform, Cobbett's rural devotions might seem overly reductionist. Perhaps they were. But for the village worker who was otherwise without representation in the public press, Cobbett's primitive union of 'chopsticks' was one of the most heroic stands in the annals of English labour. In former times, John Ball, Wat Tyler and Gerrard Winstanley had stalwartly represented the English peasantry, but Cobbett sustained his dialogue with village workers for more than a generation, and at the same time entered into a difficult and bitter battle with the ruling class in the name of the labourer. If his cottage charter was ignored by Whigs, Tories and most of his fellow Radicals, it was owing to an urban bias that prevailed at Westminster and the urban hustings alike.

Marx's observation that Cobbett was 'a plebeian by instinct and sympathy' carries the significant implication that Cobbett somehow transcended the high politics of radicalism.[56] In what manner Cobbett achieved this transcendence, Marx declined to speculate, but without such recognition Cobbett's instinctive plebeianism has only an abstract relationship to the culture and politics of the rural radical platform. Cobbett's reform agenda, if read independently of his instincts and experiences, contains little new or original. It was the Country Party platform that induced him to seek political stewardship from the independent country gentlemen; it was Major Cartwright who inspired him to endorse parliamentary reform; it was Henry Hunt who encouraged him to challenge the economic interests of the landlords; it was a speech by Samuel Bamford in 1817 that formally moved him from householder to universal adult male suffrage; and it was Thomas Paine who inclined him against the funding system and paper money.[57] Indeed, we can erode Cobbett's political originality even further: the Jacobin lecturer John Thelwall proclaimed during the 1790s virtually everything that Cobbett would ever say in way of criticism of the Pitt system, boroughmongers, commerce, the national debt, unmerited sinecures, the funding system and old England.[58] Where Cobbett stood apart from other Radicals was not in the broad subject matter of reform but in his efforts to create a national reform platform that belonged as much to the countryside as to London and the industrial towns. In the end he had more to say about the village than the town, but this was in a conscious and heroic attempt to redress an imbalance that throve in his own day as much as in our own.

CHAPTER 2

THE MAKING OF A RADICAL

The *clock* was gone; the *brass kettle* was gone; the *pewter dishes* were gone; the *warming pan* was gone ... the *feather bed* was gone; the *Sunday-coat* was gone! All was gone! How miserable, how deplorable, how changed that Labourer's dwelling, which I, only twenty years before, had seen so neat and so happy!

PR, 7 September 1816, p. 308.

WILLIAM Cobbett was born and raised 'a sort of labourer'.[1] Although less proletarian than most other farm workers (his father was a publican and small farmer) he experienced at first hand the toil and culture of late eighteenth-century agricultural workers. His later recollections of his youth, confirmed by the memories of other family members, were dominated by his setting off to the field in his blue smock-frock and woollen spatterdashes, together with his bread, cheese and wooden bottle of small beer. Like other country boys he graduated from bird-scaring and hoeing to 'the honour of joining the reapers in harvest, driving team, and holding plough'. For most of his boyhood years he was not less than a 'real and good and true ploughboy'.[2]

According to one of his brothers the young William showed tendencies of 'uncommon intelligence', but there was 'nothing about him of the prodigy'.[3] This accords with later portraits, for in his mentality and physical appearance Cobbett was infused with 'the ploughboy that continues to warm my veins'.[4] Even his very pen was held between fingers 'somewhat bent, from having been ... so often in close embrace with the eye of the spade and the handle of the hoe'.[5] We know from other witnesses that something approximating the nineteenth-century stereotype of Hodge was imprinted upon Cobbett's very countenance. At a public meeting in 1813 a Tory adversary, who had read Cobbett but never set eyes on him, nearly passed him over as one more 'bacon-eater' from rural parts:

I myself never saw this extraordinary character but once – It was at a county meeting in Hampshire ... If he had not been pointed out to me by one who knew him, I should probably have passed him over as one of the *innocent bacon-eaters of the New forest*; but when I knew that it was Cobbett, you may believe I did not allow his placid easy eye and smile to take me in.[6]

Twenty years and some twenty million published words later, a similar description was provided by another witness; this one perhaps the more significant for being drawn as Cobbett sat in uncontrived repose upon the benches of the House of Commons:

Never were the looks of any man more completely at variance with his character. There was something so dull and heavy about his whole appearance, that any one who did not know him would at once have set him down for some country clodpole ... who had never read a book or had a single idea in his head.[7]

The customary starting point for contemporary descriptions of Cobbett is Hazlitt's famous observation that he was the most powerful and eloquent political writer of his day,[8] but what escaped Hazlitt was Cobbett's association with the cultural and psychological world of the village worker. The personified or contrived dimensions of Cobbett's mentality, as both of the above witnesses inadvertently implied, was not his bacon-eating appearance but rather his forty years in public life.

In 1784, Cobbett's twenty-first year, he abandoned the plough for the musket, enlisting in a marching regiment which was garrisoned in New Brunswick for most of his seven-year tenure. The abandonment of the plough has been said by one of his biographers to contradict his later claim of happiness in rural life at his native Farnham.[9] This is unjust. Cobbett himself admitted that he had begun to long for new horizons and adventure, but not before his accidental sighting of the Royal Navy at Portsmouth in 1782:

I had, before my Portsmouth adventure, never known any other ambition than surpassing my brothers in the different labours of the field; but it was quite otherwise now; I sighed for a sight of the world; the little island of Britain seemed too small a compass for me. The things in which I had taken the most delight were neglected; the singing of the birds grew insipid, and even the heart-cheering cry of the hounds ... was heard with the most torpid indifference.[10]

A temporary ambivalence towards rural life was not unique to Cobbett; his own regiment, the West Norfolk, contained many other 'lads from the plough tail' who had similarly exchanged the smock-frock for the

2 Cobbett while resident in Newgate in 1810–12. Reproduced by permission of the Trustees of Botley Market Hall.

Cobbett's son James believed that this portrait by John Raphael Smith resembled his father in figure and dress, 'but the air of seriousness in his face has too much of the crabbed, and not sufficient of the full and florid in complexion' (J. P. Cobbett, 'Memoranda relating to Life & Times of Cobbett', 1855. Estate of General Sir Gerald Lathbury). A 'full and florid' complexion was Cobbett's frequent boast. After a rural ride or a day on the farm he would write 'I am as red as a rose', or 'my face is as hard as a farmer's heart' (Cobbett to Nancy Cobbett, 6 August 1832, 14 September 1826, Nuffield).

red-coat. A song of the 1870s, still in circulation among some country singers, tells their story:

> Once I was a merry ploughboy going to plough the fields all day,
> Till something came across my mind: I'd like to run away.
> For I was tired of country life and the places that I'd seen,
> So I came to be a soldier for her Majesty the queen.
>
> So I threw aside my old white slop and I threw aside my hoe;
> I threw aside my old white slop, no more to reap or mow.
> No more I'll work in the harvest fields or go and reap the corn,
> For I've been and took the shilling, boys, and I'm off tomorrow morn.[11]

Cobbett's uniqueness lay not in his decision to depart rural England but in his resolve to endure hunger and harsh discipline on sixpence a day, while many other of the ploughboy-soldiers opted to desert, sometimes out of 'sheer hunger'.[12] Yet it would be far-fetched to suggest that his perseverance, together with his part-time studies of English grammar and of the Country Party ideals of Swift and Pope, disqualify him as a countryman or 'a sort of labourer'.[13] His ambitions to get ahead were characteristic of most nineteenth-century working-class improvers.[14]

In 1791, upon returning to England and receiving his requested discharge, Cobbett encountered Paine's newly published *Rights of Man*, which propelled him 'headlong' into republicanism and democracy.[15] Likewise it was Paine's commendation of America that inspired Cobbett to choose the new Republic as his asylum from a probable court-martial in England for having attempted to launch one of his own against the officers of his former regiment.[16] But soon after migrating to Philadelphia in 1792 he began to feel betrayed by the new Republic's boosters: the landscape was displeasing, the climate 'detestable' and the people obnoxious. England, as he had discovered during his army years, had its corruption in high places, but here was an entire population that seemed 'worthy of the country – cheating, sly, roguish gang', he wrote bitterly.[17] If this was the cultural effect of republicanism and democracy, Cobbett did not want any part of these creeds. Furthermore, the important issue at hand, he believed, was to undertake a self-appointed diplomatic mission to prevent France and America from collaborating against Britain in the French Revolutionary Wars.[18] Ideology, as he later explained to William Pitt, was not his motivation:

> I was actuated, perhaps, by no very exalted notions of either loyalty or patriotism; the act was not much an act of refined reasoning, or of reflection; it arose merely from feeling, but it was that sort of feeling, that jealousy for

the honour of my native country, which I am sure you will allow to have been highly meritorious.[19]

Given his object of effecting an Anglo-American alliance, Cobbett could not be so iconoclastic as to eschew all association with high American politics. His diplomatic purposes most closely coincided with those of the pro-British Federalist faction led by Alexander Hamilton. It therefore befell Cobbett publicly to endorse the Federalist domestic platform, principally its ideal of strong central government under the direction of the merchants and manufacturers of the eastern seaboard. It followed in turn that he should distance himself from Thomas Jefferson's pro-French Republicans, including their commitment to democracy, decentralized government and the cultural virtues of the American frontier. But a suggestive hint on Cobbett's personal preferences is provided in his private expression of contempt for 'the base spirit of commerce'.[20] Further, his autobiographical *Life and Adventures of Peter Porcupine*, written and published in 1796, provides abundant notice that he associated moral rectitude and political independence with rural society and culture. Clearly, 'Peter Porcupine' (as Cobbett called himself in America, though Paine thought 'Peter Skunk' more appropriate)[21] had not altogether cashiered his early predilection for the Country Party platform.[22]

Cobbett's notorious attacks upon Paine and the French hardly touched upon political ideas, and his representations of Burke's *Reflections* styled the British monarch into a virtual democrat who smiled 'with equal warmth on the palace and the cottage'.[23] The cottage of rural America did not much concern Cobbett, but the little that he did know of it, when set beside his memories of Surrey during the 1770s and early 1780s, left him convinced that farmers and labourers in England were better 'fed, clad and lodged than people of the same description in Pennsylvania'.[24] It could be assumed, of course, that he was engaging in more political grandstanding, but his comparative assessment of standards of living accords with the findings of English agricultural commentators who toured America during the 1790s. Yet between them is one essential difference: the English agricultural visitors observed that the situation was moving fast in reverse as food scarcities at home reduced the standard of living of English rural workers.[25] Ignorant of this development, but full of anti-Jacobin promise, Cobbett returned to England in 1800.

Within days of docking at Southampton, Cobbett began to sense that something was changed from his boyhood years. At his native Farnham he found two of his brothers, small farmers both, to be obliged to 'work very hard' and 'far from being in easy circumstances'. As he offered them financial help, he learned that two of the three largest estates in the area had passed from the landed aristocracy into the hands of upstart merchants. And as he approached the public house he heard ordinary farmers trumpeting the high price of wheat and livestock.[26] These scenes were new to Cobbett, and dramatically out of step with the English rural society that he had described only four years earlier in *Life and Adventures of Peter Porcupine*. For now, however, he had other things on his mind, such as dinner engagements with prominent anti-Jacobins who flocked to pay him homage for his unsolicited services in America. He met with William Windham, George Canning, William Huskisson, Robert Jenkinson (the future Lord Liverpool) and William Pitt himself. At first overwhelmed by his enormous advance from ploughboy to dinner with the Prime Minister, he was gradually sobered by his realization that many leading anti-Jacobins were in receipt of government remuneration, and that at least two of them, Windham and John Reeves, held Pitt and his 'system' in private contempt. Government moneys, Cobbett alleged, were offered to him too, which he declined (though he did accept approximately £3,000 from Windham to begin a newspaper) on the grounds that he could more effectively contribute towards the destruction of republican principles from a position of obvious independence.[27]

In his daily newspaper *The Porcupine*, which carried the motto 'Fear God, Honour the King!', Cobbett resumed his diatribes against republicans, democrats and the 'perfidious and sanguinary' French. His paper was expressly intended for 'persons of property, rank, and respectability', but as the life of *The Porcupine* coincided with the great food scarcity of 1800–1, Cobbett periodically lowered his sights to the common people. Since even his own household was obliged to make do with a coarser loaf, he could not deny the reality of scarcity, but still he urged the gentry to proceed apace with enclosure and other 'improvements'. At the same time he denounced popular demands for peace and plenty as the result of Foxite and Jacobin foment of the 'swinish multitude' and 'vile rabble'. Throughout the scarcity Cobbett upheld a free market economy, and attributed the escalating poor-rates less to food shortages than to a new trend of idleness among working people. The English labourers, he maintained, had 'lost all that manly sense of independence, which *formerly* made them revolt from the idea of becoming a burthen to the parish'.[28]

What happened to change Cobbett? Can it be agreed with George Spater that he 'became a reformer by the same process that had earlier made him a reactionary'?[29] Not at all, for the two processes differ fundamentally. The slide from *Rights of Man* to political reaction had three roots: his wartime devotions to the British Crown, his disdain for

American politics and manners, and his ignorance of the state of rural England since his departure from Farnham. Expression of contempt for the common people was almost a prerequisite of anti-Jacobin discourse, and Cobbett was genuinely of the opinion that English workers had grown self-seeking, disloyal and even anti-English. Thus, while the process by which he had glided towards an anti-Jacobin conception of politics and of the 'rabble' had been only a matter of weeks in the autumn of 1792, his arrival at radicalism was a slow and painstaking process that simply cannot be characterized as opportunistic or arbitrary. Cobbett's radicalism was rooted in a set of experiences, accidentally obtained, involving popular rural sports, the Napoleonic invasion fright, the common land of Hampshire, pauper statistics and Poor Law reform. These several experiences informed him of the causes and extent of poverty among English farm workers, and from there he moved to his broader mandates as a political Radical with a national profile.

The early *Political Register* did not entertain the problems of the labouring poor. Its focus was on high politics, and its great object was to undermine Jacobinism at home and abroad. At Cobbett's side was his patron and mentor William Windham whose parliamentary speeches were given extensive publicity in the *Register*'s columns. But late in 1802, with the *Register* only months old, and with Cobbett a novice at social and cultural commentary, Windham temporarily departed from high politics and stepped forward as the leading parliamentary opponent of the evangelical campaign to reform the sports and recreations of the common people. Although at first unclear as to why Windham was taking up the subject, Cobbett felt obliged to side with his ally, and in the process received a lesson in the cultural and economic priorities of the dominant culture.

The rural society that Cobbett remembered, and the one that he thought was still in place, took great pride in its bruising and 'manly' recreations. Rich and poor, or so he thought, shared a taste for blood, whether divulged in fisticuffs, cudgels, cock-fights or bull-baits. This was not an inaccurate understanding of the middle decades of the eighteenth century, when as John Chamberlayne observed, the English labourers sought their evening recreation in 'Football, Cricket, Prison-Base, Wrestling, Cudgel-Playing, or some such-like vehement Exercise'.[30] Cobbett had shared in these pastimes during his youth; and he perceived them as expressions of the gladiatorial temper of the English, who with the patronage of Elizabeth and the nourishment of roast beef had defeated the Armada and achieved English supremacy of the high seas. But beginning in the 1770s and 1780s many country gentlemen took hard aim at the sports of the people, first by withdrawing their patronage and then by enlisting the aid of legislators and magistrates to crush the people's own sporting initiative.[31]

Harold Perkin claims too much in his remark that England was transforming during Cobbett's years from 'one of the most aggressive, brutal, rowdy, outspoken, riotous, cruel and bloodthirsty nations [into] the most inhibited, polite, orderly, tender-minded, prudish and hypocritical'.[32] But between 1780 and 1840, numerous writers complained of a middle-class conspiracy to steer popular culture in the directions of dandyism and effeminacy. Pierce Egan, for example, appealed for a restoration of the courageous recreations of old, with rich and poor sharing the same venue. Boxing, wrestling and village brawling remained, many sports writers observed, but the retreat of baits and cudgels was leaving a cavity in rural life, for the poor were without the means and authority to stage baits and cudgels on a community scale. The response of the Evangelicals was that the poor should be encouraged by force of law towards passive and Christian recreations which focussed attention on the spirit and self, whereas rural communities preferred robust and outgoing games, such as in the sporting relics sponsored and organized by Cobbett himself.[33]

Between 1805 and 1808 the dying martial game of single-stick was resurrected by Cobbett in his new village of Botley in Hampshire. The object of the tournaments, he declared in the advertising handbills, was 'to encourage, to reward, and to honour bravery and hardihood, from whatever part of England they might come'.[34] As much as 30 guineas – the average annual wage of a Hampshire labourer – was awarded for first prize, while out-of-county participants received at least their travel expenses. Thousands of spectators from all over the South travelled to Botley to witness this post-harvest spectacle of two combatants at a time, each with one arm tied behind his back, and equipped in the other with a stout stick, attempt to 'break' a head by drawing one inch of blood from the skull of the opponent.[35] Defeat was not readily conceded – the 1805 competition providing an example in the form of a Wiltshire labourer who entered the quarter-finals with his head 'not broken according to the rules of the match [but] swelled to an enormous size: one eye was closed up, and both arms and both sides were very much bruised'.[36] One competitor, Cobbett gleefully reported to Windham, even swallowed a broken tooth out of fear that to spit out the enamel would free blood to run the fateful inch.[37] Incidents like this, whether 'manly', foolish or both, do imply a formidable courage. More importantly, the combatants were said by *The Sporting Magazine* to retain a charitable disposition towards one another: verbal rancour and unpleasantries were almost unknown. 'The feats upon the stage', remarked an on-the-spot reporter in 1806, were too powerfully attractive of admiration, too well calculated to inspire feelings of the higher order, to suffer the intrusions of the petty passions ... For one day, at the close of the harvest, care and labour gave way to the exhibition at Botley, whence the spectators, retiring in every direction, carried to their families and their neighbourhoods the lessons of bravery and of fortitude that they had that day received.[38]

The cultivation of old English hardihood, within a context of regional rivalry, suited the labourer-contestants as much as it suited Cobbett and the other farmer sponsors. The labourers demonstrated their own solidarity by dividing the prize money among all contestants.[39]

The Evangelicals, meanwhile, were hard at work to repress the rougher of the popular sports, especially bull-baiting. In 1802 Sir Richard Hill appealed to the House of Commons to put an end to the 'barbarous custom'.[40] Baits *were* mean business, but the case of the abolitionists did not rest with the welfare of animals. William Wilberforce and the Evangelicals, long-standing opponents of even non-violent popular recreations, were no less concerned about large crowds, lost work-time and supposed immorality. Both Windham and Cobbett were quick to see that the Evangelicals' case against baiting was only one expression of an attempt to reform the manners and work-discipline of the common people. The cultural reformers, they argued, would have the labourers eat, sleep, work and nothing else, while reserving for themselves the violent hunt and rowdy horse race.[41] In Windham's words to Parliament, the poor could justly say:

> why interfere with the few sports that we have, while you leave to yourself and the rich so great a variety? You have your carriages, your town-houses, and your country-houses; your balls, your plays, your operas, your masquerades, your card-parties, your books, your dogs, and your horses to amuse you – On yourselves you lay no restraint – But from us you wish to take the little that we have?[42]

The campaign of Windham and Cobbett can be counted among the last great efforts by Country Tories to maintain fair play as an ideological canon of rich and poor alike. Their purposes were not without objectives of social control, but they cannot be reduced to this alone. Theirs was a strategy consistent with their opposition to most species of innovation; and in light of the number of popular songs that celebrate cultural co-operation between élite and non-élite, it is probable that they expressed the wishes of most village workers.[43]

On the subject of popular sports Cobbett grew as hostile to the Evangelicals as to the Radicals, lumping them together as mutual enemies of

Englishness and of physical hardihood.[44] For the time being he ranked Englishness and hierarchy ahead of class, but the sporting issue neverthe-less challenged some of his fundamental assumptions about English so-ciety. It taught him that 'innovation' could be cultural as well as political, and that not all anti-Jacobins were prepared to exercise fair play towards those who provided the comforts of the élite. Of course, Cobbett remained in Tory ranks; the campaign against rural sports did not drive Windham towards radicalism, nor would it alone propel Cobbett there. And yet, though a keen defender of cultural interaction between peasant and peer, Cobbett even now entertained a notion that seems more radical than Tory: 'something must be left', he contended, 'and something ought to be left, to the sense and reason and morality and religion of the people'.[45] Here, very quietly, he differed with Windham and that part of the Country Party platform which promoted independence for the gentry, dependence for their workers.

Cobbett's willingness to allow a degree of cultural independence to the common people was guided by his understanding – a mistaken one – that the labourers of England were naturally committed to the preservation of all traditional institutions in church and state. Even during his American days he had remained convinced that working people were decidedly in favour of the established order, and that they were innately loyal, passive and ill-disposed towards protest. Indeed, it was this understanding that induced him to limit his anti-Jacobin energies to the established press; he did not yet appreciate that radical ideology could arise independently of print. Once again, he was victimized by his twenty-year absence from rural England.

Although far from embracing radicalism, Cobbett was beginning to explore ideological currents that he would later enlist in radical service. In America he had declared that 'I have no pretensions to *patriotism*', by which he meant that he was 'guided by truth' rather than the 'public will', and that he rejected the Country Party allegations that the English govern-ment was corrupt and its Constitution imbalanced.[46] But even as an anti-Jacobin propagandist, he was nearer to the eighteenth-century Coun-try Party opposition than he liked to admit. During his youth and army service he spent much of his spare time reading the Augustan satires of Swift, Pope and the early Samuel Johnson, and it was surely these writings that convinced him of the virtues of independence from the public will on one hand, and from government remuneration (whether in the form of pensions or places) on the other. This Country Party understanding of 'patriotism' as entailing the 'independence' of the élite was of course oppositional to Pitt's government, but by the 1770s, as Hugh Cunningham

has shown, both government supporters and Country Tories had abandoned the language of patriotism to Radicals, for whom the word meant
the natural and historic rights of freeborn Englishmen.[47] In 1800 this was
not Cobbett's understanding of patriotism, but when during the invasion
scare of 1803–4 the government made a bid to reclaim patriotism in the
name of single-minded loyalty to the established political order, Cobbett
used the semantic dislocation as an opportunity to discuss the need for
independence at all levels of society, whether from the parish rates or from
government funds.

The return of armed conflict with France in the summer of 1803 permitted
Cobbett little time to involve himself directly with the problems of village
workers. As the threat of French invasion mounted, he became increasingly preoccupied with national defence. The same was true of numerous
other writers who plied the labourers with security propaganda.[48] Wilberforce, Richard Sheridan and Hannah More – all vocal critics of popular
sports – were among the first to solicit the rural poor to take up arms.[49]

The ruling class was aware that farm workers were without rational
cause to fight for England. Thus in reply to the argument that the poor had
nothing to lose from French occupation, they would resort to half-truths
and exaggerated alarms. The poor, reasoned one commentator, are always

> the first victims of a violent and protracted War; because they always
> constitute the bulk of a nation, and are least able to bear the hardships of
> Plunder and Desolation. When the Rich are pillaged, the Poor lose the price
> of their labour; and when daily employment fails, Death stares the poor in
> the face.[50]

The French will take your mahogany tea-chest, your pewter tea-spoon,
and your Sunday apparel, said one writer; they will lower wages and
increase taxes, declared another.[51] On went the conjecture in the manner
of *A Lesson for Labourers*:

What is a day-labourer's condition at present?
If he is industrious and careful, he has always a little before hand...
If he chooses to throw himself upon the parish, the laws provide for his mainten-
    ance, when ever he is unable to maintain himself.
It is his own fault if he has not a tight dwelling over his head, warm clothing, and
    plenty of wholesome food...
If one master treats him amiss, he has his liberty, and can go to another.
If a rich man uses him ill, he can make him pay damages...
These are things worth defending.

Each of these statements misrepresented the recent experience of rural workers. More in theory than practice did they have freedom of movement and recourse to the courts of law; nor was parish relief as automatic and flexible as the propaganda made out. Therefore the author invoked the fear of God, telling of how the French soldiers would rape labouring women, set fire to cottages and push the inhabitants 'back with pikes into the flames'.[52] Likewise, Hannah More, fortified by her conviction that 'an endeavour to amend the morals and principles of the poor is the most probable method of preserving us from the crimes and calamities of France',[53] broke into some frightful verse in her 'Ploughman's Ditty':

> I've a dear little wife,
> Whom I love as my life,
> To lose her I should not much like, Sir;
> And 'twould make me run wild,
> To see my sweet child,
> With its head on the point of a pike, Sir.[54]

The best-known tract that sought to exploit the labourer's passions was entitled *Important Considerations for the People of this Kingdom* – an anonymous broadside sent under the royal seal to every officiating minister of every parish in the Kingdom. Congregations throughout Britain were subjected to its dire message from the pulpit, hearing of how the French reserved their 'direst malignity' and 'sharpest bayonet' for the labouring classes, and of how the murder of parents was deferred so that they might hear their children 'shriek amidst the flames'. So compelling and tragic was this story that a copy of the broadside version was still found to be hanging in a Southampton church in 1809. In the same year a rather sheepish Cobbett confessed to its authorship.[55]

There is more than a little irony in the fact that Cobbett's most widely circulated piece of writing should be a government-endorsed exercise in cautionary propaganda.[56] But Cobbett, at this stage, was a most valuable ally for the Pitt administration, not only because of his anti-Jacobin politics, but because his experiences and instincts as a labourer and countryman provided him with insights into labouring culture, including the unbounded love of parents for children – a cultural quality that he would later put to radical use. The people must be shown warriors, he advised Pitt:

> What, for instance, induced me, when so far distant from my country, voluntarily to devote myself to her cause? ... It was the name and fame of England. Her laws, her liberties, her justice, her might, ... but above all her deeds in arms, her military glory ... There is not, perhaps, a ploughman in England, who has not a hundred times repeated the names of Drake and

A2935

ASSOCIATION
FOR PRESERVING
LIBERTY AND PROPERTY.

CROWN AND ANCHOR, JULY 25, 1803.

AT A MEETING OF THIS COMMITTEE,

JOHN REEVES, Esq. in the Chair;

Upon reading a Printed Paper, intituled, IMPORTANT CONSIDERATIONS FOR THE PEOPLE OF THIS KINGDOM, the Committee RESOLVED, That the said Paper, being full of the most important Truths, and calculated to explain completely the designs of the French, and the true Interests of this Country, should be printed, and circulated by this Society, in such manner, as will make it very generally known: and that the Chairman be requested to take such measures, as shall appear to him proper, for carrying the same into immediate execution.

Wm. COBBETT

IMPORTANT

CONSIDERATIONS

FOR THE

PEOPLE OF THIS KINGDOM.

Published July 1803, and sent to the Officiating Minister of every Parish in England.

SOLD BY J. DOWNES, TEMPLE-BAR; J. SPRAGG, KING-STREET, COVENT-GARDEN; J. ASPERNE, CORNHILL; AND J. HATCHARD, PICCADILLY.

Price 2d. or 1s. 6d. per Doz.

3 Cobbett's *Important Considerations*, published as a pamphlet and broadside, received the endorsement of the Association for the Preservation of Liberty and Property against Republicans and Levellers. Reproduced by permission of Nuffield College.

Marlborough; and of the hundreds of thousands of them, there is not one, perhaps, who ever heard ... the name of Cecil or of Godolphin.[57]

Cobbett in his youth was nourished upon the same penny chapbooks, the same 'glorious deeds of our admirals and sailors',[58] that dominated the oral and printed culture of the labouring poor. He was well positioned to exhort Pitt to 'turn over the page of history, and then say, whether those princes who have been the greatest warriors have not also been the greatest favourites, more especially of the lower classes'.[59] These observations had one important shortcoming, for not yet did Cobbett realize that the physical condition of rural workers had deteriorated to the point where traditional symbols alone were insufficient to herd them into battle. In the end, the labourers did shoulder a musket or pike in defence of their homeland, but they did so under protest. First, resentment abounded over the ballot system – a form of conscription from which the wealthy could purchase exemption.[60] Second, labouring people were not blind to their poverty and mistreatment. They resisted government propaganda and assessed the wartime situation for themselves:

> I am a brave fellow, I love my country and king,
> And wish to do right to both country and him;
> But I still love the poor, that I always will do,
> And them that don't join me they're not true blue.[61]

Patriotism, in this verse, is not confined to the uncritical love of homeland that dominated Cobbett's *Considerations*. Additional requisites are care for the poor, liberty for all and sturdy commitment to the traditional diet of Englishmen. The defaults of the élite meant that workers enlisted with half a heart, and Cobbett failed to see that they took up arms more to invest in the future than to endorse their position in the recent past.

As one would expect of a former soldier, Cobbett paid careful attention to the parliamentary debates on national defence. In his view a well-trained regular army was superior to a semi-trained body of volunteers. But only for logistical reasons did he criticize the volunteer armies: ideally he wished to see a regular force of 'the hardy and unsophisticated peasantry' under the command of the 'ancient gentry'. 'The peasants of this country are brave', he advised Pitt, 'their forefathers were so, and notwithstanding the incessant efforts of cant and effeminacy to eradicate every manly sentiment from their minds, the sons also are brave.'[62] Windham took a sterner view of the labourers among the volunteers: he questioned not only their training but also their loyalty, bravery and hardihood.[63] It was Cobbett's opinion, however, that the labourers were better endowed for battle than any other class, including the 'grovelling wretches in and about great towns and manufacturing places'.[64] The near reality of invasion, furthermore, enhanced his appreciation of the labourers who prepared themselves to defend their native land against foreign intrusion. Although he did not observe in rural workers the same degree of loyalism that he remembered from his youth, he perceived them as truer patriots than the ruling class. The more he studied and collected parliamentary debates of past and present, and the more he saw fund-holders receiving interest payments, the closer he embraced the old Country Party understanding of 'patriotism', declaring it to be independent of a 'desire to get a contract or a job', or of 'anxiety for the funds like that of the patriotism of Lloyds'.[65]

This revised understanding of the source of 'patriotism' was approaching that of the Radicals. For William Frend, patriotism was to be encouraged by 'wise legislation, just administration of the laws, manly exercises, and above all by the people having a share in the government'.[66] Not yet would Cobbett have concurred with the democratic note, but in the wake of the invasion scare he mounted the Middlesex platform on behalf of 'Burdett and Independence'.[67] For the first time his *Register* began to secrete sustained dissatisfaction with taxes, sinecurists, placemen and the thin edge of what he would later call Old Corruption. The public response to the invasion scare, together with his exposure of numerous examples of wartime profiteering by self-proclaimed 'patriots', made it difficult for him to accept that loyalty was the preserve 'of those who depend upon [and] always support every measure and every pretension of the minister of the day'.[68] Although edging towards what would become his reform position, Cobbett was far from alone in his graduation. During the invasion fright and its immediate aftermath, there appeared a flood of songs which criticized Pitt, sinecures, taxes and, most vigorously of all, the continuance of the war. Cobbett did not endorse this popular agitation; his support for the candidacy of the aristocratic Burdett in the Westminster election of 1804 was defined almost exclusively on Country Party grounds, especially the claims of Swift, Pope and Johnson.[69] But at the same time he was beginning to wonder if he belonged on the urban platform in any capacity.

By the summer of 1804, countrymen in general, and village workers in particular, were emerging in Cobbett's estimation as the personification of his ideals of hardihood and of economic disinterest in the preservation of Englishness. Meanwhile, he was coming to believe that much of the talk against Jacobinism and sedition was grossly exaggerated: Bonaparte was stalking Europe and the Treasonable and Seditious Practices Act had done its work at home. As his understanding of sedition narrowed, Cobbett felt sufficiently relaxed to begin to broaden the Country Party mandate of the

Political Register so as to include the exposure of all disloyal and self-seeking individuals, 'whether proceeding from clubs of jacobins, companies of traders, synagogues of saints, or boards of government'. His special attention to the 'sedition' of the labouring people was now relinquished, and when Napoleon abandoned his plans to invade, he was ready to take a closer look at this patriotic class.[70]

The sport debate and the invasion fright prepared Cobbett for a more sympathetic approach to working people and their economic problems, but his references to labouring life remained sparse, ill-informed and nigh drowned in a sea of political commentary. Until the summer of 1804 he continued to accept the conventional wisdom on the state of the labourer, declaring the two previous years to be ones 'of *comparative* ease, not to say of idleness', in rural labouring life.[71] It was in the autumn of that year, while on a working holiday in southern Hampshire, that he met with the people, the data, and the landscape that would cause him to revise this opinion, and ultimately to orient his politics around rural England. At the start of this three-month excursion Cobbett was still in his Tory career; the *Register*, though critical of Pitt's administration, rested its opposition on the shadow of the Peace of Amiens, that brief respite from war which in Cobbett's opinion did irreparable damage to the glory and security of England. Government, as he saw it, should 'lead the people' rather than yield to popular cries for 'peace and plenty' or 'peace and a large loaf'.[72]

Ever since his American days, Cobbett had taken issue with the popular claim that war and high prices marched hand in hand.[73] Borrowed statistics and dubious mathematics supported his conclusions; but as the fear of invasion began to subside, and as the people again called for 'peace and plenty', he resolved to put his case 'beyond all dispute'.[74] Thus while visiting Hampshire he occupied himself with detailed study of long-term movements in the price of bread; and to his own satisfaction at least, he disproved the correlation (but only by dividing price trends by decade, rather than by years of war and years of peace):

	s	d
Average price of the quarter loaf, during the ten years ending with 1760, was	o	$5\frac{3}{4}$
During the ten years ending with 1770	o	$6\frac{1}{2}$
During the ten years ending with 1780	o	7
During the ten years ending with 1790	o	$7\frac{1}{2}$
During the thirteen years ending in July, 1804	1	o

Although concluding that war had no effect on the price of bread, Cobbett

neglected to exploit his price table in line with his original purpose, for he
had discovered that peace and war aside, the price of bread – 'that article
of the poor man's subsistence' – had almost doubled since his taking leave
of Farnham twenty years earlier.[75] It was on the basis of this data that
Cobbett began, slowly at first, to investigate the social effects of taxation,
the funding system, the national debt and paper currency. Although such
topics were not inherently radical (they had long constituted a centrepiece
of the Country Party critique), they did leave him ideologically vulnerable,
for he sought information on these topics from a wide variety of perspectives, including that of Thomas Paine, whose opinions on English finance
he had viciously attacked several years earlier from America. Anti-Jacobin
days were too near to hand for Cobbett to make positive public reference
to Paine's doctrines, but the poverty of the cottage table induced him
privately to rethink Paine's arguments about the inflationary effects of
paper money (Cobbett appears to have read at least parts of Paine's
Decline and Fall of the English System of Finance as early as 1797). At the
same time as he was beginning to regret his assaults upon Paine he was also
starting to question his early trust of Pitt's economic promises, especially
his assurances of 1799 that the war could be conducted indefinitely
without additions to the national debt.[76] For the time being, however, his
primary concern was whether wages had kept pace with price rises. At first
he took some solace in the claims of a Hampshire agricultural writer that
wages were effectively indexed to bread prices. But he resolved to look into
the matter for himself, taking 'some pains' to ascertain rural wages. His
research revealed that a recent 60 per cent rise in the price of bread was
accompanied by no wage rise whatsoever.[77]

At Michaelmas 1804, soon after conducting his investigations into rural
wages and prices, Cobbett spent the most formative day of his political life.
Still in southern Hampshire, partly to enquire into farms to purchase, he
occupied a Sunday afternoon by strolling around the common land at
Horton Heath. By Hampshire standards the common was small, some 150
acres, but around its borders were some thirty cottages, each with a small
garden of corn and fruit trees encroaching on the common. The cottagers
also had livestock: altogether 100 bee-hives, some 60 pigs, 15 cows and
their calves, and some 500 poultry. All of this, including the gardens, was
peripheral to the common proper, which was grazed by the cattle and
sheep of local farmers. But according to Cobbett's figuring the cottagers'
bees alone were worth more than the annual production of the common:
'my calculation was, that the cottages produced from their little bits, in
food, for themselves, and in things to be sold at market, *more than any
neighbouring farm of 200 acres*'. From this moment Cobbett ceased his

praise for enclosure. He had witnessed at first hand the great productive capacity of cottage agriculture, and at a time 'when the madness for enclosures raged most furiously'.[78]

Although Horton Heath was only one common in one parish, there is a wider significance to Cobbett's findings. Recent scholarship on enclosure has indicated an increase in agricultural production upon the enclosure of open fields, but it is far from conclusive that enclosure of the common lands produced the same result. The break-up of the old commons meant an increase in wheat production, but fuel, poultry, milk and garden vegetables often became more expensive and scarce, requiring as they did the constant care and intensive labour afforded by cottage production. Moreover, it must be remembered (as Cobbett often informed his readers, and as Mick Reed has so convincingly shown) the produce of cottagers or 'household producers' was not always intended for the commercial market, for a great portion of their economy rested upon neighbourhood exchanges of commodities and services – honey for milk here, a day's labour for some bacon there. Indeed, if the cottagers' losses to enclosure could be factored into the larger picture of agricultural production, it might be that the allocation of common lands to larger landholders added little or nothing to the nation's overall food supply.[79]

Cobbett's experience at Horton Heath went beyond agricultural production to the cultural worth of common land. It being a Sunday, he was able to visit with cottagers as their children romped about the edges of the common. Some families invited him indoors, where the scenes to meet his eyes, he later recalled, propelled him deeper into political revisionism:

> I myself, in the early part of my writing life was deceived ... but, when, in [1804], I revisited the English labourer's dwelling, and that, too, after having so recently witnessed the happiness of labourers in America; when I saw that the clock was gone; that even the Sunday-coat was gone; when I saw those whom I had known the most neat, cheerful and happy beings on earth, and these my countrymen too, had become the most wretched and forlorn of human beings, I looked seriously and inquired patiently into the matter; and this inquiry into the causes of an effect which had so deep an impression on my mind, led to that series of exertions, which have *occupied my whole life, since that time*, to better the lot of the labourers.[80]

Much of Cobbett's early anti-Jacobinism had rested upon his assumption that the eighteenth-century social and economic order was alive and well in the early 1800s. Some material deprivation, he now allowed, might be the consequence of wartime exigencies, but the impoverishment of the cottage was of revolutionary proportions. American farm workers, whom in 1800 he had held to be in worse condition than those in England, now appeared the better off. Furthermore, the well-kept cottages and gardens of Horton Heath testified to the fact that idleness – the great charge of the Regency élite against the rural poor – was not its cause.

This was an important moment in Cobbett's evolution towards radicalism. H. T. Dickinson observes that 'the shift from a Country Platform to a radical plan of parliamentary reform occurred gradually and there was never a clear dividing line between the two'.[81] This is true, though it applies only to radicalism as a *political* process. Cobbett approached radicalism, not from political ideology alone, but also through the totality of the labourers' economic and cultural experiences, or what he called the great 'instructor' of 'daily experience'.[82] Had Cobbett's radicalism sprung from high ideology alone, he would not have spent the month of August 1804 among the rural people of Hampshire; he would have been in London, preparing his speeches and papers on behalf of the 'Burdett and Independence' platform in the Westminster by-election of September. Although he would indeed take an active part in the Westminster campaign, the agrarian base of his radicalism was taking a distinct shape.

In choosing Windham as the recipient of his documentary survey of the productive but impoverished cottagers of Horton Heath, Cobbett served notice that he still regarded the Country Tories as the spokesmen and custodians of the first seven decades of the eighteenth century that he would come to call 'old England'. But the alliance between Cobbett and the old Tories was wearing thin. Within weeks of the trip to Horton Heath he encountered a recent parliamentary report on the Poor Law which revealed that in the year ending at Easter of 1803, England and Wales were home to more than one million paupers. This not only proportioned paupers at one in ten of the population, but exposed a concentration of relief claimancy in his own rural South: one in seven in Hampshire, one in five in Wiltshire and Berkshire, one in four in Sussex. Repeatedly from October of 1804 onwards, Cobbett reminded his readers of these statistics, and especially of the doubling of pauper numbers since his departure from Farnham in 1784. 'Yes, in England!', he bawled, 'English men and women and children! More than a million of them! One eighth part of our whole population!'[83] Cobbett did not reflect upon the increases to pauperism brought by the food scarcities of 1795 and 1800–1; nor did he allow for the strain on living standards caused by the rise in rural population. But two things he did know: that the farmers were wealthier than they had been during his youth, and that neither unemployment nor underemployment was responsible for the labourer's material hardship.

It was still possible for Cobbett to make a 'Tory' response to the pauper statistics. Certainly he would not have sided with Malthus or Burke, both of whom sought to reduce, if not abolish, the Poor Law itself.[84] But more positive and liberal proposals for reducing the number of paupers had been advanced in 1796 by William Pitt, whose scheme included the foundation of industrial schools for children, the recovery of wastelands for the use of the poor, and even loans from the rates for the purchase of a cow.[85] For Cobbett, however, these proposals seemed a half measure in the promotion of cottage independence; moreover, they were advanced by a Prime Minister who had done much to destroy independence in other spheres, beginning with politics. Between 1800 and 1804 Cobbett had complained of a sinecure here and a pension there, but only with the appearance of the Poor Law report did he begin directly to relate pauper numbers to taxes, boroughmongers, sinecures and the funding system. This was a new application for the Country Party platform. For Country Tories such as Windham the major evil of pauperism was the threat it presented to domestic peace and popular devotion to the war effort; so long as the country gentlemen maintained their political independence while curbing it in their workers, the pauper matter was a non-issue. But Cobbett, convinced that pensions and taxes moved hand in hand with pauperism, injected a radical dimension into Country ideology. For him the rapid increase of pauperism was the first symptom of the decline of England, and all of his economic programme, including his obsessions with the national debt, paper currency and the 'funds', was henceforth related to pauper numbers or to hungry labourers.[86] His desire to abolish the 'Pitt system' was still partly moved by the Country Party ideology which championed independence, but in Cobbett's mind the labourer's impoverishment was the paramount national concern. In 1805 he purchased a farm at Botley in Hampshire, where he pursued the life of an independent country gentleman, physically removed from the commercial and political intrigue of the 'Wen'. But these genteel appearances can deceive, for Cobbett had taken a large step towards an ideological transformation. If the country gentlemen were to deserve their political and social privileges, as well as their custody of the reform movement, it was necessary that they attend to the poverty of the cottage.

It was without regret that Cobbett received news of the death of Pitt in January of 1806. For it was this man, he argued, who introduced the 'taxing and pauperizing system', and who 'perfected the system of degrading the labourers'.[87] What should be expected of a new administration? As early as November of 1804, Cobbett had called for a public enquiry into the state of the nation, with the results to be communicated 'to every cottage of the kingdom'.[88] For Tory and Whig, such accounting between rich and poor was unnatural and dangerous; but when a new ministry took office upon the death of Pitt, Cobbett was on hand with a further list of recommendations. To the farm worker he gave first priority. 'The plain fact is', he informed Grenville and the Ministry of All-the-Talents, 'that a man with a wife, and with four children that are unable to work cannot now, out of his labour, possibly provide them and himself with the means of living.' Not only are they without comfort, he argued, they cannot even *'sustain life'*:

> There are hundreds of thousands of the people of England who never taste any food but bread and vegetables, and who scarcely ever know what it is to have a full meal even of these. This is *new*: it was not so in former times: it was not so even till of late years: the causes are obvious, and they ought to be removed.

'That this is not an exaggerated picture', he continued,

> will, I think, be readily believed by any one who will bestow a single minute in contemplating the situation of the agricultural labourer. His weekly

4   Cobbett's house at Botley as it appeared in 1817. There he accommodated about twelve farm servants at a time. Married labourers lived in surrounding cottages. Reproduced by permission of Hampshire Record Office.

wages (for I shall suppose him *never to lose a day's work*, either from recreation or *sickness*) is, upon an average 12 shillings, putting it at the very highest. The average price of the quarter loaf is eleven pence. Here, then are the means of purchasing 58 pounds of bread in a week, which is a little more than 8¹/₂ pounds a day for a *working* man, his wife, and 4 children! Absolutely not enough to support life. *Nothing* for drink; nothing for clothing: nothing for bedding; for household goods, for fuel, for a house to rent! The evident conclusion is, that some of them must die, unless they are supported in existence by the parish, or by voluntary alms.[89]

The foremost duty of government, as Cobbett now saw it, was not the maintenance of traditional establishments in church and state (which is to say that he had ceased to qualify as a Tory or an anti-Jacobin), but rather the promotion of the well-being of the labouring poor. He no longer saw political creeds or government boasts about 'national wealth' as having any rationalization independent of the circumstances of the cottage. And yet, if no longer a 'Tory', neither was Cobbett a Radical, for he had not yet arrived at the realization that Parliament was unable to reform itself. In 1806 he campaigned on behalf of an independent and non-aligned candidate in a by-election at Honiton, whilst remaining cautiously hopeful that the Whigs in the new ministry could be convinced to examine the interior of the cottage, and to cease their 'boasts about the *flourishing* state of a country with 1,200,000 paupers'.[90]

Grenville's ministry was no more attentive to the rural poor than were the last administrations of Pitt. Its greatest deed – the abolition of the slave trade – was for Cobbett an example of misplaced benevolence. The West Indian slave, he argued, was better fed, clothed and lodged, and was better treated by his master, than was the farm worker of England. Such racial bigotry was an unfortunate way of illustrating his point that freedom was a mirage in the English rural community. More sensibly, he drew the government's attention to an advertisement in a Hampshire newspaper:

> The Visitors and Guardians of the Poor of Sixteen United Parishes, whose House of Industry is situated at [Easebourne], near Midhurst, Sussex, are desirous of immediately receiving Proposals from Persons willing to *contract* for providing the Diet and Clothing, and for *taking the Labour* of the Paupers in the said House, at a specific sum weekly for each pauper, for One Year ... The Contractor will be paid constantly for Seventy Paupers at the least, and will be repaid the price exceeding twenty shillings per load for all Wheat consumed for Pauper's Food.[91]

'Now Sir,' said Cobbett, turning to Wilberforce, 'these are our own country people; our own flesh and blood and skin. Why, then, while they are thus contracted for and let out; why should we seek for objects of compassion elsewhere?' After a trial of almost a year, Cobbett began to wonder whether Whigs were any more emotionally or ideologically equipped than Tories to consider the needs of the labourers. It was the moral duty of all statesmen, he argued, to give this heed:

> Persons, who do not examine or reflect; persons, who, in certain situations of life, can know nothing of the distresses and miseries of the labouring part of the people, may be excused for paying no attention to them; but, such inattention in a statesman is, at all times, and particularly at a time like the present, inexcusable. Experience, daily observation, minute and repeated personal inquiry and examination, have made me familiar with the state of the labouring poor, and, sir, I challenge contradiction when I say, that a labouring man, in England, with a wife and only three children, though he never lose a day's work, though he and his family be economical, frugal, and industrious in the most extensive sense of these words, is not now able to procure himself by his labour a single meal of meat from one end of the year unto the other. Is this a state in which the labouring man ought to be?[92]

Had members of Grenville's government, which included Windham as secretary of state for war, shown even a modest interest in the labourers' poverty, it is possible that Cobbett would have remained, at least for a time, on the fringe of either established party. He still entertained a paternal sensibility and venerated a legislature composed of the landed aristocracy. But the 'Talent' administration was tainted by an attempt at social reform which caused him to abandon all hope in either of the conventional parties.

Samuel Whitbread, a Foxite Whig, was well known as a dedicated, if erratic, friend of the rural poor. In 1795, and again in 1799, when the labourers faced food scarcity and the introduction of the Speenhamland allowance system, he proposed that local magistrates be empowered to fix a minimum agricultural wage. In 1807 he again stepped forward in the cause of the rural poor, this time with a bill for a far-reaching reform of the Poor Law. Unlike the earlier proposal, however, the plan of 1807 was closely attached to that strand of Whig hostility to popular culture which would later take more definable shape in Utilitarianism and the educational programmes of the SDUK.

Whitbread's panacea for rural poverty was the foundation of a national network of parish schools. Loans for the purchase of cottage cows he thought impractical; savings banks were a much superior method of assuring popular solvency. He wished to see vestries endowed with a system of plural voting, whereby the largest rate-payers would have the most say in the disposition of parish funds. He also suggested a scheme of rewards and punishments – the former to exalt the unrelieved labourer, and the latter to humiliate and degrade the 'criminal' claimant. Even the 'unfortunate poor', regardless of their needs, were to have their relief 'confined to necessities'.[93] On went the plan, consuming fifty columns of *Hansard*, without a single reference to high food prices and low agricultural wages, the primary causes of early nineteenth-century rural poverty. Cobbett was dumbfounded. Privately he noted: 'It is the foolishest and wickedest [plan] that ever was heard of. Damn them, they would put badges upon us all. The poor are yet too free for them. They want to have them all tamed to their hands like chickens, that they may devour them at pleasure.'[94] Whitbread's proposals put Cobbett in mind of the industriousness and decency of the cottagers upon Horton Heath. It was not the rural workers but parliamentarians like Whitbread who were in need of reform: 'This former patriot, this zealous prosecutor of corruption, this reformer of parliament, is now ... occupied with a plan for reforming, not the House of Commons, but *the people*! ... They cry for bread, and he would give them a primmer [*sic*]: they ask for freedom, and he would give them a badge.'[95] At one stroke Cobbett lost political confidence in the Whigs and especially in Whitbread, whom he now called the 'worst enemy' of reform. The plan, Cobbett was quick to see, rested upon Malthusian precepts, which for all their valid attention to population growth, failed to recognize the role of wages and prices in rural poverty.[96] The plural voting at vestry, which for Whitbread was the means of injecting 'decency and order in the meetings themselves', was seen by Cobbett in truer light as an attempt to channel the administration of relief into the hands of the parish élite. He also condemned the scheme for rewards and punishments, whether in the form of certificates for good behaviour, loans for the purchase of a cow or cottage visits by ostentatious philanthropists. For Cobbett, these proposals were destructive of the very independence championed by Whitbread himself.[97]

Cobbett stood alone in making these arguments, but he had company in his attack on the education clauses of Whitbread's Bill. Other critics argued that instruction would cause the poor to 'despise their lot in life', while Windham (no longer Cobbett's ally and mentor – like other Country Tories he had done nothing to assist the labouring poor) thought that teaching the poor to play the fiddle would do as much as formal schooling to reduce poverty. Cobbett agreed, but not because he joined Windham in wanting to keep the poor politically quiescent; his fear was that education schemes would distract legislators from more genuine causes of rural poverty.[98] He was also suspicious that ideas of passive obedience might reach the poor through their instructors and texts. Unlike the Whigs and their heirs the Liberals, he preferred that if popular politics was not supported by an independent and reform-minded press, then let it be a spontaneous process, with the labourers deriving their ideologies from their daily experiences. Here Cobbett moved another step closer to distinctly radical terrain. The ruling class, whether Whig or Tory in name, was not to be trusted as an educating agency, for it would abstract the value of labour, debase the radical usages of patriotism and construe popular politics as anathema to true religion. Whitbread's programme of public education, furthermore, entailed a further extension of state power, which in its present form was exercised without regard for popular will. To Cobbett's mind the state was the nation and the nation was the people; the people could educate themselves, and why not first and foremost in the ways and means of reform?

As an alternative to Whitbread's Bill, Cobbett advanced his own scheme for reducing pauper numbers and for regenerating the labourers. Interestingly, he did not deny all of Whitbread's preliminary observations. Habits of industry, independence and honesty, he admitted, were not as he remembered them:

> To become chargeable was [formerly] a reproach; and never to have been chargeable was a subject of proud exultation. The feeling, which was almost universal, was the parent of industry, of care, of economy, of frugality, and of early habits of labour amongst children . . . [Now, the labourer] takes care to spend all as fast as he gets it, makes himself as poor as he can, and uses all the arts that he is master of to cause it to be believed, that he is still more miserable than he really is.[99]

The comment is candid, even censorious in tone. But unlike Whitbread, Cobbett would neither suggest nor imply that the labourers were themselves responsible for their deficiencies. The negative traits, he emphasized, were of recent development; and as an enlightened environmentalist he set out to locate the external conditioners. These he found in the allowance system: 'the great obstacle to the restoration of the labourers to their former independence of mind, is, that their wages, generally speaking, are partly paid in the shape of relief'. Cobbett anticipated numerous critics: '"Well," some overgorged upstart will say, "and what matter is it, so that they are supported, whence the support comes." The matter is this, that the labourers are humbled, debased and enslaved.'[100]

As a farmer and employer of labourers, Cobbett believed that all of rural society could prosper out of the land. On his own farms, as we will see, he lived well himself *and* paid the full wages of his workers, without recourse to the rates. But this example was unpopular with other employers, many of whom preferred to pay part wages, leave the parish to pay the balance and to divert their profits into new habits of consumption. Occasionally, as if to apologize for their promotion of class society, the farmers would raise parochial subscriptions for the poor, but Cobbett wanted no part of this charity. During the Royal Jubilee festivities of 1810 he declined to join other Hampshire farmers in treating the poor, arguing that 'when I treat a poor man, I treat him under his own roof, or in case of sickness, send what I have to give him, to his own house, and never expose him to the humiliation of this kind of public and pauper-like relief'. Publicly to regale the labourers was 'to keep pauperism in countenance', and to seek to reconcile able-bodied people to a life of dependence and servility.[101]

Cobbett's paternalism was in abeyance by 1810. He wanted to see the labourers with at least partial economic independence; he wanted them to have (or in some cases, to have *back*) cottage gardens, pigs, brewing utensils and the traditional array of common rights. But neither farmers nor legislators were interested in the restoration of partial economic independence to the rural workers. Nor were they accepting of Cobbett's invitation to join him and the country labourers in campaigning for a radical reform of Parliament. Since they too were prospering from the wars, and to some extent from the 'system', they left Cobbett to go his own way with the labourers.

The 'chopsticks', among whom Cobbett counted himself, were highly instrumental in his transition to radicalism. Part of the Country Party platform, submerged during his stay in America, resurfaced after 1800 to provide ideological clothes for his attack on Old Corruption. But in Regency England, a Country platform alone would have left Cobbett a liberal-Tory hybrid, not a Radical edging towards democracy. To that position Cobbett was moved by empirical contact with the plight of the country workers. If radical ideology is conceived in the recognition that parliament is unable or unwilling to reform itself, and that only extra-parliamentary action by the common people can expose the root causes of injustice, then Cobbett was a Radical by 1806, when the Ministry of All-the-Talents failed adequately to respond to the labourers' poverty and to the leviathan of political dependence and corruption promoted by Pitt. Conservative remnants would remain with Cobbett always; for even as a Radical, as Olivia Smith has shown, he retained in his discourse a conservative imagery and rhetoric akin to that of Burke, and a righteousness not far removed from that of his adversary Hannah More.[102] These traits, however, do not serve notice that Cobbett was either a 'Tory' or a 'Tory

Radical'; nor do they show that he never fully graduated from the politics of 'independence'; they merely serve to demonstrate that his radicalism was a process, that he was educating himself as he educated his readers, and that many of these readers, like Cobbett himself, were more receptive to radical ideas in politics and economics than in matters social, cultural and moral.

It has been suggested by Edward Thompson that Cobbett's move towards radicalism 'entailed a certain opportunism'.[103] This is perhaps true to the extent that on the metropolitan platform, Cobbett was more follower than leader – that he 'was not initiating but flowing *with* a new reforming tide'[104] – but meantime he volunteered as a radical leader in the countryside, where the stock of radical political traditions was smaller and more diffuse than in the towns. As Roger Wells and John Bohstedt have shown, radical expression was far from absent in the countryside during the 1790s,[105] but the fact that Cobbett was occasionally reduced to despair of the countryman's indifference to national politics[106] serves notice that he was making a conscious effort to lead rather than follow. If, as has often been stated, emolument and national fame were Cobbett's primary objects, he would have been better off on the urban platform, where publicity would have been greater and his disciples more. It was not 'opportunism' but preconceptions of justice and fair play, applied to his own rural memories and his objective witness of the reduced circumstances of the cottage, that moved and framed his opposition to the state as constituted and maintained under Whig and Tory management. Yet the unprecedented powers that the state adopted during the 1790s do not alone account for the origins of Cobbett's radicalism;[107] for while he vigorously denounced Pitt's repression of popular politics, he would have suffered the aristocratic monopoly of office to continue had it not been accompanied by a sustained disregard for the cottage table that had not been characteristic of eighteenth-century governments or economic thought.[108] Finally, it is worth remembering that Cobbett is one of the few public figures of modern English history to evolve in middle-age (he turned forty in 1803) from Right to Left. The great bulk of the traffic of political maturity (there are of course exceptions: among them William Gladstone, David Lloyd George, Charles Dickens) typically runs in the opposite direction, and especially among witnesses of the French Revolution. This further testifies, albeit in an impressionistic way, to the transforming power of the cottage.

Cobbett was always at pains to declare that his radicalism contained nothing new, but this was a psychological crutch for a man who, like the farm workers for whom he spoke, could more readily accept innovation in politics than in culture and economic tradition. In fact, Cobbett demanded innovations on an enormous scale. In 1804, whilst defending Burdett's platform, he declared that 'nobody censures Pope or Gay or Akenside or Goldsmith or Johnson for the lashings which they so plentifully bestowed upon court-sycophants, parasites, pensioners, bribed-senators, directors, contractors, jobbers, hireling-lords, and ministers of state'[109] – all of which is to say that he saw himself as the heir of the Country Party. But the *methods* of attaining reform were new. According to the eighteenth-century Country platform, the desired sponsor of reform was the patriot king, as Bolingbroke called him, but aristocratic sponsorship of the reform movement was not Cobbett's vision by 1804. For the next twelve years he held out hope that independent country gentlemen would join in the campaign for parliamentary reform; but when their commitment proved wanting he advised the common people to go it alone. This was radical, and dramatically so.

Similarly, Cobbett defended Jacobinism on the grounds that it, too, contained nothing new. Here again he played fast and loose with English political traditions. In an effort to salvage the reformers' credibility in the Middlesex election of 1804, he confessed that Burdett's language in the 1802 election had been 'seditious to a degree bordering upon treason', and that he had then chosen 'to disgrace his cause by appealing to the worst passions of the worst part of the people'. But Burdett had learned the error of his ways, said Cobbett, for he no longer sought to disrupt 'the established order of things'.[110] By 1805 Cobbett was adding new dimensions to his argument, claiming that Jacobinism was dead and irrelevant, indeed that it had been the invention of Pitt's governments. This convenient explaining away of his own political past makes him a bad historian of Jacobinism, but the fact remains that he did much to translate its discourse into 'our rights', 'our labour' and 'our oppressors'. For his own cultural comfort, as well as that of his audience, Cobbett personalized Jacobinism, deconstructed some of its abstractions and replaced its cosmopolitanism with self-evident Englishness. 'It has long been a fashion amongst you', he informed English merchants in 1815,

> to call every friend of reform, every friend of freedom, a *Jacobin*, and to accuse him of *French principles* ... What are these principles? – That governments were made for the people, and not the people for governments. – That sovereigns reign legally only by virtue of the people's choice. – That birth without merit ought not to command merit without birth. – That all men ought to be equal in the eye of the law. – That no man ought to be taxed and punished by any law to which he has not given his assent by himself or by his representative. – That taxation and representation ought to go hand in

hand. – That every man ought to be judged by his peers, or equals. – That the press ought to be free. Now I should be pleased to know how these came to be French principles ... Ten thousand times as much has been written on the subject in England as in all the rest of the world put together ... To Tooke, Burdett, Cartwright, and a whole host of patriots of England, Scotland and Ireland, imprisoned or banished, during the administration of Pitt, you can give them the name of Jacobins and French principles. Yet, not one principle have they ever attempted to maintain that Hampden and Sydney did not seal with their blood.[111]

The contrast between Cobbett's anglicized version of Jacobinism and the charter Jacobinism of Thomas Paine takes us to the heart of Cobbett's methodological populism. Unlike Cobbett, Paine invoked political theory with confidence. Paine was also comfortable with the rationalism and progress theories of the Enlightenment; Cobbett was not. Paine had little interest in documenting a cultural, national or historical basis of his reform programme; Cobbett insisted upon it. Cobbett derived his radicalism from empirical workshops in the countryside, using theory to *rationalize* his ideology. Paine was the opposite: he embroidered his ideology with empirical example, and by way of rationalizing his theory, not as its engine. And yet, despite the differences between the two writers, Cobbett would say of Paine: 'at his expiring flambeau, I lighted my taper'.[112] He meant two things by this: first, that Paine was the source of many of his economic doctrines, and second, that Paine 'awakened, in the common people of this country, the spirit of enquiry'.[113] But Cobbett also knew that some of Paine's doctrines were a liability upon the reform movement. Republicanism, his American years had taught him, was not in itself a guarantee of virtue, liberty and good government. Although after 1805 he did not go to great lengths to defend the monarchy (except for the personal throne of Queen Caroline), he continued to charge republican Radicals with deranged priorities.[114] Towards rational religion he was similarly cautious. From time to time he invoked Paine's *Age of Reason* as an anti-clerical club, but he always stopped short of public endorsement of heresy and infidelity.[115] Lastly, on the subject of internationalism, Cobbett was clearest of all: it was treasonous and culturally repugnant. In the inaugural pamphlet of his American career, he advised Joseph Priestley that 'a man of all countries is a man of no country ... he who has been a bad subject in his own country ... will neither be trusted nor respected'.[116] Radicalism and old age did not temper his opinions. 'I am no citizen of the world', he confessed in an 1831 essay on the nationalist struggles in Poland,

It is quite enough for me to think about what is best for England, Scotland and Ireland. I do not like those whose philanthropy is so enlarged as to look,

as Rousseau said, to Tartary for objects of affection and commiseration,
while their own countrymen are starving, or existing on sea-weed and nettles
... [Poland] is too distant, too out of the way of our affairs, that we would
take one single meal from a weaver or ploughman for the sake of doing good
to the Poles.[117]

It was in the face of his own essential agreement with popular culture on
the subjects of republicanism, rational religion and world citizenship that
Cobbett disinterred the very 'carcass' of Paine that he had once consigned

5   Caricaturists were quick to lampoon Cobbett for recovering Paine's
bones and transporting them back to England.

to everlasting perdition. 'Let this be considered', he said of his nocturnal deed,

> the act of the *reformers of England, Scotland, and Ireland*. In their name we opened the grave, and in their name will the tomb be raised. We do not look upon ourselves as adopting *all* Paine's opinions upon *all* subjects. He was a *great man*, an *Englishman*, a *friend of freedom*, and the *first and greatest enemy of the Borough and Paper system*. This is enough for us.

But Paine was *too much* for many Englishmen, despite the qualification in Cobbett's manifesto. Upon returning to England with the box of bones, he found little support for his public subscription to erect a 'colossal statue, in bronze' in honour of Paine's memory; nor was there overwhelming support for his scheme to manufacture jewellery containing lockets of Paine's hair. Quietly at his farmhouse, he slid Paine's coffin beneath his bed, muttering all the while that Paine was a man of 'distinguished talent' who would eventually be redeemed by 'the *healing* hand of *time*'.[118]

The bones fiasco was the closest that Cobbett ever came to compromising his cultural conservatism for the sake of political radicalism. He had gambled that the English worker was prepared to distinguish between Paine's religious, economic and political doctrines; but more than he had anticipated, the ruling class had succeeded in directing popular opinion against most things Paineite, with labouring people themselves volunteering the Gallophobia already current in English popular culture. But if Cobbett failed to restore popular dignity to Paine's legacy, he did succeed in deconstructing Jacobinism, and in transplanting many of its principles into the post-war radical movement. Like the village workers for whom he spoke, Cobbett preferred a made-in-England reform programme.

CHAPTER 3

DISCOVERING CLASS: COUNTRYMEN, LABOURERS AND NEW-FASHIONED FARMERS

It is well known that, generally speaking, your labourers hate you as they hate toads and adders. They regard you as their deadly enemies; as those who robbed them of their food and raiment, and who trample on them and insult them in their state of weakness; and they detest you accordingly ... You know that you merit their deadly hatred; and then, proceeding upon a principle of the most abominable injustice, you hate them, and you destroy them, if possible, because you know that they hate you.

'To the Bull-Frog Farmers', *PR*, 11 September 1824, p. 671.

They hate me, because, and only because, I have pleaded the cause of their poor labourers.

PR, 24 May 1834, p. 450.

I N 1802 the minor romantic poet Samuel Jackson Pratt published a poem entitled *Bread; or, The Poor*. It paints a picture of a healthy and contented peasantry yielding to 'a different race: the wretched paupers of the Present Hour!' Pig, chicken, cow and garden have vanished from the cottage economy; yet surrounding the impoverished cottage is a new 'insidious train' of 'farmer-gentlemen' – 'proud', 'vain', and the enemy of the 'lowly swain'. A decade later, Cobbett would use similar language to describe the new-fashioned farmer, but in 1802, when reviewing Pratt's poem, he took exception to its presentation of the farmer as the 'natural enemy' of the labourer. Cobbett did not deny the existence of wealthy and insolent farmers, but he stoutly resisted any incitement or even observation of conflict and ill-feeling between classes.[1] 'I persist in looking upon the government and people as one', he had once told the Americans; the King and Executive are Britons, he reasoned, and therefore to abuse them is to abuse the British people or nation.[2] But shortly after his return to England in 1800, he began to purge the ruling class from the 'nation', the 'people' and the 'country'. These terms, he argued, encompass not the few but the *whole of the people*. England's rulers, he claimed, 'are not

England: they are not my *country*; my country is unhappy, in misery, sinking in character'.[3]

These re-definitions have significant implications for the familiar claim that Cobbett was a model John Bull, or in Marx's words, an 'inveterate' one.[4] This is not a misleading identification if we take it to mean that Cobbett was a plain-speaking, hard-nosed countryman who opposed cultural internationalism, who thought free trade 'stupid' and war among nations inevitable, and who trumpeted the English as the hardest-working people on the face of the earth.[5] But we must be careful when treating of Cobbett's portraits of an English national character, especially if we allow them to blind us to his discovery of class society and politics. Nation and class, as Linda Colley has recently reminded us, were 'not antithetical but two sides of the same historical processes'.[6] If Cobbett's laudatory portraits of the English character are removed from their political context (as is often done in anthologies of his 'opinions') he can appear as a nation-builder who served the class interests of the ruling élite.[7] But this would mislead: radicalism was inseparable from Cobbett's Englishness and understanding of 'nation'. As long as the élite maintained its monopoly of political office, he pursued an international dialogue with American reformers, and even enlisted their country's navy as an ally in his efforts to overthrow the English ruling class. But when the prospects for reform improved, he adopted a different tack, warning his Yankee friends that one of the first orders of business of a democratic England would be to put Americans in their place: 'I wish them all the happiness that men can enjoy in this world; but a nation may be very happy without being permitted to swagger about and be saucy to England.'[8] Had John Bull symbolized a democratic England, or at least have continued to personify the old English ideology of fair play, Cobbett would have offered him his undivided devotions, but during the war years the national mascot was divested of his former Country ideology and transformed by the ruling class into a guardian of ideological conformity who in the name of beef and beer demanded unconditional loyalty to an abstracted state.[9] Furthermore, as Cobbett and the village workers saw, John Bull had changed employment during the war years. He was no longer the fustian-coated and pint-tilting husbandman of mid-Georgian times, but rather a shopkeeping townsman who preferred town to country, and who stereotyped village workers as weak-minded and disloyal 'clodhoppers'.[10]

So who were the quintessential representatives of Englishness for radical Cobbett? The sport debate, as we have seen, saw him narrow the field, eliminating Methodists, Evangelicals and all other opponents of 'manly' recreations and of social and cultural interaction between élite and non-élite. Industrialists and manufacturing workers, whose supposedly effeminate employments rendered them unsuitable for maintaining the war effort, were likewise denied access to the English essence. And as the patriotic Englishman could not confuse national interest with private gain, it was not possible for fund-holders, stock-jobbers and boroughmongers to qualify.[11] Finally, Cobbett's model of archetypal Englishness excluded the permanent inhabitants of towns, especially of the Metropolis, whose residents were defiled by their proximity to the heart of the 'system' and by the cosmopolitanism and conspicuous consumption which he selectively observed on its streets and by-ways. As he crossed the threshold to radical-ism, Cobbett distilled from the ranks of English society a vertical configur-ation of countrymen – including landlord, farmer, labourer and village tradesman – which he defined, not according to relationships with the means of production, but according to rural residence, a love of the land and a shared opposition to the culture and ideology of the city.[12]

Cobbett was not the first or the last social commentator to divide a society between town and country. Gramsci observed in his native Italy 'an urban ideological unity against the countryside', with 'hatred and scorn' for the peasant; he also observed a reciprocal aversion by country people for the city, and for 'all the groups which make it up'.[13] Marx, too, observed an ideological conflict between town and country, affixing much of the blame upon the peasant, whose predilection for small-scale production, he be-lieved, retarded the development of class society in the rural world.[14] Almost certainly, Marx would have applied some of his assessments of the Continental countryside to rural England, where there were few peasants in objective economic terms but many in aspiration. Cobbett inverted Marx's later model, suggesting that it was petty bourgeois impulses that attracted workers into the towns and kept them there.[15] While Marx trusted that migration to the industrializing city would rescue rural so-ciety, and especially the 'peasantry', from 'the idiocy of rural life', Cobbett trusted that the return of town workers to the status of small producers in the countryside would rescue them from the idiocy of urban life.

A countryman consciousness, Cobbett believed, was not at odds with radicalism. Life on the land, he argued, produced economic co-operation and a sort of natural democracy among all countrymen, regardless of their proximity to the means of production:

Rural affairs leave not a day, not an hour, unoccupied and without its cares. The seasons, which wait for no man; the weather, which is no respecter of persons, and which will be what it will be, produce an habitual looking forward, and make the farmer *provident*, whatever might have been his natural disposition. The farmer's cares are pleasing cares. His misfortunes can seldom be more than lessons. His produce consists of things wanted by all mankind. His market is a ready-market one. No day-books, bills, and ledgers haunt his mind. *Envy*, that accursed passion, can in a natural state of things, find no place in his breast; for, the seasons and the weather are the same to all; and the demand for his produce has no other measure than the extent of his crops.[16]

Conflict, class distinctions and market capitalism stood in sharp contradiction to this rural vision. Agriculture was a natural pursuit, and the pursuit most natural to the English. Therefore it was nonsense, in his opinion, to speak of the landed interest or the 'agricultural class', though in explaining his reasons he did exactly that, pitting agriculture against industry:

> Why, the land is the *country*, is it not? 'Class', in their silly teeth! It *is the people of the country*; for though there are great numbers of manufacturers, what are they compared with the whole of those who own, who occupy, who till the land, and who prepare the tools and make the buildings for the land?[17]

The essential and important conflict in English society, therefore, appeared not along the horizontal borders of class but along the vertical seam dividing town and country. That conflict, according to Cobbett, was generated by urban appropriation of what might be called the 'surplus value' of the countryside. In his rural rides he often calculated the extent of these appropriations, such as for the parish of Milton in the valley of the Avon:

> Here is, then, bread for 800 families, mutton for 500, and bacon and beer for 207. Let us take the average of the three, and then we have 502 families, for the keeping of whom, and in this good manner too, the parish of Milton yields a sufficiency ... Now, then, according to the 'Population Return', laid before Parliament, this parish contains 500 persons, or, according to my division, *one hundred families*. So that here are about *one hundred* families to raise food and drink enough, and to raise wool and other things to pay for all other necessaries, for *five hundred* and *two* families! ... What injustice, what a hellish system it must be, to make those who raise it *skin and bone and nakedness*, while the food and drink and wool are almost all carried away to be heaped on the fund-holders, pensioners, soldiers, dead-weight, and other swarms of tax-eaters![18]

This was town-based rather than class-based appropriation. All countrymen, whether labourers, farmers or landlords, were legitimate economic producers. Non-countrymen might also be admitted to the rank of producer, but the nature of their employment had to conform to his premise – which pertained as much to culture as to economics – that agriculture constituted 'the main pillar of every great state'.[19]

The most significant and problematic of Cobbett's exclusions from the productive social order was the worker engaged in export manufactures. During his stay in America he had publicly celebrated English commerce while privately denouncing its 'base spirit';[20] he also privately rejected the claim of Prime Minister Pitt that the mercantile and martial spirits were mutually supportive.[21] An opportunity to give economic structure to these cultural reservations appeared in 1808 in the form of William Spence's pamphlet *Britain Independent of Commerce*, which, taking its cue from the French Physiocrats, asserted that agriculture was the only source of a nation's wealth, and that foreign commerce should altogether be abandoned by Britain. Cobbett liked the idea, claiming that commerce (by which he meant foreign trade, though he quickly broadened his criticisms to include all town-based manufactures) benefited only a few rich people while contributing nothing to national wealth. In his own village of Botley he was aware of only a dozen people who were engaged in export manufactures, and even these few were occupied in the readily dispensable task of manufacturing hoops for West Indian rum casks. Such workers should return to the land, he reasoned, and thereby reduce England's dependence upon imported food. Nationally he took the same view, calculating that the annihilation of commerce would oblige only 400,000 pairs of hands to exchange 'the shuttle for the spade'. Close encounters with enclosed commons, large farms and great tracts of untilled wasteland convinced him that the land could provide a living for all 400,000, and that an even greater number could be absorbed by a more intensive cultivation of existing enclosures.[22]

Cobbett's anti-commerce essays of 1808 appeal for a drastic reduction in the structures of industrial and commercial capitalism. He did not even bother to suggest ways by which the approximately 13 per cent of national income generated by commerce would be made up;[23] nor did he care to consider the impact upon industrialists of his plan to restore all domestic manufacturing to the country cottage. In his view it was sufficient commendation that labourers of town and country should be restored to an independent and more prosperous cottage economy. Upon being restored to the land, industrial workers would cease to be the 'slaves' and 'abject dependents [*sic*]' of the 'cotton-lords'.[24] And since they would be granted title to their allotments from the wastelands, and since urban consumption of agricultural produce would decline in proportion to the relocation of factory workers, all countrymen would receive a fairer share of the produce of the land and of their labour. Finally, the destruction of commerce and large-scale manufacturing would ease the ill-effects of industrial depression. Accordingly he advised the Luddites to make haste for the countryside, spade in hand.[25]

Cobbett did not construct his opposition to commerce upon the right of the poor to property in land. There was to be no redistribution of the property of existing landholders, nor even a very viable plan for assisting the relocation of industrial workers. Yet there was an incisive and meaningful radical critique in Cobbett's scheme.[26] Marx, who does not seem to have been aware of the 'perish commerce' essays, would say that

> what [Cobbett] did not see, was that the epoch of the pretended decline of the English people coincided exactly with the beginning ascendancy of the middle class, with the development of modern commerce and industry ... The great changes attending the decomposition of the old English Society since the eighteenth century struck his eyes and made his heart bleed. But if he saw the effects, he did not understand the causes, the new social agencies at work. He did not see the modern *bourgeoisie* ... They were the prime motors of the decline of England, and the degradation of its people.[27]

But Cobbett *did* see the agency of mercantile finance, industry and the modern bourgeoisie in the degradation of the English worker. Central to his anti-commerce argument was the annihilation of merchants, cotton-lords and the majority of the urban middle class. Even country shopkeepers would be reduced in number; barter and non-monied exchange would thereby be restored, and the appropriations of market capitalism reduced. But Marx was half-right, for Cobbett did not understand that landholders were fast becoming the allies of the 'modern bourgeoisie', hence his confidence (for the time being at least) that he could create a rural radical platform on the basis of agricultural value rather than labour value.

Cobbett's first object in promoting reductions in commerce and the return of manufacturing to the land was to promote the well-being and independence of country workers. The plan of Willian Spence, he argued, predicated that the farm workers were 'no more useful than the French valets and Italian singers'.[28] Nonetheless, Cobbett emerged from the 'perish commerce' essays without seriously challenging his vertical profile of rural society. He conducted the debate on behalf of all countrymen, arguing that commerce 'destroyed the natural influence of the proprietors and cultivators of the land'. But for many apologists for capitalist agriculture, most notably Arthur Young, Cobbett's anti-commerce doctrines were also anti-agricultural, for they seemed to threaten the loss of markets for farm produce, or, in Young's words, to jeopardize an 'agriculture animated by a great demand'. Commerce and industrial manufacturing, Young informed Cobbett, were 'sister employments ... which constitute that demand'. Further to increase demand, Young vigorously defended a general enclosure bill, describing it as 'a MONUMENT OF NATIONAL WISDOM' in contradiction of Cobbett's argument that it would constitute 'a monument of national folly'. In the spring of 1808 they again locked horns – this time on the subject of a proposed bill to replace barley with West Indian sugar in the distilling industry, to which Young and his agricultural lobby were steadfastly opposed on the grounds that it would decrease the demand for barley, and consequently its price. Cobbett, given his prejudice against commerce, might have been expected to support the agricultural lobby, but he sided with the proposed bill, arguing that it might go some way towards reducing the threat of scarcity. The exchanges with Young on the 'Grand Distillery Question' revealed to Cobbett a pervasive self-interest among large capitalist farmers, who feigned alarm about scarcity while opposing a measure that would help guard against it. Young, argued Cobbett, was the 'oracle' and 'grand war-horse' of an agricultural interest that looked no further than the immediate profits of the landholder: 'Have [the farmers] found any want of a market? Has not their corn borne a good price? Do they not drink wine? Do not their wives have their parties? Do not their daughters make a villainous noise upon the piano?' Cobbett's opposition to the anti-sugar lobby was as cultural as it was economic, indeed it was Young who made the more careful and convincing arguments about the possible effects of the proposed measure on crop rotations and on the lack of alternative use for inferior soils that could grow barley alone among cereal crops. The point that Cobbett stressed, however, was that farmers and landlords had a duty to support the interests of all rural society.[29] Clearly, he was going to have to re-evaluate his operative assumption that all countrymen possessed similar economic interests.

For the farm workers there was nothing new in Cobbett's arguments against commerce. They had long since come to reject ruling-class propaganda on behalf of commerce and manufacturing, whether emanating from the speech from the throne or from the well-known song 'The Roast Beef of Old England':

> For while by our commerce and arts we are able,
> To see the Sir-Loin smoking hot on our table,
> The French may e'en croke like the Frog in the fable,

> O the Roast Beef of Old England,
> And O the Old English Roast Beef.[30]

Labourers were usually game for a poke at the French, but they rejected out of hand the claim that commerce was a foundation of national wealth or even a legitimate national endeavour. Cobbett agreed: the text of 'Roast Beef' was arrant nonsense, he claimed, for beef itself was neither shipped to England nor assembled in a factory. The song needed revision: 'spade' and 'plough', he argued, should be substituted for 'commerce' and 'arts'.[31] This he impressed upon the national culture while the village workers were making a similar point in 'The Painful Plough' – one of the most popular of country songs during the nineteenth century:

> Behold the wealthy merchant that trades in foreign seas,
> And brings forth gold and treasure for those that live at ease,
> With finest silks and spices, and fruits and dainties too,
> They are brought from the Indies by virtue of the plough.
>
> For they must have bread, biscuit, rice pudding, flour, and peas,
> To feed the jolly sailors as they sail o'er the seas,
> Yet ev'ry man that brings them here will own to what is true –
> He cannot sail the ocean without the painful plough.[32]

Cobbett's defence of agriculture and his ambivalence towards town-based manufacturing and handicrafts were informed by rural popular culture and by his confidence in the productive capacity of cottage farming. He made polite but firm replies to townspeople who declined to admit the case for the primacy of the plough. Cobbett and the labourers were not surprised to find townspeople taking issue with their claims, for it was an old and familiar debate in town and country. The seventeenth-century ballad 'The Husbandman and Servantman', which was current in rural workers' repertoires throughout the nineteenth century, tells of a vigorous dialogue between a domestic servant and a husbandman on the subject of the economic utility of their respective occupations. After fifteen hard-bargaining stanzas it is the servant who concedes:

> Well, but Sir, I must confess, and allow you your request,
> Whatever man's station is upon,
> Though ours is not so painful, yet yours it is so gainful,
> I wish I was a husbandman.[33]

Use of the term 'husbandman', which in this context encompasses all countrymen who live by the sweat of their brows, suggests an affinity of interest among farm servants, day-labourers and lesser yeomen. It is clear from the text that the husbandman is 'downright', that he follows the plough himself, and is proudly 'neither Lord, nor Duke nor King'. No distinction is made between the labourer and working farmer, regardless of their relationship to economic production.

Other traditional symbols spoke to the same federation of countrymen through the symbol of the 'plough' or 'ploughman'. Registered at the Stationers' Company in 1630 was a song entitled 'The Poor Man Paies for All',[34] which would pass into oral culture and remain a prayer of the farm workers throughout the nineteenth century:

> The King he governs all,
> The Parson Pray for all,
> The Lawer [sic] Plead for all,
> The Ploughman Pay for all,
> And feed all.[35]

Occupations from kingship to carpentry were obliged to honour husbandry on the judgement day of economic valuation. 'Adam was a ploughman', sang the labourers, and so too was 'Cain the eldest son';[36] subsequent generations who abandoned the plough were deserters. Cobbett concurred:

> we are All, we who are at anything else, *deserters* from the plough. God said to mankind: 'this is ground, there are ploughs, *use the latter* on the former, and bread and meat and flax and wool and leather and wood shall come; and you shall eat, drink, be clad and be lodged'. So that this was the business of us all; and all who do not follow it are, in fact, *deserters*.[37]

The Regency labourer expected the farmer to join him in field labour and in lyrical refrain against the unproductive classes of the city. Where such was the case, the labourers were generally accepting of countryman status, singing such songs as 'The Jolly Thresherman' or 'The Nobleman's Generous Kindness' which look upon the farmer as a benevolent soul who presents the labourer with a gift of 30 acres.[38] But by the 1810s, as large farmers defaulted on daily labour and joined in the hunt, the trend in the labourers' songs was towards a class-oriented vocabulary: 'countryman' and 'husbandman' give way to 'labourer' and 'farmer', with the latter sub-divided into old-fashioned and new-fashioned.[39] Since obeisance and deference were no longer producing evident reward, the labourers shifted away from the received notion of belonging to the same countryman order as the farmers, taking their cue from a new genre of songs which addressed economic and cultural conflict between employer and worker:

> There was a time the farmer would work all day at plough,
> His wife would to the meadows go, with her pail to milk her cow,
> But work and him are now fell out, he makes poor men to jump,
> And his wife looks like a scare-crow with a bustle on her r——.[40]

God speed the *Plow*,
and bless the *Corn-mow*.

OR,

A new merry Dialogue between a
Plowman and a *Servingman*.

The Servingman most stoutly doth dispute.
The Husbandman his speeches doth confute
The Servingman sayes his Calling is the best,
The Plowman sayes in that he does but jest,
But in conclusion as I do understand
The Husbandman he got the better hand.

The tune is,   THE DUKE OF NORFOLK.

MY noble friends give ear,
　If mirth you love to hear,
　Ile tell you as fast as I can
A story very true,
Then mark what doth ensue,
　concerning of a husbandman.

Servingman.
A Servingman did meet
A Husbandman i'th street,
　and thus unto him he began
I pray you tell to me
Of what calling you be
　or if you be a servingman.

Husbandman.
Quoth he my brother dear
The Coast I mean to clear,
　and the truth you shall understand
I do no one disdain,
But this I tell you plain,
　I am a Husbandman.

Servingman.
If a Husbandman you be,
Then come along with me
　and Ile help you as soon as I can
Unto a gallant place
Where in a little space,
　you may be a Servingman.

Husbandman.
SIr for your diligence
I give you many thanks
　then answered the plowman again
I pray you to me show
Whereby that I may know
　what pleasure hath a Servingman

Servingman.
A Servingman hath pleasure
Which passeth time and measure
　when ỹ Hawk on hi[s] fist doth stan
His Hood and Uarvils brave
And other things he have,
　which yields joy to a servingman

Husbandman.
My pleasure's more then that,
To see my Oxen fat
　and to prosper well under my hand
And therefore I do mean
With my Horses and my Team
　to keep my self a Husbandman.

Servingman.
O 'tis a gallant thing
In the prime time of the Spring
　to hear the Huntsman now & than
His Bugle Horn to blow
And the Hounds run all arow
　that is pleasure for a servingman.

Servingman.
To hear the Beagle cry
And to see the Falcon fly
　and the Hare trip over the plain
While the huntsman and the hound
Make Hills and Dales rebound,
　that is pleasure for a servingman.

Husbandman.
'Tis pleasanter you know
To see the Corn to grow,
　and to grow so well on the Land,
The plowing and the sowing,
The reaping and the mowing
　yields pleasure to the husbandman

Servingman.
At our Table you may eat
All sorts of dainty meat,
　Pig, Cony, Goose, Capon & Swan
And with Lords and Ladies fine
You may drink Beer, Ale and Wine
　that is pleasure for a servingman.

Husbandman.
While you eat Goose and Capon
Ile feed on Beef and Bacon,
　& piece of hard cheese now & than,
We Pudding have and Souse
Alwayes ready in the house
　*which contents the honest husband*man

Servingman.
At the Court you may have
Your Garments fine and brave
　and Cloak and gold lace laid upon
A shirt as white as milk,
And wrought with finest silk
　thats pleasure for a servingman.

Husbandman.
Such proud and costly Gear,
Is not for us to wear,
　mongst ỹ briers & ỹ brambles many
　one
A good strong Russet Coat
And at your need a groat
　will suffice the honest husbandman

Husbandman.
A Proverb here I tell
Which likes my humor well
　and remember it well I can
If a Courtier be too bold
He may want when he is old
　then farewell the servingman.

Servingman.
It needs must be confest
That your Calling is the best
　no longer discourse with you I can
And henceforth I will pray
By night and by day,
　heaven bles the honest husbandman

Servingman.
To end my Ditty now
I say God speed the plow
　for thats the chief stay of our land
And he that takes the pains
Deserves to have the gains
　which is the honest husbandman,

And thus my loving friends
My Story now it ends,
　according as I first began.
There's none that passeth by
Can say my Song's a lye,
　concerning of the Husbandman.

Printed for W. GILBERTSON *at the sign of the Bible in* GILT-SPUR-STREET.

6   Since the mid-seventeenth century 'The Husbandman and Servantman'
was sung and published in a variety of editions and titles, including 'God
Speed the *Plow*'. The ballad declined in popularity among farm workers
over the course of the nineteenth century. Reproduced by permission of the
Librarian, Glasgow University Library.

𝕿𝖍𝖊 𝕹𝖔𝖇𝖑𝖊𝖒𝖆𝖓'𝖘 𝕲𝖊𝖓𝖊𝖗𝖔𝖚𝖘 𝕶𝖎𝖓𝖉𝖓𝖊𝖘𝖘:
OR,
The Country Man's Unexpected Happiness:

Giving a true Account of a Nobleman, who taking notice of the Poor Man's Industrious Care and Pains
for the maintaining of his Charge, which was seven small Children, meeting him upon a Day, discoursed
with him, and invited him and his Wife, with his Children, home to his House, and accordingly
bestowed upon him a Farm of thirty Acres of Land, to be continued to him and his Heirs for ever.

To the Tune of, The Two English Travellers. Licens'd according to Order.

A Nobleman liv'd near a Village of late,
Hard by a poor Thresher, whose Charge it was great,
He had seven Children, and most of them small,
And none but his labour to keep them withal.

He never was given to idle and lurk,
This Nobleman see him go daily to work,
His flail, with his bag, and his bottle of beer,
As cheerful as those that had Hundreds a Year.

Thus careful and constant each Morning he went
To his daily labour with joy and content,
So jocund and jolly, both wistle and sing,
As blithe and as brisk as a Bird in the Spring.

One Morning this Noble Man taking his walk,
He met with this poor Man, and freely did talk;
He asked him many a Question at large,
Familiarly talking concerning his Charge:

Thou hast many Children I very well know,
Thy labour is hard, and thy wages is low,
And yet thou art chearful; I pray tell me true,
How you do maintain them so well as you do?

I carefully carry home all that I earn;
Now daily experience by this I do learn,
That though it is possible we may live poor,
We still keep a ravenous wolf from the door,

I reap and I mow, and I harrow and sow,
Sometimes I to hedging and ditching do go;
No work comes amiss, for I thresh [an]d I plow:
Thus I eat my bread by the sweat of [my] brow.

My Wife she is willing to pull in the yoak,
We live like two Lambs, and we never provoke
Each other; but like to the labouring Ant,
We do our endeavour to keep us from want.

And when I come home from my labour at night
To my Wife and Children, in whom I delight,

To hear them come round me with tatling noise;
Now these are the riches that poor Men enjoys.

Though I am as weary as weary may be,
The Youngest I commonly dance on my knee:
I find that content is an absolute feast,
I never repin'd at my Charge in the least.

The Nobleman hearing then what he did say,
Was pleas'd, and invited him home the next day;
His Wife and his Children he charg'd him to bring,
In token of favour he gave him a ring.

Then thanked his Honour, and taking his leave,
He went to his Wife, who would hardly believe,
But that this strange story himself he might raise,
Yet seeing the ring she was then in amaze.

Betimes in the morning the good Wife arose,
And made them all fine with the best of their Cloaths:
The good Man and Wife, with his Children small,
They then was to dine at the Nobleman's Hall.

And when they came there, as the truth doth report,
All things was prepar'd in a plentiful sort:
And they, at the Nobleman's table did dine,
With all sorts of dainties, with plenty of Wine.

All this being over, he soon let him know,
What he then intended on him to bestow:
A Farm, with full thirty good Acres of land,
And gave him the writings then with his own hand.

Because thou wast careful and good to thy Wife,
I'll make thy days happy the rest of thy life;
It shall be for ever to thee, and thy Heir,
For why? I beheld thy industrious care.

No tongue then was able in full to express
The depth of their joy, and their true thankfulness,
With many a courtesie and bow to the ground.
But such Noblemen there is few to be found.

London: Printed for *E. Brooksby, at the* Sign of the Golden-ball, in *Pye-corner.*

7 Ballads about benevolent squires were commonplace in nineteenth-
century village repertoires. The majority of the labourers' protest songs were
directed against farmers. Reproduced by permission of the Librarian,
Glasgow University Library.

Until the late eighteenth century, 'God Speed the Plough' had served as the mutual prayer of the owners and followers of the plough. The rich Regency farmer, however, toasted success to master ploughshare without reference to his workers, who in turn responded with class expressions of their own:

> Some pity the farmers, but I tell you now,
> Pity poor labourers that follow the plough.[41]

Even songs such as 'A Country Lad Am I', which in title suggests a theme of unity among countrymen, instead acknowledges the farmer's absence from the fields, while threatening him with having to plough himself unless wages are lifted above 18d. a day.[42] Such appeals for solidarity among workers were now commonplace. The new moral and economic resolve of the labourers was that

> He that by the plough would thrive,
> ... himself must either hold or drive.[43]

Along with the labourers Cobbett was edging from a vertical to a horizontal perspective of rural society; in other words exchanging his countryman consciousness for class consciousness.[44] In the same manner as the labourers' songs he illustrated this new consciousness by remarking upon the tendency of employers to withdraw from labour and to honour the plough independently of the plough*man*:

> the worst of it has been in England of late years, that when the fat, red-cheeked, and purse-proud fellows, have been giving the toast at their sheep-shearings and cattle-shows '*honour the plough*', they meant not to include the plough-*man*. They meant, if they meant anything really belonging to that implement of husbandry, the wood and the iron and the horses, and never the man. So, likewise, when they give the toast '*speed the plough*', they have meant, literally, the wood and iron to be got along through the ground themselves ... Now, this was not at all the meaning of the prayer in old times. The meaning was, success to the works of the plough; happiness and good living to those who till the land; and the plough, having been, in all times, the chief implement of husbandry, the word plough was made use of as a short, and, at the same time, comprehensive designation, of the whole of the affairs and of the things and persons appertaining to husbandry.[45]

The new-fashioned farmer rejected social, cultural and economic identification with the ploughman; he sought to cultivate the land with the fewest 'hands' possible (prizes for this achievement were commonly awarded by the agricultural societies), and he praised his own class, and the agency of capital, as the mainstays of agriculture. Accordingly the new-fashioned farmers ceased to sing the songs in praise of unity among countrymen,

THE NEW-FASHIONED FARMER.

Good people all, attend awhile,
  Whilst I relate a story,
How the farmers in old England
  Did once support their glory,—
When masters lived as masters ought
  And happy in their station ;
Until at length their stinking pride,
  Has ruined half the nation.

CHORUS.

Let's pray that hungry bellies may
  Be filled when they are empty;
And where a servant gets ten pounds
  I wish he may get twenty,

A good old fashion'd long grey coat
  The farmers use to wear, sir;
And old Dobbin they would ride
  To market or to fair, sir.
But now fine geldings they must mount
  To join all in the chase, sir;
Dress'd up like any lord or 'squire,
  Before their landords' face sir.

In former times, both plain and neat,
  They'd go to church on Sunday;
And then to harrow, plough or sow,
  They'd go upon a Monday.
But now, instead of the plough-tail,
  O'er hedges they are jumping;
And instead of sowing their corn,
  Their delight is in fox-hunting.

The good old dames,—God bless their
    names?—
Were seldom in a passion;
But strove to keep a right good house,
  And never thought on fashion.
With fine brown beer their hearts to
    cheer,
  But now they must drink swipes, sir;
It's enough to make a strong man weak,
  And give him the dry gripes, sir.

The farmers' daughters used to work
  All at the spinning-wheel, sir;
But now such furniture as that
  Is thought quite ungenteel, sir.
Their fingers they're afraid to spoil
  With any such kind of sport, sir:
Sooner than handle mop or broom,
  They'd handle a piano-forte, sir.

Their dress was always plain and warm,
  When in their holiday clothes, sir;
Besides, they had such handsome faces,
  As red as any rose, sir;
But now they,re frilled and furbelowed
  Just like a dancing monkey :
Their bonnets and their great black veils
  Would almost fright a donkey.

When wheat was just a guinea a-strike,
  The farmers bore the sway, sir;
Now with their landlords they will ride
  Upon each hunting-day, sir:
Besides, their daughters, too, must join
  The ladies to the ball, sir:
The landlords say, we'll double the
    rents,
  And then their pride must fall, sir.

I hope no one will think amiss
  At what has here been penned, sir;
But let us hope that these hard times
  May speedly amend, sir.
It's all through this confounded pride
  That has brought them to reflection:
It makes poor servants' wages low,
  And keeps them in subjection.

8 'The New-Fashioned Farmer' was one of the most widely printed of the labourers' protest songs of the early nineteenth century. Reproduced by permission of the Syndics of Cambridge University Library (Madden Collection of Ballads).

directing their attention to the 'anti-Boney' songs (which often recalled with favour the high wartime price of wheat) and to the drawing-room refrains of Charles Dibdin.[46] Indeed, by 1820, the traditional songs in praise of ploughmen had a solitary venue: the post-harvest village feast.

The new-fashioned farmer was too enamoured of class respectability and too much the beneficiary of proletarian labour to will a permanent restoration of the countryman bond, but his sponsorship of one evening of solidarity between worker and master would not seriously compromise the cash nexus; it might even have the effect of discouraging his workers from emigrating or changing employers.[47] For their part, the labourers were reluctant to turn their backs on a sponsored feast; and for convivi-ality's sake, they even suspended outward expressions of contempt for old 'Jolterhead'. 'It did not do to look beneath the surface' at harvest home, said Flora Thompson in the later nineteenth century,[48] but it is by no means clear that her advice was followed in Regency times, even when

> ... masters [levelled] with their men,
> Who push'd the beer about, and smok'd and drank.[49]

The master, seated at head-table, played the leveller the only way he knew how: by recourse to traditional song. In charge of the evening's repertoire, he crooned some of the new bourgeois verse, patriotic and pastoral, or recalled the valour of General Gage or Lord Nelson. Then came the traditional songs in praise of old England and solidarity on the land: 'God Speed the Plough', 'The Farmer's Boy' and finally that anthem of harvest home, 'We're all Jolly Fellows that Follow the Plough':

> 'Twas early one morning at the break of day,
> The cocks were crowing the farmer did say,
> Arise my good fellows, arise with good will,
> Your horses want something their bellies to fill.

> We jump out of bed and put on our clothes,
> And into the stable each nimbly goes,
> There's a rubbing and scrubbing I swear and I vow,
> We are all jolly fellows that follow the plough.

> When six o'clock comes to breakfast we go,
> With good beer and cheese and the best stingo,
> Besides fill our pockets I swear and I vow,
> We are all jolly fellows that follow the plough.

> We harness our horses to plough we then go,
> So nimbly we trip o'er the plain boys we go,
> With our hands in our pockets like gentlemen go,
> And see which of us the best furrow can draw.

TIMES ARE ALTERED.

Come all you swag'ring farmers wherever you may be,
One moment pay attention and listen unto me;
It is concerning former times that I to you declare,
So different from the present times if you with them compar

CHORUS.

For lofty heads and paltry pride I'm sure 'tis all the go,
For to distress poor servants and keep their wages low.

If you'd but seen the farmer's wives 'bout 50 years ago,
In home-spun russetlinsey were clad from top to toe,
But now-a-days the farmers' wives are so puff'd up with prid
In a dandy habit & green veil, to market they must ride.

Some yeart ago the farmers' sons were lea.nt to ploufh and
                                                        sow   (mow,
And when the summer time was come likewise to reap and
But now they dress like squires' sons their pride it knows no
                bounds,   (hounds,
They mount upon a fine blood horse to follow up the hounds,

The farmers' daughters formerly were learnt to card & spin,
And bo their own industry good husbands theoy would win,
But now the card & spinning wheel are forced to take their
                chance,   (to sing and dance,
While they are hopp'd off to boarding school far to learn

In a decent black silk bonnet to church they used to go,
Black shoes and handsome cotton gown stockings as white as
                snow,

But new silk gowns and coloured shoes they must be (ought
                for them,
Besides they are frizz'd & fnrbelow'd ust like a friesland hen,

Caeh morning when at preakfast each master and each dame
Down with the se,vants they woul sit & eat & drink the same
But now with such good old thengs thdy've done them quite
                away,
Into the parlour they do go with coffee, toast, and tea.

At the kitchen table formerly the farmer he would sit,
And carve for all his servants good pudding and good meat,
But now all in the dining room so closely they are box'd in.
But if a servant was to peep it would be thodght a sin.

Now in these good old fashion'd times the truth I do declare,
The rent and taxes could be paid & money for to spare;
But now they keep the fashions up they look so very nice,
Although they cut an outside show they are as poor as mice.

When Bonaparte was in vogue poor servants could engage,
For l16 a year my boys and that was handsome wage,
But now the wages are so low & what is worst of all,
The masters cannot find the cash so do not pay at all.

When 50 acres they did rent then money they could save,
But nhw for sy support their pride 500 they must haye;
If those great farms were taken and divided into ten,
We then migut see as happy days as ever we did then.

' W. Clift, Printer, Cirencester.

9 'Times are Altered' (*c.* 1820). Vanity and pride among the farmers was a leading complaint among agricultural workers. Reproduced by permission of the Syndics of Cambridge University Library (Madden Collection of Ballads).

Then the farmer comes round and to us doth say,
What have you been doing this long summer's day,
You've not done an acre I swear and I vow,
You're all idle fellows that follow the plough.

The plough boy turns round and makes his reply,
What you have been saying is a big lie,
We have plough'd an acre I swear and I vow,
We are all jolly fellows that follow the plough.

The farmer turns round with a smile and a joke,
'Tis past four o'clock boys 'tis time to unyoke,
Unharness your horses and rub them down well,
And I'll give you a cup of good brown ale.[50]

We cannot know for certain what passed through the labourers' minds as they harmonized with these verses, but a clue might lie in the recollections of two twentieth-century singers from Sussex, who offered opposite accounts of their state of mind as they sang 'Jolly Fellows' at harvest home. One implied that he was thankful for the feast and had no quarrel with the farmer, which is to say that not all labourers, either of the nineteenth or twentieth centuries, were conscious of conflict or of the objective experiences of class society. The other singer, however, suggested that he was not at all a jolly fellow, that he disliked rising at four o'clock in the morning, and that he was put out of humour by twelve hours of toil in a rain-soaked field. Above all, he was displeased with his employer's paternalism. For this latter labourer, 'Jolly Fellows' represented class antagonism under the guise of deference.[51] If we project this coding back to the early nineteenth century (though the anachronism of these examples must certainly be admitted), it becomes easier to understand why traditional countryman narratives could co-exist in the labourers' repertoires with the newer, class conscious, protest verse.

Cobbett's vertical perspective on rural society began to crumble at the conclusion of the commerce and agriculture debates of 1807–8, but its demise was a gradual affair. The same can be said for the countryman consciousness of the labourers. Much of their energy during the 1820s was devoted to appeals for the restoration of cultural unity among countrymen. They were not certain that they wanted its restoration, but traditional farmer–labourer relations seemed the quickest way forward for a partial proletariat which was caught without its own class culture when their employers opted for one of their own. It was not that the labourers enjoyed the company of the gentry and farmers but that their proletarian experience seemed somehow ameliorated by a direct line of

THE POOR
LABOURERS.

YOU sons of old England, now list to my
  rhymes,
And I'll sing unto you a short sketch of
  the times,
Concerning poor labourers you all must
  allow,
Who work all the day at the tail of the
  plough.

CHORUS.

O, the poor labourers, pity poor labourers,
That are working for five or six shillings
  per week.

There's many poor labourers to work
  they will go,
Either hedging or ditching to plough or to
  sow,
And many poor fellows are used like a
  Turk,
They do not get paid for half a days
  work.

And many poor labourers I'm sorry to say
Are breaking of stones for eightpence a
  day;
Bread and water's the fare of the poor
  labouring man,
While the rich they can live on the fat of
  the land.

Some pity the farmers, but I tell you now,
Pity poor labourers that follow the plough,
Pity poor children half starving and
  then,
Divide every great farm into ten.

There are many young fellows you'll see
  every day,
For snaring a hare they are banished
  away,
To Van Dieman's land or to some foreign
  shore,
And their wives and children are left to
  deplore.

There's many a farmer that's making a
  fuss,
While the poor are starving, can scarce
  get a crust,
Do away with their hounds and their
  hunters so gay,
And give the poor labourers a little fair
  play.

Fair play in a stranger these many years
  past,
And pity's bunged up in an old oaken cask
But the time's fast approaching, it's very
  near come,
When we'll have all the farmers under our
  thumbs.

JOLLY MORTALS
FILL YOUR GLASSES.

Jolly mortals fill your glasses!
  Noble deeds are done by wine:
Scorn the nymph and all her graces,—
  Who'd for love or beauty pine?

Look within the bowl that's flowing,
  And a thousand charms you find,
More than Phillis has though going.
  In a moment to be kind.

Alexander hated thinking,
  Drank about at council-board,
He subdued the world by drinking,
  More than by his conquering sword.

Henson, Printer, &c., Lower End Bridge Street
Northampton.

10 In the songs of the 1820s and 1830s the words 'husbandman' and
'countryman' gave way to 'labourer' and farmer'. Fair play and small farms
were among the leading demands of the cottage charter. Reproduced by
permission of the Syndics of Cambridge University Library (Madden Collection of Ballads).

communication with those who paid their wages and negotiated their perquisites. Bailiffs and stewards corrupted this direct line; in the words of one labourer, 'masters never give us a chance to speak to them'.[52] Knowing the importance of free and easy relations between master and man, Cobbett recommended his own practice of paying the labourer his wages 'at the fire-side, over a familiar mug of ale, as in former times; and not half-wages, handed to him by a bailiff from one of the out-house windows of Daddy Coke's agricultural villas'.[53] He also advised farmers to forego their 'get out of my way or by G-d I'll run over you' attitude that he encountered so often on his rural rides, recalling with favour the farmers of his youth who either walked to Farnham market or meandered there aboard a tired mare.[54] It was likewise in the labourer's memory:

> The farmers to market did once used to walk,
> Amusing each other with old-fashioned talk,
> But now on fine geldings are mounted so gay,
> To ride over poor folks if they stand in the way.[55]

The labourers did not aspire to possess gigs, carpets or parlour-bells of their own, but they understood with Cobbett that 'since the piano-fortes and the parlour-bells and the carpets came into the farmhouse, the lot of the labourers has been growing worse and worse'.[56] The labourers would not have considered accepting the farmer's luxuries were they offered them, but they freely cursed them for removing the farmer and his family from the traditional culture of the community.[57] Cobbett, too, ridiculed the daughters who attended horse races, election balls, and who clasped their hands and leered 'at the ceiling in reading the soft balderdash of Southey or Walter Scott'.[58] Rural labourers knew nothing of Southey and Scott, but they were at one with Cobbett's recommendation that farm girls light the oven with their novels and return to the knitting-needles by the rush-light. Indeed such was Cobbett's reverence for the traditional farm woman that when in Wiltshire he spotted a young woman at work on a cheese press, he leapt from his horse and squeezed her hand with joy. For Cobbett and the labourers, such women embodied the times when women were collectively known as 'women, wenches and girls', and individually as 'Moll' or 'Bess'.[59]

The Regency farm workers were not new to a consciousness of exploitation,[60] but the consumerism and ostentation of the farmhouse were now more visibly financed by extractions from the labourer's wages. During the early stages of the wars, recalled a Suffolk labourer, the rich farmer was a rare sight – the exceptions in his parish being one farmer in top-boots and another in dog-skin gloves.[61] It was the increase in these scenes that caused

THE JOLLY

Plough Boys

Harkness, Printer, Church Street, Preston.

'Twas early one morning by the break of day,
The cocks were crowing the farmer did say,
Arise my good fellows arise with good will,
Your horses want something their bellies to fill.

We jump out of bed and put on our clothes,
And into the stable each nimbly goes,
There's a rubbing and scrubbing I swear and vow,
We are jolly fellows that follow the plough.

When six o'clock comes to breakfast we go,
Whith good bread and cheese and the best stingo,
Besides fill our pockets I swear and vow,
We are all jolly fellows that follow the plough.

We harness our horses to plough then we go,
So nimbly we trip o'er the plain boys we go,
With our hands in our pockets like gentlemen go,
And see which of us the best furrow can draw.

Then the farmer comes round and to us doth say,
What have you being done this long summer's day,
You've not done an acre I swear and I vow,
You're all idle fellows that follow the plough.

The plough boy turns round and makes his reply,
What you have been saying is a big lie,
We have plough'd an acre I swear and I vow,
We are all jolly fellows that follow the plough.

The farmer turns round with a smile and a joke,
'Tis past four o'clock boys 'tis time to unyoke,
Unharness your horses and rub them down well,
And I'll give you a cup of good brown ale.

11 'The Jolly Ploughboys' or 'We're all Jolly Fellows that Follow the Plough' was commonly sung at nineteenth-century harvest homes. Reproduced by permission of the Syndics of Cambridge University Library (Madden Collection of Ballads).

the labourers to enquire more directly into the origins of the farmer's property:

> Where does it come from but out of the poor,
> It is they that works for it and must work for more.[62]

As Cobbett explained, agricultural wages in 1790 were on a scale of two bushels of wheat per week, and that in 1814, with wheat fetching 15s. a bushel, wages should have been at 33s. instead of 13s. Of the 20s. difference, a few shillings were returned to the labourers in the form of parish relief, leaving the employer a net gain of about 15s. to finance improvements, top-boots and the bailiff.[63] In the words of one farmer, every shilling spent on labour during the war returned two to the employer,[64] or in the more direct language of Cobbett, the new level of profit was extracted from the 'flesh and blood and bones' of the labourers.[65]

Among the greatest sources of alienation between labourer and farmer was the increasing reluctance of the latter to share their board and roof with their workers. It was the labourers' perception that

> The farmers and the servants together used to dine,
> But now they are in the parlour with their pudding, beef, and wine,
> The master and their mistress, their sons and daughters all alone,
> And they will eat the beef and you may pick the bone.[66]

The songs suggest that class consciousness among employing farmers was the primary cause of the decline of living-in, though some recent work by Mick Reed suggests that it was sometimes by mutual agreement.[67] This accords with Cobbett's observation that the 'manners and principles of the working class are so changed that a sort of self-preservation bids the farmer (especially in some counties) to keep them from beneath his roof'.[68] As regards living-in with small farmers, the labourers had few objections, providing that they received an ample board, fair contracts and a blind eye towards nocturnal absenteeism. In early nineteenth-century Bedfordshire, according to an agricultural surveyor: 'it is common for the servants to dine at the same table as their master, wherever the farms are not very large: some little distinction is made occasionally; but the servants seldom look forward with eager expectations to the pleasures of a separate table'.[69] Social control was implicit in the tradition of living-in, including Cobbett's own maintenance of a standing army of farm servants, but he and the labourers looked upon it as a right to accept or decline for themselves. 'These fellows in nail shoes do the work', Cobbett reminded employers, 'and it is the bounden duty of Landlords to take care that they have their due and honest share of the produce of the land.'[70] An aggrieved

Herefordshire farmer, who wrote in to the *Register* to reprimand Cobbett for telling the labourers that they held a *right* of residency in the farmhouse, complained that the exercise of such right would dispossess him of his authority over his household, and reduce him to a 'servant and tenant' of his men. All to the good, replied Cobbett, either the servant has the right and option to live-in or he must have some land given up that 'he may cultivate it for himself!'. If the employers refused to grant this right at the labourer's request, then 'the *right of nature returns*: that is to say, the *right of the strongest*'.[71]

For the labourers and Cobbett the decline of living-in was one of the most irksome symbols of the new class formations in the countryside. Although many employers attempted to disguise their own role in the affair by describing indoor servants as an affront to the delicate sensibilities of the nuclear family, the great underlying cause of the decline (in the words of an Oxfordshire cleric) was 'the difference in station resulting from large Farms being held by Capitalists'.[72] As a Shropshire farmer apologized, farmers were now 'a superior set of men to the farmers of former days who were in no ways distinguishable from the peasants who sat at their board'.[73] Farmer and labourer, needless to say, had long been distinguishable at the point of access to the produce of the land, but class consciousness had hitherto been postponed by shared board, common toil and a spirit of countryman unity.

The post-war county agricultural meetings were convened and dominated by large farmers and landlords who were bound hard and fast in an anti-Cobbett and anti-labourer alliance. Their object, in most cases, was to petition Parliament against falling corn prices, especially by the early 1820s when the Corn Laws ceased to be in full effect.[74] Cobbett was not well-disposed towards this agricultural lobby, for it was predicated upon the class notion that the agriculturists (a word he deplored, preferring the term 'agriculture-asses', which he thought more apt and more grammatical) were 'a most valuable class of men'. The so-called agriculturist, he argued, was not one bit more valuable than the labourer, and no more deserving of legislative favour.[75] The landholder, he argued, had been privileged for long enough, and it was plainly immoral that he should seek 'to perpetuate his *extravagant gains*' by a refurbished Corn Law.[76]

It was farmers and landlords who collaborated with the government and the urban middle class, whether by investing in the funds or by riding in the yeomanry cavalry, whom Cobbett wished to see ruined by the post-war fall in agricultural prices. The small farmers who remained outside a cultural and ideological alliance with the middle class, he predicted, would not be brought down.[77] It was only the labourers and small farmers who could make sense of this argument, which paradoxically invoked class in an attempt to undermine its objective determinants. Cobbett and the labourers sought the impoverishment of large farmers to the point where they would be forced to recognize that the labourers were their 'only rampart against their natural foes, the dealers in money and funds'.[78] If this made no sense to the landlord and farmer, it made complete sense to labourers such as John Clare, who discerned 'some very sensible arguments' in Cobbett's anti-farmer protests.[79]

Large farmers and landlords refused to yield to any argument that did not seek to maximize the price of corn, and in constructing their case they falsely represented the labourer as the friend of the high-priced bushel. But the experience of the labourers (confirmed by the recent work of Keith Snell) was that real wages declined during the war years. Further, as Cobbett's fellow anti-Corn Bill lobbyist Henry Hunt recalled, the farmers' antipathy to reformers 'increased in proportion to the high price of corn and bread'.[80] The claims of landholders that higher prices were in their labourers' interests did not pass Cobbett unnoticed. Parliamentary committees investigating protection, he advised, should not enquire into whether the farmer be low on capital (which he equated with 'asking a drunkard if he be thirsty'), but into the date when living-in and home-brewing fell into decline, and when it was that potatoes and tea replaced bacon and bread on the cottage table: 'And, if you find that all these took place at the time when farmers began to wear shining boots, white cravats, and broad cloth coats, instead of spatterdashes, red handkerchiefs, and smock-frocks, ought you not to recommend that which will bring prices still lower?'[81] This was the labourers' voice on the question of protection. As a Suffolk labourer put it, 'men worked on the same farm when corn sold low and when corn sold high, and they found that wages never kept pace with the rise in prices'.[82] John Clare remembered that when corn was dear during the wars, farmers combined to freeze wages at 1os.[83] As a class the labourers understood that they had more to lose than gain by a rise in agricultural prices:

> Should corn again be dear, which God forbid,
> Would wages rise as fast? They never did.[84]

Cobbett repeated the point, contradicting the farmers and landlords in the name of the labourer's experience: 'the labourer of England knows well, that, whether corn be dear or cheap, he shall be allowed no more wages and rates, than will just enable him to feed his young and to perform his work'.[85] Although Cobbett was himself a corn farmer who stood to gain from a new schedule of protection, he wanted no part of a measure that held no benefit for the labourers, and which might enable the urban middle class to buttress its economic and political power by collecting more taxes from agriculture.[86]

The caricatured landlord and farmer of Cobbett's *Register* and of the labourers' songs were not without prototypes at the county agricultural meetings. Among them was the Wiltshire landowner John Benett, whose estates generated annual rents of approximately £10,000, and who served as county magistrate, sheriff of Wells and president of the Wiltshire Agricultural Society.[87] In 1817 Benett threatened to re-locate to France if further legislative protection for agriculture was not forthcoming; he would not tolerate, he declared, a reduction in the social and economic station of 'the gentlemen of landed property'. At the same time he flatly rejected a suggestion that the labourers might benefit from allotments. And as a rate-payer and employer of labour, he vowed that he would sooner demolish the cottages on his estates than allow more labourers to obtain a settlement in his parish; indeed he admitted to averting many additional settlements by hiring labourers for a fixed term of less than a year. Further to reduce claimancy on the rates, Benett authored in 1812 a penurious allowance scale of a gallon-loaf and 3d. per person per week.[88] Although such relief scales were not uncommon in the rural South, Cobbett would not allow this particular one to be forgotten; henceforth it was 'gallon-loaf' Benett or 'the stupid ass'. Cobbett wielded a sharp pen, but he was prepared to come clean on his own farms, using the occasion of Benett's remarks to re-state his commitment that 'no labourer of mine shall ever live upon *a pound and a quarter of bread and a half penny a day*'.[89] The likes of Benett were not numerous, but they wielded much influence over local wage levels and relief scales. They were represented in popular song as the loud-mouthed and big-bellied men who swaggered about the market and grieved about drunkenness, idleness and profligacy among labourers. In 1830 they became the favourite target of Captain Swing (as happened to Benett himself, who attributed the fires to Cobbett's writings).[90] They read Cobbett and they feared him, not just because he had a sound grasp of agricultural economics, but because he accepted capitalist farming only on the condition that all labourers receive a decent living out of the land. Above all, they were afraid of Cobbett's proven ability to engage the language of rural popular culture and to look over the heads of landholders to their workers. 'When I see a great farmer', Cobbett declared, 'I know that he has from 40 to 100 poor wretches of *paupers* or of half-starved labourers at home ... with their rags and long beards and lank jaws and sunk eyes and scabby heads.'[91] Much to the dismay and anguish of landholders, it was these people whom Cobbett saw as the worthiest representatives of agriculture.

A special problem for the landholders was that Cobbett personified aspects of their own past. Dressed as a yeoman farmer, and able to converse on all agricultural matters, he put them in mind of the days when there was no improvement for improvement's sake, and when the word 'capital' was seldom heard. Many older farmers knew well the rural England that Cobbett wished to see restored, and by no means were all of them opposed to such a restoration. The union with the urban middle class, which had worked to the farmers' advantage during the wars, was now faltering as the government seemed to give priority to industrial and commercial enterprise. But landlords and large farmers, particularly those who attended the county agricultural meetings, had overly committed themselves – financially, culturally and ideologically – to an alliance with the middle class and to the promotion of class society. They were not disposed to reverse these investments at Cobbett's behest.

The post-war county meetings were generally restricted to freeholders, so that to qualify for attendance at these assemblages, Cobbett had either to tell falsehoods about his county property holdings or else perform some swift shuffles on the freehold market; he did both.[92] A small minority of the meetings (Cobbett attended at least twenty in 1822 alone) were open to non-freeholders, in which case he had support to the extent of their numbers. In Salisbury in 1815, as the Corn Bill passed through Parliament, a crowd of many hundreds crammed into a hall to hear his speech and petition against 'rapacious landlords'.[93] At Norwich in 1821, despite contrary recommendations by Thomas Coke, the crowd carried Cobbett's petition in all its particulars, including its call for the enfranchisement of the rural workers, whose property, he argued, was in their labour.[94] At a Surrey meeting in 1823, support for Cobbett's petition came from the non-freeholder side of the hall, which votes were discounted by the presiding Lord Ellenborough. 'Who ever knew a labourer working for three shillings per week?', asked Cobbett at this meeting; 'they work for two shillings' returned a voice from the audience.[95] At most of the meetings, however, Cobbett had to speak *for* rather than *with* the labourers, whose presence was generally neither welcome nor official. On these occasions Cobbett reminded landholders that their profits and produce were owing to their workers. He asked them to remember that the labourers paid more in taxes in proportion to their means than did any other class: as much as one half of their net earnings. He asked employers to cease to define poor-rates as a tax; they were wage-funds and as such they should be understood. He asked employers not to reduce wages as a means of paying tithes, rents and taxes, for the labourers held first claim to the produce of the soil. He reiterated the 'law of nature' and the 'law of God' that no one should starve in a land of plenty. 'Were I pushed even to the very verge of ruin', he claimed, 'my labourers would share with me to the last . . . I would pay my tradesman in full; and as to the landlord and tithe-owner, they must . . . take the rest.' He asked his audience to treat the labourers with 'gentleness and justice', and to exchange class preoccupations for making common cause with their workers.[96] At his native Farnham he reiterated his appeal for solidarity among countrymen:

> Instead of looking into the [labourers'] misery, those who inveigh against them seem to regard them as a separate cast of beings; as a distinct and different breed of animals. But I trust, Gentlemen, that all we who are here present . . . shall not fail to reflect, that it may be owing to accidental circumstances, that we are not exposed to the humiliation of receiving parish relief. For my own part, you must well know, that it was owing to accident that I was not a labourer all my life. I feel this at any rate; and unnatural should I be, if I had not great consideration for all that class of men, who, performing as they do, the toils of the community, are entitled, when they experience distress, to our most solicitous regard and kindest compassion. At any rate, it is cowardly, as well as unjust, to throw upon the defenceless the blame which is wholly due to the powerful.[97]

At best the farmers and landlords would hear him out. Often they showed signs of disapprobation, as at Salisbury, where his exhortations for mercy to the labourers 'met with sour looks from a part of my hearers'. But he persevered: 'I knew that my doctrines were not generally palatable; but I despised frowns and sour looks when put in the balance against my duty. My great object was to plead the case of the labourers.'[98]

His most formidable perseverance was in eastern Sussex, where the meetings were firmly under the control of the 'bull-frogs' (so-called by Cobbett for their deep-throated capacity to gulp down small farmers). At one of their gatherings in 1821, chaired by the fair-minded Earl of Egremont, a number of speakers criticized the labourers for causing recent rises in poor-rates. This was an old claim, but amidst the proceedings emerged the further revelation that the parish overseers felt themselves in constant danger from the physical violence of the paupers. It was further disclosed by the Glynde farmer John Ellman Jr that a number of labourers were set to work by overseers in drawing beach-gravel, with the lead drawer being suited with a bell, so that the overseer might better know when the men were stopped. Cobbett was enraged:

> here is much more than enough to make me *rejoice in the ruin of the farmers*; and I do, with all my heart, thank God for it; seeing, that it appears

absolutely necessary, that the present race of them should be totally broken up, in Sussex at any rate, in order to put an end to this cruelty and insolence towards the labourers, who are by far the greater number; and who are *men*, and a little *better men* too, than such employers as these, who are, in fact, monsters in human shape![99]

This, in turn, was too much for the east Sussex farmers, who were already frustrated by the refusal of the paupers to be ordered about at the will of rate-payers. The spirited poor threatened the lives and limbs of overseers, and refused seriously to work at parish-sponsored work schemes, especially at those tasks in which they were harnessed to carts or set to crushing rocks for the construction of roads, which indignities they revenged by leaning on the carts or by playing at games. 'They must and will have *food*', said Cobbett, 'and the farmers have their choice, whether they will give the food in *exchange for labour*, or give it for nothing.'[100]

Cobbett was not representing the Sussex labourers in vain, for much to the dismay and irritation of farmers and landlords, they demanded relief as a *right*. At the time of the 1821 meeting there was a presentation of nineteen men before the Brighton Bench for allegedly coercing an overseer into awarding them relief. The men were lectured by a magistrate about idleness and drunkenness, as well as reprimanded for not having saved a portion of their earnings for the winter months. All nineteen men were outwardly silent to the reprimand; Cobbett articulated their reply:

> My forefathers were not paupers, and yet nobody, in their day, had the face to interfere with them as to the disposal of their summer earnings . . . [They] found in their *wages* the means of decent living; the means of securing a warm back and a full belly. If they earned more in summer than in winter, they lived better during the season of hard work; and, they expended the *surplus* in articles of ornament for their wives and daughters; never suspecting, that the winter was to be a season of *distress*. They spent, and had a right to spend, some part of their time at *fairs* . . . and, we should think it no harm to do that now, when we read of so many *grand dinners, routs, balls* and *masquerades*, giving [sic] by persons who notoriously do no *work at all*.

All nineteen men, Cobbett assured the justices, were thinking these thoughts, which were a part of nature and 'never to be driven out of the head'.[101] On these particulars the Sussex farmers could not contradict Cobbett, but at their meeting at Lewes of 9 January 1822, some of their number read aloud from the *Register* its diatribe against them. And when the author of that diatribe showed up at the meeting in person, the audience approved a motion for his eviction – the execution of which became another matter when their visitor rose to his feet in order 'that they might see the man that they had to put out'. Cobbett was suffered to stay and to deliver his speech, in which he reminded the landholders (or at least those who did not join the walk-out when he took the floor) that they owed their all to the labourers, and that he himself was bred at the plough-tail.[102] In the end, the petition framed at the Sussex meeting said nothing about the labourers, but Cobbett rejoiced in his achievements: 'I beat the cocks upon their own dung-hill', he wrote privately.[103] Eight years later, during the Captain Swing revolts, the Sussex landholders came to see that in rejecting Cobbett in 1822 they had rejected the wants and aspirations of the entire class of agricultural workers.

On no subject is Cobbett more quoted than on his declared veneration for a traditional social order where everyone knew their place and was happy in their station. Yet the social model that he praised in theory was not the model that he recommended in practice. It is true that he declared an unbroken chain of connection from the richest to the poorest to be the social order decreed by God and by Nature. He also wrote of the social necessity of rank, order and gradation in civil society, while repudiating 'the ridiculous doctrine of equality either in rank or estate'.[104] These were strong words, but his eighteenth-century model of society was so loaded with conditioners and riders as to make it unworkable and almost mean-ingless as a code of social and economic behaviour. His invitation to workers to defer to their superiors and to forego demands for equality in property were made conditional upon these superiors abiding by a long list of duties and responsibilities, including payment of fair wages, commit-ment to radical parliamentary reform, and rejection of government pen-sions and sinecures. To these duties he added dozens more, including opposition to the malt tax, the game laws and the decline of living-in. According to these terms, very few of the rural élite qualified for deference from below.

Rather than promote the notion that the rich were somehow better than the poor, Cobbett sought to undermine it:

> Now, unless this feeling be changed: unless the people be cured of this baseness, nothing that can be done by men, even the most able and industri-ous and zealous, will ever render them better off than they now are . . . I shall be told that I have always been an advocate of king, lords, and commons, and for bishops, seated among the lords. Now, this is very true . . . Well, then, ought you not to cherish these orders now? Are they not what they always were? . . . Stop: yes, my friend, we have dukes, marquises, earls, and so forth still; but those that we have now are no more like those in former times, than a French crab is like a Newtown pippin.

The aristocracy had ceased to perform its social duties; they now taxed the poor for the defence of their estates; the bishops were no longer the guardians of the patrimony of the poor – 'in short, it is a prodigious band of spongers, living upon the labour of the industrious part of the community'.[105]

Cobbett's call for a partial return to a mid-Georgian social order was a shrewd radical device designed to portray the rich as the exclusive authors of class conflict. His advice to all Englishmen to remain in their station at birth was sharply contradicted by his own career and by his efforts to make smallholders out of proletarians. The great purpose of Cobbett's feigned veneration for a static and hierarchical society was not to pin working people to a low social station but to incite them to rise above it by demanding a pulling-down of new-fashioned farmers and of others who had 'risen recently from the dung-hill'.[106] He cornered the aristocracy too. In the event of all things being equal with the reciprocal rights and duties of former times, he would have been pleased to honour his commitment to uphold the privileges of the natural magistracy,[107] but he was too astute to think that all things could ever be equal with even the recent past. Further-more, he had all of his historical bases covered; even many members of the landed aristocracy who behaved benevolently in the here and now could be shown to be sitting on estates that had been acquired during the seizure of church lands and tithes during the sixteenth century. By not allowing a statute of limitations to apply to the acquisition of landed property, Cobbett declared war upon the aristocracy as a class. They held their estates at the pleasure of the common people, not by absolute right.[108]

Cobbett's periodic declaration of support for a natural élite does not preclude or contradict his observances of class society. He felt a degree of emotional attachment to the old gentry on account that he had been raised to honour them,[109] but he was convinced by the 1820s that radical reform could not come until primogeniture was stopped and the landed aristoc-racy be 'wholly ousted'.[110] From time to time he harked back to the virtues of the old gentry, but this was a tactical device for highlighting his special contempt for the commercial and industrial entrepreneurs who purchased landed estates. As he said himself, the only reason that he had any good to say about the old gentry was that the new ones were even more oppressive towards the poor.[111] Cobbett was aware that labourers, too, were more hostile towards the new-fashioned landholder than towards the old-fash-ioned gentry.[112] Providing that the common people were free to exercise their rights, he had no quarrel with this position;[113] but this is not to say that Cobbett spared the old nobility ('these mean, these cruel, these cowardly, these carrion, these dastardly reptiles'[114]) from a share of responsibility for the impoverishment and degradation of the English village worker.

Thus in the post-war years Cobbett came to recognize that all relations in English rural society were class relations, no matter how benevolent or well-disposed the landlord or farmer. 'I shall be told', he said to Thomas Coke of Holkham,

> that many *large farmers* treat their labourers very kindly, and even take care to see, that they are supplied with a sufficiency of *food* and *raiment*. I believe this, and I have heard, that *your* estates are remarkable for this kindness and benevolence. But, Sir, the Jamaica farmer does the same by his slaves. From a different motive, perhaps; but he *does* it. This renders slavery less cruel; but, still, a state of life which contains a *compulsion to work* without a moral *possibility* of saving something for old age, is slavery, call it by what name you will; and, one of the consequences of such a state of things, is, that *a large standing army is required in a time of profound peace*. The *social* tie being broken; the tie of *content* being no longer in existence, its place must be supplied by *force*. Hence our two *armies*, the army constantly on foot, composed of Labourers who have sought bread in the ranks; and the army of farmers, landlords and traders, who are called *yeomanry*.[115]

This was as distinct an observation of class and of class conflict as the vocabulary of the early 1820s would allow. The labourers were no longer seen as fellow countrymen by the farmers and landlords, but as a distinct and inferior class.[116] But class conscious though they were, the old land-lords offered Cobbett his only hope for representation of the labourers from within the ruling class. Thus at the same time as he forecast the passage of all landed estates to the labourers, he urged the aristocracy to remember that the labourers were their natural friends, allies and protec-tors.[117] This was not the voice of one who failed to see the 'modern bourgeoisie' (if we hark back to Marx's words); by 1820 Cobbett saw it clearly, but he also recognized that for the time being the labourers needed allies among countrymen, for they were not yet representing themselves in the high politics of Westminster.

In 1800 the labourers' dominant ideology was a recognition of their importance as producers. They articulated this ideology, not as a class, but as countrymen who joined farmers and landlords in expressing antag-onism towards the culture and economic appropriations of the towns. As the labourers' songs show, this common discourse broke down during the Regency years, and when the labourers acquired control of their own cultural media, they began to articulate an appreciation of class conflict which outweighed all other species of conflict within the varied economic ranks of farm workers. Like a traditional peasantry, Cobbett and the labourers continued to look upon the townsman with a degree of cultural reservation, and they maintained their peasant-like aspirations for customary rights and non-wage forms of subsistence. Yet it is highly questionable whether village workers can be described as a class of 'low classness',[118] even relative to the consciousness of the industrial proletariat. The evidence of the songs, together with the work of Mick Reed and Roger Wells, suggests that the Regency labourers were keenly aware of economic conflict with their employers, and in particular of their displacement from a shared community culture.[119] They viewed their own class consciousness as a negative and hopefully temporary construction, but it was class consciousness all the same. Cobbett, too, invoked class consciousness in an effort to undermine its objective economic determinants. He knew that during the 1820s the labourers were not always in a position to translate their common consciousness and solidarity into overt collective protest, being 'chained to the spot and the plough, and [with] no means of *combining*, or *turning out*, or of making, in any way, a stand against the horrible oppression',[120] but he ultimately trusted that while 'victory may appear frequently to change sides, the millions must, in the end, prevail'.[121] The more pragmatic option in the short term, and the one he pursued on the county agricultural platform of the 1820s, was to promote the restoration of a common culture and economic interest among countrymen. Although not until the Captain Swing revolt would he formally exchange a countryman model of rural society for a class model, he knew that the farm workers of the 1820s were inclining towards a sophisticated recognition of class society in rural England.

The ultimate historical lesson in all this is that the farm workers, together with Cobbett on their behalf, emerged with class consciousness rather sooner than is sometimes thought. During the decade after Waterloo they came to see clearly (contrary to the claims of one of their most recent historians) that their interests were in sharp conflict with those of their employers,[122] and that this conflict would not abate even if the farmers again saw fit to grip the plough or to bless it speed in the guise of a jolly fellow. Entreaties for the restoration of the old countryman bond did not vanish (indeed they survived in many popular rural repertoires throughout the nineteenth century), but in the post-war years these traditional verses lost ground to the new genre of protest songs which condemned and ridiculed the new-fashioned farmer, and which advanced prescriptive statements on the need for economic and cultural solidarity among workers.[123] Thus the labourers cannot be said to have postponed class consciousness until the middle decades of the century, much less to have awaited the arrival of Joseph Arch and the National Agricultural Labourers' Union in the 1870s.[124] As Cobbett saw (though he alone among radical leaders), the Regency farm worker was developing a political and class consciousness that rivalled that of the weaver, the miner and the cabinet-maker.

CHAPTER 4

THE BATTLE FOR THE PEDLAR'S PACK

The People do not at all relish little simple tales. Neither do they delight in declamatory language, or in loose assertion; their minds have, within the last ten years, undergone a very great revolution.

PR, 27 January 1820, p. 738.

I remember my mother being in the habit of reading Cobbett's *Register*, and saying that she wondered why people spoke so much against it; she saw nothing bad in it, but she saw many good things in it. After hearing it read ... I was of my mother's opinion.

James Watson, 'Reminiscences of James Watson' (1854), in David Vincent (ed.), *Testaments of Radicalism* (London, 1977), p. 110. Watson was a farm worker in his early years.

A QUARTER century ago Edward Thompson dubbed the mass reform movement of 1816–20 as 'the heroic age of popular radicalism'. Thompson championed the metropolitan and provincial working-class organizers of this half-decade without eulogizing their national leaders, who, in his much-quoted phrase, 'rarely looked heroic and sometimes looked ridiculous'. For Thompson the least ridiculous of the radical leaders was Cobbett, whom he elevated as the most articulate and plausible spokesman of a radical convocation on that pragmatic terrain between the revolutionary experiments of the Spenceans and the liberal propensities of the Benthamite reformers.[1] More recently, several historians of Regency popular politics have extended the study of the radical platform to the metropolitan cell, the trade club, the tavern and the blasphemous chapel,[2] yet Cobbett has not been granted a central or even a significant position on this broadened platform. Nor will he be unless the platform is further enlarged. Cobbett, after all, had little faith in Utilitarian reform (he fell out sharply with Francis Place in 1810) or in the retreating radicalism of Sir Francis Burdett; similarly he had little contact with either the Hampden Clubs or with the underground associations of London's ultra-Radicals.[3]

And most significantly of all, his last great co-operative venture with Henry Hunt was on the county platform of 1815, after which Hunt shifted his attention to what John Belchem calls the 'historic programme' adopted at Spa Fields.[4]

Thus even on the extended radical platform Cobbett continues to be presented as a chronicler of the heroic age, and as one who ensured the safety of his own skin by sometimes pushing others, Hunt in particular, into the more dangerous outreaches of radicalism. In part it is an interpretation that Cobbett helped to bring on his own head. On the urban platform he was often self-serving, temperamental in his leadership, and even unclear himself about the ideological perimeters of the reform movement. Two years in Newgate (1810–12) for publicly criticizing flogging in the militia left him cautious in his programme and uncertain about his future in popular politics. And when the dark clouds of repression loomed in 1817, he fled once more to America, which cost him further credibility within the radical movement, especially among those who faced down Lord Sidmouth or stoically endured their prison sentences. Then, upon his return to England in the wake of Peterloo, he sought to restore himself on the radical stage, first with the talisman of Paine's bones (which failed to work) and subsequently with the cause of Queen Caroline (which temporarily did). Yet for all this Cobbett was a consistent and important contributor to the radical platform during the decade after Waterloo, though to recognize it we must extend the radical platform into the country pedlar's pack.

It has been observed by John Stevenson that the Queen Caroline affair marked 'the last of the old-style metropolitan agitations in which London gave a lead to the rest of the country'; and from which followed 'the relatively calm years of the eighteen twenties'.[5] Yet on account that Cobbett never invested all of his political eggs in the metropolitan basket, his political career cannot be charted according to the oscillations of London politics. Throughout the heroic age itself, and unabated even during the apparent lull in popular politics during the 1820s, Cobbett pursued a political mission in the countryside that was almost invisible from the vantage point of the city or town. In the name of the reform movement he undertook the difficult but important task of designing a new working relationship between rural experience, oral tradition and democratic ideology. It was a platform that was not subject to control by the gallows, but nor was it Cobbett's platform by default, for the ruling class was determined to maintain its hold upon the politics of the people. In the end, the battle for the pedlar's pack amounted to the most heroic of all Cobbett's radical endeavours.

Samuel Bamford left us perhaps the most comprehensive account of the effect of the scarcity, de-mobilization and slashed relief scales of 1816 upon the post-war radical movement. Yet his much-cited chronicle is incomplete, for what revitalized and co-ordinated Cobbett's radicalism was the rural and agricultural story that Bamford largely ignored. Cobbett's entry into the heroic age was inspired by his experiences in his own village of Botley, which in the summer of 1816 he found to be swarming with ragged and unemployed beggars. 'What is it', he asked himself, 'that can have changed men in this manner?'[6] A want of parliamentary reform was his answer, but of what use is it, he further asked, to recommend such a course in a periodical priced well beyond the reach of most workers? The stamp laws seemed to prevent the *Register* from being priced at less than a shilling, but it was learned by Cobbett that the tax did not apply to broadsheets treating of opinions rather than news. During October he experimented with a small run of unstamped *Registers*, printed on both sides of an open sheet, price twopence.[7] As he contemplated making this a weekly issue the uppermost thing on his mind was a recently published survey by the Board of Agriculture which confirmed his impression that distress among the rural poor was nation-wide. Of the 273 replies to the Board's queries, 237 reported misery and destitution among farm workers. Yet this hardship did not deter the correspondents, mainly landholders, from taking issue with the labourers' character. A typical witness was one Dr MacQueen of Bedfordshire who declared that the Poor Laws were 'coupled with the idleness and depravity of the working classes', that the run of labourers were 'careless', 'improvident' and spendthrift and that 'the doctrine of equality and the rights of man is not yet forgotten, but fondly cherished and reluctantly abandoned'.[8] Cobbett was unsurprised but livid: 'to hear these gentlemen railing,' he argued, 'one would suppose, that the people were at least, comfortably fed and clothed and lodged'.[9]

Thus unlike Bamford, and contrary to what is usually argued or implied about Cobbett's political motivations in 1816, it was in the name of the country workers that he launched the inexpensive radical periodical press, and with these much-quoted words:

> Whatever the pride of rank, of riches, or of scholarship may have induced some men to believe, or to affect to believe, the real strength and all the resources of a country, ever have sprung, and ever must spring, from the labour of its people ... With this correct idea of your own worth in your minds, with what indignation must you hear yourself called the Populace, the Rabble, the Mob, the Swinish Multitude ... Shall we *never* see the day when these men will change their tone! I trust that they will change their tone, and that the day of the change is at no great distance![10]

The politics of Cobbett's early two-penny broadsheets was familiar to the ruling class – they had long been hearing the same message from the stamped *Register*. What they were not accustomed to (quite apart from the prodigious sales of the sheets) was Cobbett's variance with the idiomatic conventions of serial journalism, and especially his rapid and confident deployment of first and second person pronouns: 'I', 'you', 'we', 'us', 'our' – one after the other. Cobbett took as his mandate the expression of two decades of popular ill-feeling towards the 'insolent men, who call us the *"Lower Orders"'*. Speaking more directly to rural popular culture than ever before, he lashed out at pejorative words such as 'peasant' and 'the poor', which latter implied a smug disregard of poverty and a perception of the labourers as '*a distinct and degraded class of persons*': 'I, in behalf of the labourers, reject this appellation with scorn.'[11] He drew poignantly upon the recent past by observing that the farm workers at Waterloo were heralded as heroes rather than as seditious and profligate drunkards – for 'all the qualities of the swine are cast off with the smock-frock'. But the abuse returned with the smock:

> Have not the labourers, as well as their employers, liberties and lives to defend? Do they not mainly assist to fight the battles of their country by sea and land? Are they not called out to serve in the militia and local militia? Have they not wives and children whom they love to see happy? ... Have they not a right to happiness, and shall I be accused of *sedition*, because I endeavour ... to point out to them how to obtain and secure that happiness?[12]

In mimicking the dominant culture's pejorative reductionism of the common people into 'swinish multitude' and 'rabble', while maintaining in his own discourse the colloquial usage of 'chopstick', Cobbett moved squarely into the vernacular of rural popular culture.[13] Whereas the rich had long abstracted the common people into one cacophonic orchestra, Cobbett turned the practice on its head by caricaturing the ruling class as an undifferentiated and vincible assembly whose animus was the crucifixion of popular rights. They required no more detailed definition than 'they' or 'them'.

Vended by hawkers, the broadsheet *Register* was injected directly into the bloodstream of popular culture. It entered into democratic cultural dialogue with working people through its personalized prose, its defiance of abstractions and its polarization of 'us' and 'them'. And yet its ideologies, though politically democratic, were economically conservative and almost neutral on the subject of class. An express purpose of Cobbett's sheets was to direct the common people away from the turbulence that was

THE

LABORING MAN.

Tune—The Roving Bachelor.

William Pratt, printer, 82, Digbeth, Birmingham.

You Englishmen of each degree,
One moment listen u. to me ;
To please you all I do intend,
So listen to those lines I've ped'e
From day to day you all may see,
The poor are frown'd on by degrees ;
By them you know, who never can
Do without the labouring man.

CHORUS.

Old England's often led the van,
But not without the labouring man.

In former days you all must know,
The poor man cheerful used to go ;
Quite neat and clean upon my life,
With his children and his wife.
And for his labour it is said,
A fair day's wages he was paid ;
But now to live he hardly can,
May God protect the labouring man.

There is one thing we must confess,
If England finds they're in a mess,
And has to face the daring foe,
Unto the labouring man they go.
To fight their battles, understand,
Either on sea, or on the land ;
Deny the truth, we never can,
They call upon the labouring man.

Some for soldiers they will go,
And jolly sailors, too we know ;

To guard old England, day and night,
And for their country boldly fight.
But when they do return again,
They are looked upon with great disdain,
Now in distress throughout the land,
You may behold the labouring man.

When Bonaparte, and Nelson too,
And Wellington, of Waterloo :
Were fighting both by land and seas,
The poor men gain'd those victories.
Their hearts are cast in honours mould,
The saillor's and the soldier's bold ;
And every battle, understand !
Was conquered by the labouring man.

The labouring man will plough the deep,
Till the ground, and sow the wheat ;
Fight the battles when a-far,
Fear no dangers or a scar.
But still they're look'd upon like thieves,
By them they keep at home at ease ;
And every day throughout the land,
They try to starve the labouring man.

Now if the wars should rise again,
And England is in want of men ;
They'll have to search the country round,
For the lads, that plough the ground.
Then to some foreign land they'll go,
To face and drub the daring foe ;
Let England do the best they can,
They can't do without the labouring man.

12   It was commonly complained by the labourers that they were respected
more on the battlefield than on the land. Reproduced by permission of the
Syndics of Cambridge University Library (Madden Collection of Ballads).

reducing England to something 'approximating a civil war'. He informed labouring people of their misguidance in attacking bakers, brewers, millers, farmers and landlords, who, he claimed, were the 'innocent neighbours and fellow sufferers' of working people. Dismissed without a hearing was the people's traditional mistrust of the dealing strategies of middlemen, who for centuries had been among the first targets of food rioters. This was contentious advice, despite the ailments of the old moral economy. Moreover, he took issue with the protesters' next port of call: employers' wages. These were much too low, he admitted, but he trusted that employers would hire workers at adequate pay if only the government would ease up on taxation. It was sinecures, pensions and the national debt, not middlemen, employers or machinery, which were bringing working people to grief.[14]

The earliest two-penny *Registers* have often been described as the foundation texts of the post-war radical movement, yet they are among Cobbett's most inconsistent and confused writings. During most of his radical career, including in the Captain Swing revolt, he lent his support both to 'modern' political activity and to the spontaneous, food-oriented or 'pre-industrial' disturbances that he now denounced.[15] Further, he downplayed in 1816 the class antagonisms that were such a central feature of his speeches and writings from the agricultural platform. These contradictions can be accounted for only if we bear in mind that in the early cheap *Registers* Cobbett sought to unite workers and employers of town and country in the reform movement. In addressing the latter-day 'Luddites' Cobbett spoke to the merits of machines on the basis of his experience of their utility in farming, and even more oddly, pointed to falling prices for wheat and livestock in explanation of hard times in industry and handicrafts.[16] His advice to the destroyers of industrial machinery was to leave off their misguided activities and to divert their energy to peaceable petitions for Parliamentary reform (it is therefore not surprising that Henry Brougham should later seek Cobbett's permission to circulate the *Letter to the Luddites* in reply to Captain Swing, so expressly did that text contradict Cobbett's advice to the country workers[17]). As to who might lead the petitioning campaign in industrial and urban areas, Cobbett was vague and uncertain, perhaps masters and factory owners might be interested; but in the case of rural workers he was much more decisive and assured: if 'the "decent fire-side" gentry' remain aloof, he enjoined, 'proceed by yourselves'.[18] Thus while it can certainly be said that Cobbett communicated a language of popular rights that was meaningful to industrial workers and artisans,[19] he found himself locked into rural images and experiences that he had neither the will nor the ability to escape.

The advent of the broadsheet *Register* in the autumn of 1816 has been said to have instituted a 'revolution in press history'[20] and a 'new era in radical journalism'.[21] These captions convey the impression that the two-penny *Register* has only two contexts: that of serial journalism and the overt political expressions of the radical platform. But the cheap *Register* was not exactly serial journalism (although a periodical, it avoided the stamp laws by treating of opinions rather than news) and it was more than a transcript of radical politics. Its operative context was the pedlar's pack, from where it was vended at hiring-fairs, market-places and public houses, together with other cultural productions such as chapbooks, almanacs, broadside songs and other assorted expressions of a magico-religious world-view.[22] Cobbett knew well that most of his readers preferred broad-sheets to books,[23] but the popular format obliged him to keep company with a traditional literature that did not always meet with his approval. One vanity that Cobbett did not give himself was to imagine that he held an instant monopoly on the cultural and intellectual repertoire of his audience.

Chapbooks, for their part, were not in direct competition with Cobbett's broadsheets, for they catered to a dimension of popular culture which at worst did not impede a political sensibility. Indeed, many of these abridged histories, such as the ever-popular Robin Hood stories, accorded with Cobbett's sheets in commending the old English ideology of fair play, as well as in their didactical conclusions (much played out in Cobbett's own narratives) that good must triumph over evil. The almanac, however, seemed in direct competition with Cobbett's political objectives. Coincid-ing with the publication of the *Address to Journeymen and Labourers* was the 1816 edition of *Moore's Almanac* which asserted that affairs of government were regulated by the 'Configurations of the Planets', and that 'Mundane Affairs' were in turn indicative of 'how the Planets incline'.[24] Cobbett did not pretend to approve of these circular debilitations of popular intuition and experience. 'If your pupil live in the country', he informed ruling-class advocates of popular literacy,

> his standard book will, in all likelihood, be MOORE'S ALMANACK, that universal companion of the farmers and labourers of England. Here we will find a perpetual spring of knowledge; a *daily* supply, besides an extra portion monthly. Here are *signs* and *wonders* and *prophecies*, in all which he will believe as implicitly as he does in the first chapter of Genesis. Nor will he want a due portion of politics. To keep a people in a state of profound ignorance; to make them superstitious and slavish, there needs little more than the general reading of this single book.[25]

Moore's Almanac doubtless far outsold the two-penny *Register*, but Cobbett overstated the capacity of the almanac to negate popular appreciation of human agency. He failed to observe that Moore's astrological forecasts sometimes augured well for the reform movement, and that the fortunes of farmers were sometimes made contingent upon the extent of their goodwill towards their labourers. The prophecies themselves were ostensibly rationalized by the zodiac, but these rationalizations had counterpoints, such as in alternative versions of *Moore's Prophecies*:

> He says, cold weather may begin this year,
> Tells us to fill our bellies with good cheer,
> Clothe well your backs, and have your feet kept warm;
> And this advice, he says, can do no harm.
> He might have said that it can do no good
> To those who neither can get clothes nor food.[26]

The history of secular rationalism in rural popular culture has yet to be written; nor perhaps can it be without recourse to simplistic Whiggish models that would do more harm than good to the history of mentalities. But whatever the agency of conventional almanacs and chapbooks, they were never so pervasive as to cripple an appreciation of human agency or even a popular political consciousness. During the mid-seventeenth century, George Herbert lamented a tendency among country workers 'to think that all things come by a kind of naturall course; and that if they sow and soyle their grounds, they must have corn; if they keep and fodder their cattel, they must have milk and Calves'. By way of remedy he informed the country parson 'to reduce them to see God's hand in all things, and to believe that things are not set in such an inevitable order, but that God often changeth it according as he sees fit, either for reward or punishment'.[27] More than a century later, John Wesley similarly despaired of the labourers' tendency towards a rational empiricism, which he took to mean that the 'the generality of peasants' were 'extremely dull', 'usually unhappy' and 'grossly, stupidly ... brutishly ignorant, as to all the arts of life, but eminently so with regard to religion and the life to come'.[28] When God or Francis Moore appeared to fail the farm workers, or was monopolized as a spokesman for the élite, they turned elsewhere for mascots and patrons, often to the highly personable and folk-created Robin Goodfellow. When nature served them with hardship, they were disposed to turn to magic and religion; when man or ideology served them with hardship, they were inclined to turn against that man or that ideology.

It is too often assumed that traditional popular culture, especially its oral productions, cultivated superstition and ignorance at the expense of political will. Many nineteenth-century working-class autobiographers invite this impression, for part of their purpose was to accentuate their own importance within the reform movement, and to convince others of the utility of their struggles for bread, knowledge and freedom. But as an historical model of popular culture it amounts to back-door Whiggery. All belief systems contain tensions between the rational and non-rational: the farm workers had their non-rational convictions as did the miners and the town artisans. Country superstitions, as the late George Ewart Evans demonstrated, articulate the relationship, or more accurately, the *lack* of an *obvious* relationship, between hard work and nature's caprice.[29] Superstitions are symbols of inexplicable extra-mural agencies; they do not in themselves corrupt political consciousness. If they did, one would expect to find village workers more politically conscious in Victorian than in Regency times, for by the later nineteenth century, superstitions were much reduced as allusions in popular songs. Regency workers, however, articulated a political consciousness of equal sophistication to that of their Victorian sons and daughters, and at a time when almanacs and chapbook stories about 'Jack the Giant-Killer' shared the pedlar's pack with the more expressly political discourse of Cobbett's *Register* and of broadside songs.

Far from proving a cultural or intellectual liability, it was chapbooks, almanacs and broadsides that introduced the printed word to rural popular culture (and thereby revealed the deception in William Howitt's claim that 'the clodhopper has no library').[30] By the end of the eighteenth century, broadsides were everywhere, whether in the form of a king's speech, a report of a public meeting, a dose of political propaganda or an account of a murder or execution. Radical politics also had representation in a battery of Paineite songs during the 1790s; and at least twice prior to 1816, Cobbett himself had recourse to the broadsheet format.[31] But as Cobbett knew, this plethora of popular print did not cause the labourers to abandon oral culture. The two-penny *Register*, like popular song, was adapted to auditory reception by means of lyrical phrases and the punctuating repetition of personal pronouns. The reader of the *Register* did not have to pause for words and lines, for Cobbett drew upon a familiar store of formulaic phrases and themes which the reader and audience had heard combined in a variety of ways. The outcome was a text which conformed readily to rural patterns of speech, and which presented ideologies in a down-home idiom which harmonized with the forthright language of villagers. Cobbett's methodological 'secret', recalled a bitter Charles Knight, lay in his auditory technique:

> The 'Register', in November, 1816 became a Twopenny publication ... Gaping rustics would eagerly listen to some youngster who had learnt to

read since the days of Bell and Lancaster, as he poured forth the racy English, in which there were no fine words or inverted sentences ... As Scarlett always won a verdict by getting close to the confiding twelve as if he were a thirteenth juryman, so Cobbett forced his 'Register' into every workshop and every cottage, not only by using the plainest English, but by identifying himself with the every-day thoughts – the passions, the prejudices – of those whom he addressed. It was very long before any of us who aspired to be popular instructors learnt the secret of his influence.[32]

Even then the ruling-class educators only partly understood Cobbett's 'secret'. They did not discern his appreciation that a text required traditional signs and symbols to acquire currency in oral and printed culture, and that its politicizing potential lay in its capacity to rally those traditional symbols and canons on behalf of experienced injustice.

Print and orality, the rational and the non-rational, were not mutually exclusive genres or world-views within rural popular culture. John Clare, probably the earliest collector of folk songs in southern England, gathered songs from oral culture and from printed culture, without distinguishing between them as to veracity or currency. In youth a farm worker himself, Clare participated in the superstitions and protests of the songs he recorded, revising some to suit his taste, and at least on one occasion, composing himself a petitional ballad. As a collector of popular narratives, Clare preferred traditional love songs and the fabulous stories of the chapbooks to the more topical and pragmatic strains of the white-letter broadside verse. Yet his veneration for oral narratives and traditional lore did not prevent him from reading and approving of Cobbett's agrarian platform, though he remained outside any visible or mass agitation.[33] It was the same for the majority of Cobbett's rural readers: quietly within their communities they attached their daily experiences to his political strictures.

It was Cobbett's understanding that a political education did not depend upon direct access to the printed word. Literacy itself, he appreciated, could be squandered on gallows literature or ghost stories. Even more importantly, it rendered popular politics more vulnerable to sabotage by the dominant culture, whether by the manipulation of school texts or by the controls of the stamp laws. Yet as Cobbett's own career testifies, literacy represented the only avenue to public acknowledgement of a worker's ascendancy over the non-literate or semi-literate masses. Thus the arts of reading and writing often became all-consuming to the autodidact, tempting him or her into conflict with an oral culture that took little account of the intellectual property of individuals. In oral societies, as

Jack Goody remarks, 'the individual signature is always rubbed out in the process of generative transmission'.[34] This refers to a purely oral culture, which was altogether extinct in England by the nineteenth century, but the Regency farm workers continued to subsume the discourse of individuals into the broader and collective culture of the community. Cobbett himself admitted as much when he denied a suggestion that his two-penny *Register* proceeded from an entire class: not so, he replied, it proceeds entirely from me.[35] Resident in each village were a core of singers and politicans who were prepared to lead their class from within the context of an oral culture, and without the sort of fame and acknowledgement to which Cobbett aspired.[36] These were persons, in the words of a Suffolk labourer, 'who worked for their daily living – men of genius who are seen on rare occasions among the poor, and who are in a small way lions among their fellows'.[37] As of yet we know very little about these 'lions', but it seems that they served as the local custodians of Cobbett's tracts, which they blended with the more anonymous expressions of popular protest, songs in particular.

The autodidact in quest of individual recognition must withdraw, at least in part, from oral cultural forms. Stephen Duck, the eighteenth-century labourer and poet, invested all of his spare moments in reading and study. Even the easy-going John Clare invested much of his spare time in reading and study, sacrificing friendships in an effort 'to gain notice or triumph over my fellows'.[38] And later Joseph Arch, who though attending day-school between the ages of six and nine, sought to extend his knowledge by evening study. 'There were no slack half-hours for me,' he boasted, 'no taking it easy with the other lads. To make more money, to do more, to know more, to be a somebody in my little world was my ambition and I toiled strenuously to attain it.'[39] Self-righteous enterprise of this sort was no less pronounced in Cobbett. During his stay in the army, he complained, 'I lived amongst and was compelled to associate with the most beastly of drunkards, where liquor was so cheap that even a soldier might be drunk every day, yet I never, during the whole time, even *tasted* of any of that liquor.' Amidst the 'talking, laughing, singing, whistling, and brawling of at least half a score of the most thoughtless of men', he pursued the study of grammar with 'unceasing assiduity'. His seat was his bunk, a board his desk, and a knapsack his book-case; the purchase of pen, paper and ink meant that he had 'to forego some portion of food, though in a state of half-starvation'.[40] The autodidact, once weaned from orality and from the more ribaldrous productions of popular culture, certainly proved more diversified in communications skills – Cobbett perhaps more so than any autodidact in English history. But with literacy and book-knowledge came pressure to surrender to the cultural and ideological controls of the dominant culture, including subscription to the élitist caricature of Hodge.

Cobbett's uniqueness lay in his refusal to surrender, but many others relented. The one-time farm worker John Britton, upon having graduated to the world of high letters, announced to his new constituency that 'the genuine rustics ... have little more sagacity than the animals with whom they associate'.[41] Stephen Duck, upon receiving the patronage of the Court and the adulation of established Augustan poets, was diverted in his poetry from the dignity of agricultural labour to the trappings of urban life.[42] Literary ambition also enticed the Suffolk labourer-poet Robert Bloomfield into the editorial clutches of his patrons. His poem *The Farmer's Boy*, strongly praised by Southey and Hazlitt as an innocent and virtuous celebration of the beauties and mysteries of rural life, contains hostile declarations against metropolitan culture, enclosure and the refinements of new-fashioned farmers. Bloomfield demands that 'labour have its due' and that the cottage be restored to independence from wage tyranny.[43] Not in so many words does *The Farmer's Boy* call for political reform, but when removed from the earshot of his patrons, Bloomfield would privately condemn the accumulation of wealth by one class at the expense of another as evidence of 'an inefficiency in the Laws of this or any Country where it happens'. In high politics he might even have been more adventuresome than Cobbett, for in December 1816, a month following the launching of the cheap *Register*, he privately grumbled that 'I see no reviews, no papers, but *Hunt* and the mild moderate *Cobbett*.' Five years later, however, when informed that his patrons were bailing out on account of rumours that he read the wrong papers and was lapsing into deism and republicanism, he followed the advice of a friend to step forward in denial. 'Cobbet and Hunt', he now said, 'are men I would not trust with power, they are too eager to obtain it. Universal suffrage is an impracticable piece of nonsense.'[44] It was certainly possible for both an agricultural labourer and a radical reformer to mistrust Cobbett and Hunt, but disparagement of universal suffrage as 'impracticable nonsense' is moved by some deeper mediator than 'natural' Tory sensibilities or even political ignorance. It is the language of a patronized obeisance.

It is well known that Cobbett could track down parliamentary corruption from great distances; it is less well known that he traced the tentacles of 'Old Corruption' all the way to the cottage door:

> The cause of the people has been betrayed by hundreds of men, who were able to serve the people, but whom a love of ease and of the indulgence of empty vanity have seduced into the service of the bribing usurpers, who have

spared no means to corrupt men of literary talent from the authors of folios
to the authors of baby-books and ballads. *Caricature-makers, song-makers*;
all have been bribed by one means or another. Gillray and Dibdin were both
pensioned. Southey, William Gifford, all are placed or pensioned. *Play-
writers, Historians*. None have escaped. Bloomfield, the Farmer's Boy
author, was taken in *tow*, and pensioned for fear that he should write for the
people.[45]

Cobbett appreciated that the political autonomy of villagers had always
been compromised by the ruling class, whether by the provision of patronage for peasant poets or by state censorship of the contents of the pedlar's
pack. What concerned him now was that the ruling class was undertaking
new initiatives to offset the printed politics of the labouring poor.

When in 1800 Cobbett was offered editorial control of a government-
owned newspaper he came face to face with government dominion over
high journalism. The same interference was at work in the popular press,
with Pitt himself taking a hand in the operations by instructing the dramatist and song-composer Charles Dibdin to compose loyalist war songs for
distribution among the people. Assisting these designs was the Vice Society
and the Association for the Preservation of Liberty and Property against
Republicans and Levellers. The Association, remembered Francis Place,
printed and distributed loyal songs free of charge, and helped in bundling
off to a magistrate those ballad-singers who persisted in retailing the old
songs. Magistrates, according to Place, 'admonished' the hawker and
reminded him or her that the loyalist productions could be obtained free of
charge, and with the compliments of authority. This campaign to cleanse
the pedlar's pack was effective and beneficial, recollected Place: 'the
bawdy songs, and those in praise of thieving and getting drunk were
pushed out of existence'. In turn the 'loyal songs were succeeded by
Dibdin's Sea Songs',[46] so that by 1835 (when Place was writing), the
people themselves would cause any singer of the older songs 'to be rolled in
the mud'.[47]

Place got some things wrong. In the first instance he exaggerated the
bawdiness of traditional song. It is true that some London pubs were well
known as homes of pornographic verse, but these strains were not typical
of popular song. Second, Place was handicapped by his ignorance of rural
England, where after 1815, simultaneous with the appearance of the
two-penny *Register*, there appeared a wave of protest songs against new-
fashioned farmers, taxation and pauperism. Some of these songs were
authored by the labourers themselves; others were the work of Grub Street
muses who patrolled the countryside and composed broadside songs on

the basis of the labourers' protests.[48] Thus by 1815, rural song was becoming a class genre: the farmers sang loyalist and drawing-room refrains in the privacy of their homes while the labourers sang protest verses in their cottages and pubs.

But Place was right about the determination of wartime governments to exercise a greater influence over popular prints. If Cobbett needed any convincing of this, he need have looked no further than his own government-disseminated broadside *Important Considerations for the People of this Kingdom*. By 1805, however, the tables were turned as Cobbett himself became one of the favourite targets of the conservative propagandists, while the popular song market as a whole was inundated with diversionary appeals to roast beef, frog's legs and the virtues of the ruling-class version of John Bull. In the stamped *Register* Cobbett denounced the '*abject submission*' encouraged by the 'pensioned rhyme-makers' who 'puked' their 'national braggings' upon the public,[49] but between 1805 and 1816 he opted not to enter the broadside market. The decision was both faint-hearted and pragmatic, for he knew well that it was a battle that he could not win so long as Bonaparte was on the loose and Gallophobia rampant among the people. As H. T. Dickinson has recently reminded us, conservative and loyalist propaganda should not be ignored or explained away. In sheer volume, and in mass influence besides, it far surpassed that of radical literature, despite its inability to alter the base of economic experience.[50] The war years were not only frustrating ones for Cobbett but he did not readily forget them. Indeed his very anxieties about the wisdom of launching the broadsheet *Register* in 1816 (he attempted to recall the *Address to Journeymen and Labourers* on the day after its release to the provinces) were doubtless moved by a fear that he was opening himself to destructive rejoinders, or at the very least committing himself, despite the conclusion of the war and the obvious upturn in the fortunes of radicalism, to a long and bitter struggle over the control of popular political expression.

An important agent in the cultural and ideological contamination of wartime print was Hannah More and her associates in the Cheap Repository Tract Society. More was an enthusiastic sponsor of peasant poets, or at least of the poetry of those rustics who deferred to her ideologies and moral strictures.[51] By the mid-1790s, however, she became convinced that patronized peasant poetry was inadequate apology for the established order. 'Vulgar and indecent penny books were always common,' she grieved in 1796, 'but speculative infidelity, brought down to the pockets and capacities of the poor, forms a new era in our history.' She grew alarmed by the 'impatience' with which country workers awaited the pedlar's broadsides on liberty and equality, 'and with what avidity his poison was swallowed'. Even the more 'innocent' of the broadsides, she complained, achieved 'more harm than good', treating as they did of 'ghosts, dreams, visions, witches and devils'. Thus More launched her 'Plan', as she called it, to compose 'safe' songs and stories for the poor, and to have them vended 'along side of the dirty and indecent stuff'.[52] As a minor literary figure in her own right, and generously funded by her supporters in church and state, she intruded into the popular song market, carefully styling her verses and selecting her wood-cuts in such a way as to make her productions indistinguishable, at a glance, from the 'seditious' and 'bawdy' productions. In all she composed some fifty songs and tracts; they infiltrated popular culture throughout England, and even reached America, where they were proudly retailed in Peter Porcupine's Philadelphia bookshop.[53]

For many of the same reasons that Cobbett and Hannah More exchanged compliments and promoted one another's writings during the 1790s, they later became principal antagonists in a tug-of-war for the pedlar's pack. Both aspired to the vernacular by emulation of the unaffected and unelaborate language of the Augustan satirists. Although More saw herself as a popularizer of Burke, she stopped short of his bombastic abstractions and crude debasements of the lower orders. If she did not join Cobbett in mimicking Burke's slogans against the poor, nor did she condone them. Indeed, More presented the common people as valuable for their labour and as conscious agents in the construction of a national culture and ideology. Her politics were conveyed in dialogues between non-caricatured individuals who articulated plausible scenes and experiences from rural life: scarcity, riot, domestic joy, hardship. Almost invariably her village dramas concluded with ideological negotiations between two or more actors; and while the outcome of these negotiations was thoroughly contrived, the very presence in her discourse of ideological debate lent a certain verisimilitude to her tracts and songs. In her early writings it was generally a reactionary farmer who convinced a radical labourer or artisan to mend his political ways, but as class consciousness took hold among country workers, she wisely transferred the voice of orthodoxy to working-class ranks.[54]

Most conservative propaganda was limited in its effectiveness by fashionable and abstract language, cultural misrepresentations and gross violations of common sense. More's songs were vulnerable on ideology alone. The fact that they looked and sounded like popular literature reduced the criteria for their acceptance or rejection to the ideological vigilance of the people. Hannah's trojan horses were skilfully camouflaged, and Cobbett knew it. No more distant a figure than his own wife Nancy, though unable to read, enjoyed having read to her the stories and songs of More, much to her husband's disgust.[55] Also too close for comfort was the cottager on the Cobbett farm who accepted as truthful a tract signed 'Jesus Christ' which warned against popular meddling in political topics.[56] Print, as both Cobbett and More realized, worked for and against their respective ideological models. That careful observer of rural popular culture, John Clare, was familiar with both acceptance and rejection of the 'white lies that are suffered to be hawked about the country to meet the superstitions of the unwary – & though it may make the weak shake their heads & believe it – others will despise the cant & pity the weakness of those who propagate such absurditys'.[57] Knowing that More's tracts and songs were the main competition of the two-penny *Register* (More, for her part, saw Cobbett as 'my mortal enemy'),[58] his tone was uncharacteristically nervous:

> One of the '*Tracts*', put forth by those canting hypocrites who pretend to exclusive grace, is entitled '*The Life of Peter Kennedy, who lived on, and saved money out of eighteen pence a-week.*' And this to his *praise*, mind! Why, he might *exist* in this way; but, can it be called living? What could the creature do? What *strength* could he have? What was he any more than a snail in winter? Such a thing ought not to be called a man ... I despise such creatures.[59]

Cobbett could not deny the existence of the likes of Peter Kennedy,[60] but he could counter them with more representative biographies of hard-working and provident labourers whose experience was debt and hunger. He had on his side the experience of most farm workers, but lest they suffer the loyalist tracts to offset their experience (as had indeed happened during the wars), he maintained a relentless confrontation with the tract-writers themselves, labouring to convince himself, in the first instance, of their limited influence among the people:

> Has it been intended, that these people, should read nothing but Hannah More's *Sinful Sally*, and Mrs. Trimmer's *Dialogues*? Faith! The working classes of the people have a relish for no such trash. They are not to be amused by a recital of the manifold blessings of a state of things, in which they have not half enough to eat, nor half enough to cover their nakedness.[61]

During the heroic age of popular radicalism Cobbett spent almost as much time berating the tract-writers as he did the denizens of the unreformed Parliament. He ridiculed their claims that the governing class was sufficiently charitable, that the government was neither responsible nor accountable for the labourer's poverty, and that the poor should extract their politics from their betters. The authors of anti-Cobbett tracts, meanwhile, including More, were not helping their own cause. They made errors of fact, such as when More had her protagonist Tom Hod sing 'O the Roast Beef of Old England' upon his conversion to anti-Jacobinism, whereas the experience of the labourers was that roast beef had long since vanished from the cottage.[62] They also mistakenly assumed that their labouring audience turned to popular print in search of consolation for life's tribulations. Half wages and half a cottage, decreed More, was superior to no wages and no cottage.[63] Or, as she entitled another of her songs: 'The Riot; or, Half a Loaf is better than no Bread', which concludes with a labourer professing that 'I'd rather be hungry than hang'd.' The labourers found solace in ballads during times of bereavement or of forsaken love, but More's brand of consolation was an insult to their intelligence and experience. They did not want to be hungry *or* hanged, but they were prepared, especially by the 1820s, to risk the gibbet to ameliorate hunger. Cobbett, meanwhile, like any responsible and dutiful labour leader, urged workers to be vigilant against compromise and consolation: half a loaf, he argued, '*is no bread*: it is worse than no bread; it can only deceive, only enthral; only prolong your degradation'.[64]

If consolation is a principal function of folk song, it is not apparent in the struggle for the pedlar's pack. The majority of new songs which entered the pedlar's pack in the post-war years demand bread and beer, not political silence or ephemeral consolations. They argue the efficacy of protest, even the destruction of the very food that they wished in greater supply upon the cottage table – a point which Hannah More sarcastically diverted into the question of 'whether *destroying the flour* will make *bread plenty*'.[65] 'Oh no,' retorted Cobbett, challenging her sophistry,

> to destroy flour will not make bread plenty; neither is that what the parties *expect*. They are not fools enough for that. Their object is to *make their own treatment better*. They do not calculate upon direct, but indirect good; and, it is perfectly beastly to reason with them, as if they believed, that they should *fill their bellies* by the burnings of stacks.[66]

In challenging the tract-writers Cobbett upheld the very strategies of popular protest which he had denounced in the opening two-penny *Registers*. If he did not altogether agree with 'pre-industrial' protest strategies, he saw a need to maintain a united popular front against the established order.

Upon fleeing to America in March of 1817 Cobbett proclaimed victory in the battle for the pedlar's pack.[67] As if to agree, More received news of his departure as 'too good to be true'. But since her adversary continued his

The *RIOT;*

Or, HALF a LOAF is better than no BREAD.

In a DIALOGUE between *Jack Anvil* and *Tom Hod.*

To the Tune of " A Cobler there was," &c.

TOM.

COME neighbours, no longer be patient and
　　quiet,
Come let us go kick up a bit of a riot;
I am hungry, my lads, but I've little to eat,
So we'll pull down the mills, and seize all the meat;
I'll give you good sport, boys, as ever you saw,
So a fig for the Justice, a fig for the law.
　　　　　　　　　　　　Derry down.

Then his pitchfork Tom seiz'd—Hold a moment,
　　says Jack.
I'll shew thee thy blunder, brave boy, in a crack.
And if I don't prove we had better be still,
I'll assist thee straitway to pull down every mill;
I'll shew thee how passion thy reason does chea
Or I'll join thee in plunder for bread and for meat.
　　　　　　　　　　　　Derry down.

What a whimsey to think thus our bellies to fill,
For we stop all the grinding by breaking the mill!
What a whimsey to think we shall get more to eat
By abusing the butchers who get us the meat!
What a whimsey to think we shall mend our spare
　　diet
By breeding disturbance, by murder and riot!
　　　　　　　　　　　　Derry down

Because I am dry 'twould be foolish, I think
To pull out my tap and to spill all my drink;
Because I am hungry and want to be fed,
That is sure no wise reason for wasting my bread;
And just such wise reasons for mending their diet
Are us'd by those blockheads who rush into riot.
　　　　　　　　　　　　Derry down.

I would not take comfort from others distresses,
But still I would mark how God our land blesses;
For tho' in Old England the times are but sad,
Abroad I am told they are ten times as bad;
In the land of the Pope there is scarce any grain,
And 'tis still worse, they say, both in Holland and
　　Spain.
　　　　　　　　　　　　Derry down.

Let us look to the harvest our wants to beguile,
See the lands with rich crops how they every
　　where smile!
Mean time to assist us, by each Western breeze,
Some corn is brought daily across the salt seas,
Of tea we'll drink little, of gin none at all,
And we'll patiently wait and the prices will fall.
　　　　　　　　　　　　Derry down.

But if we're not quiet, then let us not wonder
If things grow much worse by our riot and plunder;
And let us remember whenever we meet,
The more Ale we drink, boys, the less we shall eat
On those days spent in riot no bread you brought home,
Had you spent them in labour you must have had some.
　　　　　　　　　　　　Derry down

A dinner of herbs, says the wise man, with quiet,
Is better than beef amid discord and riot.
If the thing can't be help'd I'm a foe to all strife,
And I pray for a peace every night of my life;
But in matters of state not an inch will I budge,
Because I conceive I'm no very good judge.
　　　　　　　　　　　　Derry down.

But tho' poor I can work, my brave boy, with
　　the best,
Let the King and the Parliament manage the rest
I lament both the War and the Taxes together,
Tho' I verily think they don't alter the weather.
The King, as I take it, with very good reason,
May prevent a bad law, but can't help a bad season.
　　　　　　　　　　　　Derry down.

The Parliament men, altho' great is their power,
Yet they cannot contrive us a bit of a shower;
And I never yet heard, tho' our Rulers are wise;
That they know very well how to manage the skies;
For the best of them all, as they found to their cost,
Were not able to hinder last winter's hard frost.
　　　　　　　　　　　　Derry down.

Besides I must share in the wants of the times,
Because I have had my full share in it's crimes;
And I'm apt to believe the distress which is sent,
Is to punish and cure us of all discontent.
—But harvest is coming—Potatoes are come!
Our prospect clears up; Ye complainers be dumb!
　　　　　　　　　　　　Derry down.

And tho' I've no money, and tho' I've no lands,
I've a head on my shoulders, and a pair of good
　　hands;
So I'll work the whole day, and on Sundays I'll seek
At church how to bear all the wants of the week.
The Gentlefolks too will lend us supplies;
They'll subscribe—and they'll give up their puddings
　　and pies.
　　　　　　　　　　　　Derry down.

Then before I'm induc'd to take part in a Riot,
I'll ask this short question—What shall I get by it?
So I'll e'en wait a little till cheaper the bread,
For a mittimus hangs o'er each Rioter's head;
And when of two evils I'm ask'd which is best,
I'd rather be hungry than hang'd, I protest.
　　　　　　　　　　　　Derry down.

Quoth Tom, thou art right; If I rise, I'm a Turk,
So he threw down his pitchfork, and went to his work.

　　　　　　　　　　　　　　Z.

―――――――――――

[*Entered at Stationers Hall.*]

Sold by J. MARSHALL,
(PRINTER to the CHEAP REPOSITORY for Moral and Religious Tracts) No. 17, Queen-Street, Cheapside, and
No. 4, Aldermary Church-Yard; and R. WHITE, Piccadilly, LONDON.
By S. HAZARD,
(PRINTER to the CHEAP REPOSITORY,) at BATH; and by all Booksellers, Newsmen, and Hawkers in Town
and Country.
Great Allowance will be made to Shopkeepers and Hawkers.
Price an Halfpenny; or 2s. 3d. per 100.—1s. 3d. for 50.—9d. for 25.

13　Hannah More's 'The Riot', published by the Cheap Repository Tract
Society in the mid-1790s.

penmanship from abroad, the aging More could not relent: she revised her *Village Politics*, composed some new songs for the periodical *Anti-Cobbett*, and informed her friend Wilberforce that Cobbett alone prevented her from retiring her pen.[68] But More had indeed lost the battle, not because of a want of strategical skills as a popular writer, but because the playing-field had tilted in Cobbett's favour. With Napoleon retired to St Helena, and with scarcity rife, the tract-writers could no longer appeal to a ring-wing version of patriotism – like Cobbett they stood face to face with the unmediated experience and common sense of the people. This worked to Cobbett's distinct advantage. Although one cannot wade far in collections of nineteenth-century broadsides without encountering an anti-Cobbett broadside or a Cheap Repository tract or song, there is little evidence that they were actually purchased and consumed by labouring people (Cobbett introduced a jocular note by suggesting that anti-Cobbett tracts were used to light pipes and for other purposes 'which it would be hardly decent to describe[69]). Francis Place, who in general approved of More's publications, informed a parliamentary committee that the people were not eager to obtain them: 'there is an immense number of them distributed and wasted'. Hannah More herself admitted that her writings were 'full as much read' by the rich as by the poor.[70]

The Cheap Repository Tract Society was not Cobbett's only adversary in the popular press. His monthly periodical *Two-Penny Trash* (1830–2) was intended in part as a counter-weight to the cheap publications of the SDUK,[71] some of whose members purported to have learned from Cobbett that popular audiences had to be addressed in popular language.[72] From the Society's presses came numerous tracts on the merits of *laissez-faire*, labour-saving machinery, Malthusian population theory and Poor Law reform. Although the tracts of the SDUK did not penetrate the rural world as they did the urban, Cobbett kept his eye upon them, urging the industrial working class to maintain control of its political and cultural forums. At the Mechanics' Institute in the Strand in 1823, he warned his audience to be vigilant against Whig theories of improvement, and in particular not to be 'humbugged, which you most certainly will be if you suffer any body but REAL MECHANICS to have any thing to do in the managing of the concern'.[73] His fears were not unfounded.The library of the Bolton Institute contained Cobbett's grammars but not his political writings.[74] Rather less subtly in 1831, he was prevented by George Birkbeck from lecturing on political subjects at the Strand Institute.[75] The middle-class patrons of the Institutes preferred utilitarian and non-partisan subjects, such as a demonstration (though this is an extreme example, most other topics were more substantial) of the volume of air that could be pumped into the body of a dead rat.[76] William Lovett, for one, was very taken with such 'miraculous' subjects, yet he was quick to disparage the superstitious traditions of the oral culture of his youth.[77] The so-called 'rational' education of the Whigs could surpass even *Moore's Almanac* in frivolousness and sensationalism. Thus in 1832 a number of Birmingham mechanics criticized SDUK publications 'for not touching on the wants and condition of the labouring class'. The mechanics demanded rational political discussion rather than dictations about the supposed harmony between capital and labour. They objected to the Society's advice that workers be content in the face of poverty. The Society's *Penny Magazine*, in their view, offended labouring people by dwelling upon things 'of a light and entertaining nature, whilst [workers] are surrounded by poverty and misery produced by an irrational and vicious system of government'.[78] Thus, despite his claim to the contrary, Charles Knight, producer of the *Penny Magazine*, had not learned much from Cobbett after all. But the mechanics had learned from him – not least in the art of circulating their protests in broadside form: a mode of popular communication which Cobbett did much to return to the control of the working class, urban as well as rural.

Cobbett denounced the so-called religious tracts without denouncing a religious education. The tracts, he argued, were not religious at all, but rather blasphemous treatises on behalf of passive obedience. He did not care to embroil himself in the great theological debates on the subject of resistance and non-resistance, but then nor did the tract-writers, whose message was therefore easy prey to Cobbettian parody:

> When frost assails your joints, by day,
> And lice, by night, torment ye,
> 'Tis to remind you oft to pray,
> And for your sins repent ye.
>
> At parching lips when you repine,
> And when your belly hungers,
> You covet what, by right divine,
> Belongs to Boroughmongers.
>
> Let dungeons, gags, and hangman's noose,
> Make you content and humble.
> Your heav'nly crown you'll surely lose,
> If here, on earth, you grumble.[79]

Convinced that the sole purpose of the tract-writers was to dissuade 'the *poor* from cutting the throats of the rich',[80] Cobbett composed his own series of inexpensive religious tracts, drawing upon his own self-righteousness and his thorough knowledge of Scripture.[81] The only short-coming of the Bible as a reform treatise, he once mused, was its lack of reference to the details of parliamentary reform.[82] It was not any potential political liabilities in Christianity that worried him but rather the 'twisting and turning' of religion for the purpose of 'pursuading the labourer that he is to die contented with an empty belly'.[83] The great purpose of his 'Poor Man's Bible' and of *Cobbett's Monthly Religious Tracts*[84] was to prove to labouring people that the Bible advised good works, full employment, a living wage and rights on the land. Turning to the dominant culture, he streamed together biblical passages in support of his point that the Bible's first imperative was justice towards labouring people,[85] and that oppressors of the poor were ear-marked for divine vengeance.[86]

Life-long membership in the Church of England did not render Cobbett fond of its clergy, and in particular of Parson Baker of Botley, whose misdeeds ranged from opposition to parliamentary reform to the mortal sin of selling farmer Cobbett a load of straw that turned up rotten.[87] But it was the political avocations of the clergy that Cobbett and the farm workers most deplored, such as those of the Suffolk parson whom one labourer indignantly remembered to have been a vocal anti-Jacobin, a member of the Pitt Club, a follower of the hounds, a county magistrate and a chairman of Quarter Sessions.[88] Inwardly Cobbett regretted the tensions between labourers and clerics, fondly remembering when the village workers were so numerous at church that the service could not begin until 'the rattling of their nailed shoes ceased'.[89] These scenes, he believed, were diminishing in inverse proportion to the humility of the parsons, who gave themselves airs and treated the poor 'like dogs'. During his country rides he usually made a point of attending church on Sunday, but only at Firle in Sussex did he encounter psalm-singing by a choir of 'chopsticks', yet such choirs, he recollected, were commonplace fifty years earlier.[90] Knowing that the labourers took great pride in their psalm-singing, Cobbett lodged personal appeals in his own parish churches for the restoration of the 'chopstick choir'.[91] His purposes were two-fold: he drew personal enjoyment from their music and he wished to stem popular diversion to the chapel.

Cobbett's renowned hostility towards Methodism is the most problematic aspect of his religious creed. Theologically, damnation teaching did not accord with his interpretation of Scripture or with his environmental interpretation of the nature of humanity. For Cobbett and the labourers, religion was neither 'abstract' nor 'metaphysical'; either it had a beneficial effect upon social behaviour or it was 'good for nothing'.[92] Methodism did affect behaviour, and usually for the better, but Cobbett chose not to look beyond those particular parsons whom he knew to be enemies of parliamentary reform and of the *Political Register*. He accused the entire Methodist clergy of attempting to distract the people from the study of the real causes of their misery by 'ranting and raving' in a manner that was 'ten thousand times more mischievous than the brawls at the alehouse'.[93] At Bagshot he heard the minister hectoring his congregation about grace, hell and the devil, while at Benenden in Kent, the shibboleth was 'houses! houses! houses!':

> 'Do you know,' said he, laying great stress on the word know: 'do you know, that you have ready for you houses, houses I say; I say do you know; do you know that you have houses in the heavens not made with hands? Do you know this from experience? Has the blessed Jesus *told you so?*' ... Some girls whom I saw in the room, plump and rosy as could be, did not seem at all daunted by these menaces; and indeed, they appeared to me to be thinking more about getting houses for themselves *in this world first*: ... *houses* with pig-styes and little snug gardens attached to them.[94]

Earlier on the same Sunday, at nearby Goudhurst, he dropped in on a Methodist Sunday School, where

> the School-master was reading to the children out of a *tract-book*, and shaking the brimstone bag at them most furiously. This school-master was a *sleek*-looking young fellow: his skin perfectly tight: well-fed I'll warrant him: and he has discovered the way of living without work, on the labour of those that do work. There were 36 little fellows in smock-frocks, and about as many girls listening to him; and I dare say he eats as much meat as any ten of them.[95]

From these experiences he deduced the cheeky principle that Methodist parsons 'dress in the best of clothes, sleep on feather beds, eat roasted beef, and drink wine'.[96]

This was not full justice by a long way, but anti-Methodist comedy had a ready market in popular culture. Exploiting this, Cobbett approved even of the more juvenile of pranks against dissenters, including egg-throwing: a ritual he might well have encountered as a youth when attending an outdoor revival meeting of John Wesley's.[97] Full credence he gave to the country yarn (which was told and re-told in rural popular culture) that Methodist preachers were attracted to the scent of bacon, and that they would contrive their entry to the cottage in order to obtain a flitch or two from an unsuspecting follower. Like all good country story-tellers, Cobbett would embellish the tale with his own imaginative accessories:

A good honest careful fellow had a spare-rib, which he intended to sup with his family after a long and hard day's work at coppice-cutting. Home he came at dark with his two little boys, each with a nitch of wood that they had carried for miles, cheered with the thought of the repast that awaited them. In he went, found his wife, the Methodist parson, and a whole troop of the sisterhood, engaged in prayer, and on the table lay scattered the clean-polished bones of the spare-rib.[98]

This was oral fiction at its finest and most compelling. From the élite, especially the politicians and historians among them, Cobbett demanded hard empirical truth; but from countrymen, especially labourers, he modified his strictures on veracity to accommodate legends, proverbs, anecdotes, and that prodigious diary which is a farm worker's memory. In cultural matters, Cobbett was ever-mindful of the labourers' own assignments of truth function. 'Yes, Sir, and it is true', was the categoric postscript of many rural singers who plied their voices before the song-collector Cecil Sharp.[99] But at least as important as the descriptive testament of a song were its ethical judgements. 'When a singer talks of truth,' observes Tony Green of today's folk-artist, he is referring to morality rather than to historical questions.[100] Doubtless the same can be said for the nineteenth-century agricultural worker. Had Cobbett restricted himself to the recounting of empirical facts, his relationship with his audience would have been passive and deferential. This it was not. Cobbett coloured as well as documented cultural experience, extracting from popular legend those moral and comic prescriptions which comprised an important function of the literature of the pedlar's pack.

Anti-Methodism was but one more commission in Cobbett's representation of rural popular culture. Yet it had also a political function in that his diatribes against leading Methodists were intended to plant a face upon the adversaries of reform. Just as he would ridicule Francis Moore without ridiculing the readers of Moore's almanacs, he would abuse the Methodist parsons without abusing the proletarians within their congregations. He warned the people to be on their guard against 'the sleek-headed Methodist thief that would pursuade you to live upon potatoes'. He condemned the parsons for plying their congregations with 'books and pamphlets', 'hobgoblins and devils', instead of encouraging them 'to discover the cause of the emptiness of their bellies and the raggedness of their backs'. The parsons talked about 'the *living bread*' when Cobbett wanted to hear about the real bread, 'made of flour, salt and yeast'.[101] Unfortunately for them, many Methodist parsons played directly into Cobbett's hands. At a time when the labourers were hungry, many preachers (especially Wesleyans) emphasized the inner and spiritual being. Their unworldly

THE

Methodist Parson

OR THE

Flitch of Bacon.

A Methodist Parson whose name it was George,
A jolly brisk tinker just come from the forge,
A virtuous woman who was George's friend,
And he often went to her, her soul to mend,
The good old woman's husband no methodist he,
But a true churchman both jovial and free,
He lov'd his brown jug like a good honest man'
And his house was hung round with bacon and ham,

George lov'd this man's wife and often went to her,
And out a good slice of bacon would do her,
Till at last her husband great notice had taken,
And found that this friend came a preaching for bacon
Then he look'd round with an eager intent,
For he was determined to know how it went,
Then he wen out as usual, they supposed him to work
But the cunning sly boots, stept aside but to lurk.

By and by he came in, and found her at prayers,
They looked very earnest devout and sincere,
Then look'd round the room he'd great reason to guess
For he plainly preceived that his bacon was less,
Then round the house so cunning and sly,
And in George's pocket he cast a quick eye,
He saw something in it tied up in a rag,
Says he honest man what is that in the bag.

Why then replied George 'tis God's holy word,
The sacred Scripture I have from the Lord,
For when I'm at home I never am idle,
But make it my duty to read my Bible,
Then pull out the Bible the churchman replied
Or else by the devil I'll Bible your bride,
A Bible like this there never was in this life,
For thy Bible is bacon which thou stole from my wife

George shuffled about till the Bible brought out.
It was a great lump of bacon lapt up in a clout,
Then he took to his heels for he must not be idle,
And from that day to this, George was preaching
    without a Bible ;
Come all you honest fellows who lead jovial lives,
I'd have you take care of your bacon and wives,
If you have a good flitch great care must be taken
For th'll preach like the devil while there's plenty of
    Bacon

Printed and Sold by J. ROSS, Royal Arcade, New-
astle-upon-Tyne; and may be had of Stewart,
Botchergate, Carlisle ; Dalton, Walmgate, York.

14 The supposed contrivances of Methodist parsons were a regular feature
of village humour. Reproduced by permission of the Syndics of Cambridge
University Library (Madden Collection of Ballads).

doctrines, normally praiseworthy, seemed to ingratiate the ruling class by reducing poverty to questions of sobriety, moral reform and thrift.

Thus a full century before Elie Halévy, even longer before Edward Thompson, Cobbett defined Methodism as a middle-class creed which called attention away from the external world and towards the inner and spiritual being. He criticized it as a hindrance to reform while excusing his pyschological opposition to its dogmas by taking asylum in traditional popular culture. Further, like Halévy and Thompson, Cobbett was unable to see that Methodism (in the words of the labourer John Buckmaster) had 'its good side as well as its grotesque side': 'it gave these poor men something to think about; it gave them comfort in time of want and suffering; it was to them the only thing which made this life tolerable, with the hope of a better'. Buckmaster did not think much of the 'ranting and groaning' and 'Amens' and 'Lords have mercy upon us' which if 'taken out of their service there was not much left',[102] but he saw further into the subject than Cobbett, whose teachings, ironically, had more in common with the secular ethos of Methodism than he cared to admit. By inadvertence, Cobbett joined the Methodists in preaching sobriety, charity, hard work, the importance of community and the worth of the labourer in the eyes of God. In his brimstone prose and self-help literature, few writers more closely approximated John Wesley than William Cobbett. Although he did not join Wesley in purporting to believe in witches and the efficacy of bibliomancy, he was prepared to make concessions to rationalism for the sake of competence in this world. Wesley would not have approved of Cobbett's emphasis upon the flesh over the spirit, but later Methodists, such as Joseph Arch, might well have. If Cobbett had lived long enough to study the political involvements of Primitive Methodists later in the century, his story would have been modified. He would have disparaged some of their religious creeds while joining them in the struggle for enfranchisement and a formal trade union of agricultural labourers.[103]

More than a few commentators, from Cobbett's day to our own, have marvelled at his attitudes towards education in general, and towards literacy in particular. The cause of this dismay is a misunderstanding of Cobbett's strategies in securing working-class control of working-class culture. 'Education', as Cobbett defined it, meant 'rearing-up' or 'breeding-up'. He liked to make the point that his wife Nancy was well 'schooled' in farm work, despite her inability to read or write.[104] Cobbett was aware that he was playing with words, but he knew that book-learned labourers were often the laughing-stock of their fellows, and that competence in the rural world (then as now) was measured more according to physical than intellectual skills. Book-study, he pointed out, might be compatible with 'weaving and divers other arts',[105] but the essence of rural learning was indoctrination in the ways of nature and the craft of agriculture. Cobbett himself had mastered the art of ploughing in a district celebrated by Arthur Young for its sophisticated tillage; while William Marshall valued the skill to the point of declaring that 'a good plowman is worth any wages'.[106] Not anyone, as Fred Kitchen observed, could hold a plough for twelve hours in opposition to the will of the horses, let alone cut the all-important straight furrow.[107] In talking with Surrey farmers, however, the agricultural surveyor William Stevenson gained the impression that the labourers were devoid of skill and utterly ignorant of agricultural practice. But upon taking the time to speak directly with local labourers, he learned that they 'not only knew and could explain very clearly the system that was followed on the farm, but in general could assign very sufficient and proper reasons for following one practice in preference to another'.[108] According to John Buckmaster, 'the labourer knew as much about farming as the farmers, but the labourers never had the chance of showing it – they remained labourers'.[109] This was Cobbett's point too; he knew of very few labourers who were 'deficient in point of capacity to conduct the affairs of an ordinary farm', including his own.[110]

Most agricultural work required sophisticated skills, but country workers maintained an elaborate hierarchy of skill and expertise. This was carefully preserved by Cobbett:

> There are *grades*, too, even in the learning of agricultural labourers, from the mere filler of a dung-cart and shoveller up of dirt, to the hedger and ditcher, the ploughman, the mower and thatcher; and lastly the woodman, whom I have always placed at the top; he being a sort of mechanic as well as a labourer, cutting the rods and poles from the stems and converting them into spars, brooms, hurdles, and hoops; and all done upon the spot, with no tools but his bill-hook and his axe.[111]

This is 'a *suitable* education', Cobbett declared, for even the woodman's four- or five-year-old son, though but an onlooker, had 'already more real sense' than Brougham and the entire cast of Whig educators. Nor could he resist making supplemental reference to a newspaper report that Lords Darnley and Fitzwilliam had accidentally cut their feet and toes while wielding axes. Had they been farm workers, Cobbett mused, they would have come gradually and professionally to the use of an axe; they would have begun their working life with bird-scaring, then have learned to slice bread, to chop the tops of rods, to remove knots with a bill-hook and finally to split rods. Only then would they have come to the axe, by which time they would have known to keep their feet clear.[112]

Cobbett's elevation of agricultural work into the realm of legitimate education was not intended for an audience of labourers, but rather for those who maligned their abilities and character. He appreciated that agricultural skills were painstakingly acquired by competitive and gruelling apprenticeship. Youngsters were instructed by elders, not always by kind words and positive reinforcement, but by stern and silent example.[113] On his own farm he once set a lad of sixteen to do some spade-work alongside of two older workers, one of them named James Ives. The lad was Ives's superior at holding plough, but not at digging; he toiled and sweated away, getting nowhere, while Ives moved along with ease. Though reluctant to interfere, Cobbett at last interjected: ' "Come Ives, why don't you show that young fellow how to dig? You were young yourself once, recollect." "Aye, sir," said he, "and *very* young, too, when I did not know how to dig." ' Although Cobbett did not altogether approve of the labourers' methods of instruction, he knew that their educational philosophy gave primacy to experience, and that their silence spoke to pride in their craft, not to misanthropy. Indeed the same James Ives would later approach Cobbett for a 12s. advance on his wages in order that he might hire a night watchman to protect the body of his recently deceased daughter from the threat of grave-robbers.[114] Each insult to the intelligence and integrity of farm workers (and these were legion in Regency England) was taken personally by Cobbett, for he was satisfied that his own rural apprenticeship was the source of his competence and capacity for hard work. Agricultural labourers possessed skills and moral arts requisite to their craft and to society as a whole:

> Is the literary man to call a labourer ignorant, because the latter can neither write nor read, and because he does not know A from B? Well, then, is not the labourer to call the literary man *ignorant* because he cannot hold a plough or make a hurdle, and because he does not know oats from barley when they are six inches high?[115]

Cobbett was too familiar with modern English usage, as well as with the manifold dimensions of the Hodge stereotype, to think that knowledge of a craft was sufficient to clear the farm workers of charges of ignorance. Thus he proceeded to illustrate the labourers' character by pointing to evidence of their sensitivity, including their '*neatly kept and productive little gardens*',[116] and their tenderness and leniency in child-rearing.[117] The domestic sensibility of the labourers that Cobbett most emphasized was their predilection for large families – a subject he cleverly politicized by arraying Cupid and the Bible against the demographic forecasts of the

Malthusians. Scripture commanded procreation, he argued, while nature provided the sexual instinct 'by the very first and most imperative laws'.[118] As a sexual populist he equated restraint, and even artificial birth control, with a wholesale denial of the labourer's right to sexual expression and family life.[119] Population control, he informed a Sussex couple during one of his rides, was one more conspiracy against labouring people:

> I stopped and looked at them for some time, and then, turning my horse, rode up to the wicket, getting into talk by asking the distance to Horsham. I found that the man worked chiefly in the woods, and that he was doing pretty well. The wife was then only twenty-two, and the man only twenty-five. She was a pretty woman, even for Sussex, which, not excepting Lancashire, contains the prettiest women in England. He was a very fine and stout young man. 'Why,' said I, 'how many children do you reckon to have at last?' 'I do not care how many,' said the man: 'God never sends mouths without sending meat.' 'Did you ever hear,' said I, 'of one Parson Malthus?' 'No, sir.' 'Why, if he were to hear of your works, he would be outrageous; for he wants an Act of Parliament to prevent poor people from marrying young, and from having lots of children.' 'Oh! the brute!' exclaimed the wife; while the husband laughed, thinking that I was joking.[120]

In his comic play *Surplus Population* Cobbett endowed the anti-Malthusian protagonists with the sensual names of Ned Maple, Patty Primrose and Mary Violet, through whom he addressed the 'bouncing girls of eighteen or twenty, with the blood ready to burst through their skins, and ... [the] young fellows that valued life itself because it afforded them the gratification of their tastes and pleasures'.[121] In 1835 he directed a troop of labourers in performances of the play, but soon discovered that magistrates in parts of the rural South were putting a stop to the performances upon seeing the advance playbill.[122] Yet Cobbett's point was made: the rural workers took exception to their treatment as indulgent breeders. In the words of a grateful correspondent to the *Register*:

> Those who have been in the habit of calling us (the poor people) the '*swinish multitude*', take it for granted that our propensities to procreation are precisely the same sort of those of pigs ... You have shown us how we became a '*swinish multitude*' [and] how we became 'paupers' ... and now you have beautifully shown us that the '*data*' of these feelosofers have been assumed in gross ignorance ... I, Sir, return you, in common with many thousands, my hearty thanks, ... [for] the sooner [the population theorists] have their heads knocked against the cow-crib posts the better.
>
> I am, Sir,
> Your constant reader
> and hearty admirer
> A LABOURER[123]

Shortly before his death, while performances of *Surplus Population* encountered resistance from local authorities, Cobbett found in Edward
Lytton Bulwer's *England and the English* a description of the author's
encounter with a Sussex labourer who allegedly spoke ill of his wife and
family. So removed was this from Cobbett's experience that twice he
challenged the author to lead him to the abusive labourer.[124] The chal-
lenges were altogether ignored, but the aspersions remained in print to
nurture the Victorian stereotype of Hodge.

Cobbett required no further proof than his own biography to realize
that a wealth of potential literary and political talent lay within the
labourers' ranks.[125] His own experience told him that a knowledge of
reading and writing was necessary for the articulation and public recognition of this talent, but prior to his victory in the battle for the pedlar's
pack, he downplayed popular literacy and formal educational schemes.
The run of school-books, he observed, were religious tracts writ large,
teaching the people 'to be *content*: to regard ragged backs and hungry
bellies as the work of *Providence*'. But in 1818 he felt safe in declaring that
'the people do not, any longer, suck this down',[126] and accordingly began
work on his English grammar. Grammatical petitions from 'we, of the
"*Lower Orders*"',who possess 'superiority in all the branches of knowledge connected with the well-governing of a nation', would undermine
'the base and blasphemous notions, that wisdom and talent are confined to
what is called high-birth, and that the few possess a divine right to rule,
oppress and plunder the many'.[127] A mastery of writing skills would at
once demonstrate the ability of the poor to share in government and
prepare them for eventual victory in the class struggle:

> Let us, when they have the insolence to call us the '*Lower Orders*', prepare
> ourselves with useful knowledge ... They have challenged us to the combat.
> They have declared war against us. They have resorted to falsehood, fraud,
> and everything that is base in order to keep us their slaves ... Our struggle
> *may* lie *long*; let us, then, make the result sure. We were, and are, quite
> willing to enjoy only our bare rights; but these we shall have, and the way to
> make sure of them is to begin directly at the foundation of all book-learning,
> and to enable great numbers of the young and ardent-minded men to acquire
> a competent knowledge of it.[128]

An early edition of the *Grammar* was praised for its lucidity and common
sense by John Clare, whose idiosyncratic syntax was not Cobbett's doing,
but some of whose consciousness of agrarian grievances was.[129] Similar
debts were owed by the Chartist John Frost whose 'mind was turned to
radicalism' by the *Grammar*, and who learned from it that 'respect was

paid to the rich and powerful men not through voluntary admiration but through fear and compulsion'.[130]

The success of the *Grammar* did not cause Cobbett to abandon his monitorship of the pedlar's pack. Whenever the dominant culture mounted a campaign to de-politicize its contents, he invoked the non-literary culture of the farm workers to discourage their efforts. 'Think of John Clodpole', said Cobbett to Henry Brougham on the subject of the cottage curriculum of the SDUK,

> with every finger as thick as your wrist, and chaps between the finger and thumb, a quarter of an inch deep, no more capable of turning over the leaf of a book than you are of turning over, with the spade, twenty rods of ground in a day; only think of poor John, coming home from hedging, with a nitch of wood upon his back, to which is appended a pair of gloves or cuffs, each as big as your brief-bag; only think of him, with a pair of shoes, weighing half a score of pounds, and with jacket impenetrable by thorns; think of poor John ... who is to sit down over his handful of fire and his farthing or half-farthing rush-light, and meditate on ... the Essays of Bacon.[131]

A bull-bait or a single-stick competition had more meaning and veri-simility in rural popular culture than did Bacon's essays, or, for that matter, Cobbett's own *Grammar*. Unlike the Whig educators, however, Cobbett did not ignore the sensorial basis of the labourers' epistemology: he therefore promoted vigorous recreations, reduced his *Register* to an open sheet, adapted its language to oral culture and grouped grammatical conventions into proverbial formulas amenable to memorization.

In a lecture to the National Union of the Working Classes in 1835, the liberal reformer John Roebuck (apparently to cheers from his urban audience) chastised Cobbett for debasing 'the poor ploughman into a mere hewer of wood and drawer of water'.[132] Similarly, some of Cobbett's Oldham electors took issue with his apparent ambivalence towards book-learning, 'for we deem it necessary, that every Man should have so much book knowledge'.[133] These spirited claims, still often encountered, mis-represent Cobbett's strategical philosophy of education. He heartily ap-proved of dissemination of literacy and knowledge, providing that 'knowledge' was not defined and disseminated by the élite alone. Just as the ruling class cannot be accused of consciously promoting ignorance on the basis of the delays brought to government grants by sectarian dis-agreements between the National Society and the British Society, so Cob-bett cannot be accused of encouraging ignorance on the basis of his ideological vetting of the educational schemes of government and church. At the same time, he wanted to demonstrate to the élite that agricultural skills, oral traditions and daily experiences were important species of learning. But above all else, he did not want any educational schemes, including his own, to ingratiate the ruling class by distracting attention from the poverty of the cottage table.

Like Marx and Engels, Cobbett and the labourers were of the opinion that humanity must eat, drink and find shelter before pursuing politics.[134] 'The "*expansion* of the *mind*" is very well,' Cobbett argued, 'but, really the thing which presses the most, at this time, is the getting of ... a little more bread, bacon and beer.'[135] The East Anglian rioters of 1816, he recalled, demanded 'Bread or Blood', not 'Books or Blood'.[136] The ranking of food over the printed word was not a conservative or an anti-educational prescription but a mere premise of the maintenance of life:

> [School] plans they are good, as far as they go,
> But the farmers should raise the men's wages thereto,
> For its useless to talk of these fanciful schemes,
> Whilst bellies are empty and to fill them no means.[137]

It was Cobbett's ideal that the labourers have *both* book-learning and full stomachs, but if it came down to one or the other: 'I would rather that the people should believe in *witchcraft* and have plenty of bread and meat and good Sunday coats, than that they should laugh at witchcraft and be fed on potatoes and covered with rags.'[138] Was this debasing of the labourer's mind? Not at all, for Cobbett never separated a radical political education from traditional culture, competence in the cottage and a hearty diet of bread, bacon and beer.

CHAPTER 5

COTTAGE ECONOMY

Homeward see him labour on his way,
And close the toil of long and tedious day;
His poor coarse meal then soon behold him take
Potatoes salted and some barley cake;
Cold water serves his painful thirst to slake,
Or Indian leaves a half-strained beverage make.
> Thomas Shoel, 'Poverty', in Llewellyn Powys,
> *Somerset Essays* (London, 1937), p. 143.

Amongst the improvements which may be derived from this garden-like system of mine, those which small farmers and even *labourers* may derive from it, are by no means the least; for it is their well-being; it is their belly-full; it is their Sunday coat; it is their comfortable fire-side and their warm bed; which ... we ought, above all things, to keep in view.
> *PR*, 2 June 1821, p. 590.

IN 1823 *The Edinburgh Review* imposed a sudden if temporary ceasefire in its fifteen-year battle with Cobbett's politics and economics by declaring his new work *Cottage Economy* to be 'an excellent little book ... abounding with kind and good feelings, as well as with most valuable information'. The *Review* (Henry Brougham was the author of the praise) recognized that Cobbett's work was addressed to 'them', or 'the labouring classes', but it encouraged the rich to enlist the text in Whig educational service as a 'really useful' publication.[1] Tories, for their part, did not publicize their opinions on *Cottage Economy*, but much of Cobbett's enthusiasm for an independent cottage economy was echoed in Robert Southey's essays on the 'peasantry' for *The Quarterly Review*.[2] Thus we might ask: was Cobbett absolving employers and the state of responsibility for rural poverty, or was *Cottage Economy* misinterpreted by the élite? Wholly the latter, this chapter will argue, for in its political suppositions, and above all in its revisionist model of agrarian capitalism,

Cobbett's strictures on cottage technology parted company with Whig improvement theory and with Tory prescriptions on the means of creating independent cottagers out of proletarian economic conditions.

Programmes of self-help, such as that espoused in *Cottage Economy*, were not the preserve of Whigs and Tories. A central theme of popular rural song throughout the first half of the nineteenth century was the struggle between economic determinism and the people's own agency in the attainment of domestic happiness. When traditional ballads treating of the chivalry of the nobility fell out of favour after 1815, the labourers turned not only to overt protest verse but to a genre of cottage songs whose heroes and heroines were humble country men and women who lived by the sweat of their brows, and who strove to maintain hospitality and happiness in the face of material hardship. At first glance the cottage songs appear to conform to the values promoted by the dominant culture's intrusions into the rural song market, but where the latter decree that the poor are too often idle and dissolute, the cottage songs suggest that these vices afflict the rich more than the poor. The songs acknowledge that honesty is an important virtue, but they proceed to remark that grinding poverty and unjust laws frequently oblige the poor to supplement their household economy by poaching and other extra-legal endeavours.[3] Happiness, the songs observe, cannot be found in the face of poverty and exhaustion, but they encourage the poor to maintain their spirits, to seek out political solutions to their problems and to do whatever they must to make cottage life bearable and efficient. Thus, contrary to the élitist caricature of the farm workers as violent and misanthropic boors, the cottage songs reveal a class of people who strove to solve their social and cultural problems according to their own values and moral priorities. Indeed, the songs underwrite Cobbett's dictum that 'though we are oppressed, there is always something that we can do ourselves'.[4]

During his twenty-two years as a practising farmer Cobbett delighted in growing two blades of grass where only one grew before; he experimented with tree culture, Tullian drill husbandry, Indian corn, cottage manufacturing and the importation of merino sheep.[5] Not all of these projects were successful (the sheep, for example, developed an incurable foot-rot on the wetter English pastures), but it is simply wrong to suggest that his agricultural projects were ill-conceived or demonstrative of his inability 'to innovate'. He was indeed 'bereft of allies' in his husbandry,[6] but only because of his opposition to the capital-intensive and market-oriented agriculture conducted at Holkham, Woburn and Petworth. As he explained to Thomas Coke, he was an improver with a difference:

[Improvement] is a mark of good taste, and it is a pursuit attended with more pleasure, perhaps, than any other. But, if the thing cannot be accomplished without producing the fall, the degradation and misery of *millions*, it is not improvement . . . The gay farmhouses with pianos within were not *improvements*. The pulling down of 200,000 small houses and making the inhabitants paupers was not an *improvement*. The gutting of the cottages of their clocks and brass-kettles and brewing-tackle was no *improvement*.[7]

In Cobbett's 'radical' husbandry, as he called it, improvement was a technological innovation which added to the food, dress and happiness of those who worked the land. While the agricultural societies of the farmers and landlords ('nests of conspirators against the labourer', in Cobbett's view)[8] awarded premiums to employers who cultivated the most land with the fewest hands, Cobbett's experiments were manpower intensive, even to the point where he once worked 100 men upon 4 acres at Kensington.[9] The great object of Cobbett's agricultural experiments was to elevate labourers into self-sufficient smallholders, and in the process to undermine the high capitalism of large farmers and shopkeepers. Not in so many words did he encourage labourers to cease waged employment, but nor did he disguise the fact that the introduction of more non-wage forms of survival would reverse proletarianization and reduce the pool of reserve labour upon which large-scale capitalist agriculture depended.

Cobbett deplored the word 'peasantry' on account of its implication of a 'degraded caste of persons',[10] but he was strongly supportive of many of the occupational characteristics that rural historians have assigned to an objective or idealized peasantry.[11] Indeed, Cobbett's assumption in *Cottage Economy* that many village workers extracted part of their subsistence from self-employments, cottage gardens and other diverse ingenuities go some way towards reinforcing the suggestions by Mick Reed and Dennis Mills that peasants or household producers were more common in nineteenth-century rural England than we have been in the habit of thinking. Cobbett certainly remarked upon a trend in his day towards a threefold tiering of rural society – namely landlords, tenant farmers and hired labourers – but he also observed that many agricultural workers in the rural South derived a portion of their livelihood by productive modes that were distinct from market-oriented capital on one hand, and from proletarian labour on the other.

For Cobbett, the most important means of self-sufficiency was access to the soil, whether in the form of common land, cottage gardens or small farms. Even at Botley, where he cobbled together farms to a total of some 600 acres (mostly during his anti-Jacobin years, but still an embarrassment to a future critic of engrossment),[12] he stood opposed to enclosure schemes which would have contributed more acres to his personal holdings. These stands against enclosure were hardly acts of great charity, but he also pursued more direct initiatives in support of landholding among the rural poor. During the scarcity of 1816, according to the vestry minutes of Bishop's Waltham, he used his influence as one of the larger landholders in the parish to call a special vestry meeting to obtain leave from the Lord of the Manor and the copyhold tenants

> to enclose small parcels of Waste-Land in order to assist them in the support of their families. *Second*, to consult on the propriety of making application to the Lord of the Manor and the tenants to grant Copies for the said enclosures, and also for all enclosures already made in the manor by Encroachers, if the said Encroachers be poor men or women belonging to this Parish.

The proposal, according to the minutes, 'was rejected, their [*sic*] being only Mr. Cobbett to vote for the Propositions'. Among those who voted against the initiatives were two leasers of pauper labour and three large farmers: the first claimed that the parcels of land would make the labourers more 'saucy', the second argued that it would cause them to breed more rapidly and the third suggested that it would lead them to demand higher wages. Not only was the plan lost but within two years the vestry voted to throw open the existing encroachments which Cobbett had sought to have certified in deed.[13]

Although not resident at Botley after his bankruptcy of 1820, Cobbett maintained a close interest in the welfare of the labourers and cottagers in his former parishes. In 1826 he opposed a petition by local farmers and landlords to enclose the 1,300 acres of Waltham Chase, on which lived a thousand cottagers who drew a large portion of their living from the cows, pigs and forest horses that they grazed on the common. The petitioners' claim that the land was 'unproductive in its present state' was sufficient word for the House of Commons, which drafted and passed a bill allowing the enclosure to proceed. Much to Cobbett's gratification, however, the Lords, to whom he had submitted evidence on both the productive use of the Chase and the hardship that its enclosure would cause, inspected the bill in committee and refused to proceed with it.[14] 'Judge you of [the farmers'] mortification', said Cobbett to the cottagers:

> You have seen an egg-sucking cur, when an egg-shell fitted with hot coals has been crammed into his mouth; and you have seen him twist his jaws about, and stare like mad. Like these curs were the graspers, when the House of

Lords refused to give them the power of robbing the poor of Waltham Chase
of the last blade of grass.[15]

It was Cobbett's experience that commons and small farms bred a spirit of
independence and self-confidence among the rural poor. His favourite
agricultural scientist, Jethro Tull, had complained bitterly during the early
eighteenth century of 'saucy' labourers who defied their masters and
insisted that they be addressed 'in a very humble pursuasive manner'.[16]
This was all to the good in Cobbett's view. While admitting that there
might be some 'inconvenience' in brashness, he much preferred 'the saucy
daring fellow' over the 'poor, crawling, feeble wretch, who is not saucy,
only, perhaps, because he feels that he has not the power to maintain
himself'.[17]

Cobbett also knew that labourers and cottagers were efficient and
productive cultivators in their own right. Turning to Coke of Norfolk as
an apologist for large farms and capital-intensive agriculture, he asserted
that ten farms of 100 acres would yield more than one farm of 1,000 acres,
for much agricultural produce, especially poultry, milk and honey, was
more the result of time and care than of capital. The large farm, he claimed,
only *appeared* more productive, with its large wagons rumbling to market
along impressive new turnpikes.[18] Large farmers knew as much, hence
their bitter and irrational denunciations of cottagers as a 'new class of
producer' who had the arrogance (in the words of one employer) to 'show
us how to farm'.[19] As one steward learned, 'it is by no means uncommon
for a farmer who holds three or four hundred acres of land to complain,
when his landlord interferes to take from him three or four acres for a
cottager, that his farm is essentially injured by it'.[20] In Wiltshire in 1806,
recalled the rector of Broad Somerford, some parcels of land that farmers
proved unable to reclaim were allotted to labourers, and soon 'cultivated
in such perfection that ... it is a disgrace to the farmer's cultivation'.[21]

Cobbett knew many instances of cottagers succeeding at labour-
intensive husbandry. Known to him since his youth were the Surrey
'Bourners' who put their spades to the tiny green patches between the
heath-covered hills to the south of Farnham. 'The land being generally too
poor to attract the rich,' Cobbett observed, 'this common has escaped
enclosure bills; and every little green dip is now become a cottager's garden
or field ... till they have formed a grand community of cottages, each with
its own plot of ground and its pigsty.'[22] Similar to the 'Bourners' were the
cottagers of the New Forest who managed a prosperous and efficient
agriculture which included a pig, sometimes a cow and pony, customary
access to peat, wood and turf, as well as rights of grazing and mast. The pig
was the certain thing: on one visit Cobbett counted some 140 within 60

yards of his horse.[23] New Forest pigs, according to the topographers Brayley and Britton, produced the best bacon in the country, and reached weights of between 300 and 800 pounds apiece.[24] Yet this dynamic economy of the foresters invited charges that they were so many thieves, prostitutes, smugglers and poachers. The agricultural improver Charles Vancouver pleaded on 'moral' grounds for the removal of the encroachers on the Forest's edge, while William Gilpin represented the entire population as 'an indolent race; poor and wretched in the extreme'. All their manifold advantages in way of fuel and livestock, he claimed, 'procure them not half the enjoyments of common day-labourers'.[25] Cobbett, on the other hand, found them 'happy and well' with neat cottages, abundant fuel, a pig or two and sometimes a cow.[26]

The pattern to emerge from Cobbett's detailed studies of forests and commons was that the poorer the soil the better off the labourers. At Swing-torn Micheldever in Hampshire he found newly enclosed commons, large farms and hungry labourers, whereas south of Winchester on the Mildmay estates, amid poorer soil, smaller farms and abundant woods and commons, the labourers had gardens, pigs and 'none of that haggard look which is so painful to my eyes in the north of Hampshire'. At Hurstbourne Tarrant the soil was rich and the agriculture advanced, but the labourers among the poorest in the county. To the south and east on the difficult soil of the Sussex woodlands, the labourers and cottagers were better off than their fellows in the corn-growing regions, for 'all is not appropriated where there are coppices and woods, where the cultivation is not so easy and the produce so very large'. In the forests near Tunbridge Wells, for example, he found that the labouring people looked 'pretty well' and had pigs in their sties; while in more arable areas, such as the Isle of Thanet, they 'suffer from the want of fuel, and they have nothing but their *bare pay*'. Scenes of poverty amid plenty were observed by Cobbett in the valley of the Avon, East Anglia and most often in north Hampshire and Wiltshire, where he found the labourers at the 'inferno potato level' with 'worse gardens than anywhere else'.[27]

Of all country workers it was the 'clay and coppice' people of the southern weald that Cobbett most admired, and it was among them that he researched and compiled the recipes and instructions of *Cottage Economy*. These workers were unlettered and superstitious, but from the awkward wealden soils they extracted a hearty living 'by hook or by crook'. They had pigs, cows in some cases, winter employment in the coppices and a ready supply of wood for fuel, pig-sties, cow-sheds and hop-poles. These people were not confronted by enclosure schemes or by engrossing farmers; they secured their subsistence independently of the rich, who despised them for it. These 'leather-legged chaps', as Cobbett called them, were neither capitalist nor proletarian; they produced for their own consumption, exchanged produce with their friends and neighbours and had only occasional recourse to the commercial market. It was Cobbett's observation that they were able to maintain their independent economy, not so much because of any uniquely 'entrepreneurial' disposition, but because their property was 'deemed worth *nothing*' by the large landholders.[28]

Much in contrast with the clay and coppice people were the labourers of arable districts who were often obliged to pay £4 or £5 a year, or a quarter of the man's earnings, for wood, peat or coal.[29] Some Wiltshire labourers, Cobbett observed, scrambled for fuel merely to boil water for tea.[30] These 'local disadvantages', as Frederick Eden glibly called them,[31] were not sympathetically treated by the labourers' critics: a Surrey farmer, for example, *seemed* to have the right idea when he urged his workers to diversify their diet by boiling rather than broiling their meat, but after a fair trial his workers complained that they could not afford the additional fuel involved.[32] Cobbett understood the problem: at Botley he included a constant supply of fuel in his workers' wages; he also ensured that his cottages were fitted with large ovens. But these were extraordinary practices; the first cottage of Joseph and Hannah Ashby, for example, had no range for cooking, 'only an open fire with a shallow oven of seventeenth-century pattern under it'. Such an obvious disadvantage, however, did not prevent a visitor to Tysoe from publicly condemning the 'improvidence and cooking of the cottage women', which charge would have gone unchallenged had not Joseph, like Cobbett, possessed the exceptional ability to launch a written defence of the skills and efficiency of his class.[33]

Ill-informed criticism of the labourers' 'improvidence' was commonplace in nineteenth-century cottage manuals. But while Cobbett's treatise was a rare exception, it did not pretend to approve of all of the labourers' domestic habits. Not intending that the book be read by employers or Whig educators, he dealt frankly with domestic inefficiencies, calling upon rural workers to make the best use of their raw materials. There 'are very few gardens of the labourers in the country', he observed, 'unless where they have been totally stripped by the bull-frog system of enclosure, which do not contain twenty or thirty rods each'.[34] He instructed his readers in how to turn these few rods to full advantage, and at the same time to cease all unnecessary indulgences which imbalanced the cottage budget. His most controversial advice pertained to bread – the '*staff of life*' which he insisted upon for every farm worker. A man earning 10s. a week, with four children, an industrious wife and a quarter acre garden, he calculated, should not have his children crying for bread, even with flour at 6d. a bushel. The woman's duty was to bake the bread; that of the man was not to complain that a coarser loaf was not good enough – 'it was good enough for his forefathers who were too proud to be paupers'.[35] These heady words were more pleasing to the readers of The Edinburgh Review than to the southern rural workers, who associated the coarse and heavy flour of Cobbett's recommendation with extraordinary scarcity, the olden times and the fare of the Midlands and North. But unlike other commentators who criticized the labourers' insistence upon the wheaten loaf, Cobbett ensured that he also offered advice on the means of securing the other two-thirds of the three Bs: bacon and beer.[36]

In a small way Cottage Economy indulged the southern farm worker by refusing to recommend the more flexible diet of the labourer of the North and Scotland.[37] It was Cobbett's boast that a Sussex labourer would not adopt a northern diet unless the rich 'broke every limb in his body', destroyed the coppices and woods and force-fed him 'oat-cakes, pea-bunnochs, and burgoo'.[38] Thus no sooner was he across the Tweed in 1832 than he began composing broadsides for the southern chopsticks about the scarcity of villages, churches, alehouses, flower-gardens, and pigs and geese, while ridiculing the bothies where the Scottish labourers kept residence and prepared their meals from their allowances of potatoes, oats, barley and milk. 'If this be the effect of [Scottish] light,' he declared, 'give me the darkness 'o' tha' Sooth', and on he went to urge the southern labourers to go to any length to preserve their gardens, Poor Laws and what remained of their bread, bacon and beer. This was indulgence of a sort, but it was also the commission of the southern labourers' own songs, which refused to relinquish a claim to the three Bs, even if it meant foregoing the more varied fare of their Scottish brothers and sisters.[39]

The Edinburgh Review was able to embrace Cottage Economy on account that its editors did not detect Cobbett's unofficial sub-text which invited the labourers to steal fuel and fodder, to poach as required and to evade the exciseman whenever possible. Such practices were condoned by Cobbett on account of his belief that the labourers already performed adequate services for their rulers and employers, who in turn bore much of the responsibility for the erosion of organic relationships within the cottage. The state taxed leather, salt, candles, soap, malt and hops, while employers often refused to break bulk or to retail small portions of food to their workers.[40] The result was a dependence upon shopkeepers which crippled the cottage budget by appending to food costs the profits of farmer, miller, mealman and retailer, which in many cases amounted to the difference between indebtedness and solvency within the cottage. A cycle was thereby set in motion that saw the labourers mortgage their harvest earnings by July, fall into debt by early winter, and have their credit vanish by the start of the new year.[41] Among Cobbett's official remedies were his campaigns against excise duties, his lectures to farmers on the virtues of the farm-gate sale and his support for the cottage cow-keeping programmes of Lords Brownlow, Carrington, Stanhope and Winchelsea,[42] but he did not hold his breath for these reforms, advising the labourers in the meantime to do what they had to do – legal or otherwise – to avoid the shopkeeper and the purchase of taxable commodities.

After the quarter-acre garden or its pilfered equivalent the cornerstone of Cobbett's writing on cottage economics was the pig. It was the national animal, according to Cobbett and the labourers – unmatched in taste and culinary versatility. Cobbett was even moved to suggest that a flitch in the larder was more important and meaningful than a complete set of the *Political Register*; it prompted peace, goodwill and happiness in a way that nothing else could.[43] As Walter Rose later observed, the flitch 'formed the purtiest picture in the house', and 'to understand why, you must know not only the labourers' habit of mind but the poverty from which his stock had sprung'.[44] Cobbett well understood this state of mind, but first he got down to advising the labourers on the means of fattening hogs upon a wide variety of fodders amenable to spade husbandry, including potatoes, pease, beans, cabbages, turnips and Indian corn, together with the familiar roadside acquisitions that inclined some Dorset farmers to declare that 'no labourer can be honest and feed a pig'.[45] It was in pig-keeping that labourers and cottagers most ably demonstrated the 'hook or crook' ingenuity that Cobbett wished to see extended to all aspects of the rural domestic experience, for despite a decline in the number of cottage pigs in some regions,[46] Cobbett found many sties still occupied, especially in Gloucestershire, Worcestershire, Kent, the Isle of Wight and the fens of Lincolnshire and Cambridgeshire. Exact figures are hard to come by, but there seems to have been a pig in about 40 per cent of cottage gardens.[47]

Like Flora Thompson, Cobbett revelled in the lore of the pig.[48] He spoke in metaphysical tone about the sagacity and discriminating palate of the hog, and happily conformed with the countryman's penchant for scratching a pig's back with a walking stick while entertaining passers-by with tall stories about the hog's wisdom. One of his yarns, though 'true beyond all doubt', pertained to a gamekeeper who had taught a pig to point to partridges and other fallen game in the manner of a pointer dog. Accordingly, Cobbett insisted upon first-class accommodation for his swine: 'When I make up my hogs' lodging place for winter, I look well at it, and consider, whether, upon a pinch, I could, for once and away, make shift to lodge in it myself. If I *shiver at the thought*, the place is not good enough for my hogs.' During his stay in America in 1817–18, he went as far as to accommodate a large sow inside his Long Island farmhouse, much to the irritation of his son John who was kept awake at night by the incessant grunts of the boarder. If in some ways Cobbett lived an absurd and obsessive life, this was not one of them: the pig is a tidy and intelligent animal maligned only by urban prejudice. Its well-being was the most important concern of a pig-keeping household; when the bacon chest ran low, Cobbett observed, the pig-keeper's discourse evolved from 'd—d hog' to 'pretty piggy'; and as slaughter-day approached, the atmosphere in the cottage became one of nervous anticipation. Along with the labourers, Cobbett remembered the procedures of the butchering with proverbs and rituals, knowing that the job had to be done methodically and with a mystical reverence, not in the haphazard and secular manner of Hardy's Jude.[49] For a small minority of countrymen, such as Joseph Ashby, the mentality associated with pig-keeping was intellectually debilitating;[50] Cobbett preferred to see it as an example of the importance of tradition, neighbourliness and good living in the village community.

Cobbett's greatest contribution to pig-keeping was his introduction to England of 'Cobbett's Corn': a dwarf variety of Continental maize which he proved would ripen in England and provide an excellent source of both animal fodder and of human food.[51] As small a crop as 10 rods, he claimed, could fatten a pig to 1,000 pounds; or if the labourer preferred, five pigs to 200 pounds. The crop had much to commend it in Cobbett's agrarian economics: it required no capital and no barn, it could be worked by women and children, with the entire family spending the winter months shelling ears at the fireside.[52] Cobbett further predicted that cottagers with 20 rods of his corn would aspire to 10 acres, and subsequently to a small farm. In this way the corn would produce '*real emancipation*: it is the *poor man's plant*: it is the *plant of liberty*; the *plant of independence*', and of insurance: 'It will *prevent the labourers from ever being slaves again*; it will inevitably re-produce *small farms*; it will make labourers more independent of their employers; it will bring back, it will *hasten* back, the country towards its former happy state.'[53] Cobbett's expectations were not met, but in the face of derision from *The Times* and the *Farmer's Journal*, the crop met with substantial, if temporary, success.[54] From his experimental farm in Surrey (the cost of the experiments ran into the 'thousands' according to his daughter Susan),[55] 'Cobbett's Corn' spread in patchwork from Scotland to the Channel Islands, enabling a number of labourers to keep a pig for the first time.[56] Early in 1831, on account of the excellent public response to the corn, Cobbett arranged to distribute free packages of seed to the Swing counties, each of which was to receive 200 ears for its labourers, with the exception of Kent, which was to receive 500 in unsubtle commemoration of the starting point of the rising. It was Cobbett's intention to distribute the corn in person, 'but I do not want to be hanged; and, I know, that no place is safe for me; which is not at a *good* distance from the ricks and barns, and furnishes me with an alibi'. When the torches were laid to rest, Cobbett hurried to the Swing-torn parishes of Sussex and north Hampshire, where he organized the planting of the corn in the face of derision from large farmers, the London press and an estranged Henry Hunt.[57] All that mattered to Cobbett was the response of the labourers, who seem to have appreciated the gesture. One elderly labourer refused to accept payment from Cobbett for two exemplary ears: 'I planted 24 corns, and I have these bunches of fine ears, I have put some short ones by for seed and Mr. Cobbett, God bless him, he is welcome to the whole of them if he wishes it.'[58] The local scribe who passed on the message might have coloured its contents to curry favour with Cobbett; nevertheless the corn was not the hoax that many alleged, even some of

15   Satirical representation of Cobbett writing to Henry Hunt from his farmyard in Long Island, New York.

16   Cobbett's house at Normandy farm, near Ash in Surrey. Reproduced
by permission of the Syndics of the Fitzwilliam Museum, Cambridge.

From 1805 until 1817 Cobbett farmed at Botley in Hampshire, where he
was derisively known as 'the Hampshire hog'. Most of the two following
years he spent in America, where he practised a cottage agriculture on Long
Island. Between 1821 and 1826 he performed his agricultural experiments
upon a 4-acre garden at Kensington; in 1826 he leased more garden plots,
and subsequently an 80-acre farm, on the south side of the Thames at Barn
Elm. After the expiry of the Barn Elm lease in 1830 he rented a farm of 160
acres at Normandy near Ash in Surrey, some 7 miles from his birthplace at
Farnham. It was there that he died in 1835.

Cobbett's political adversaries admitted as much.[59] Still, not even Cobbett
himself boasted complete success, for the new crop failed to bring an end
to the human consumption of potatoes.[60]

It is understandable that late twentieth-century Britons – the world's
foremost consumers of potatoes – [61] should find novelty and amusement
in Cobbett's diatribes against 'the root of extreme unction', but dietary
dignity is relative. If today's North Americans feel no cultural imposition
in gnawing 'Cobbett's Corn' directly off the cob, the same cannot be said
for many aghast British observers, who sometimes marvel at the culinary
simplicity and apparent indignity of the spectacle. Cobbett ate his sweet

corn directly off the cob, yet he deplored the sight of labourers unearthing potatoes, tossing them unwashed into a pot, and carrying them cold to the fields in their satchels. It was not so much the taste or the foreign origins of the potato that most unnerved him (nor its status as an innovative crop: his own sweet corn was an even newer arrival), but rather the 'slovenly and beastly habits' which he associated with its production and consumption.[62] The vigour of Cobbett's opposition to the 'villainous root' had much to do with with his recollection of a potato-free Farnham:

> I can remember when the first acre of potatoes was planted in a field, in the neighbourhood of the place where I was born; and I very well remember, that even the poorest of the people would not eat them. They called them hog-potatoes; but now, they are become a considerable portion of the diet of those who raise the bread for others to eat.[63]

Although carrying his opposition to the ridiculous heights of threatening to inflict penalties upon anyone who transported potatoes onto his own farms, he had important scientific and economic objections to the root. First, it contributed little to the organic relationships in the cottage garden, yielding no straw for pig-bedding and returning few nutrients to the soil.[64] Second, he joined the labourers in objecting to potatoes, not as a dietary supplement, but as the 'sole food of man'.[65] Finally, he strongly rejected the uncharitable idea (often expressed in Cobbett's own day, and later by J. H. Clapham) that potatoes were adequate compensation for the labourers' losses in other vegetable fare.[66] The labourers of 1830 were 'almost wholly supplied with potatoes', according to one observer: 'breakfast and dinner brought to them in the fields, and nothing but potatoes'.[67] In 1826, not a particularly hungry year, Alexander Somerville was obliged to do with his crop of potatoes 'what I intended a pig to do – eat them'.[68] Most emphatically of all, Cobbett opposed the potato because it allowed rural employers to add to the exploitation of their workers. Farmers represented the potato plot as 'a blessing to all the lower classes of the community', for it meant that their labourers might survive on 7s. or 8s. a week.[69] In the words of one agricultural reporter, the new crop kept the labourers 'more under subjection' by discouraging them from 'leaving their master during the summer; as in that case the crop would be forfeited'.[70]

Potato-eating, according to Cobbett, was not an isolated practice but 'a component part of the tea-drinking system' which cumulatively robbed the labourers of time, money and good health.[71] In advising English workers to refrain from tea, he joined the company of John Wesley, Arthur Young, Frederick Eden, William Howitt and Sir John Sinclair – Tories in the main.[72] These men looked back to an older, more virile and 'manly'

England; they parted company with Cobbett on political matters but believed in fair play and hard work, which according to most genuine countrymen, required an ample supply of beer. For William Marshall, the speed at which harvest work was performed stood in inverse relationship with the amount of beer consumed.[73] The same observation was made all over the Kingdom, including by a Shropshire farmer who after complaining of the 'excessive quantity of beverage' allowed to the farm workers of his county, proceeded to observe (without relating cause and effect) that 'there are few parts of England, where the harvest is got in with such spirit and expedition'.[74] Cobbett was in no doubt that beer was a necessity of life for those who lived by their labour. As an employer he discovered that one labourer 'well lined with meat and beer is worth two or three creatures swelled out with warm water, under the name of tea'.[75] In terms of the labourers' overall diet, he rated beer next in importance to bread and meat, and as far more important than cheese or butter.

Opposition to beer came from the advocates (mainly Whigs and Peelites) of an urban-based English culture. The younger Peel, whom Cobbett later confronted in Parliament for a repeal of the malt duty, defended tea as a moral refreshment and as 'our national beverage'. Cobbett and his men could only laugh at these suggestions; they saw the advertisers of tea in the same light as they saw temperance reformers: as 'despicable drivelling quacks'.[76] This is not to say that Cobbett approved of immoderate consumption or drunkenness.[77] He carefully calculated his workers' allowances at two quarts per day in winter, three in spring and five in summer; this much the labourers must have, he argued, otherwise they would turn to the alehouse with ruinous frequency.[78]

Cobbett was far from alone in condemning the decline in cottage brewing precipitated by the leap in the malt tax from 10s. 6d. per quarter in 1791 to 38s. 8d. in 1804.[79] Farmer John Ellman of Glynde in Sussex informed the 1821 Select Committee on Agriculture that when he began farming in the 1770s, every family in his parish brewed their own beer – 'there are few of them now that do, unless I give them the malt'.[80] Ellman was no Radical, and partly for this reason Cobbett extracted abundant mileage from the testimony, referring to it not fewer than twenty times.[81] Many other commentators supplied similar evidence. At Chailey in Sussex during the 1790s it was observed that 'since the advance in the price of malt, both the brewing and consumption of beer have been much discontinued; and tea and spirits have been very greatly substituted'.[82] In nearby Offham there was said to be tea but no beer in the cottages.[83] In Berkshire, according to David Davies, home-brewing fell off markedly during the early 1790s on account of a doubling of the taxes on malt and hops.[84]

During the 1780s, remembered an Isle of Thanet farmer, every labourer 'had a barrel of beer in his cellar', but such was not the case by the 1830s.[85] Home-brewing, said Frederick Eden in 1797, 'even amongst small farmers is at an end. The Poor drink tea at all their meals.'[86] The labourers were 'worse workmen' as a result, added a Gloucestershire farmer, 'for they have not now strength sufficient to perform their work properly, from the want of a nutritive and invigorating beverage, which the removal of the Tax upon Malt would supply'.[87]

Some of Cobbett's archest political foes, including the Hampshire MP Willis Fleming and Thomas Coke of Holkham, lamented the passing of cottage brewing.[88] Many farmers, to be sure, were less interested in cheap beer than in markets for their barley, but some were genuinely distressed at the sight of their workers attempting to quench their thirst at the water-pump. In some cases these farmers continued to brew, despite the high costs. A large Kentish farmer claimed that his brewing expenses amounted to £2,000 between 1831 and 1834; another announced that he tolerated a high malt bill because 'a man cannot work without beer'.[89] Still, such sensitivity was the exception. The Essex farmer and political reformer Montagu Burgoyne, for example, was party to a local decision to pay weekly wages of 8s. with beer, or 9s. without. 'I am laughed at by all gentlemen farmers for preferring the former', he remarked, 'I know that it is attended with inconvenience; but it is no small comfort to the poor man; and trouble, in such a case, is a duty.'[90]

Thus, while the commercial production of beer continued to rise after 1790, the decline of home-brewing meant a decrease in the rates of *per capita* consumption, which is to say that English rural workers doubtless consumed more beer in the 1720s than in the 1820s, despite a modest reduction in the malt duty in 1822. Moreover, the beer consumed in Regency times was largely purchased from the public house, where until 1830 it was taxed at the rate of 200 per cent. The bottle-crook that Cobbett had carried to the field in his youth became a rare sight. 'While this tax lasts', he argued,

> working men have *no home*; no fireside, no family; they are driven to prowl about for drink like cattle in a dry summer. In short, this tax must be repealed, or we must prepare ourselves for everlasting strife, and everlasting confusion. Tax the wine, tax the spirits, tax the sugar, tax the tea, tax anything but the malt.

The malt duty was worse than plague, famine or civil war, he claimed, it was 'the main instrument in the ruin of England'. Given cheap malt, the labourers would brew again; their beer would cost them a penny a quart and they could dispense with the tea-kettle 'that boileth without ceasing, like the bowels of Mount-Edna'. In the meantime he urged his own workers to make their own malt behind the back of the exciseman, 'and good jovial lives they led'.[91]

Along with the Poor Law Bill, the malt duty was Cobbett's first priority as a member of Parliament, and he died fighting for its repeal against the Whigs and Tories who cared little about the labourers and their mascot John Barleycorn. Home-brewing would ultimately return to the cottage, but not until later in the century, in the communities of Richard Jefferies and Flora Thompson, by which time tea was commonplace and the standing of beer reduced in rural culture.[92] Even a countryman of the calibre of W. H. Hudson would assume that neatness and civic pride in Wiltshire villages implied temperance among the inhabitants. He was surprised to learn that the villagers brewed their own beer and drank of it daily.[93] Doubtless the village was sober not despite its home-brewing but because of it, just as Cobbett would have anticipated.

The great explanation for Cobbett's long-standing opposition to Regency tax schedules lies not in the *Political Register* but in *Cottage Economy*. The approximately 40 per cent of the labourers' earnings that went to the taxman were the ways in which the 'system' contributed to the corruption of the labourers' economy. Salt quarried in Hampshire cost 2s. 6d. in the state of New York, but 19s. at the quarry itself.[94] Legislators seemed unaware that salt was required in the making of butter, cheese and, above all, bacon. The labourer Thomas Smart, in giving evidence to the 1824 parliamentary committee on agricultural wages, complained that the salt tax prevented him from keeping a pig, for the three pecks needed to salt a good-sized hog were elevated by the tax from 6d. to 10s. 6d.[95] The pig might also have to go if the farmer refused to sell the odd bushel of wheat to the labourer, for that was the source of bran that best concluded the fattening process. The demise of home-brewing also had implications for pig-keeping inasmuch as used malt was often applied to the same purpose. Without a pig, in turn, there was neither bacon in the cottage nor natural fertilizer for the garden; nor was there lard for cooking or (to return to the decline of home-brewing) yeast for the baking of bread. Cottagers had either to buy these supplies at the inflated prices of the shopkeeper, publican and baker, or they went without their traditional fare.[96]

The last great compromise of the organic potential of the cottage lay in the removal of manufacturing from the countryside. Cobbett is often criticized for his prosaic appeals for a return to 'the *dark ages*' when women spun wool and knitted stockings, but it is seldom observed that he tackled the problem directly by reviving the straw-plait industry which had entered a depression during the 1820s on account of the importation of straw hats from Tuscany.[97] His plan was to grow in England the same grasses that were used in the Italian and American manufacture, which in a limited way he succeeded in doing. Among those to prosper at his industry were two Botley girls who earned more at plaiting than did their father at agricultural labour. A crippled Kentish worker who was unable to perform field labour mastered the craft of plaiting from the book by 'Mr. Caubitt'. Even as far north as the Orkneys there was introduced the 'Cobbett-Bonnet' industry, which, according to one observer, added £20,000 a year to the regional economy.[98] For his efforts Cobbett was awarded the silver medal of the Society of Arts (he thought that he deserved the gold), which he accepted in a frank speech condemning 'that despicable cant, which was constantly dinned into the ears of the labouring classes; who, if they complained of their situation, were immediately told, that they ought to be contented with the state of paupers'. Mixed with the applause of Society members, according to *The Times* correspondent, was 'some slight disapprobation'. A certain amount of disapprobation was inevitable for Cobbett was attracted to the industry because it engendered no urban masses, 'calico-lords' or Combination Acts. He also liked the fact that it required little capital, and that it was 'a great deal better employment than singing hymns, listening to the bawling of the Methodist parson, or in reading those lying blackguard things called religious tracts'.[99]

Cottage Economy sought to rebuild the cottage as a viable economic organism at the same time as Cobbett campaigned against legislation prejudicial to the labourers' independence and happiness. At one level it is a practical text on cookery, but when set beside Cobbett's other ventures on behalf of the village economy, it becomes a highly political text in a way that *The Edinburgh Review* did not perceive. Even on points where Cobbett and the ruling class seemed to be in essential agreement, such as on the merits of the straw-plait industry, or on the virtues of home-brewed ale, they were at political and economic odds; for while most legislators and employers were not exactly opposed to improvements in the labourers' happiness and material circumstances, they were not prepared to run any risk of esteeming labour ahead of capital. Cobbett, on the other hand, perceived the cottage, and indeed the entire industry of agriculture, as a family unit of peasant production which would have all but destroyed capitalist agriculture. *Cottage Economy* worked in close collaboration with the labourers' own cultural priorities, while giving them hard advice on how to brew affordable beer (even with the malt tax in place), to build ice-houses and to keep bees. Although stopping short of the more collectivist agrarianism of the Owenites or Spenceans, Cobbett was adamant that his readers not be content as waged labourers or even as cottagers; he wanted a nation of peasants or 'household producers'[100] who exchanged goods and services in kind, cultivated their own lands with family hands and avoided the capitalist market except to sell by barter some excess produce at traditional fairs:

> I hold a return to *small farms* to be absolutely necessary to a restoration of any thing like an English community; and I am quite sure, that the ruin of the present race of farmers, generally, is a necessary preliminary to this . . . Men, not only without *capital*, but who have never so much as heard the coxcomical word, must be put to cultivate farms. Farms will be divided again.[101]

And so sang the labourers, who called for ten farms to be made of one.[102] But small farms did not return, and the primacy of capital was not reduced. Even the later allotment movement was viewed by many employers with grave suspicion: as a Suffolk labourer recalled, 'the landowners and gentry were as much against our desire for allotments as if we had claimed universal suffrage'.[103]

CHAPTER 6

OLD ENGLAND: NOSTALGIA AND EXPERIENCE

The working people of England were, when I was born, well fed, well clad, and had each his barrel of beer in his house; and, let what may be the accompanying consequence, if they be not thus again before I die, every one shall say, that the fault has not been that of William Cobbett.

PR, 3 August 1833, p. 261.

The toiling remains, but all else has given place.
'The Roast Beef of Old England' (*c.* 1820).

T**HE** most prominent stereotype of Cobbett is of a rural rider who indulged in a wayward nostalgia for some obscure and distant Eden that probably never existed. As one typical comment runs:

> [Cobbett] looked back to a legendary England; a land of peace and plenty, of hale and hearty yeomen, of home-baked bread and home-brewed ale, a country of villages and hamlets, a nation of pristine innocence and un-corrupted virtue ... Nowadays the limits of Cobbett's outlook are obvious: he idealized the England of his youth.[1]

Such unproblematic verdicts (which in turn idealize 'nowadays' empiri-cism) have assisted to reduce Cobbett's historical usages to a catalogue of pastoral sentiments and extravagant dreams about a merry English past. Many recent historians and literary critics, however, have set about decon-structing some of the social experiences and emotive stimuli that inspire a search for Eden.[2] Others, with special reference to Cobbett, have suggested that his readings of the past be understood as ahistorical exten-sions of his social and economic criticism.[3] This chapter will suggest another course: that Cobbett's histories be analysed in the context of his attempt to recover popular history from the control of the dominant culture; and that they be approached according to his own claims that they constituted accurate representations of the past and of the historical consciousness of English villagers. In the process we will attempt to bring into question the oft-heard claims that Cobbett's nostalgia was predicated upon an abiding Toryism that threatened to undermine his radicalism in politics and economics.[4]

It was argued by Raymond Williams that English history records a long line of 'golden age' thinkers, often countrymen, who cumulatively escalate the rural paradise until it falls off the edge of time.[5] This insightful metaphor should not be taken to mean that the escalator maintains an even pace or a uniform quota of human traffic. The first three-quarters of the eighteenth century, for example, was not a great age for looking back, especially among agricultural workers. During the half-century after 1780, however, nostalgic allusions to the past became commonplace in popular rural songs and autobiographies. After a brief respite during the middle decades of the century, another phase of rural nostalgia (together with the first great wave of public interest in Cobbett) accompanied the agricultural depression of the late Victorian and Edwardian decades. For the remainder of the twentieth century the escalator has proceeded by fits and starts; its pace was slowed during the middle decades but it now shows signs of a new tempo and vitality. There is no habitual or impulsive relationship, then, between rural workers and the pursuit of Edenic mysteries. It must also be remembered that not all countrymen and rural writers, even many who lived during phases of Arcadianism, were amenable to escalation. George Sturt, for example, remarked in 1910 that 'the more I examine it, the more I grow sceptical of the well-being of the people, in these "good old times"'.[6] Similar reservations were expressed by Alexander Somerville, Joseph Arch and James Hawker. Like the 'King of the Norfolk Poachers' they remembered no golden age 'except for the man with plenty of gold'.[7] These countrymen and labourers might well have expressed a minority opinion, but it deserves to be said that quests for Eden are not entirely the product of some unconscious impulse or chronic lament for the lost serenities of a traditional rural life. As Roger Wells has noted of the eighteenth century, structural change in English argicultural society and economics proceeded at too slow a pace for golden age notions to occupy the rural worker's mind.[8] Lived experiences within particular eras condition at least the dynamics of historical production and reception, even on an escalator containing an army of hand-picked countrymen stretching from Virgil to Ronald Blythe.

Cobbett's histories were composed in conscious opposition to the dominant historiography of his day. The old chapbook histories that he had known as a boy – treating of war heroes and illustrious monarchs – were innocent enough in his view, but the proliferation of penny abridgements of the works of the great liberal historians suggested to him that the ruling class was undertaking new initiatives to secure control of popular memory. Cobbett's alternative histories were intended to preserve and fortify the independence of the people's historical consciousness; in turn the ruling class confessed its designs upon popular memory by producing a nervous series of tracts (which often quoted Hume's *History* at great length) that ridiculed Cobbett's thesis of a superior past.[9]

Cobbett challenged the dominant historiography by meeting Hume and Gibbon on the high field of methodology, denouncing them as 'romancers' who communicated 'the gossip and scandal of former times, and very little else'. The great duty of historians, he argued, is to 'record facts' and to seek 'earnestly after truth'; they are to provide instruction in the origin of laws and institutions, and above all in the effects of those laws and institutions upon the people. The dominant historiography fell short of these duties:

> We do not want to consume our time over a dozen pages about Edward the Third dancing at a ball, picking up a lady's garter and making that garter the foundation of an order of knighthood . . . It is not stuff like this; but we want to know what was the state of the people; what were the prices of the food, and how the labourers were dressed in the reign of that great king.[10]

Cobbett democratized historical vocabulary by defining the nation as '*the whole of the people*', and by evaluating economic measures according to their contribution to the welfare of the majority. Thus 'national wealth' was not demonstrated when of ten persons, two were elevated into a 'coach and four', and the other eight reduced to 'misery or dependence'. Cobbett wrote class history, concentrating upon the dispossessed eight. Legislators he praised or vilified, not according to the accidental price of bread and bacon during their tenures, but according to their stand on behalf of the natural rights of labour.[11]

Cobbett was an early practitioner of a radical variant of 'people's history' who seemed to bounce between Left and Right, thus earning the praise of G. K. Chesterton while anticipating some of the themes later developed in a more socialist focus by R. H. Tawney and Christopher Hill.[12] It is therefore tempting to see Cobbett's histories as traditional in cultural matters, and as radical in politics and economics. But while such a spectrum would be broad enough to account for the veneration of Cobbett by Chesterton or Hilaire Belloc, for example, it would dissolve the essential radicalism within his historical methods. Radical ideology inhered in his notion that true and democratic history dwelt in the folk mind rather than in the historical models and 'age of improvement' hypotheses of the Whigs and Tories. As an historian it was Cobbett's great purpose to win the political present for the common people by pointing to aspects of the English past which were remembered in the people's culture, and which were readily recoverable by the dominant one.

It was the state of the farm workers that inspired Cobbett to delve into the English past. 'What I eagerly looked for in your Report', he said to Lord John Russell, chairman of the 1824 parliamentary committee on agricultural wages, 'was the cause clearly stated of the misery of the labouring classes: the cause why this is now a land of paupers.'[13] This was the operative question behind 'The Plough-Boy's History of the Church', which in a strategic concession to Daniel O'Connell's Catholic Association, he published under the title *A History of the Protestant 'Reformation' in England and Ireland*. The working title was more appropriate to Cobbett's theme, for it was not his object to apologize for the liturgical and spiritual mysteries of Rome. Although drawing heavily upon the *History of England* by the Catholic priest Dr John Lingard, he sharply rejected a proposal by some members of the British Catholic Association that he be presented with as minor a gift as a complimentary copy of Lingard's work, declaring with indignance that 'I am not to be *hallooed* on.' Moreover, he was as critical of Lingard as of Hume for writing a political and religious rather than social history of the Reformation. Religious issues, he implied, were irrelevant to himself and to the farm workers, whom he represented as mindless of 'masses and images': they think primarily about 'good treatment, good victuals, good clothing, and all those things that make life easy and happy'.[14] The principal merit of the medieval English, according to Cobbett, had less to do with their spirituality than with the fact that they 'never suffered anybody to put them to board on cold potatoes and water'.[15] The Reformation itself he represented as a cultural and economic 'devastation' that manhandled the traditional festival calendar and robbed the poor of their patrimony.[16]

Cobbett approached medieval England with circumspection.[17] He did not contradict the opinion of the Anglican establishment that monastic charity gave rise to a degree of idleness among the common people, though he did wonder whether 'it were not as good that the people should lounge about the doors of convents, as about the doors of Overseers, who send them to Bridewell on account of their poverty'.[18] Similarly, he made no attempt to deny the old legends (much encouraged by Hume) about debauchery within monastic walls, but he did pause to think that the monks were resident, that they spent a portion of their revenues locally, and that they were oblivious to the nineteenth-century art of rack-renting. Nor did Cobbett's view of medieval England incorporate the enthusiasm for peasant bondage that looms so large in the poetry and prose of

PRICE ONE PENNY.

MR. COBBETT'S
PETITION
To Parliament.

YESTERDAY (the 7th March) the following Petition was presented to the House of Lords by Lord King. His Lordship is reported to have said that he wished the Minister for Ecclesiastical Affairs had been present to hear the Petition read. The Petition will speak for itself; and I have only to add, I will not say my hope, much less my expectation; but my most earnest wish that the prayer of the Petition may be granted, and especially the latter part of its prayer.

To the Right Honorable Lords Spiritual and Temporal, of the United Kingdom of Great Britain and Ireland, in Parliament assembled.

The Petition of William Cobbett, of Kensington in the county of Middlesex, dated this 7th day of March, 1827,

Most humbly sheweth,

That, reluctant as your Petitioner is, and as it becomes him to be, to trespass upon the time of your Right Honorable House, he hopes that it is unnecessary for him to inform your Lordships, that, in beseeching your attention to the representations, which he, with all humility, is about to submit to your Lordships on the state of his Roman Catholic fellow-subjects, he can have been actuated by nothing short of that sense of duty to his Sovereign and his Country, which he is sure your Lordships will readily admit, ought to supersede every other earthly consideration.

Though, after the most mature consideration; though after the most diligent inquiry; after the most patient and most impartial historical researches; though the result of all these has, notwithstanding the early planted and deep-rooted prejudices of his youth, and even of a large part of his riper years; though the result, notwithstanding every obstacle in its way, has been a settled conviction in his mind, that the departure from the religion of our forefathers has produced, and from its outset has been producing, great injury to our country; though he cannot look at the state of England in former times, compared with its state in latter times; though he cannot look into the statutes, passed by our Catholic ancestors, and there behold the indubitable proofs of the ease, the happiness, the plenty of food and raiment, the harmony, the order, the almost total absence of crime; though he cannot, when he compares these with those things of the same nature, now existing in the same country; though, when he makes this comparison, he cannot but feel, that he should be guilty of the basest injustice, were he to withhold an expression of his opinion, *that England has suffered from the change:* still he is too well aware of the violence, the injustice, the numerous and great dangers to his country, which must necessarily arise from any attempt whatever to restore and re-establish that, the abolition of which he regards as so great an evil.

But your humble Petitioner, though he entertains no wish to see the Roman Catholic religion restored and established, in any part of his Majesty's dominions, does, nevertheless, most anxiously desire two things; namely, *first,* that his Roman Catholic countrymen may be, as to political and civil rights, placed upon the same footing with himself, and with all the rest of his Protestant fellow-subjects; and, *second,* that the revenues of that Church, which now enjoys what the Roman Catholic Church enjoyed, may, like the revenues of the Roman Catholic Church, be applied in the like manner as they were in the days of our Catholic ancestors, *to the maintenance of the destitute poor.*

As to the *first* of these, your Lordships' most humble Petitioner beseeches you to reflect, that the Roman Catholic subjects of his Majesty, suffer great privations, great degradation; and, that they suffer these solely because they adhere to the religion of their and our forefathers; because by quitting that religion, by disowning it, by apostatizing from it, they can, at any moment, remove all the privations and all the degradation, of which they so bitterly, and, in your Petitioner's humble opinion, so justly complain: he beseeches your Lordships to reflect, that we owe the colleges, the universities, the cathedrals, and churches, in which we now worship God; that we owe the division of our country into counties, hundreds and parishes; that we owe our proudly-claimed and long-exercised dominion of the seas; that we owe the common law of the land, and those courts of justice, which law and which courts have done more than every thing else done by man to make England happy and great: that we owe, in short, every institution that we really venerate, not only every institution which is worthy of our veneration, but every institution which we really do venerate: your humble Petitioner beseeches your Lordships to reflect that we owe all these; that we owe all the real renown of our country, to the institutions and deeds of our Roman Catholic forefathers: and, hoping that your Lordships will, in your benignant condescension, be pleased thus to reflect, he cannot but hope, that, thus reflecting, you may be disposed to listen to his humble prayer, that you will, at last, pass such laws as shall cause a cessation of the suffering and degradation of those of our countrymen, who suffer for no other cause than that of adhering with unshaken fidelity to the faith and worship of our Roman Catholic forefathers.

As to the *second,* your humble Petitioner, though he seeks not to destroy any of the establishments or institutions of the country, cannot behold without feelings of shame, millions of Englishmen become miserable *paupers;* and, he cannot but recollect, and your Lordships cannot but know, that PAUPER was a name unknown in England in the days of our Catholic forefathers; and, seeing that your Lordships cannot but know, that the indigent poor were wholly maintained out of the tithes and other revenues of the Church; seeing, that your Lordships cannot but know that provision was made for the indigent poor, even in the Canons which established a Roman Catholic Clergy; seeing that your Lordships cannot but know, that it was part of the duty of that Clergy to provide effectually for the indigent poor, out of the revenues of the Church; seeing that your Lordships cannot but know, that laws were made to transfer those revenues to the Clergy of the present Establishment; seeing that your Lordships cannot but know, that the Clergy of the present Establishment do actually enjoy those revenues: seeing these things, and bearing in mind the representations above humbly made to your Lordships, your Petitioner, with the most profound respect for your Right Honourable House, but with an earnestness and anxiety equal to that respect, and with that confidence in the wisdom, the justice and the mercy of your Honourable House, which it becomes him to entertain and to express, he prays, that your Lordships will be pleased to pass an Act or Acts for the accomplishment of the following purposes:

1. For placing his Majesty's Roman Catholic subjects upon the same footing, with regard to political and civil rights, as the law has placed his Majesty's Protestant subjects.

2. For causing the indigent poor to be, as they were in the days of our Roman Catholic ancestors, maintained by the Clergy, out of the tithes and other revenues of the Church; and for causing thereby, the degrading, the odious name of pauper, to be unknown amongst us, as it was unknown amongst our happy Catholic progenitors.

And your humble Petitioner will, as in duty bound, ever pray.

WM. COBBETT.

London. Printed by WILLIAM COBBETT, No. 183, Fleet-street.

17 Cobbett did not want to see the Roman Catholic Church 'restored or established' in England, but he did call for the emancipation of all Catholics and for the application of the revenues of the Established Church to the relief of the poor. The date of the petition is 1829. Reproduced by permission of the Syndics of the Fitzwilliam Museum, Cambridge.

Wordsworth, Scott and Chesterton. Cobbett had profound respect for the labourers' aspirations for freedom, seeing nothing idyllic in being tied to the soil or in owing a fixed roster of labour to a lord. At the same time he professed to seeing nothing sentimental in the Settlement Acts which restricted the movement of workers in his own day, or in the combinations of employers which tended to hold down wages and necessitate abuse of the Poor Law. In the closed paternal villages of western Sussex he found little 'freedom' to celebrate:

> Hume and other historians rail against the *feudal*-system; and we '*enlight-ened*' and '*free*' creatures as we are, look back with scorn, or, at least, with surprise and pity, to the '*vassalage*' of our forefathers. But, if the matter were *well enquired into* ... we should find, that the people of these villages were *as free* in the days of William Rufus as are the people of the present day; and that vassalage, only under other names, exists now as completely as it did then.[19]

This is far from evidence of a disabling nostalgia or of a 'mythical picture of rural England'.[20] It expresses a legitimate understanding that freedom can be compromised by capitalism and feudalism alike.

Although often alluding to the virtues of Saxon constitutionalism and the effrontery of the Norman Yoke, Cobbett's main object in turning to the Middle Ages was to obtain hard information on the legal origins of landed property, tithes and poor-rates. In the process of telling this story he dabbled with medieval living standards, citing contemporary chron-iclers who described the beer, meat and woollens that went part way towards ameliorating feudalism and chronic pestilence. In general his view of medieval England approximated that of one of his admirers and fellow travellers in the genre of people's history, J. E. Thorold Rogers, who, after several decades of tireless research on manor records, concluded that the hardship in medieval England was a common lot, and that there was then 'more hope than superficial historians have conceived possible'.[21] Without access to any corroborating documents, Cobbett shared this view. He was somehow aware that a late medieval peasant on the manor of Farnham was a virtual freeholder of his virgate or half-virgate, and that he could 'buy, sell, exchange, give, recover by process of law' the land he held from the Bishop of Winchester. Further, doubtless from oral tradition, Cobbett knew that William of Wykeham, who overcame his humble origins to become Bishop of Winchester and Lord of Farnham manor, was charitable towards the poor, and that he exercised only 'mild authority' over his tenants.[22] Thus, in honour of this great commoner, Cobbett and his son Richard performed a pilgrimage to the Bishop's tomb in Winchester

Cathedral. As they rode away Richard's eye was drawn back towards the Cathedral: 'Why, Papa, nobody can build such places *now*, can they? No, my dear, said I. That building was made when there were no poor wretches in England, called *paupers*; when there were no *poor-rates*; when every labouring man was clothed in good woollen cloth; and when all had a plenty of meat and bread and beer.'[23] There might well be empirical deficiencies in Cobbett's narrative, but the enshrinement of the Bishop in Cobbett's consciousness and in popular memory was a powerful, informed and shared historical exercise.

Along with country workers, Cobbett's formal historical memory began with Tudor times, particularly the reign of Elizabeth, whom he braved to represent as a 'gross, libidinous, nasty, shameless old woman' whose foremost bequest to England was her 'pauper and ripping-up reign'. But after denouncing her as 'the worst woman that ever existed in England', he proceeded to admit the claims of popular culture that the labourers of her reign were 'but *partially* poor', that they had roast beef and plum pudding, and that the word 'labourer' was not then synonymous with 'pauper' or 'poor man'.[24] Similar views were expressed in the popular versions of the patriotic anthems of the dominant culture which applauded the permanence of roast beef and ale on the national menu. Richard Leveridge's mid-eighteenth-century ballad 'The Roast Beef of Old England', for example, which bullishly honoured the cuisine of the English while denouncing the frog's legs of the French, was revised in early nineteenth-century popular culture so as to address the loss of English roast beef:

> In Queen Bess's days, and at much later date,
> How happy indeed was an Englishman's state,
> For although he toiled both early and late;
> 'Twas for the roast beef of Old England.
>
> A labourer's cottage used then to display,
> A bright copper-kettle, and coal-scuttle gay,
> And bright pewter dishes whereon he did lay,
> The famous roast beef of Old England.
>
> Of saucepans and candlesticks too he'd a stock,
> And what he most valu'd, a good eight-day clock,
> In cellar a barrel of beer upon cock,
> To drink with the roast beef of Old England.
>
> His garments, though homely, did comfort denote,
> He'd holyday linen and holyday coat,
> A good featherbed, too, his rest to promote,
> Besides the roast beef of Old England.

> Now, instead of roast beef, a red herring you see,
> And a most wretched hovel, entirely free
> Of every comfort that used to be
> The boast and the pride of Old England.
>
> Alas! what a change, and how alter'd the case!
> The toiling remains, but all else has given place
> To that which to mention bespeaks the disgrace
> Of those who have ruled Old England.[25]

The provenance of revised 'Roast Beef' songs in collections of early nine-teenth-century broadsides is far from conclusive proof that Elizabethan cottages were blessed with happiness and abundance. Early nineteenth-century labourers doubtless claimed too much for the quality of life in the past, but they were moved to make their reflections by their misery in the present, and by the false claims of the dominant culture that roast beef and 'improvement' was the popular experience of Regency times.[26]

It is not too much to say that the 'Roast Beef' songs amount to versified abridgements of Cobbett's historical writing. 'Is this the country of roast beef!', he asked, 'Is this the same nation that used to laugh at the frog-eaters of France?': ' "*The Roast Beef of Old England*" was [formerly] a sort of proverb, or maxim, which meant, that English people lived better than any other people. There were, in fact, no people in England, who could, with strict propriety, be called *poor*. Now we are a mass of paupers with a few rich people.'[27] Cobbett would not have traded his own age, including its institutions, for that of the 'long-nailed she-tyrant', who in his view ruled a country of roast beef by inadvertence. Yet as much as possible he deferred to popular sensibilities, weaving the English workers' ideal of a superior past into a strong if subordinate historiography that claimed both a truth function and the more presentist agenda of supplying the infor-mation by which the people might compare their own condition with that of their ancestors.[28]

True and relevant history, Cobbett believed, could not be assembled within the halls of the social, economic and political establishment. Mean-ingful and democratic history dwelt in the folk mind, where it was orally conveyed from generation to generation with minimal interference from either the dominant culture or the 'novelty of experience'. 'What a man has not actually seen himself,' he declared, 'his father or grandfather has seen':[29]

Everything of tradition; all the old sayings of the country, which come down from father to son, show, that England was, in all former times, a country singularly happy ... The words '*English hospitality*' had not their origin in

The ROAST BEEF of *Old - England*,

A C A N T A T A.

Taken from a celebrated Print of the Ingenious Mr. Hogarth.

'TWAS at the gate of Calais, Hogarth tells,
 Where fad defpair and famine always dwells;
A meagre Frenchman, Madame Grandfire's Cook,
As home he fteer'd his carcafe, that way took;
Bending beneath the weight of fam'd Sir Loin,
On whom he'd often wifh'd in vain to dine :
Good father Dominic by chance came by,
With rofy gills, round paunch and greedy eye,
Who, when he firft beheld the greafy load,
His benediction on it he beftow'd :
And as the folid fat his fingers prefs'd
He lick'd his chaps, and thus the Knight addrefs'd.

A I R.
(A lovely Lafs to a Friar came)

Oh rare ROAST BEEF ! lov'd by all mankind,
 If I was doom'd to have thee,
When drefs'd and garnifh'd to my mind,
 And fwimming in thy gravy,
Not all thy country's force combin'd,
 Shou'd from my fury fave thee.

Renown'd SIR LOIN, oft times decreed
 The theme of Englifh Ballad ;
On the e'en Kings have deign'd to feed,
 Unknown to Frenchman's Palate :
Then how much does thy tafte exceed,
 Soup-meagre, Frogs and Sallad!

RECITATIVE.
A half-ftarv'd Soldier, fhirtlefs, pale and lean,
who fuch a fight before had never feen.
Like Garrick's frighted Hamlet, gaping ftood,
And gaz'd with wonder on the Britifh Food.
His morning's mefs forfook the friendly bowl,
And in fmall ftreams along the pavement ftole :
He heav'd a figh which gave his heart relief,
And then in plaintive tone declar'd his grief.

A I R
(Foote's Minuet)

Ah, facre Dieu ! vat do I fee yondre,
 Dat look fo tempting, red and vite ?
Begar it be de ROAST BEEF from Londre;
 Oh grant to me von letel bite.

But to my guts if you give no heeding,
 And cruel fate dis boon denies,
In kind compaffion unto my pleading,
 Return, and let me feaft mine eyes.

RECITATIVE
His fellow guard, of right Hibernian Clay;
Whofe brazen front his country did betray ;
From Tyburn's fatal tree had hither fled,
By honeft means to get his daily bread.
Soon as the well-known profpect he defcry'd,
In blubb'ring accents dolefully he cry'd.

A I R
(Ellen a Roon)

Sweet BEEF, that now caufes my ftomach to rife,
Sweet BEEF, that now caufes my ftomach to rife,
 So taking thy fight is,
 My joy fee tho fight is,
To view thee, by pailfuls runs out at my eyes.

While here I remain my life's not worth a farthing,
While here I remain my life's not worth a farthing,
 Ah, hard-hearted Loui !
 Why did I come to ye ?
The Gallows more kind, wou'd have fav'd me from
 Starving.

RECITATIVE
Upon the ground, hard by, poor Sawney fat
Who fed his Nofe, and fcratch'd his ruddy pate ;
But when Old England's Bulwark he efpy'd,
His dear lov'd Mull, alas ! was thrown afide ;
With lifted hands he blefs'd his native place,
Then fcrubb'd himfelf and thus bewail'd his cafe.

A I R
(The Broom of Cowdenknows)

How hard, oh Sawney ! is thy lot,
 Who was fo blithe of late ;
To fee fuch Meat as can't be got,
 When hunger is fo great.

O, the BEEF, the bonny bonny BEEF,
 When roafted nice and brown ;
I wifh I had a flice of thee,
 How fweet it would gang down !

Ah, Charley ! had'ft thou not been feen,
 This ne'er had happ'd to me ;
I would the de'el had pick'd mine ey'n,
 E'er I had gang'd wi' thee.

O the BEEF ! &c.

RECITATIVE
But fee ! my Mufe to England takes her flight,
Where health and plenty focially unite ;
Where fmiling Freedom guards great George's throne,
And whips and chains, and tortures are not known.
Tho' BRITAIN's fame in loftieft Strains fhou'd ring.
In ruftic Fable give me leave to fing.

A I R

As once on a time, a young FROG pert and vain,
Beheld a large OX grazing on the wide plain,
He boafted his fize he cou'd quickly attain.
 O the ROAST BEEF of Old England,
 And O the Old Englifh ROAST BEEF.

Then eagerly ftretching his weak little frame,
Mama, who ftood by; like a knowing old Dame,
Cry'd "Son, to attempt it you're greatly to blame."
 O the Roaft Beef, &c.

But deaf to advice, he for glory did thirft ;
An effort he ventur'd more ftrong than the firft,
Till fwelling and ftraining too hard made him burft.
 O the Roaft Beef, &c.

Then BRITONS be valiant, the moral is clear ;
The OX is OLD ENGLAND, the FROG is MONSIEUR.
Whofe puffs and bravadoes we never need fear.
 O the Roaft Beef, &c.

For while by our commerce and arts we are able
To fee the SIR-LOIN fmoking hot on our table,
The French may e'en croke like the Frog in the fable,
 O the ROAST BEEF &c.

18 'Roast Beef' songs were sung by rich and poor alike during the eighteenth century. The version here is by Richard Leveridge. Reproduced by permission of the Syndics of Cambridge University Library (Madden Collection of Ballads).

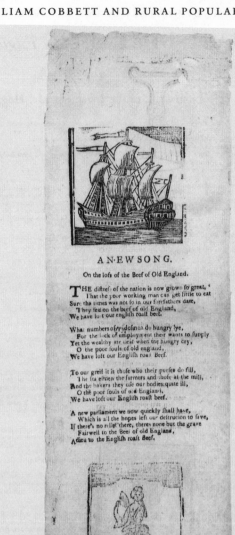

19   By the early nineteenth century the farm workers turned to songs treating of the loss of roast beef. Reproduced by permission of the Syndics of Cambridge University Library (Madden Collection of Ballads).

nothing. The capaciousness of the cellars in ancient houses; the capaciousness of the kitchens; the old songs, whenever they treat or allude to matters of this sort, all show that good living was a great characteristic of the nation.[30]

Cobbett was, in fact, a highly innovative historian, engaging proverbs, songs and archaeological evidence, not only in an attempt to escape the controls of the dominant culture over printed sources, but as vehicles of meaning and historical insight in their own right. The certainty with which he expressed his findings is not reducible to 'bad' history; for his historical treatises shared in the thought patterns of labouring people, who he knew did not 'split straws' but rushed 'at once to conclusions' which they ascribed in 'short and pilthy phrases'.[31] Even had Cobbett been able or willing to adopt the scholarly demeanour of a Hume or a Gibbon, he could not have afforded to adopt a dispassionate narrative style. Such a method might have produced 'better' history, but it would also have rendered his narratives more vulnerable to the progressivist models of the dominant historiography.

There was little abstract or ill-defined about the primary golden age of Cobbett and the rural workers: it dated from 1720 to 1785. The latter half of these good times was remembered by Cobbett directly, while he learned of the former half from his day-labouring grandparents. The London press had only scorn for Cobbett's treatment of the eighteenth century, but this was less true of provincial papers, where there frequently appeared observations such as this one from *Jackson's Oxford Journal* in 1830:

> The wages of agricultural labour in the year 1732 were from 6s to 7s. a week. The price of wheat was then from 18s. to 25s. per quarter, or 2s. 9d. per bushel; malt from 15s. to 22s. per quarter, or 2s.6d. per bushel. In 1829, 1830, the price of wheat is from 6s.6d. to 8s. a bushel; malt, 8s. to 9s. a bushel; wages of labour, *seven to nine shillings* a week ... It is plain from the above statement that the labourer can *now* procure only *one half* the quantity of bread and *one fourth* the quantity of beer he could in 1732.[32]

The food of the labourers, according to a German visitor in 1748, was the very roast beef and plum pudding that Cobbett and the labourers claimed for old England.[33] By the mid-1780s, however, the old diet was in disarray. In 1787, elderly Berkshire labourers informed David Davies that their earnings had maintained them in much superior condition at mid-century.[34] More specific was a farm worker from Bury who recalled that his former weekly wage of 5s. had purchased a bushel of wheat, a pound of butter, a pound of cheese, a bushel of malt, and a small supply of tobacco; whereas in the scarce year of 1800, his weekly wage of 15s. (one third of which was paid by the parish) was insufficient to buy the wheat alone.[35] According to the Essex parson John Howlett, a labourer's real wages in 1796 were half their value of 1750. Four years later, at the time of Cobbett's return from America, Howlett reported a further decline in real wages, declaring himself witness to the most widespread rural poverty in living memory.[36]

This was far removed from the years of Cobbett's youth, when weekly wages at Farnham were 9s. and the price of bread and beef 2d. and 4d. per pound respectively.[37] Then a family of five, in which the secondary wage-earner contributed 2s. or 3s. to family earnings, could get by without a budgetary deficit. In parts of Dorset during the 1780s, for example, the husband earned 6s. a week at daily agricultural labour while the wife earned the same sum at spinning. In 1831 the husband earned 7s. and the wife nothing, the spinning having been removed to the factory.[38] Real as well as nominal wages were falling: at Farnham between 1765 and 1800, food prices rose 40 per cent while wages were up by only half that figure.[39] In the decade of Cobbett's birth, wages for nine days of work would buy a bushel of flour, a pound of bacon, a pound of cheese and a bushel of malt; the prices of these articles in 1809 amounted to nineteen days' wages.[40] To express it in the measurements used by the labourers themselves, they were remunerated at the rate of two bushels of wheat per week in 1743, one and a half bushels in 1760, two-thirds of a bushel in 1800–1 and three-quarters of a bushel in 1824.[41] Or, as Cobbett explained to the ploughmen, wages were 9s. in 1792, but they advanced only to 15s. after prices tripled, leaving a reserve capital of about 27s. to be divided among the farmers, landlords and parsons.[42] This enormous victimization, moreover, was peculiar to agricultural workers. As William Marshall learned in 1800, 'all ranks of people, FARM WORKERS ONLY EXCEPTED, have had an increase of income, with the increase of the prices of the necessaries of life'.[43]

Joanna Innes has recently suggested that we should not be too hasty to assume that the late eighteenth century witnessed an increase in objective poverty. Reminders of this nature are helpful, for poverty is in part a subjective construction. Indeed, one of the reasons why we know more about the Regency than the Tudor cottage is owing to the development at the end of the eighteenth century of more sophisticated methods for studying the rural economy. At the same time we must be aware that post-1780 enquiries into rural England were often motivated by notions of control or improvement. Frederick Eden, for example, sought not only to report on the condition of the poor but also to ascribe a portion of rural poverty to the labourers' own inefficiencies. Finally, we must also attend to the memories of rural folk themselves: they studied both good times and bad, real wages and nominal wages, as well as their own criteria for cottage happiness. The great methodological difficulty (and this is precisely where the old standard of living debate fell down) is to blend all three enquiries, and in particular to merge quantitative and qualitative data in the manner of Keith Snell's *Annals of the Labouring Poor*. As his study makes abundantly clear, the late eighteenth century witnessed an increase in rural poverty in the rural South-East, not only relative to the expectations and aspirations of labouring people, but also in terms of objective changes in the structure of the rural economy, which produced new periods of impoverishment into the life-cycle of villagers. Snell has further shown that real wages rose during the middle third of the eighteenth century, stabilized during the 1770s and 1780s, and then retreated during the war years.[44]

The usual explanation that scarity and a superabundant workforce were the cause of the downturn is simply untenable in light of the almost full employment that prevailed during most of the war years. Throughout the wars, newly class conscious farmers sought to augment their capital from the labourers' wages, customary rights and cultural traditions; and it was these traditions and superior wages that Cobbett and the labourers claimed for the eighteenth century – or what they meant by 'old England'. Not often after 1790 does one encounter in the local press a harvest home on the scale of John Ellman's in 1793, where upwards of eighty men, women and children were served with '15 or 16 stone of beef; 6 or 8 stone of mutton; besides more than 1 cwt. of plum pudding; 40 or 50 gallons of strong beer; and bread, &c. in proportion'. John Ellman Jr, with whom Cobbett frequently quarrelled, declined to cultivate the hospitality of his father, instead devoting his energies to lobbies of Parliament on behalf of the new-fashioned farmers of eastern Sussex.[45] A similar rift between an old-fashioned father and a new-fashioned son is evident in the career of the Hertfordshire farmer John Carrington (1762–1810). When not laid up with the gout, or preoccupied in denouncing the French, Carrington indulged in 'stakes', 'moton chopps', 'sassages' and 'Rose Beef'. As an employer he paid the going rates, though he was active as a parish officer to ensure the delivery of food, beverage and fuel to needy parishioners. During the scarcity of 1800 he took the initiative of promising his less fortunate pub-mates that he would lower the price of his wheat to 10s. a bushel, for which he became the hero of market-day, while other farmers and dealers were heckled and abused. But when in the following week he promised a repeat performance, his son, who managed the farm along the lines of improvement, stepped in to block the transaction in the name of market forces.[46]

The new-fashioned farmer felt pressured to conform to local wage-rates; he was uncertain about the durability of high prices and he did not wish to be ridiculed by his fellows for interfering with the market or for rejecting a class culture. As Cobbett often lamented, farmers too were pressured by increases in taxes and rents, but their luxuries and improvements were proof of their ability to pay higher wages, if not at the rate of 1780, then at the rate of 1792. Nothing like this was attempted, he argued; instead was launched the allowance system, which if in part a last gasp of the old moral economy, was also a measure to render farm workers more stationary and pliable in the workplace. Whether prosperous or hard pressed, the farmers claimed to have nothing more for the labourers, which at the very least raises the question posed later in the century by Thomas Hardy:

> If a farmer can afford to pay thirty per cent more wages in times of agricultural depression than he paid in times of agricultural prosperity, and yet live, and keep a carriage, while the landlord still thrives on the reduced rent which has resulted, the labourer must have been greatly wronged in those prosperous times.[47]

For Cobbett and the labourers 'old England' was a construction of class experience and of their perception of relative economic prosperity in the past. They conceived their golden age on the basis of the degree rather than the principle of exploitation, which is to say that they would have largely been satisfied by a cask in the cellar, a flitch in the pantry and the restoration of the farmer to the plough. Employers knew that these were not tall or seditious demands, but even a minor yielding to old English symbols, no matter their financial cost, would have compromised their new undertaking that the maintenance of class society required constant vigilance to take every opportunity to make absolute economic gain at the expense of the weakest members of the community. Accordingly, the golden age of the farmers, 1793 to 1815, began where that of the labourers left off. Whereas the year 1795 was remembered in rural popular culture as the time of scarcity, Speenhamland and the terminal date of old England, farmers would come to reflect upon it as 'a very great year'.[48]

The historical reflections of Cobbett and the labourers became radical and progressive at the point where they sought to reduce the scale and accumulation of agrarian capitalists. Their nostalgia was accompanied by activism rather than wistfulness, for they knew that their aspirations were both plausible and attainable. Keeping alive the hopes of Cobbett and the labourers were the likes of the yeomanry of Devonshire, who in 1794 were said to 'exercise without parade, that old English hospitality which the refinements of modern manners have banished from many other parts of the kingdom'.[49] Even higher up the social order were durable practitioners of old England whom the farm workers did not wish to alienate from their cause. Among these was Thomas Law Hodges (1776–1857) – Kentish magistrate, Whig MP and notable agricultural improver. Hodges, like Cobbett, dated the great decline in the labourers' circumstances from the start of the French Wars in 1793. During the 1780s, he recalled, most workers resided with the farmer, while those living in cottages managed to support themselves on their daily wages of 1s. or 1s. 6d. The day-labourers brewed their own beer: 'I never saw a teapot in any man's cottage', Hodges recalled, whereas by 1831, home-brew had been 'universally' replaced by tea. Hodges went beyond the cultural trappings of old England to observe that many labourers had formerly risen into the ranks of smallholders; indeed most of the farmers of his own village of Benenden had 'sprung from labourers'. This state of things, he remarked, 'has entirely gone by'. By the 1830s, Hodges was a lone voice among large landholders; and he was the only one of their number in whom Cobbett, during his last years, was prepared to confide.[50]

As a proud alumnus of old England who remembered 'the cask in the cellar and the flitch in the pantry', Cobbett strove to maintain the ways and means of old England on his own farms. His economic practices were capitalist, though modified by the bartered exchanges and remunerations in kind that he remembered from his youth and still saw practised in parts of the rural South. At Botley, Barn Elm and Normandy farms his conventions were to pay an adult man a minimum of 15s. per week, or some 20 per cent above neighbouring rates. On average between 1804 and 1817, he also paid £200 a year in poor-rates, none of which went to his own workers (with the exception of one family over one winter) on account of his resolve to have no paupers in his employment.[51] The traditional role of the Poor Law was fulfilled by the Cobbett family, including the payment of sickness benefits and old-age pensions.[52] Thus in Cobbett's farm records we find him providing a worker with 10s.6d. a week, 'well or ill to do as much as he can for it'.[53] Elsewhere we find him refusing to send a family out of his farmhouse on account 'they must all go to the Workhouse pell mell if I do'.[54] When in Newgate in 1811 he received news of incompetence in his carter he advised his foreman to go easy:

> Tell him, that I by no means would expose him to any distress. He is unable to do what he has been doing lately. He cannot take care of horses. He has

not the power to do it, and my horses suffer under his hands. But, God forbid, that I should turn him and his family out upon the road, or expose them to any hardship. Therefore tell him, that he can remain where he is 'till Spring, if he chooses it; but, that he must work at job work, and have what he can earn. He may, if he dislikes my work, or my prices, get work from any body else; and, still he shall live in the house rent-free 'till the spring of the year; but, if he gets work with any body else, he cannot reasonably expect, that I should find him in fuel.[55]

The price of this fair play was a demand for good workmanship, discipline and obedience to the terms of employment. On at least three occasions Cobbett appealed to magistrates against workers whom he held to be in breach of contract; and in 1809 he went as far as to form a posse to track down a decamped farm servant – a deed for which he was deservedly exposed in the anti-Cobbett press.[56] Anyone to exploit his reputation as a fair-minded employer was brought up short:

A lazy English fellow, whom I set to dig some ground one day, and whom I reproached for his laziness, replied by saying, 'I thought *you* were a *friend of the poor*'; 'Yes,' said I, 'but not a friend of *rogues*; and you are a real rogue, who are cheating me out of the wages I give you.'[57]

On the more positive side, Cobbett employed any beggar that came to his door; he served his workers with 'good words' when they did a job well; and he never suggested that he was moved by charitable or paternal disposition to pay superior wages. 'One of my labourers', he freely admitted, 'is worth two or three half-famished creatures.'[58]

Many of Cobbett's workers had pigs and cottage industries of their own, with the blessing and encouragement of the master. At the cost of £40 apiece he built several new cottages at Botley, complete with gardens, ovens, sitting-rooms and bedrooms. Each household received a constant supply of fuel and sometimes of malting barley – the latter in defiance of the excise officer.[59] The best off of his labourers were those who matched their employer in ambition and energy, such as the suitably named stock-keeper at Botley, James Cowherd. On top of a weekly wage of 18s., Cowherd earned extra income for 'vermin extinction', warding off poachers and Sunday work with the stock. He received a rent-free cottage, a good-sized garden, and a constant supply of fuel laid at the door. Mrs Cowherd was casually employed in field work, cottage industries and in selling some of her poultry and garden produce to the Cobbett household. The Cowherds and Cobbetts maintained a dynamic ledger of debits and receipts, usually expressed in cash terms but often redeemed in goods and services.[60] It might well have been that some of Cobbett's workers grew

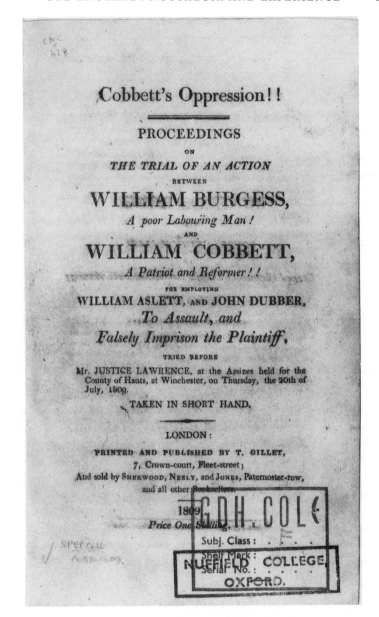

20   Cobbett insisted that his farm servants fulfil all the particulars of their contracts. In 1809 he invoked the law to recover the services of a decamped farm servant named Jesse Burgess. Much to the delight of the anti-Cobbett press, the servant's brother William launched an action in connection with the affair. Reproduced by permission of Nuffield College Library.

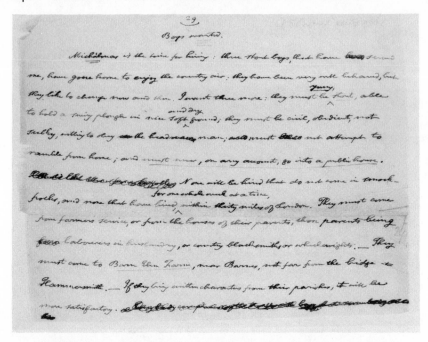

21   Manuscript of Cobbett's advertisement for farm servants (1829). Reproduced by permission of the Syndics of the Fitzwilliam Museum, Cambridge.

tired of his resolve to pay them 'out of the land' (it was alleged by Henry Hunt that Cobbett once paid for some casual labour with 'stinking cheese'), but his payments in kind were generally a supplement to wages. Remuneration 'out of the land' worked principally to the benefit of the twelve or so farm servants who lodged with the Cobbetts at any one time. Cobbett himself took a direct hand in attending to their needs, especially in the brewing of the approximately 700 gallons of beer consumed annually in his extended household.[61] In return the servants were expected to obey their contracts, to rise early (he once enforced this by withholding candles from a servant) and to behave with civility and obedience. He did not want 'Saints', as he put it, but he did advertise for sobriety and competence:

BOYS WANTED

They must be *young, stout,* able to hold a swing plough in nice, soft and dry ground; they must be civil, obedient, not sulky, willing to obey the head man; must not attempt to ramble from home; and *must never, on any account, go into a public house.* None will be hired that do not come in smock-frocks; and none that have lived, for one whole week at a time, within thirty miles of London. They must come from farmer's service, or from the houses of their parents; those parents being labourers in husbandry, or country blacksmiths, or wheelwrights.[62]

The thing that Cobbett most insisted upon was farm experience. Despite his strictures about the alehouse, he suffered his men to attend, including James Cowherd (who eventually fell from grace, but only because of his deficiencies as a ploughman) and John Dean, who rose from hedge-clipper at Botley to become Cobbett's secretary in London at an income of £100 a year.[63]

Although a strict employer, Cobbett was rewarded with long records of service. Sir Richard Phillips, a frequent visitor to Botley, observed that Cobbett paid his labourers 'liberally', adding that 'I have never anywhere seen such excellent cottages, gardens and other comforts, appropriated by the labouring classes, as those which he erected on his estate.'[64] Another frequent visitor, Henry Hunt, submitted that Cobbett was 'one of the *kindest*, and *best*, and the *most considerate masters*, that I ever knew in my life'.[65] As to the word of the labourers themselves we have only those of Joseph Carter, a farm worker (and future Swing-rioter) who informed Alexander Somerville that Cobbett was 'a good master. I ha' nothing to say agin he. I lived with him at Botley, and would never wish to serve a better master.'[66] The most that can be said for Cobbett's employment practices is that they represented the best and worst of old England. On the credit side was his provision of good wages and year-round hospitality in accordance with his precept that 'the first business of the farmer is to *live well*: to live in ease and plenty; to "keep hospitality" as the old English saying was. To *save money* is a secondary consideration.'[67] On the debit side he installed the regimen of old England from the top down, even to the point of ordering his workers to abstain from tea, potatoes and adulterated beer. Indoor servants, for example, were expected to attend local fairs on the master's terms. Thus while elated to see his men and women 'all decked out' for Guildford fair, he bid them to have their 'fill of pleasure, for by heavens, I mean to give them a belly full of work, next week'.[68] For Farnham fair the work had to be accomplished beforehand, with the workers allocated one shilling apiece 'to go and have *one pint* each, in the [public] house in which I was born'.[69] The fact that old England was partly an extension of Cobbett's ego is perhaps most apparent in his intention to write an autobiography that bid 'the "PLOUGHBOYS OF ENGLAND" to be sober, industrious, early rising, merciful to the horses and oxen; to be obedient to their masters in all their lawful commands; and ... to perish, if

22 Cobbett kept detailed records of the tasks he assigned to his workers.
Reproduced by permission of Nuffield College Library.

necessary, rather than live upon POTATOES, SALT, AND WATER'.[70] It is in moments such as these that we are reminded of Cobbett's capacity for self-service; yet it was his uniqueness to know that his private aspirations for the labourers accorded with the terms of the cottage charter.

For all their supposed idealism of the past, the labourers did not see old England as a free ride: something for nothing was neither their expectation nor their request. If they could have traded places with Stephen Duck, who lived in the heart of the golden age, they too would have realized

> ... how rarely's Happiness compleat,
> There's always Bitter mingled with the sweet.

For Duck, work was a 'drab' and 'painful' affair, but this would not have scared away the Regency farm workers, whose first claim for old England was the bread, bacon and beer that Duck observed to be the provision of his time.[71] Accepting this fare as sufficient grounds for their nostalgia, the labourers turned repeatedly to the 1730s and 1740s, or as they expressed it in their songs of the 1820s, 'ninety years ago'.[72] The song 'Time's Alteration', composed during the early seventeenth century by the ballad-writer Martin Parker, was revised during the early 1820s so as to replace Parker's generic complaints about 'the decay of the times' with specific and dated criticisms of low wages, the decline of living-in and the enclosure of the commons. Rather than gaze misty-eyed towards some vague and forgotten past, the new rendition, entitled 'My Old Hat', stares directly at the period 'almost fourscore years ago', approximately 1740.[73] By the late 1820s and early 1830s, Cobbett and the labourers abbreviated their golden age, articulating a willingness to accept the rural world of the early 1790s. Then, at least, pauperism was not commonplace, and farmers were only beginning to constitute themselves as a class; home-brewing was still in place and enclosure seemed to know limits. As the post-war songs put it:

> About twenty years ago when the corn began to rise,
> Horses, sheep and cattle, butter and cheese like-wise
> Farmers they set down and sung and smok'd their pipes also,
> In some Horses we will buy and a hunting we will go.[74]

This gradual escalation of the golden age to the 'bout 50 years ago' of the songs of the 1830s[75] was an attempt by the labourers to meet the ruling class half-way, but they would escalate no further on account of their understanding that old England had breathed its last during the 1790s, and that it was now the turn of their employers to demonstrate the extent of their commitment to merry England.

It was not country workers but middle-class rural writers, such as William

23 Wages and piece-rates were carefully recorded in Cobbett's farm account book. Reproduced by permission of Nuffield College Library.

Cobbett's son William would remind his father in 1835 that 'you have, for now upwards of thirty years that you have employed labourers, never had a single labourer who received relief from the parish; in the dear times you gave 15s. a week, with cottages of the most perfect construction ...; and to married men 18s a week; and to both, those occasional additional benefits which are advantages belonging to the service of every good master ... You have thus paid in wages thousands more than you were compelled to do ...; you have chosen that the loss should fall upon you, and not upon those who are in no way recognized by law as having suffrage in the electing of those who make the laws (PR, 4 July 1835, pp. 15–16).

Howitt, who lapsed into vague and romantic effusions about the past. Cobbett and the labourers were not vague: their sense of the eighteenth-century past was grounded in experience and oral traditions rather than in a chronic and wistful impulse to recover the past for the past's sake.[76] They invoked eighteenth-century England, as perceived and as lived, to inform radical programmes for the present and future. Their method of obtaining their background information – by oral transmissions from ancestors – was traditional in character, but the inferences they drew from this data were thoroughly radical, especially in the context of the disposition of the Regency élite against the poor person's property. The mutual calls by Cobbett and the labourers' songs for the restoration of the cow, the pig, the joint-stools and the broad-cloth Sunday coat might not leave us with a definitive inventory of the Regency cottage, but they do reinforce Michael Ignatieff's point that Cobbett's historical writings illustrate that 'the dynamics of dispossession were deeply understood in popular historical consciousness two generations before *Capital*'.[77] Further, Cobbett and the labourers assigned dates and radical meanings to that dispossession.

For Cobbett and the labourers, history was an inductive study: they remembered a better life and they wanted it back. They traced the crest of their dispossession to the 1793–1800 period, while the remainder of the eighteenth century became part of old England in popular rural culture. Henceforth the labourers joined Cobbett in wanting 'to see the poor men of England what the poor men of England were when I was born'. This phrase, often quoted by way of ridiculing Cobbett's nostalgia and inflated ego, should not be allowed to obscure the countless times that he depersonalized old England and objectified its material provisions: wages at 7s. a week, a gallon loaf for 9d., mutton at 4d. a pound and malt at 4d. a bushel.[78] His usages of the past did not consist of the hearsay and innuendo of the traditional chapbook, but rather of his boyhood experiences in 'a less *splendid* and more *happy* land'.[79] Like the labourers, Cobbett did not seek to restore the past for the past's sake; what he wanted was radical reform, and by that he meant not nostalgia but simply 'a *change for the better*', whether that meant going forward or backward. Certainly he was not as comfortable as Paine or Owen with the idea of progress, but we have only to witness his agricultural innovations to realize that he did not reject progress out of hand. What he did reject was an historical theory of continuity and incremental reform, which as Christopher Hill showed some years ago, was claimed by Whig and Tory for conservative political purposes.[80]

Old England as Cobbett defined it was an aspiration peculiar to the farm workers.[81] Artisans, miners and industrial workers, though having

HONEST PLOUGHMAN.

COME all you jolly husbandmen and listen to my song,
I'll relate the life of a ploughman, and not detain you long,
My father was a farmer, who banish'd grief and woe,
My mother was a dirty maid—that's ninety years ago.

My father had a little farm, a harrow and a plough,
My mother had some pigs and fowls, a pony and a cow,
They didn't hire a servant, but they both their work did do,
As I have heard my parents say, just ninety years ago.

The rent that time was not so high, but far as I will pen,
For now one family's nearly twice as big as then was ten.
When I was born my father used to harrow, plough and sow,
I think I've heard my mother say 'twas ninety years ago.

To drive the plough, my father did a boy engage,
Until that I had just arrived to seven years of age,
So then he did no servant want, my mother milk'd the cow,
And with the lark I rose each morn, to go and drive the plough.

The farmers wives in every part, themselves the cows did milk,
They did not wear the dandy veils, and gowns made out of silk,
They did not ride blood horses, like the farmers' wives do now,
The daughters went a milking, and the sons went out to plough.

When I was fifteen years of age, I used to thrash and sow,
I harrow'd, plough'd, and harvest time I used to reap and mow,
When I was twenty years of age, I could manage well the farm,
I could hedge and ditch, plough and sow, or thrash within the barn.

At length when I was twenty five, I took myself a wife,
Compelled to leave my father's house, as I have chang'd my life,
The younger children in my place, my father's work would do,
Then daily as an husbandman, to labour I did go.

My wife and me tho very poor, could keep a pig and cow,
She could sit, and knit, and spin, and I the land could plough,
There nothing was upon a farm at all, but I could do,
I find things very different now—that's many years ago.

We lived along contented, and banish'd pain and grief,
We had not occasion then to ask for parish relief,
But now my hairs are grown quite grey, I cannot well engage,
To work as I had used to do, I'm ninety years of age.

But now that I am feeble grown, and poverty do feel,
If for relief I go, they shove me in a Wig Bastile,
Where I may hang my hoary head, and pine in grief and woe,
My father did not see the like, just ninety years ago.

When a man has laboured all his life, to do his country good,
He's respected just as much when old, as a donkey in a wood,
His days are gone and past, and he may weep in grief and woe,
The times are very different now to ninety years ago.

Now I am ninety years of age, if for relief I do apply,
I must go in a Whig Bastile, to end my days and die,
I can no longer labour, as I no power have,
Then at the last, just like a dog, they lay me in my grave.

London ; Printed at the "Catnach Press," by W. S. FORTEY, Monmouth Court, Bloomsbury. The Oldest and Cheapest House in the World for Ballads (4,000 sorts) Children's Books, Song Books, &c.

24   The labourers of the 1820s and 1830s often invoked the mid-eighteenth century in evidence of a superior material life in the past. Reproduced by permission of the Syndics of Cambridge University Library (Madden Collection of Ballads).

MY OLD HAT.

I am a poor old man, in years, come listen to my song,
Provisions are full twice as dear as when that I was young,
It was when this old hat was new that sits upon my brow,
O what a happy youth was I when this old hat was new.

'Tis almost four-score years ago, the truth I will declare,
When men could take each others words, and thought it very
        fair,
No notes or bonds did they require, their words were so true,
This was in my youthful days, when this old hat was new.

Brotherly love it did abound, oppression ne'er was heard,
But O the misery of the poor, they scarcely can get bread;
Poor children crying out for food, & know not what to do,
This cruelty did ne'er abound, when this old hat was new.

There's velvet bonnets and silk veils, lace caps upon their
        heads,
But O the misery of the poor, they scarcely can get bread,
Which makes them wander up and down, for want of work to
        do,
This cruelty did ne'er abound when this old hat was new.

But when the time of harvest came, and we went out to reap,
How often were we merry made, with cider, ale, and beer,
And when the corn it was brought in and set upon the mow,
Reapers paunches were well fill'd when this old hat was new.

The master at the board would sit, the table for to grace,
The servants as they all came in, they took their proper place,
The good old dame, with cheerful heart, gave to each man his
        due,
Where plenty then did abound when this old hat was new.

But now the times are altered much, and the poor are quite
        done o'er,
The men do get their wages paid, like beggars at the door,
Inside the house they must not come, if they be o'er so few,
Which cruelty did ne'er abound, when this old hat was new.

When Romans reigned in this land, the commons they did
        give
Unto the poor for charity, to help them for to live,
But now they've taken the poor man's ground, that certainly
        is true,
Such cruelty did ne'er abound, when this old hat was new.

New the commons they are taken in, and cottages are pulled
        down,
And Molly has no wool to spin her linsey-woolsey gown ;
The winter cold, and clothing thin, and blankets very few,
Such cruelty did ne'er abound, when this old hat was new.
        Ward, Printer, Ledbury.

25 'My Old Hat' or 'When this Old Hat was New' lamented low wages, the decline of living-in and the enclosure of the commons. Reproduced by permission of the Syndics of Cambridge University Library (Madden Collection of Ballads).

golden ages of their own, were more reserved about the virtues of the past, even if some of them concurred with Cobbett's plans to restore them to the land. Among other radical leaders, only Henry Hunt, a farmer himself during the 1790s and early 1800s, understood the extent of the labourers' dispossession, but he showed few signs of wishing to incorporate old England into his urban platform. Openly scornful of Cobbett's nostalgia was Francis Place who joined the Whigs in repudiating the past, and who was eager to see reformed the popular culture (but less so the objective experiences) that provided the context and media for articulating old England.[82] Richard Carlile also criticized Cobbett's veneration for the past, complaining of the 'disease in this gentleman to think well of past times, and to see retrogression and not improvement in society'.[83] Cobbett saw retrogression, not because of 'disease' but because few important or valued dimensions of the labourer's life were changed for the better during his lifetime. For this reason alone, not according to some dogma of reaction, he announced himself to be 'a great hater of change',[84] for nearly all change experienced by the labourers was negative, whether in wages, popular recreations, customary rights or the Poor Law. In the labourers' vocabulary, 'change' was synonymous with man-traps, spring-guns and hired overseers. 'The people venerate things long established', said Cobbett. 'Of all the people in the world none dislike innovation so much as the country people in England. Improvement when it is real, and even manifest finds great difficulty in making its way amongst them, because it necessarily implies change.'[85] The early nineteenth-century ruling class chose not to demonstrate the positive face of change, innovation and progress. Thus rather than be in a position to look ahead, Cobbett and the labourers had always to fight a rearguard action in defence of what remained of their living standards. And when something new did become their pursuit, such as parliamentary reform, they often cloaked it as something old, merely to give it credibility among themselves.

A genuinely conservative or 'Tory' view of the past was represented by Robert Southey, who hankered after some vague and undatable era when the 'peasants' were supposed to have prospered.[86] For Cobbett, who was neither a latent Tory nor a 'romantic medievalist', this was meaningless, though like Southey he was ambivalent towards many aspects of modernization, including commerce, industrialization and pauperism. While Southey called for the revitalization of an old social order in which the labourers were firmly under the thumb of the parson, landlord and farmer, Cobbett revolted against the idea that workers 'must be everlastingly watched and superintended as if they were babies'.[87] Southey, like Cobbett's former associate William Windham, wanted the common people out of politics altogether, and though a self-avowed friend of the 'peasantry', he was one of Cobbett's most vocal critics outside of Parliament. The old England of Southey and the Tories was less an affair of liberty and good food than of paternalism and condescension on the one hand, obeisance and subordination on the other.

CHAPTER 7

'RURAL WAR': COBBETT AND
CAPTAIN SWING

The history of the whole world contains not one single instance of oppression being put an end to by the humility of the oppressed.

PR, 19 February 1825, p. 476.

I know the country people well; and I know that they will not lie down and starve quietly, and God Almighty forbid that they should.

PR, 20 February 1830, p. 241.

You may depend upon it, it will never be forgot, all round about here, to the end of the world.

A Hampshire labouring woman (c. 1860), recalling the hanging of Henry Cook, in Charles Roach Smith, *Retrospections, Social and Archaeological*, 3 vols. (1883–91), II, p. 45.

FOR twenty-five years Cobbett appreciated that the farm workers had due cause to turn to violent insurrection.[1] By the mid-1820s he began to prophesy a major rural rebellion, and by 1828 he was dating it to the winter of 1830–1. He was not expecting a repetition of the East Anglian bread and wage riots of 1816 or of the machine-breaking incidents of 1822. The pending revolt, he predicted, would be more widespread and have a broader mandate on account that hunger and unemployment (probably no worse in 1830 than in 1816 or 1822) were now joined by a heightened political consciousness and by a series of oppressive innovations that humiliated village workers in the name of the Poor Law.[2] Central to Cobbett's prognostications was the roundsman system, the labour auction and the employment of paupers in parish-sponsored work-schemes. In 1828 a farmer of the soon riotous parish of Ash in Kent observed that 'I have seen thirty or forty young men in the prime of life degraded in their own estimation, as well as in the estimation of their beholders, hooked on to carts and wheelbarrows, dragging stones to the highway because they could not get employment elsewhere.'[3] In February of 1830 the subject of degrading parish employments was raised in the House of Lords, but a proposal for a parliamentary enquiry was rejected on account that the labourers appeared to submit (in the words of the Bishop of Bath and Wells) 'with such patience and fortitude to the privations of their conditions'. Cobbett advised differently, suggesting that the labourers were finding no solace in their fortitude or in the religious tracts which asserted that stone-breaking was a virtuous and ennobling occupation which served the greater glory of God and man.[4] The observant contemporary would have noticed in the public press that some hired overseers were being assaulted, even shot at, for engaging paupers as beasts of burden; and that in 1831 a Hertfordshire worker, improperly harnessed to a cart, was dragged beneath its wheels and crushed to death – all without attracting a word of attention in Parliament.[5]

Throughout the latter half of the 1820s, Cobbett found degrading parish employments almost everywhere, including in his home parish of Kensington.[6] Rate-payers and employers, he remarked, view the labourers 'not as *men* and *women*, but merely as animals made for their service and sport'. 'I have known', he continued, 'twenty different projects for correcting the "*evil of pauperism*", but never of one project for making the lot of the labourer better ... There must be a day of *justice*: this ill-treatment of millions of good people never can pass off without producing some signal event.' That event was eighteen months away, though each week Cobbett intensified his warnings to farmers and landlords who would submit the labouring poor to the economizing whim of paid overseers. The question was not the possibility of insurrection but 'how long can the peace last?'[7]

The years 1826 to 1830 saw further deterioration in the labourers' material circumstances, despite the post-1825 optimism of J. H. Clapham and most recently Alan Armstrong.[8] The case for improvement rests upon the assumption that the retreat of bread, bacon and cottage gardens was more than adequately redeemed by potatoes, tea and an allotment in the form of an unused corner of a farmer's field. It might well be (as Armstrong suggests) that pottery, household utensils and cotton clothing were dramatically reduced in price during the 1820s,[9] but one has only to review the labourers' songs and the grievances of Captain Swing to realize that these items were of low priority in the cottage charter; indeed the labourers wanted back their pewter dishes and their heavy woollen coats. Moreover, the humiliation they suffered at the hands of legislators and parish officers is not accessible from the dark alley of real wages. How, for example, does one quantify the parish cart or the Dead-Body Bill that

TO THE

RATE-PAYERS

OF

KENSINGTON.

GENTLEMEN,

I see that the men who are on the poor-book, in our parish, are used as *beasts of burden.* I pay my rates for their *relief,* and not to enable any body to treat them in this manner. This mark of national degradation, of which, as exhibited in the country parts, I have been complaining for years, is, at last, come to my own door, and exhibited side by side with the most insolent luxury, derived from those taxes which are in part wrung from the toil of these our unfortunate neighbours.

Gentlemen,---I am of opinion, that it is *unlawful* to compel a man to act the part of a *beast of burden,* as the condition of receiving parish relief; and I know that it is *disgraceful* to us, to our village, and to our country; that it is painful to me, and, I hope, it is painful to you.

Therefore, Gentlemen, I propose to you to join me in endeavours to obtain a meeting of the Vestry of the Parish, in order that measures may be taken for putting an end to this disgrace.

A *requisition,* in the following words, lies at my house for the signature of such gentlemen as may choose to sign it:---"To the Vicar and " Churchwardens of the Parish of Saint Mary Abbot's, Kensington.---We, " whose names are hereunto subscribed, request that you will cause a Vestry " of the parish to be called, for the purpose of inquiring why it is that men, " who apply for parish relief, are, as a condition of receiving it, compelled to " be used as *beasts of burden.*"

If you join me, Gentlemen, in this application, we shall, I trust, vindicate the character of our parish. At any rate, I am resolved that no part of the disgrace, belonging to the transaction, shall remain on the head of,

Gentlemen,

Your most obedient

And most humble servant,

Kensington, Feb. 27th, 1830.   WM. COBBETT.

Mills, Jowett, and Mills, Bolt Court, Fleet Street.

26   Petition by Cobbett against the use of labourers as 'beasts of burden'. Reproduced by permission of the Syndics of the Fitzwilliam Museum, Cambridge.

caused some rural workers to subscribe their pennies to hire night watchmen for the graves of their families and fellow workers?[10] Or how can one express in statistical form the privations of tea and potatoes? Alongside of

27   Cobbett in 1830. Reproduced by permission of Lady Lathbury.

these new grievances, furthermore, remained the old. Just prior to the start
of the labourers' revolt, for example, Cobbett was cheering on the first
instalments of the Otmoor fence-throwers' sixty-year fight against the
enclosure of their common.[11] Anticipating a day of reckoning, he warned
the gentry of Oxfordshire that they would soon regret their perseverance
with the enclosure. 'My advice to those who have made *this enclosure* is, to
let the people throw it open, and *say no more about it*. Let them be assured
that *times are changed*.'[12] It was the combination of old and new

complaints that caused Cobbett to define the labourers by 1829 as '*land-slaves*' whose material and emotional well-being had passed beyond the most prudent habits of cottage economy: 'no toil, no frugality, can save them'.[13] This is not to say that Cobbett invested in insurrection at the expense of his strong suit of pragmatism. In 1829, as a direct result of the new level of oppression, he at last came out in qualified support of the emigration of the poor, which he had hitherto opposed on the grounds that all English men and women possessed a right to a decent living in their native land. His *Emigrant's Guide* (1829) did not ask the labourers to forego their rights or to submit to compulsory emigration; it merely set before them a series of lively letters by Sussex emigrants who contrasted the hunger of rural England with the plenty of the United States. It remained Cobbett's preference that the labourers *not* emigrate (for it pained his soul – 'my cheeks burn with shame' – to recognize that Americans had become the custodians of old England) but he thought it his duty to suggest alternative courses to insurrection, which by 1828 he knew to be imminent.[14]

In his role as a prophet of the revolt Cobbett did not deny class consciousness or leave off his animosity towards large rural capitalists, but he did wish to make one last effort to re-create a working alliance of countrymen, wherein landlords and large farmers would have the responsibility of conducting the revolt from the parishes to Westminster. His own forecasts allowed him twelve months to forge a rural consensus on the objects of the rising. In November of 1829 he warned farmers that they would soon be called to account for their class formations and indulgences of the 'system':

> You and the tax-gatherer have taken from [the labourers], by degrees, every article of decent clothing and of household stuff; you have taken from them their cows and pigs and hens and bees; you have cut them off from every inch of *common*; you have enclosed all, you have grasped all to yourselves; and, after this you complain (as in Sussex the other day), that they will not stir to extinguish the flames that are consuming your barns and your stacks![15]

These pilot fires were a timely omen for the winter to come. As early as May (ordinarily not a hungry month) of 1829, protests against distress were being voiced by the farm workers of Bedfordshire, Buckinghamshire, Sussex and Kent.[16] What Alun Howkins calls 'seasonal structural conflict', particularly acute during winter months, was manifesting itself in new parts of the agrarian calendar during the late 1820s. More obvious than at any other moment in Cobbett's lifetime was the year-round exploitation of worker by master, with the farmer resolved to provide the labourers with an absolute minimum of wages and allowances, and the labourer equally determined to supply 'no more labour than the food they obtain is worth'. 'This is the sort of struggle that has been going on for the last seventy years,' observed Cobbett, 'but more conspicuously for the last forty, and now more so than ever.'[17]

It was a struggle that the farmers and gentry could not win by and for themselves. Rural class formations would exclude them from the insurrection unless they sided with the labourers and petitioned Parliament on behalf of the preliminary manifesto of Captain Swing. Should they choose to stay in bed with the 'system', Cobbett warned, they will bear the brunt of the labourers' wrath, who 'are the *millions*, recollect; they have all the country smiths, wheelwrights, and collar-makers with them; all the country journeymen of every description; and every small farmer, where there happens to be one, not yet devoured'.[18] Thus at the same time as he was making overtures towards employers, Cobbett re-stated his plenary definition of 'chopstick' as encompassing all members of the village community who engaged in manual labour. His own experience in the parishes confirmed that the shoemaker and the tailor were in communion with a wider political network than was the average ploughman, whether through the 'linkmen' identified by Andrew Charlesworth or the village craftsmen who communicated directly with Cobbett in order that they might keep the agricultural workers informed of political developments in London.[19] Cobbett understood (and without condescension) that ploughmen were often inclined to focus their wrath upon their immediate employer. 'The *poor* have no quarrel with the *Government*', he went as far as to say, 'their quarrel is with the farmers and the rest of the middle class.'[20] Many correspondents to the Home Office would offer the same opinion, but Cobbett deliberately understated the labourers' politicization as part of his campaign to bring farmers into alliance with their workers against the government. At the same time he did not deceive himself into thinking that all labourers coped equally with abstract talk about high ideology or distant politicians: 'we cannot find *them*', he anticipated some labourers saying, 'the farmers withhold the food from us; we must *go to them*'.[21]

It was because Cobbett did not altogether agree with this strategy of 'pre-industrial' protest that he sought to reinforce the political wing of the cottage charter. The farmers deserved to have their property razed, but so too did the inhabitants of Parliament, Whitehall and the City. Thus in February, anticipating the revolt eight months hence, he set farmers an example by taking every man and woman in his agricultural employment to the Surrey county meeting at Epsom, where he explained, in country-man language, that 'we must all be relieved, or all continue to suffer together'.[22] In the same manner he helped seven of his workers (including

PETITION.

To the Honourable the Commons of the United Kingdom of Great Britain and Ireland, in Parliament assembled,

The Petition of the undersigned Labourers at Barn-Elm Farm, in the parish of Barnes, in the county of Surrey.

Most humbly showeth,

That your petitioners have perceived, that there is a proposition before your honourable House, for mortgaging the poor-rates, and for imposing taxes, in order to raise money for the purpose of sending a part of the working people out of the country, upon the ground, that, owing to their *excessive numbers*, they cause a charge upon the land so great as to threaten to swallow up the whole of the rents.

That your petitioners have heard, and they believe, that, out of about eleven thousand parishes, in England and Wales, there are one thousand and four, the population of which is, on an average, under a hundred souls to a parish; and that they know that you have, in the evidence given before your committees, the statements of experienced farmers, that there are not too many work-people to cultivate the land properly, but that the taxes take from the farmer the means of giving the work-people wages sufficient for their proper maintenance, and that from this cause the land is not cultivated so well as it used to be, and does not yield so much as it used to yield, while the labourers are compelled to resort to parish relief.

That, deducting the amount of the country rates, militia charges, highway rates, church-rates, and the law expenses, the poor-rates, that is to say, the money actually paid in the way of *relief to the poor*, does not, especially if we deduct the salaries paid to hired overseers, amount to *six millions* of pounds, in the year; while the other taxes, imposed by the Parliament and collected by the Government, amount to *sixty millions* a year; and that, therefore, your petitioners cannot but think it strange, that your honourable House should be alarmed at the prospect of seeing the rents absorbed by these *six millions*, while you appear to be under no apprehension at all of those rents being absorbed by the *sixty millions*, especially as they cannot for the life of them imagine how it is that your honourable House can fail to perceive that it is the burden of the sixty millions; which is the real and evident cause of the necessity of raising the six millions; daylight not being more evident than the fact, that it is the enormous taxes which disable the farmer and trader and manufacturer to pay sufficient wages to their work-people.

That your petitioners have been told, that of late years, one million and six hundred thousand pounds, or thereabouts, have been voted by your honourable House, out of the taxes, for the *relief of the poor clergy* of the church of England; that they have just seen millions upon millions voted by you for the support of half-pay people and their widows and children; that they have been told, that there are numberless women and children, as well as men, maintained as pensioners and sinecurists; that there are many of these men (who have no pretence to have rendered any service to the country) each of whom receives more, every year, than would be sufficient to maintain two or three hundred labourers and their families; and that, while all these are thus supported in part on the fruit of our labour; while all these, who do not work at all, have our dinners, in fact, handed over to them by the acts of your honourable House, we cannot very patiently hear of projects for sending us out of our native land, on the ground that we threaten to swallow up the whole of the rental.

That your petitioners have recently observed, that many great sums of the money, part of which we pay, have been voted to be given to persons who render no services to the country; some of which sums we will mention here; that the sum of 94,900*l.* has been voted for disbanded *foreign* officers, their *widows* and *children*; that your petitioners know, that ever since the peace this charge has been annually made; that it has been on an average, 110,000*l.* a year, and that, of course, this band of foreigners have actually taken away out of England, since the peace, *one million and seven hundred thousand pounds*, partly taken from the fruit of our labour; and if our dinners were actually taken from our table and carried over to Hanover, the process could not be to our eyes more visible than it now is; and we are astonished, that those who fear that we, who make the land bring forth crops, and who make the clothing and the houses, shall swallow up the rental, appear to think nothing at all of the swallowings of these Hanoverian men, women, and children, who may continue thus to swallow for half a century to come.

That the advocates of the project for sending us out of our country to the rocks and snows of Nova Scotia, and the swamps and wilds of Canada, have insisted on the necessity of *checking marriages* amongst us, in order to cause a decrease in our numbers; that, however, while this is insisted on in your honourable House, we perceive a part of our own earnings voted away to encourage marriage amongst those who do no work, and who live at our expense; that 145,267*l.* has just been voted as the year's pensions for *widows of officers of the army*; and that your petitioners cannot but know that while this is the case, few officers will die without leaving widows, especially as the *children too* are pensioned until of a certain age; that herein is a high premium given for marriage, and for the increase of the numbers of those who do not work; that, for this purpose, more than *two millions of pounds sterling* have been voted since the peace, out of those taxes, more than their due share of which your petitioners have had to pay; that, to all appearance, their children's children will have to pay in a similar manner for the encouragement and support of similar idlers; and that to your petitioners it does seem most wonderful, that there should be persons to fear that we, the labourers, shall, on account of our numbers, swallow up the rental, while they actually vote away our food and raiment to increase the numbers of those who never have produced, and who never will produce, any thing useful to man.

But that, as appertaining to this matter of *check marriages* and the *breeding of children*, the vote, recently passed, of 20,986*l.* for the year, for the Royal *Military Asylum*, is worthy of particular attention; that this asylum is a place for bringing up the *children of soldiers*; that soldiers are thus encouraged and invited to marry, or, at least, to have children; that while our marrying and the children proceeding from us are regarded as evils, we are compelled to pay taxes for encouraging soldiers to marry, and for the support and education of their children; and that while we are compelled, out of the fruit of our hard work, to pay for the good lodging, clothing, and feeding of the children of soldiers, our own poor children are, in consequence of the taxes, clad in rags, half-starved, and insulted with the degraded name of *paupers*; that, since the peace, *half a million* of pounds sterling have been voted out of the taxes for this purpose; that, as far as your petitioners have learned, none of your honourable members have ever expressed their fear that this description of persons would assist to swallow up the rental; and that they do not now learn, that there is on foot any project for sending out of the country these costly children of soldiers.

That your petitioners know that more than one-half of the whole of their wages is taken from them by the taxes; that these taxes go chiefly into the hands of idlers; that your petitioners are the bees, and that the tax-receivers are the drones; and they know, further, that while there is a project for sending the bees out of the country, no one proposes to send away the drones; but that your petitioners hope to see the day when the checking of the increase of the drones, and not of the bees, will be the object of an English Parliament.

That, in consequence of taxes, your petitioners pay sixpence for a pot of worse beer than they could make for one penny; that they pay ten shillings for a pair of shoes that they could have for five shillings; that they pay seven-pence for a pound of soap or candles that they could have for three-pence; that they pay seven-pence for a pound of sugar that they could have for three-pence; that they pay six shillings for a pound of tea that they could have for two shillings; that they pay double for their bread and meat, of what they would to pay, if there were no idlers to be kept out of the taxes; that, therefore, it is the taxes that make their wages insufficient for their support, and that compel them to apply for aid to the poor-rates; that, knowing these things, they feel indignant at hearing themselves described as *paupers*, while so many thousands of idlers, for whose support they pay taxes, are called *noble Lords* and *Ladies, honourable Gentlemen, Masters*, and *Misses*; that they feel indignant at hearing themselves described as a nuisance to be got rid of, while the idlers who live upon their earnings are upheld, caressed and cherished, as if they were the sole support of the country.

That your petitioners know that, according to the Holy Scriptures, even the ox is not to be muzzled as he treadeth out the corn; that God hath said that the labourer is worthy of his hire; that the poor shall not be oppressed; that they shall be fed out of the abundance of the land.

That, according to the laws of the Christian church in England, according to the canon law, according to the statute law, the poor of every parish were to be relieved out of the tithes; that they ought to be relieved now; that, at any rate, the laws of England say, that no one shall perish from want; that, if unable to work, or to obtain work, a sufficiency of food and raiment and other necessaries of life shall be furnished to the indigent person, by the parish; and that, therefore, your petitioners have, in case of need, as clear and good a right to parish relief as the landlord has to the rent of his land; and that, if your honourable House choose to continue to take the *sixty millions* a year in taxes; if you choose to cause the working-people to be made poor in this way; if you choose to reduce us in this manner to appeal to the parish rates to support our lives: if you choose to continue to compel us to give more than half of our wages to the tax-gatherers; if this be your decision, we hope that you will not blame us for pressing on the rates and the rental.

That your petitioners are constantly liable to be called out to serve in the *militia*; that they are compelled to give in their names to the parish constable, in order that they may be called out whenever the Government may choose; that they are thus liable to lose their time in the prime of life; to quit their homes, their aged parents, their wives and helpless children; and to submit to military command, military law, military punishment, and, if need be, loss of limb or loss of life in fighting; that they are thus compelled to serve and to suffer on the ground that it is necessary either to the defence of the country against foreign foes, or to the security of property against internal commotion; but that we possess no property but in our labour, which no foe, foreign or domestic, can take from us; and that, if we be to be regarded as having no right to a maintenance out of the land in exchange for our labour, if we be to be looked upon as a nuisance to be got rid of, is it just, we would ask, that we should be torn from our homes, and compelled to waste the prime of our lives, subjected to military command and military punishment, for the purpose of defending that land?

That, about twelve years ago, an act was passed by your honourable House changing the mode of voting in parish vestries, and another act, about eleven years ago, establishing select vestries; that by these two acts, your petitioners were deprived of a great part of their rights; that, by the latter act, *hired overseers*, strangers to the parish, were introduced with salaries, to be paid out of the rates destined for our relief; that these overseers are generally paid *much* in proportion as they give *little* relief; that, hence have come oppressions and insults on us without end; that in some cases, the labourers wanting relief have been compelled to draw carts and wagons like beasts of burden; in others they have been compelled to carry large stones backwards and forwards in a field, merely to give them pain and to degrade them; in others they have been shut up in the parish-pounds, and, in short, they have been fed and treated far worse than the dogs of those who live in luxury on those taxes, a large part of which are wrung from the sweat of your petitioners; and that, at last, we have seen a bill passed by your honourable House, authorising these overseers to dispose of our dead bodies for the purpose of being cut up by the surgeons, thereby inflicting on poverty the ignominy due to the murderer.

That, while we know that we have a clear right to relief in case of need, we wish not to be be compelled to apply for that relief; we desire not to bear the degrading name of pauper; we wish to keep our wages to our own use, and not to have them taken away to be given to idlers; we wish to be well fed and clad, and to carry our heads erect, as was the case with our happy forefathers; we are resolved, at any rate, not to be treated like beasts of burden, and not to be driven from our country; and, therefore, we pray that your honourable House will repeal the two acts above mentioned; that you will take from our shoulders, and from those of our employers, the grievous burden of taxes; and that you will be pleased to begin forthwith by relieving us from the taxes on malt, hops, leather, soap and candles.

And your petitioners will ever pray.

THOMAS BRIDGES, + his mark.
JOHN KEMP.
JOHN DABINE.
RICHARD HOLDEN, + his mark.
JOHN LAING, + his mark.
EDWARD LICKFORD, + his mark.
WILLIAM CARTER, + his mark.

LIST OF MR. COBBETT'S BOOKS.

An English Grammar, price 3*s.* 6*d.*—A French Grammar, price 5*s.*—An Italian Grammar, price 6*s.*—Cottage Economy, price 2*s.* 6*d.*—The Woodlands, a Treatise on Forest Trees, price 14*s.*—The English Gardener, price 6*s.*—The "Year's Residence in America," price 5*s.*—Twelve Sermons, 3*s.* 6*d.*—"The Poor Man's Friend," price 1*s.*—"Paper against Gold;" the History of the Bank of England, and the Funding System, price 5*s.*—The Protestant Reformation; a History of that Event, price 4*s.* 6*d.* Part the Second of this work, price 3*s.* 6*d.*—Tull's Husbandry, price 15*s.*—The Emigrant's Guide, price 2*s.* 6*d.*—A Treatise on Cobbett's Corn, price 5*s.*—Advice to Young Men, Sixpence each Number, of which Nine Numbers are already published.—A set of the Register, complete from Vol. I. up to the present time, is also to be sold.—For all, or either, of the above, apply to No. 183, Fleet Street, or to any Bookseller.

Printed by Mills, Jowett and Mills, Bolt Court, Fleet Street, London.

28 Cobbett's petition on behalf of seven of his farm workers, five of whom signed with their crosses. Reproduced by permission of the Syndics of the Fitzwilliam Museum, Cambridge.

five who were unable to read or write) to compose a petition to Parliament against indirect taxes, hired overseers, compulsory emigration and innovations in the Poor Law.[23] The petition did not directly implicate the farmers in the perpetuation of the 'system', for that might have compromised the primary object of his tour of the eastern counties during the late spring of 1830. Here, in one final pitch, drawing heavily upon local experience as he moved from town to town, Cobbett pleaded with farmers not to complain of the six million pounds of poor-rates when the tax-collector took sixty million. He informed his audiences of his recent encounter with a group of labourers who toiled upon a road for a few pennies per day, while visible over the hedge were 200 fat sheep, tempting him to say 'help yourselves'. These scenes of poverty amid plenty put him in mind of his experiences in France at the start of the Revolution, and he warned farmers that an English version of the Great Fear could only be prevented by a rise in wages and the removal of parish carts and threshing machines.[24] At St Ives in May he encountered a handbill advertising the sale of farm equipment, including 'a *fire-engine* and several steel man-traps, all in *excellent* condition'. That evening he made reference to the sale, suggesting that 'dismal indeed were the times become when fire-engines and man-traps formed part of the *implements of husbandry*'. When things were in their 'natural state', he observed, rural peace could be maintained by the 'constable's staff' and the 'sheriff's wand', but nothing could save the farmer's stacks from permanent and unmitigated conflict: 'I, therefore, besought them to think of these things *in time*; and, with all the force that I was master of, I urged them to cast from them the vain and the cruel thought of being able to keep the labourers in a state of half-starvation by means of *man-traps* and *fire-engines*.'[25] With this Cobbett prepared to take his leave of the farmers, advising them that time was short and their petitions too few.[26] Many labourers, for their part, had joined Cobbett in attempting to erect a common country platform. From Battle in 1830 a government informer reported that 'in order to enlist the farmer on their side, [the labourers] are willing to support him in his complaint against the tithe owner'.[27] This was going more than half-way, but as a class the farmers refused to reciprocate by standing up for the labourers' interests. Cobbett, therefore, bowed out of the negotiations, warning 'better be a dog than a farmer next winter'. Either change your ways now, he ordered, or 'we shall be wide awake about the middle of next winter. The "*grand rousing*" will come from the fellows with hob-nails in their shoes.'[28]

The coming to pass of these events was not a matter of chance: Cobbett had never before prophesied a major rural revolt, much less dated one. It is worth remembering, too, that these forecasts were made before the Continental revolutions of the summer and the English reform crisis of the autumn. In due course, these events would contribute to the ideological direction of the rising, but it was the poverty and degradation of the farm workers that set the revolt in motion. Our current preoccupation with distinguishing between food riots and political disturbances does not do justice to the rural insurrection, for it combined indigenous politics with sheer hunger and memories of a superior past. As Roger Wells and Andrew Charlesworth have shown, some village workers were in dialogue with urban Radicals,[29] and Cobbett himself did his part in this way by delivering eleven lectures at the theatre of the Rotunda, Blackfriars Road, on the subject of the French and Belgian Revolutions,[30] but he took his leave of farmers on a knife and fork note, declaring that the labourers 'will never again suffer so much as they have suffered. Last winter they reached the lowest point. Horse, foot, and artillery, will never make them touch that point again.'[31] In October, as the first wave of fires illuminated the Kentish horizon, the labourers said exactly that: 'they boldly declare their wants shall not be stopped by instruments of force; that they cannot endure longer – they have strong arms – they have almost been suffered to starve, whilst the rich have plenty of supplies, and the wants of the people are never thought of'.[32]

At the start of the rising Cobbett resumed his place among village workers, visiting and lecturing them as the burnings and breakings proceeded from Kent to Sussex and on to Hampshire and the West. He had done everything in his power to advise the farmers to discard their class formations, but as he remarked as early as 1824, there must sometimes 'be a cause more powerful than *advice*'.[33] For the benefit of non-agricultural society, including the Rotunda audience, he stressed the experiences and ideologies that moved the insurrection, pleading with urban and industrial workers to appreciate the hardships and resolve of their rural brothers and sisters:

> When men are assembled in great masses, as in Lancashire and the West Riding of Yorkshire, they are more easily managed. The knowledge that there are a few soldiers in the neighbourhood, keeps them quiet ... It is not thus with country people. The manufacturers, thousands upon thousands, talk well, think well, are sprightly and full of intelligence; but they live in crowds, and their hands and their skins are soft; they live before good fires, and are contented in a state of unwholesome warmth. The country people, less intelligent and less talkative, are accustomed to all that hardens man: their hands are hard as sticks; they bear cold like cattle; they live detached in lanes or amongst woods; they are accustomed to move about in the dark,

and are not easily frightened at the approach of danger; they have been used to eat meat, they are thoughtful, and are rendered resolute by suffering. Each man lives near about where his grandfather lived; every one hears of the change that has taken place; and, above all things, every man and woman and child old enough to understand any thing, looks upon his parish as being partly his; and a sufficiency of food and raiment he looks upon as his inheritance. Never, let what will happen, will these people lie down and starve quietly.[34]

At least in principle this commentary turns on its head the 'natural' deference and rural isolation hypotheses that are too often invoked to account for the farm worker's apparent reluctance to engage in mass protest. If overt protests were fewer in the countryside than in the towns, it was not because the farm workers possessed (in the erroneous assessment of one of their most recent historians) a 'sense of identity with the interests of their employers'.[35] Individually and collectively they possessed a quiet confidence that they would not starve; if their right to a living out of the land was not honoured by their employers, they would extract that living by extra-legal measures, or, if need be, by force of arms. In the countryside more so than in the towns, radical ideologies were expected to serve the cause of old England and the cottage table; but it is to take a very narrow view of radical ideology to suggest that it excludes the dictates of hunger and daily experience. Cobbett was able to predict the rising for the simple reason that he did not share the almost universal assumptions that farm workers were innately deferential, reconciled to poverty and devoid of a sense of popular rights.

The cultural and ideological disposition of the labourers was known only to Cobbett among prominent reformers. Although himself raised to respect traditional culture and to imitate deference, he knew that 'for a long while men submit, they are brought, by degrees, to greater and greater suffering, till the suffering be so great, that *life*, in such a state, becomes not worth preserving'.[36] Tradition, the law and the gallows, he understood, hold 'no terrors for men who see starvation before them', and especially before their children:

> There is no man who knows the English labourers so well as I do. I not only know all their wants, but their dispositions, their tempers; and I always said, that, when it came to be a question whether they should *see their children starve, or run the risk of death*, they would choose the latter.[37]

The labourers were 'tender parents' and 'unassuming, modest, and content in their state of life', but they will not, he assured his readers, 'live on damned potatoes while the barns are full of corn, the downs covered with sheep, and the yards full of hogs created by their labours'.[38] It was not so much new ideologies (experience had long instructed the 'chopsticks' in a labour theory of value) that caused the labourers to abandon their traditional caution, but hunger and ideological ferment within view of full barns:

> Hungry guts and empty purse
> May be better, can't be worse.[39]

The rioters observed that 'we can't be worse off – if we are took we shall have summat to eat'.[40] As to assisting to dowse the flames: 'What is the use of our assisting? Whether it is burned or not it makes no difference to us – we are as badly off as we can be, and it is impossible for us to be worse: therefore it may take its chance.'[41] Even those few workers who were disposed to battle the flames, as at a fire in Berkshire, were found to be 'under-fed, feeble, without shoes, and altogether in a shocking plight'.[42] In Cobbett's estimate the labourers asked one another whether they would rather be hanged or starved. '"To be hanged." "Well, then, come along with us."'[43]

The fact that Captain Swing caught leading urban Radicals by surprise (though Henry Hunt had a brief involvement in the Hampshire protests of 1830, and Richard Carlile jumped belatedly on Swing's bandwagon),[44] suggests that they were not only ignoring Cobbett but also the labourers' own expressive culture. Rural songs of the late 1820s and early 1830s foreshadow the platform of Swing by threatening soon to have the farmers 'under our thumb'.[45] The songs also express displeasure about influxes of Irish workers, threshing machines and hunger amid plenty:

> When the harvest had used to come, O that was the working-man's joy,
> But now for to reap & mow, it's strangers they all do employ,
> A man that stops in his own parish has scarce any work for to do,
> While his family they are half-starving,
> O what will old England come to.

> Such confounded schemes and contrivance they do invent every day,
> If a poor man he owes but a trifle, he cannot get money to pay,
> And when that the cold winter comes on, what causes poor workmen to rue,
> It's all through these thrashing machines,
> O what will old England come to.[46]

As another song observed, there was the further problem of parish work-schemes at low rates of pay:

WHAT WILL
Old England
COME TO?

COME all you jolly young fellows and listen awhile to my
    song,
I'll warrant you'll say it's true, and I will not detain you long,
It's concerning the rigs of the farmers, which cause poor
    servants to rue,   [England come to ?
Its all through their pride and ambition. O! what will poor

When my grandmother was a young woman, O then what
    doings were there ?   [cider and beer,
When servants did eat with their master, and drank the best
But now they're shov'd in the back kitchen the coarsest
    provision to chew,
And are forced to drink belly vengeance. O what, &c.

Whan the harvest had used to come, O that was the work-
    ing-man's joy,
But now for to reap & mow, it's strangers they all do employ ;
A man that stops in his own parish has scarce any work for to do,
While his family they are half-starving. O what, &c.

It's plenty of good beef and mutton to the field they used to
    bring,   [whistle and sing,
With plenty of good beer and cider, 'twould make a man
But now it s black bread and skim cheese as tough as the sole
    of a shoe,
With a drop of small beer and sour cider. O what, &c.

Now when that the corn is cut the rakers the ground they
    run o'er,   [the poor,
And scarce leave an ear for a mouse, instead of a loaf for
Such doings they will have an end, and the d—l he must
    have his due,
He'll shake them for robbing poor people, O what, &c.

Such confounded schemes and contrivance they do invent
    every day,   [pay,
If a poor man he owes but a trifle, he cannot get money to
And when that the cold winter comes on, what causes poor
    workmen to rue,
It's all through these thrashing machines. O what, &c.

Their daughters as grand as a duchess away to the market
    will ride,   (faces for pride,
Dress'd up in their habits and veils you can scarce see their
Poor men that like negroes do work get it all by the sweat of
    their brow,   (come to.
But if that their pride it should fail, why then what will they

So now to conclude and to finish, the truth I think to come
    near it,   (ple to wear it,
If the cap some should happen to fit, why those are the peo-
Let us pray that old times may revive, and improvements
    soon be seen,   [the Queen.
And success to each master and mistress, God prosper & live

W. and T. Fordyce, Printers, Dean-street, Newcastle.
To be had also at No. 43, Myton Gate, Hull.

29 Songs of the late 1820s foreshadow the terms and conditions of the
Captain Swing revolt. Reproduced by permission of the Syndics of Cambridge University Library (Madden Collection of Ballads).

> Many a village and town you know,
> Young men on the roads do go,
> And there they allow them six-pence a day,
> Out of that they have lodgings to pay,
> While there's plenty of work upon the land,
> That they might employ ev'ry man,
> They drive them to rob against their will,
> They are resolved to keep the prisons full.[47]

The revolt of 1830–1 had advance billing in rural popular culture; it was not the work of strangers roaming the countryside (as was often alleged by politicians and landholders) but of sustained popular enquiry into the root causes of unemployment and pauperism. Moreover, contrary to the opinion of urban reformers such as Francis Place, and even of some historians of the revolt, the labourers were not so mired in 'local' grievances as to eschew class solidarity with town workers. In January of 1831 one William Smith of the Isle of Wight was presented at Hampshire Quarter Sessions for having assembled a hundred of 'His Majesty's liege subjects', and to them

> wickedly maliciously and seditiously did sing utter pronounce and declare a certain false scandalous and malicious song, containing among other things certain malicious and inflammatory words in substance as follows 'When the people are obliged to apply for Parish Relief it is time to raise the Fiery Cry in contempt of our said Lord the King.'

According to the scribe, this 'evil-minded' and 'wicked' man 'traduced' and 'vilified' the aristocracy, particularly that great adversary of parliamentary reform, the Duke of Wellington. Next he is said to have invited attention to a song:

> For such distress in England,
> Was never known before,
> For thousands are forced to beg,
> From door to door.
>
> The Tradesman and the Labourers,
> Are sorely now oppressed,
> All for want of employment,
> They are in great distress.
>
> Their children crying out for bread,
> Alas! what shall I do,
> 'I have got none,' the Mother cries,
> 'You Fathers ought to do!'
>
> In Country Town and Villages,
> The Poor they are oppressed,

> For machinery is all in use,
> The Poor men to distress.
>
> Machinery is all the go,
> In Country and in Town,
> For to distress poor working men,
> They keep their wages down.[48]

It was not the metropolitan radical chieftains but individuals like Smith (a tradesman one suspects) who joined Cobbett in seeking to co-ordinate the urban and rural platforms. For their part, most London Radicals were preoccupied with Continental affairs, the hardline Toryism of the Duke of Wellington, and the ideological discord within their own ranks.[49]

Urban working-class leaders had no just cause to doubt the rural workers' ability to participate in the cut and thrust of radical politics. Francis Place, for example, was in possession of evidence that the rural workers had arrived at a level of confidence and class solidarity that rivalled that of their urban fellows. Among his papers is an 1830 newspaper report of a Surrey yeoman whose arrival at a village alehouse caused the labourers to halt in mid-verse. After a brief silence one of them cried out 'Who cares?':

> A shiny night is my delight,
> In [this] season of the year

and on they went to make their nightly poaching arrangements. Hearing their bold song, the yeoman warned that the unlawful taking of game was destined to 'a bad end':

> 'Bad End, Sir!,' said one, 'you are like the rest of the people who have their belly full; there are *plenty* of people who will preach to us about the badness of it, but *none* who will give us work that we may earn something. There is not one of us but who would gladly give it up – but we can't starve – work we are not afraid of – get us employment, and we will never – no never', said he (striking the table with vehemence), 'again set a snare or shoot a bird, but we won't starve *in a free country*. It ain't our faults but the faults of our betters.'

With this the men set off on their night's work, leaving their fathers to explain to the yeoman that they had not turned to poaching until recently, and that the only available employment was roadwork at 10d. a day.[50] Place, however, did not allow himself to be informed by such testimony; instead he ascribed the labourers' revolt to 'utter ignorance' and surplus population.[51]

Cobbett's representations of the rioters' logic and motivations constituted the only public rebuttal of the anti-Swing broadsides and pamphlets that poured into the countryside and denounced the rioters as 'wicked', 'unprincipled', 'stupid' and 'idle'.[52] In a tract signed 'Not by a follower of William Cobbett', it was asked: 'how can you let people make such fools of you, as to think that putting down the rich will do anything but make you poorer?'[53] Reminiscent of Hannah More, the anti-Swing tracts charged the rioters with stupidity for setting fire to the very food stores that provided potential relief from hunger. In rejoinder Cobbett vigorously denied that the labourers were 'ignorant of what they have been doing, or of the consequences, remote as well as near, of their acts'. They were aware that threshing machines deprived them of employment in 'the dead of winter', he argued, and that in theory it was 'ignorant' to set fire to human food, but they also understood the need for something extraordinary to 'bring people to their senses'. The labourers' rationale for the fires was the 'homely reasoning', as he called it, that 'I work twelve hours a-day to *produce their food*; I do *all* the real labour; and you, who stand by and look over me, deny me even *subsistence* out of it: no, if you give me none of it, you shall have none yourself, at any rate.'[54]

The diverse grievances of Captain Swing – including threshing machines, potatoes, impersonal bailiffs, high cottage rents and parish carts – had long been subjects of harsh comment in the *Register*. 'And *now*,' said Cobbett in November 1830, 'though it has come slowly, the verification of all my doctrines has arrived.'[55] Belittled and maligned in the anti-Swing literature, and deemed eccentric in his views on potatoes and beer, it is not surprising that he should find some satisfaction in the rioters' demands. In Kent the banners read 'WE WILL NOT LIVE UPON POTATOES'.[56] At Overton in Hampshire a crowd of 'several hundred' exclaimed that 'they have been starving long enough on potatoes and bread'.[57] At Pulborough the resolution was that 'we have been starving on potatoes long enough, and there must be an alteration'.[58] At Ringmer in Sussex the riot leaders asked:

> Have we no reason to complain that we have been obliged for so long a period to go to our daily toil with only potatoes in our satchels, and the only beverage to assuage our thirst the cold spring; and on returning to our cottages to be welcomed by the meagre and half-famished off-springs of our toil-worn bodies?[59]

'We want bread, we want work, and to be paid sufficient to keep our families', said the labourers of Kent; we 'cannot endure longer'.[60]

Phrases such as 'long enough' and 'cannot endure longer' are supportive of Cobbett's observations that the labourers would not again suffer their 'lowest point' of 1829. They suggest, too, that the rioters' programme was informed by their experiences over the long term. In eastern Sussex, for example, where the riots struck in early November, there were bitter memories of long-standing parish work-schemes. At Battle there was a tradition of cruelty towards paupers, likewise at Brede and Northiam, where by 1824 the labourers were described as so many paupers, thieves and road-workers, without meat and without beer.[61] In 1828 the workers of the latter parish displayed a 'refractory spirit' by barging into the vestry and demanding relief. According to a Poor Law Commissioner, 'these men at one time were required to bring up bags of beach on their shoulders for mending the roads, and were shut up in the workhouse yard, the object of which was to prevent imposition on their parish by their receiving parish pay as unemployed, when they were, in fact, getting relief from the farmers'.[62]

These bitter memories were central to the revolt in the South-East, though its timing might have owed something to Cobbett, who in October performed a lecture-tour of several towns in Kent and eastern Sussex. Among his stops was Battle, where he lectured to an audience of 500, about one third of which was attired in smocks. The local conveners, having been refused an indoor venue, erected a booth out of sails and hop-poles: 'I was really at home here', reported Cobbett, for 'here were assembled a sample of that part of this honest, sincere, kind and once

Arouse, People of England!

let not *your Character* be lost, by listening to the *artful* advice of a few evil-disposed Persons, that are employed by *Foreigners*, who are travelling about the Country to do all the Mischief they can, by making the Labourers and others act *wickedly*.

Ask yourselves for a moment, What good will it do us by burning the bountiful Harvest *the Almighty* has given us for Food, and also ruining our *Neighbour*? The answer is, NONE, but making things *worse;* for if the Farmers are injured, they will be less able to employ Labourers, and it will assuredly bring a *Famine* and *Misery* on *themselves* and *their Families*.

Think of these *Truths*, and return to your Duty, and be *honest good Men* of

OLD ENGLAND FOR EVER!

Printed by Hickman and Stapledon, Henley.—Price One Shilling per Hundred.

30 In 1830–1 there appeared numerous handbills denouncing the destruction of food stores and attributing the riots to 'foreigners'. Reproduced by permission of the Kress Library of Business and Economics, Baker Library, Harvard Graduate School of Business and Economics.

happy people, amongst whom I was born and bred up, and towards whom my affections have increased with my age.' His speech began with reference to the burnings in Kent, which he predicted would spread swiftly into Sussex if the rioters' grievances were not attended to. He praised the 1830 revolution in France and pressed at the need for reform in England, reiterating his support for universal male suffrage and the ballot, as well as his opposition to the 113 privy councillors whose salaries he estimated at an annual worth of £20 for every working family in Sussex. Turning to local matters, he criticized the labour auctions, the parish carts and the separation of husbands and wives within workhouses. He had strong words against the game laws, the Dead-Body Bill and particularly enclosure, which he condemned for robbing the poor of cows, pigs and fuel. These oppressions, he claimed, were the true causes of the fires; and either the farmers would join the labourers in the reform movement or they would witness even more fires and an eventual allocation of land to working people.[63]

It was an inflammatory performance that left the local élite in no doubt that Cobbett was a public enemy, if not Captain Swing himself. 'An Englishman' reported to *The Times* that

> I was present at a lecture delivered at East Bourne, in Sussex, by Mr. Cobbett. In that lecture he told his hearers (who were principally labouring men), that a revolution must inevitably take place in this country; 'and,' says this dangerous man, 'it must be worked by such men as I see before me'. At Battel [*sic*] also, in addressing a labouring man, he asked him 'if his shoulder was strong enough to bear a musket'. Thus, not only by oblique hints did he inflame their minds, but openly did he predict that that and every other part of the country would be visited with similar outbreakings as to those then raging in Kent. Up to that time no appearance of disorder had taken place.[64]

Approximately a hundred members of Cobbett's audience would later put their signatures or crosses to a declaration stating that he had not urged them to set fires.[65] Others, including Thomas Goodman, setter of five fires in the Battle district, seemed less certain: 'I, Thomas Goodman,' he allegedly claimed,

> never should of thought of douing aney sutch thing if Mr. Cobet had never given any lactures, I believe that their never would bean aney fires or mob in Battle nor maney other places if he never had given aney lectures at all ... [This made] a verrey great imprision on me and so inflame my mind and i from that time was determined to set stacks on fire.[66]

At least one of Goodman's three 'confessions' appears to have been extracted at the behest of the King, who proposed a pardon for Goodman in exchange for his anti-Cobbett testimony.[67] Yet despite the machinations of the state and of Sussex magistrates (there is sufficient variation in the editions of Goodman's confession to bring its authenticity into question) Cobbett's lectures were almost certainly foul of the law. In the opinion of G. D. H. Cole, 'Cobbett did not praise the burnings',[68] but it is a very close call, for he did argue that they achieved 'great good', which is to say, by the standards of common sense, that the more fires the better. At his lengthy trial for inflaming the 'minds of the labourers' and for inciting them to 'acts of violence riot and disorder and to the burning and destruction of corn grain machines', he was saved by his older, much more conservative addresses to the Luddites, which for their rebuke of machine-breaking were sought by Henry Brougham for republication in reply to Captain Swing. Disclosure of Brougham's request for Cobbett's permission of copyright, together with non-disclosure of the fact that the author had implicitly repudiated his earlier position, went heavily against the Crown, and William Cobbett, 'labourer', as the indictment read, went free.[69]

Besides the lectures there was the *Register* itself, which even in stamped edition (price 7d.) was taken into the rural alehouses and political clubs so that (in the words of Attorney-General Denman) 'all may have an opportunity of reading it'.[70] More affordable was the abridged and unstamped version *Two-Penny Trash* which Cobbett revived in July 1830 to preside over the revolt and to press the case for parliamentary reform. The latter publication, according to a Gloucestershire magistrate, was 'read in every Country pothouse',[71] while from Kent it was reported that Cobbett was 'read and commented upon by the lower classes, who ... allow no publications of a contrary tendency to be brought into the [public] house'.[72] Two Leicestershire overseers attributed the riots to 'inflammatory speeches from Messrs. Cobbett and others', while in Norfolk the cause was said to be 'the disseminations of Cobbett's and other vicious Tracts'. A parson magistrate in Surrey suggested that the *Register* had 'much to do' with the disturbances; while assorted commentators from Sussex, including the assistant overseer of Brede, attributed the revolt to Cobbett's lectures or 'Cobbett-political agitation'. 'Could Cobbett's works be suppressed,' suggested a Suffolk correspondent, 'I think the Country would then soon get quiet.'[73] Sharing this view was Lord Carnarvon of Highclere in Hampshire who complained that Cobbett's writings were 'distributed all over the neighbourhood and had undoubtedly caused the incendiary spirit'.[74] John Benett of Wiltshire agreed, adding that Cobbett's presence in the popular press had caused him to purchase insurance for his standing crops as well as for his stacks.[75]

COBBETT'S

TWO-PENNY TRASH;

OR,

POLITICS FOR THE POOR.

VOLUME I.

FROM JULY 1830, TO JUNE, 1831, INCLUSIVE.

LONDON:
PRINTED BY THE AUTHOR, AND SOLD AT No. 11, BOLT-COURT, FLEET-STREET, AND MAY BE HAD OF ALL BOOKSELLERS.

1831.

31   The grievances of the labourers were a central concern of Cobbett's
Two-Penny Trash (1830–2). The title played to the epithet bestowed upon
the two-penny *Register* of 1816–20 by Cobbett's Tory adversaries.

Although much of this comment has the ring of hearsay, Cobbett
enjoyed a formidable influence in the countryside. Scarcely an anti-
Cobbett broadsheet or pamphlet does not confess to this, and his own
petition to the King of 1830 was among the most widely circulated
documents during the rebellion.[76] When Attorney-General Denman
pointed out at Cobbett's trial that the *Register* had 'a prodigious effect'
upon labouring people, the defendant replied: 'I hope in God it has.
Nothing has given me more delight than to hear him say that.'[77] Rather
than disguise his rural influence, Cobbett exaggerated it:

> There is *not one single village*, however recluse, in England, where my name
> is not known as the friend of the working people, and particularly of the
> farming labourers; and if ever man deserved any thing, I deserve this
> character ... I have stated their hard case, I have argued, I have supplicated,
> in their behalf, with as much earnestness as if my own life depended on the
> result. They all know this, they know, too, how I have *suffered* for these my
> endeavours; and they respect and confide in me accordingly.[78]

Yet Cobbett's egotism knew limits, for he identified the revolt as belonging to the labourers themselves. He was prepared to make common cause with them and to share in the recrimination, but he was not about to reduce the importance of the labourers' experience in the revolt by overstating the importance of his leadership. The awkward thing for the ruling class was that the revolt was *not* reducible to Cobbett's pen. 'Our labourers understand Cobbett but do not read him', reported a Norfolk correspondent to Francis Place;[79] and in the view of Lord Carnarvon of Hampshire, *Two-Penny Trash* proceeded not from Cobbett alone, but from an entire class.[80]

Cobbett's involvement in the labourers' revolt is perhaps best presented in the context of the heroic struggle in a clutch of adjacent parishes in the north of Hampshire: Micheldever, Stoke Charity, Wonston, Sutton Scotney and Bullington. In these 'hard parishes', as Cobbett called them, a cottage living had little support from nature or from local farmers; the soil was flinty, fuel scarce and the farms large and arable. Among the farm workers of the hard parishes were the brothers Joseph and Robert Mason of Bullington, aged thirty-two and twenty-four respectively, who lived with their mother as well as Joseph's wife and daughter. During the day the Mason brothers laboured for local farmers, spending their evenings on their rented smallholding of $3^{1}/_{2}$ acres, where they kept a cow, some pigs and some bees. The Masons were comparatively well off: they were not paupers and they were seldom hungry. They were also adept at reading and writing, having received instruction from their mother, a former schoolteacher.[81]

The Masons put their learning to good effect as leading members of a political club that convened in cottages and alehouses in the vicinity of Bullington. As a rule the meetings began with beer and song, progressing to local political subjects and the latest *Political Register*, which was read and discussed in earnest.[82] At Michaelmas 1830 these 'enthusiastic admirers of Cobbett', as they would later be called, convened a meeting at the Swan Inn in Sutton Scotney, where they adopted Cobbett's advice to petition the King for parliamentary reform (see Appendix II). Joseph was delegated to draft the petition, and he used as his blueprint Cobbett's 'Letter to the King' (an extrapolation of the fourth of Cobbett's lectures on the French and Belgian Revolutions), which had appeared in the stamped *Register* of 18 September. From Cobbett's essay Joseph acquired information on sinecures, taxation, tithes, church property and the national debt; he put this information into his own words, appended a variety of local grievances, and added some thoughts of his own about hunger amid plenty:

A

TRUE ACCOUNT

OF THE

Life & Death

OF

SWING, THE RICK-BURNER;

WRITTEN BY ONE WELL ACQUAINTED WITH HIM.

TOGETHER WITH THE

CONFESSION OF THOMAS GOODMAN,

**NOW UNDER SENTENCE OF DEATH, IN HORSHAM JAIL,
FOR RICK-BURNING.**

See Page 22.

THE NINETEENTH EDITION.

LONDON:

PRINTED BY R. CLAY, BREAD-STREET-HILL;
Published by

ROAKE AND VARTY, 31, STRAND.

Price Two-pence, or 1s. 6d. per Dozen.

CONFESSION OF THOMAS GOODMAN

" I Thomas Goodman under sentence of death Aged twenty years Bread and born in Battel hoop maker by trade had bean working the last year and A half for Mrs Eldrig in Battel and had latley had fifteen shillings a week i hird of one Mr Cobbit going a bout gaving out lectures at length he came to Battel and gave one their and their was a great number of Peopel came to hear him and I went to and he had a great deal of conversation concerning the states of the People and the cuntry telling that that they were verrey mutch impose upon and he would tell them how to get the better of it or they would sone be starved he said it would be verrey Propper for everrey man to keep a gun in his house espesealey young men and that they migh Prepare them selves i readdyness to go with him When he called on them and he would show them the way to get their rights and liberals [liberties] and he said that the Farmers must expect their would be Firs [fires] in susex and in Battel as well as other Places and is conversation was all as sutch to inflame the Peopels minds they thinking that he would be A friend to them which made A verrey great imprision on me and so inflame my mine and i from that time was detrmined to set stacks on fire and sone afterwards their was three firs in Battle and that same night the last fire was at the Corsbarn whent and set fire to Mr B Watts is stack with A candel and lantern and some few days afterwards i was standing A talking to three more Persons their came a verrey gentel man on horseback and he rode up to us and said why you have had a fire hear i said yes we have he said well how do Peopel seame to like theas firs or do they seam eneways A larmed at them i said yes they do but some of them are verrey mutch harden in it and think their will be no more he said i am sorry that they should think so Becaus they have but gust [just] made A beginning he ask Wether we had hird of any Person being takin in Battel that day on suspicion of theos firs i said i did not know he ask if we though [thought] the Poor Peopel would asist to find those Persons out that set theas places on fire if the farmers was to gave them to shillings a day we said we did not know and he seamed so verrey much Pleased a bout theas firs he stopt a haf a nower his hole conversation was as sutch he was a Person welldresst and verrey good horse new saddel and Bridel Wich made more imprission on my mind and some little time after i was at a publick house in Battel wich Mr —— ockvpies their was severel People their Which among them their was one   and   i new them both verrey well i whent out and they came after me and son fell into conversation concerning theas fires had been —— said he wish some one woust set fire to the premises of Mr —— and Mr —— —— said he would do it if he could do it Privat —— said he would make one to help he said he would go with me to set Muster Watts his bildings on fir if I would go i said if i did any sutch thing i should do it by myself.

" THOMAS GOODMAN."

32 and 33   One of at least three different editions of Thomas Goodman's 'confession'. King William IV proposed that Goodman be pardoned in exchange for evidence that might serve to gain a conviction against Cobbett. Reproduced by permission of the University of London (Goldsmiths' Library).

34 Cobbett emerges from his village 'office' and hands a copy of *Two-Penny Trash* to a ragged labourer. Ricks blaze and rioters march in the background. From the title-page of *Imposture Unmasked* by 'A True Englishman' (1831). Reproduced by permission of the British Library.

That many of us have not food sufficient to satisfy our hunger; our drink is chiefly the crystal element; we have not clothes to hide the nakedness of ourselves, our wives, and our children; nor fuel wherewith to warm us; while at the same time our barns are filled with corn, our garners with wool, our pastures abound with cattle, and our land yields us an abundance of wood and coal; all of which display the wisdom, the kindness, and mercy of a good Creator.

Attached to the 1,500-word petition were 176 signatures gathered from the village workers of Wonston, Bullington and Barton Stacey. Not fewer than eighteen of these names would later appear upon the indictment rolls of the Winchester Special Commission.[83]

An offer to carry the petition to the King, then at Brighton, was made by Joseph, who with 17s. subscribed for his expenses, set off on the 60 miles by foot. Arriving at the door of the Pavilion on 21 October, he was kept waiting as Sir Herbert Taylor, the King's private secretary, composed a note declaring that 'the Secretary of State for the Home Department is the proper and official channel of such communications to His Majesty'. Disillusioned and without the time or money to walk another 60 miles to London, Joseph entrusted a copy of the petition with an acquaintance in Brighton, who in turn would pass it on to Cobbett.[84]

On 13 November another meeting was held at the Swan Inn at Sutton Scotney. Angrily discussed was the rejection of the petition at Brighton, and there was determined talk about the 'sovereign people'. Afterwards Joseph read out a letter which urged the men to strike for higher wages and to destroy the 'sheens' of the farmers. According to some of those present, the letter had come from Overton, though in the opinion of Joseph Carter (a former labourer of Cobbett's at Botley), 'we did not then know who it came from. But we knows, all [of] us now in this here place, that old [Diddams] had a hand in't. He was a great friend of Mr. Cobbett. He used to write to Mr. Cobbett.'[85] The letter, whether authored by Enos Diddams, a local radical shoemaker and a signatory of the petition to the King, or by a representative of the workers of Overton, assisted to throw the 'hard parishes' into open revolt against employers and Parliament. The first object of the men was to wreck the threshing machines, for each one of them, according to Carter, threw two men out of work.[86] Second, the rioters wanted a living wage: 12s. a week for married men, 9s. a week for the unmarried.[87] Third, they wanted pecuniary donations, partly to finance refreshment and partly as a token of the goodwill of the élite. Lastly, they wanted to expedite parliamentary reform.

A particularly tumultuous day was 19 November, when a small crowd assembled at Sutton Scotney, ready to march. An early port of call was Stoke Charity, where the local curate, the Reverend Cockerton, was invited to listen to the men's grievances and to contribute a sum of money to their cause. Cockerton refused both courses. Not forcing the issue, the crowd moved on, though in a less conciliatory frame of mind. As it proceeded it swelled in size to 700 or 800 persons, some being pressed into service, others going voluntarily. At Sir Thomas Baring's estate at East Stratton the crowd broke threshing machines and negotiated a £10 levy in lieu of an attack upon the mansion house. Pleased with their doings thus far, the labourers decorated their hair with laurel leaves and looked 'all very gallant'. At Micheldever more machines were destroyed, higher wages demanded and more levies received. According to Sir Thomas's eldest son, Francis Thornhill Baring (a magistrate and a recently appointed lord of the treasury), his father's tenants were reduced to 'desperate alarm' by the proceedings. Similarly unnerved was Sir Thomas himself, who discerned 'not distress but a revolutionary spirit' at work. 'We are going to have another constitution', he heard the rioters say: 'the heads have been in power long enough, and now it is our turn.' Some of the younger rioters went further by demanding blood, though the closest thing in this way occurred at Northington where the crowd was confronted by Sir Thomas's nephew Bingham Baring, JP, MP, who in a scuffle was struck by a hammer wielded by a ploughman named Henry Cook. Moving on to Barton Stacey, the crowd was pleased to receive a pecuniary donation from the Reverend James Joliffe, who was informed that 'you have it and we want it. We have been living on potatoes long enough and we must now have something better.' Returning to Sutton Scotney the crowd put its griev-ances to the Reverend Newbolt, an alderman and magistrate from Win-chester who had come up expressly to negotiate with the men. After hearing them out, Newbolt ordered farmers to stop their use of threshing machines and to pay the demanded wages of 12s. On this note the crowd was pleased to dissolve.[88]

The main role of Joseph Mason in the rising was to serve as spokesman for the crowd at Sir Thomas Baring's estate, where the £10 levy was peaceably obtained from the steward. He was later involved in the distri-bution of a £2 levy from a Mr Dowding.[89] Robert was rather more active: he was said to have served as a leader in wage negotiations with farmers, and to have participated in the selection of threshing machines for de-struction. According to the Reverend Cockerton, Robert declared that 'you would not have believed a week ago we could have done what we have, we can do more yet'.[90] The only charge against Joseph and Robert, however, was that of 'demanding money' or 'robbery', for which sentences of death were recorded by the Hampshire Special Commission. Pros-ecuting Joseph was Sir Thomas Baring and his steward; while Robert was targeted by the Reverend Joliffe, who, apparently at the behest of Sir Thomas, demanded retribution for his being bullied out of 5s. In a letter from Winchester gaol, Robert pleaded with Joliffe to forget the matter: 'Five shillings could not have been a great loss to you, – there were not the least injury done or threatened to your person or property, not a saucy or disrespectful word uttered as I heard. You was thanked for your dona-tion.'[91] At the trials Joliffe confirmed that Robert sang in the church choir and had never before committed a breach of the peace. Nevertheless, he was transported for life, and without being able to attribute his pros-ecution to anything more substantial than a disgreement between Joliffe and Mrs Mason about the allocation of school pupils.[92] Only after the sittings of the Special Commission did the larger truth begin to emerge: in a later fact-finding tour of the 'hard parishes' Cobbett learned that 'part of the crime of the Masons was telling the *parson* that they had read the

Protestant "Reformation" and that it had taught them all about *tythes.* The parson at Micheldever ... swore three men's lives away.'[93]

Transportation was also the sentence of Joseph, who, said the Baron Justice Vaughan, 'is a person moving in a better class, and ought to have set a different example. He, therefore, must not expect any further mitigation of his punishment than that of sparing his life.' The injustice and class vengeance of it all was evident to Robert, who stated to the Grand Jury that 'If learned counsel, who has so painted my conduct to you was present at that place and wore a smock frock instead of a gown and a straw hat instead of a wig, he would now be standing in this dock instead of being seated where he is.'[94] The Jury was not moved. Their foreman was none other than Cobbett's adversary of long-standing, John Benett of Pyt House in Wiltshire, whose own estates were visited by Swing, and whose legacies to the labourers included his notorious relief scale of a gallon loaf and 3d. per week. The chief law officer was Sir Thomas Denman, who as Attorney-General would prosecute Cobbett as riot leader. The accuracy of some of Denman's information on the Hampshire disturbances can be gauged from the fact that he informed Parliament that Henry Cook was a carpenter in receipt of 5s. a day, when Cobbett would prove by affidavit from Henry's father, John Cook, that the lad was unemployed during the rising, later to become (at the time of his arrest) a ploughman at the wage of 5s. a *week*.[95] Never far behind Denman was Sir Thomas Baring, head of the country branch of the family of merchant bankers, who took very seriously his duties as a magistrate and member of Parliament.[96] As was characteristic of his class, Sir Thomas attributed the fires to a conspiracy to overthrow the Constitution and the landlords; thus he was very active in the aftermath of the revolt in identifying rioters, organizing arrests and witnessing depositions. Robert Mason looked upon Sir Thomas Baring as 'our worst enemy'.[97]

Apart from assisting in the prosecution of the Masons, Sir Thomas was closely involved in the fate of Henry Cook, a labourer upon Sir Thomas's own estate who had struck (but not seriously injured) Sir Thomas's nephew Bingham Baring, a magistrate and member of Parliament in his own right. Cook's arrest was carried out by Thomas's son Francis, who had marched into the hard parishes at the head of a troop of soldiers. Much to the irritation of all three Barings, Cobbett recruited John Cook as a witness for the defence in the King versus Cobbett. In turn Sir Thomas obtained a statement, allegedly voluntary, from John's wife Ruth:

> My Son, Henry Cook told me that he had struck Mr. Bingham Baring where he intended that he should have killed him, but that he was prevented by

being pushed forward by the other men. My son said the day before he was executed 'Mother it is not Mr. Baring who hangs me for he has done everything in his power to save my life' and I, Ruth Cook believe if it had not been for Cobbett's papers that my son would have been alive now altho he says in his papers that Mr. Baring caused him to be hanged. Cobbett sent a man by the name of Diddums [sic] to my Husband to tell him to go to him in London which he did. Cobbet gave him money and gave me clothes and Diddums told me that Cobbet would be a friend to us as he had been to a woman of the name of Mason of Sutton whose sons were transported and that he would put up a stone over my son's grave. I do not wish it. I know it is only to spite Mr. Baring and not for my Son. I wish it not to be done and my husband who is very ill is of the same mind. I have been and so has my husband very uneasy in our minds at Cobbetts papers in which he says Mr. Baring caused my Son's death and I wish to make it known for I believe from what my son told me that it is false. I hope my statement will be made public. I wish Cobbet would let me alone and my son rest in peace. Cobbet's talk stirred up the people and my poor boy who was no scholar ran headlong with the rest for which he was very sorry but it was too late.

Sworn before me   Ruth Cook
the 25th October 1831.   X
Thos. Baring   Her Mark[98]

Cobbett might indeed have exploited the plight of the Cooks for political ends, but this document rings of improbability and contrivance. There is no evidence, for example, that Sir Thomas Baring did 'everything in his power' to save Cook's life, or that Bingham took seriously his promise to Mrs Cook that Henry 'shan't be hanged'. As the people of Micheldever recalled a half-century later, Bingham Baring 'could have saved' Cook, but he chose instead to accept the Commission's case for a capital conviction.[99] Furthermore, how familiar was Ruth Cook, apparently unable to read or write, with 'Cobbett's papers' that spoke ill of Thomas Baring? She might indeed have wished that Cobbett would leave her in peace, but how did she come to construe a planned monument to her son as a rebuke of Sir Thomas? These questions are without answers, but we do know that the statement was obtained after Cobbett assisted to expose the Barings to national ridicule for their cover-up of the hypocritical conduct of Bingham Baring, who, five days after being 'felled' by Cook, committed a wanton assault of his own upon the small Hampshire farmers Mr and Mrs Deacle.

At an early stage in the revolt the Deacles had given of their time by composing petitions and carrying them from house to house for signatures. Unhappy with this development, Bingham Baring assembled a posse of strongmen and made for the Deacle farm, where he arrested,

35 Sworn deposition by David Lovell, a labourer of Northington in Hampshire, that Henry Cook struck Bingham Baring on the rim of his hat, that no other blows were attempted, and that Bingham Baring was seen later on the same day to be in 'perfect good health'. Reproduced by permission of Nuffield College Library.

298 parishes. — houses 49,516 — Ag. Pop. 116,078.—
Able labourers — 29,019.

2 killed.

135 Trans.

73 Widows.

294 Fatherless Children.

504

Nearly 2 victims to every parish.

1 Victim to every 98 houses.

1 Victim to every 220 souls in Agriculture.

1 Able Labourer killed or transported out of
    every 211 in the county.

Cook —

It was to prevent these things that the whole
    article was written.

Sutton 4 copper pennies. — See page 40. — Just
    the same punishment as Goodman.

— If so pressing — why not Hilary Term?

36   Cobbett's jottings on the doings of the Hampshire Special Commission.
     Reproduced by permission of Nuffield College Library.

handcuffed and then verbally and physically abused the couple while bundling them off to prison. Immediately upon hearing of the incident, Cobbett went to work on the Deacles' behalf: he publicized their story in the *Register* and *Two-Penny Trash*, while arranging for their legal support and composing some of their public statements and petitions to Parliament.[100] As Bingham Baring himself detected:

> Mr. Deacle's first petition bears evident marks of having been drawn up by a person who has long been busy, in his weekly journal, with indulging his impotent malice against me and my family; and who probably never took the trouble of ascertaining the facts, I speak of the malice of Mr. Cobbett.[101]

The awkward thing for the Barings was that Cobbett *had* ascertained the facts, and that he was not alone in his indignation. So compelling and blatant was the injustice served upon the Deacles that Francis Place and Cobbett overlooked their feud of twenty-five years to work jointly on the case.[102] By degrees they succeeded in capturing the sympathy of not only the radical movement but of the nation, though Parliament denied their appeal for an official enquiry and though Bingham Baring was fined £50 while Henry Cook was hanged for not grossly dissimilar offences.

After the proceedings of the Barings and the Special Commission, the workers of Hampshire were devastated. Henry Cook was hanged and so was the alleged Cobbettite James Cooper. Transported from the county were 135 men, who left behind them, according to Cobbett's calculations, 73 widows, 294 children and 157 parents. Rural people had no idea, Cobbett declared, that transportation or the gallows awaited them 'for merely assembling in bands of sturdy beggers, and frightening people out of a little money without touching, or attempting to touch, a hair of their heads to do them harm'.[103] Cook had gone further than most rioters by attempting to strike a magistrate, but the episode had mitigating circumstances: he was merely a lad of eighteen, without regular work at the time, and (according to village memories a half-century after his hanging) 'as quiet, civil, honest, and industrious a young man as ever lived'.[104] The worst response anticipated by Cobbett was the three-day prison sentence imposed upon Kentish rioters by Sir Edward Knatchbull during the early weeks of the rising; and ideally Cobbett hoped for the example of the Bishop of Winchester, who, when held up for a levy, made straight for home, hired twenty-four additional workers, commenced an allotment scheme, and threw open the doors of Farnham castle to relieve the poor. Common sense of this order was uncommon in the Hampshire Special Commission, whose juries were informed by the justices to disregard 'grievances' such as parish carts and potato diets.[105]

The Special Commissions were wide of the mark in their presentation of Captain Swing as a violent and vindictive drunkard who lived in the beershops. Even after sentencing, the first concern of the Mason brothers lay with their frail and elderly mother, whose well-being they attended to by appealing to their friends and allies of Bullington. Joseph had the additional concern of the welfare of his wife, who he expected would have to enter farm service for the remainder of her days. Both brothers were consoled through the proceedings by their religious faith, regularly quoting Scripture in order to exhort their friends and menace their enemies. 'Sure I am that the Lord will avenge the poor and maintain the cause of the helpless', quoted Robert from Psalm 140 to the Reverend Joliffe. For Sir Thomas Baring's edification he recommended a chapter of Isaiah; and in Job 24 he found apt descriptions of the present state of 'the labouring poor'. Justice having eluded him in this world, Robert hoped that 'God will never overlook the innocent blood that have been spilt; all those tears that have wet the cheeks of new-made widows, and sighs that have issued from the hearts of Fatherless children, Mothers, Sisters, Brothers, Fathers, and Friends; nor all their frequent prayers.' Robert's faith in organized religion was delivered a blow by the co-operation of the clergy with Thomas Baring and the Hampshire Commission; after receiving sentence he abandoned the church as 'the resort of the hypocrite and profane'. Joseph grew similarly disillusioned with the church, but rather than abandon public worship he converted to the Methodist chapel upon his arrival in New South Wales.

Religious faith, common decency and a Cobbettian education gave to the Masons their political determination, their caring dispositions and their will to triumph over their class enemies. Writing to his mother, Robert exhorted that 'we are not to be cast down at a trifling reverse of fortune nor repine at the triumph of proud and haughty men over us'. The 'great rich men', he observed, 'are far more wicked than the poor', and they will not 'triumph for ever' on account that 'the people of the world are resolved to enjoy more freedom than in times past'. Thus in his absence he called upon his friends and family to 'maintain a bold and enterprising spirit', to continue the struggle for reform, and to get Cobbett and other 'compassionate men' elected to Parliament. True to Robert's commission, as we will see in the next chapter, the labourers of the hard parishes remained active in the struggle for democratic reform.

Life in New South Wales was not as grim as Robert and Joseph had anticipated. Like the other prisoners they were assigned to a master who supplied them with employment, clothing and accommodation. Robert was set to work for a magistrate in Port Macquarie, from where he wrote home about low prices, good wages and the 'cangaroos'. In 1841 he married, shortly after receiving a pardon. Joseph was set to work for a gardener at Parramatta, writing home that 'I have no reason to complain as yet I receive very good treatment. I have plenty of Bread and Beef. I live in a hut in the garden with another man and we have to cook our victuals and wash our own clothes.' Although not delighted with the arrangements, Joseph appreciated that he was better off than many of his friends in England, for 'it is better by far to have to cook your own victuals than to have none to cook'. Still, the brothers carried to their graves an enormous sense of the injustice served upon them. That something had gone terribly wrong is evident in Robert's remark that the convicts said among themselves that 'the better the men the more severe the sentence'. Try as they might, they could not understand why they should be banished from their native land for advocating the cause of those 'who lived in a land of plenty, yet never knew what it was to have enough'.[106]

Cobbett, meanwhile, campaigned unsuccessfully to have the Masons and the other prisoners returned to England, while doing what he could to ensure that Mrs Mason, and many other labouring families in Hampshire, had a bountiful harvest of his Indian corn.[107] His audience with the farm workers inspired jealousy and fear; even Henry Hunt took time out from the urban platform to conduct an anti-Cobbett campaign in the hard parishes.[108] For its part, the Whig and Tory press angrily acknowledged Cobbett's dialogues with the village community, but quickly warned everyone against joining 'his desperate band of revolutionists'.[109] Given his prominence in the countryside, Cobbett was in a position to rally the farm workers to his own political advantage, or at least to threaten the ruling class with a rural militia under his private command. Such an opportunity presented itself at a Hampshire county meeting in October 1831, where Cobbett's advertisements drew a thousand village workers to a meeting on behalf of parliamentary reform. After a technicality prevented him from addressing the gathering, the mood of the workers deteriorated to the point where Cobbett, by pushing his case to be heard, could have incited a battle which would have worked to the disadvantage of the Whigs and Tories in the short term, the labourers in the long. Instead he exercised restraint, informing his son John that 'it wanted only a drawing in two opposing bodies to bring them to blows ... and that would have brought out the soldiers'. 'The Chopsticks', however, 'were very angry at my having been prevented from making that reply', and they suffered no one else to be heard for the duration of the meeting.[110]

In the aftermath of the transportations and hangings, Cobbett's tone was subdued as he shared in the labourers' grief. He knew that transportation was 'little, if anything, short of *death* for a labouring man'.[111] Villagers, he knew, had long memories:

> [Their] constant participation in each other's hardships and toils tends to bind them more firmly to one another: if you commit an act of injustice towards one, the whole village feels it individually and collectively. Even the villages themselves are connected with one another; and thus a whole county or district is imbued with one and the same vengeful feeling. Is any man so stupid as to imagine that there is a single soul in Pewsey, man, woman or child, who will not remember the transportation of eleven men in that village.[112]

Immediately upon the conclusion of his own trial, Cobbett made for the hard parishes, looking in on Mrs Mason at Bullington and enquiring at Micheldever into the welfare of the Cooks. He wrote to his wife of his discovery that at Henry Cook's funeral procession, '6 young girls in *white* and 6 young men in their white smock-frocks met the corpse a mile from the village, and the whole of the working people of all the parishes and about assembled and followed the corpse to the grave! It is a story enough to arouse the blood of a stone.' After speaking with the villagers he came away convinced that Cook's 'blood will never be forgotten'.[113] And so it is in the hard parishes today – some six generations after Robert Mason penned his tribute to Cook's memory:

> Sweet innocence
> Upon the surface ever wilt thou swin,
> Whilst guilt, black guilt will sink and be forgot.[114]

The labourers were not alone in remembering the fires and riots. The Reverend Robert Wright, a Winchester magistrate who assisted to commit the Masons, grieved that 'I shall remember the riots to the day of my death.'[115] Even at Micheldever in 1831, where hearts were heavy and countenances long, Cobbett observed that 'the victory of the labourers is complete. They are here *well-off*. Never was revolution so complete.'[116] Throughout Hampshire he discovered that workers received 'a much larger share than they did; and, notwithstanding the dreadful doings of the law, in 1830, they carry a bolder front than they did'.[117] Many employers concurred, lending credence to Cobbett's estimate that the revolt added between £4 and £8 a year to the annual wage of a southern worker.[118] Since the 'revolution of 1830', complained some Sussex farmers, the labourers 'dictate the rate of relief as well as wages'. 'They are the rulers', others complained. At Rye, where the first anniversary of the rising was celebrated in November 1831, the 'restless spirit' of the labourers was said to keep the farmers at bay; while at Battle the labourers were reported to be enjoying 'great improvement' in their condition on account that employers and overseers were careful not to transgress the labouring poor. The word of some Sussex workers was that 'if you do not relieve us we shall help ourselves'.[119] In Cambridgeshire in 1836, it was complained by an employer that 'we are paying 50 per cent more for labour than we ought to do, as a sort of premium of insurance, to prevent our farms being burnt down'.[120] In Warwick in 1834, farmers were said to give generously to beggars 'for fear of having their ricks and barns burnt'.[121] In Northamptonshire it was claimed that the burnings of 1830 'have so intimidated the farmers that they have nearly given up all control over the poor'.[122]

Perhaps the most remarkable about-face occurred in Cobbett's old parish of Bishop's Waltham, where fifteen years earlier he had received no support for his proposition that the cottagers of Waltham Chase be granted title to their encroachments on the edge of the common (see chapter 5). Not only was Cobbett's land plan dusted off and implemented with dispatch at the outbreak of the revolts, employers and parish officers agreed to 'maintain the labourers without parochial aid, and ... earnestly entreated their more wealthy neighbours to find work for the poor during the ensuing winter'.[123] It is too much to say (as did one clergyman) that the 'labourers gained their own terms' in 1830–1,[124] but it was nevertheless a monumental victory for English rural labour that would be remembered in the villages as 'the improvement of the fires'. Cobbett was pleased to find landholders 'solicitous' of the poor in the wake of the revolt, especially as the New Poor Law Bill threatened to make its way through Parliament.[125] Even John Benett, for example, uncharacteristically opposed the Bill, as if to say that he did not relish the prospect of again being stoned by an angry crowd, as happened at his own gates in 1830.[126] Finally, the revolt did something to alter the disposition of the Whig and Tory press towards rural workers. *The Morning Chronicle*, for example, had for years needled Cobbett by supporting enclosure, large farms and by denouncing his memories of old England as 'pig's meat'. No less vigorously, the paper condemned the Swing rioters as ignorant and misguided. 'But the demoralization of the labourers was not calculated on', the *Chronicle* now apologized, 'we must retrace our steps.'[127]

It is understandable that Cobbett should have been ambivalent towards those persons who responded to the physical force of Swing but had long ignored his own writings and the labourers' advance billings of their grievances. He was even of two minds about the allotment movement, probably the most lasting effect of the rising. Although pleased to find that organizations such as the Labourer's Friend Society sought to end the fires

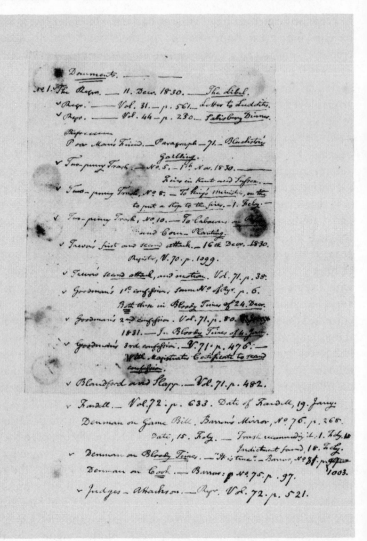

37   Cobbett conducted his own defence at his 1831 trial. Here he lists some
of the documents that he planned to lay before his prosecutors and the jury at
his trial of 7 and 8 July 1831. Reproduced by permission of Nuffield College
Library.

The indictment charging Cobbett with seditious libel was returned on 17
February 1831 by the Grand Jury at the Old Bailey. It singled out the
following passage from an essay entitled 'Rural War' which had been
brought to the attention of the Attorney-General by the anti-reform MP for
New Romney, Arthur Trevor:

But without entering at present into the *motives* of the working people, it is unquestionable that their acts have produced good, and great good too. They have been always told ... that their acts of violence, and particularly the burnings, can *do them no good*, but *add to their wants*, by destroying the food that *they would have to eat.* Alas! they know better: they know that one thrashing-machine takes wages from ten men; and they also know that *they* should have none of this food; and that *potatoes and salt* do not burn! Therefore, this argument is not worth a straw. Besides, they see and feel *that the good comes*, and comes *instantly* too. They see that they *do* get *some* bread, in consequence of the destruction of part of the corn; and while they see this, you attempt in vain to persuade them, that that which they have done is *wrong.*

(*PR*, 11 December 1830, pp. 937–8)

The jury of twelve proved unable to return a unanimous verdict; six were of one mind and six of another. Lord Chief Justice Tenterden announced an acquittal.

with gardens rather than with indictments and transportations, he could not help but feel cynical towards schemes which would provide the labourers with a quarter of an acre while leaving untouched the farm of 500 acres, as well as the 5 million acres that had been enclosed by act of parliament since his birth. No scheme for social melioration in the countryside was at once more nostalgic and mindful of cottage independence than the allotment movement, which is to say that the Cobbett of the 1810s might well have supported it. But the allotment movement was too little too late, and wrongly motivated in the estimation of Cobbett, who was now less conciliatory, and more confident that the labourers could turn their recent gains into a more comprehensive recovery of their economic and political rights. It was his understanding, seconded in popular rural song, that farm workers wanted genuine farms, which for post-Swing Cobbett were to be obtained either by demand or by the forced elevation of wages to the point where no landholder could possibly afford hired labour. The employing farmer would therefore be obliged to sell out, and the sub-division of land proceed.[128]

For the rest of his days Cobbett often presented the cottage charter under the heading of 'Rural War', suggesting that the rural revolution would be ongoing until a variety of measures were adopted: the abolition of the malt

38   Cobbett in the dress that he wore at the 1831 trial. Reproduced by
permission of the Trustees of Botley Market Hall.

Cobbett trusted that his acquittal and freedom would prove 'to the lasting
benefit of the industrious, virtuous and hardly-used labourers of England,
amongst whom I was born and bred, and to prevent whom from being
reduced to live on the soul-degrading potato and water, instead of the bacon,
bread and beer, of which our fathers had plenty, I have constantly and most
earnestly laboured, during thirty out of the sixty five years of my life, always
having regarded it as my bounden duty to use all the lawful means in my
power to better their lot, be the consequences to myself what they might'
(PR, 30 July 1831, pp. 257-8).

duty, the removal of all additions to the game laws since 1760, the introduction of legislative incentives to restore living-in, the abandonment of the New Poor Law Bill, the reform of Parliament and the pardon of all those convicted during the riots. Either grant this, Cobbett demanded, or there will be further realization that the tinder box provides the labourers with a 'comparatively safe remedy' for their grievances.[129] Such was the discovery of the Hampshire landholder the Duke of Wellington, who had received his estate from a grateful nation. But now, rather than accept the need for parliamentary reform, he chased down rioters, monitored rural Radicals and hired six watchmen to patrol his estate by day, ten by night. Still his ricks went up in smoke. In contrast, Cobbett hired no watchmen at Barn Elm and Normandy farms. His corn-filled barns had the best in-surance of all: 'the good-will of the working-people'.[130]

Despite the many contemporary claims to the contrary, Cobbett was neither Captain Swing nor the primary cause of the revolt. No number of *Registers* or rural lectures could have induced the labourers to rise before they were ready. Yet Cobbett knew exactly when they *were* ready. His role in the affair was to articulate and co-ordinate Swing's programme while soliciting urban radical support and defending the movement as a whole, including those of its practices with which he did not wholly agree. Like the Mason brothers, he refused to separate the food, wage and parish cart question from the so-called modern protests of high ideology, but this is far from saying that he ignored politics or that the revolt itself was 'predictably primitive'.[131] Cobbett personified Swing's stand on behalf of traditional culture and high politics, assuming the role of a responsible and dutiful trade union leader. As Hobsbawm and Rudé have remarked,

> up to 1830, and perhaps 1835, the labourers' agitation was essentially a sort of movement which could and ought to have been trade unionist, since it was an organized (though informally organized) demand for better wages, better conditions of life and better employment. But it was at no point *formally* a trade union movement.[132]

Cobbett was the nearest thing the labourers had to a formal leader. He predicted the rising in advance, stood by his membership throughout, negotiated with employers and legislators and stood trial himself during the recriminations. He also championed the village martyrs while remind-ing the labourers that their struggle was both worthwhile and heroic. Most importantly of all, we must remember that Cobbett did not speak for himself alone. In this context, Lord Carnarvon's remark bears repeating: *Two-Penny Trash* proceeded not from Cobbett alone, but from an entire class.

CHAPTER 8

TOWARDS REVOLUTION: THE REFORM BILL, THE POOR LAW AND THE COTTAGE CHARTER

> If all the poor of Owslebury,
> For rising of their wages,
> I hope that all their enemies,
> May live for want of places.

'The Owslebury Lads', collected from a Swing rioter by the Rev. T. Roach, in 'The Riots of 1830', *Hampshire Notes and Queries*, vol. 8 (1896), pp. 97–8.

IN the village world of George Eliot's *Felix Holt*, where the *Political Register* was said to circulate, affairs of government were declared to be 'no business' of the labouring poor: their 'solar system was the parish'.[1] It was this dimension of the Hodge stereotype that Cobbett had in mind when he observed the 'great error' in the assumption that people were 'rendered stupid by remaining always in the same place'.[2] If common sense inclines us to believe that a parish-bound village worker could not possibly divine a political consciousness from a roster of proletarian experiences, then common sense has failed us. Back in the mid-eighteenth century, Thomas Bewick observed that the rural labouring poor had 'little intercourse with the World', yet he went on to observe that their ballads and cottage readings entailed a level of intellectual activity that was foreign to their employers, who devoted their undivided attention to the management of their lands.[3] If we move on to the mid-nineteenth century, we find that the solar system of Elizabeth Ashby extended no further than 16 miles from Tysoe, yet she was a great reader and a learned cottage economist.[4] Similarly bound to his parish was Henry Burstow of Horsham, who by his late sixties had never left town, except once for a week. This same man, however, knew upwards of 400 songs, many of them spiked with radical political comment.[5] It was likewise with a Suffolk farm worker who acknowledged that most members of his class 'knew little except of their own narrow district'; but as his autobiography makes clear, he was not suggesting that this inhibited political enquiries by his class.[6]

The Hodge stereotype is not simply a prejudice to be regretted and left at that. It was (and still is) the most important determinant in the modern history of English rural workers, constituting both cause and effect of their poverty and degradation. Objective poverty on the scale of the early nineteenth century had been experienced by farm workers in earlier times; indeed the main reason that we know more about rural poverty since the late eighteenth century is owing to the development of what Joanna Innes calls 'empirically-informed, conceptually-sophisticated' investigations of English rural society.[7] But this plethora of enquiries into rural poverty was not inspired by romantic impulses or by a new-found appreciation of the importance of country workers. It was more closely the reverse. The so-called 'mercantilist' thinkers of the eighteenth century had no shortage of harsh words for the supposed idleness and insubordination of village labourers, but behind their criticisms stood a strong and sincere recognition of the rural worker's importance to the national economy. This recognition was not altogether dead by 1800 (writers such as Arthur Young carried it with them as they progressed from mercantilist economics to *laissez-faire*), but post-1800 economic literature tends to downplay the labourers' economic worth.[8] At the same time, a new focus on manners and élitist constructions of education – manifested in a new genre of cultural enquiry into rural England, typified by such writers as William Howitt and Edward Lytton Bulwer – subjected the already economically devalued labourer to cultural reduction, portraying him or her as a plodding boor who possessed no 'library', imbibed sedition and embarrassed the age of improvement.

The modern stereotype of farm workers bears upon the labourers' political sensibilities in two crucial ways. First, it herded the labourers into the company of livestock, where they were viewed from a distance as 'stupid, brutal and licentious', or as little more learned 'than the horses they work with'.[9] Second, these caricatures have been inherited by our own time, where they have conditioned certain models of agrarian history that by-pass the labourer's expressive culture in order to re-register the claim that 'a natural harmony of interest' is a static characteristic of worker–employer relations since the late eighteenth century.[10] It is certainly an acceptable point that farm workers held their old country ideology in reserve, but it is simply wrong to perceive this as a rejection of class consciousness or as a species of political incompetence.

A major reason why farm workers have passed into recorded history as vessels of political ignorance is that they refused to abstract the relationship between ideology and what Cobbett called the 'great teacher, experience'. This should not be associated with simple-minded politics, for, as Cobbett knew, the ruling class itself would only abstract or theorize politics when it served to dilute the claims of labour. Thus Burke would refuse a conceptual or historical basis to the rights of man on the grounds that popular rights were unconfirmed by tradition and by the requisites of daily life. There could be no more direct an appeal to experience than this; and Cobbett knew that experience alone could challenge it:

> Nature tells [the country labourer], three times in every day, that he has *a right* to more than a sufficiency to feed himself and family as a return for his labour, seeing that, if left to plow and dig at his pleasure, he could raise with his own hands enough in one year for himself and a family to eat in five years. And thus instructed, he will not be *content* without a sufficiency and *something to spare*.[11]

The experiential basis of Cobbett's politics was not a populist device but a direct response to the empirical claims of the dominant culture. In 1816 the government was encouraged by one of its own newspapers to reprint and disseminate Burke's tract *Thoughts and Details on Scarcity*, in which it was claimed that the abolition of every sinecure and pension in the Kingdom would add not a morsel of bread or cheese to one meal of a labourer. Cobbett was more discriminating. He never pretended that the abolition of pensions and sinecures would alone relieve rural poverty, but the dominant culture's distortion of experience forced him into more empirical and less ideological emphases. Accordingly, he defined a sinecurist as one whose income was '*partly* paid by the miserable labourer who goes to the field with cold potatoes in his wallet'. This was nearer the truth than was Burke's stricture; moreover, it accorded with the experience of the elderly Sussex labourer who complained to Cobbett that he was denied relief so long as he refused to sell his cottage, and who seethed with anger upon being shown a list of sinecures held by the aristocracy.[12]

Cobbett's lectures and writings did not initiate political complaint in the villages but they did embolden it and standardize its vocabulary. In 1830, as far north as Wigton in Cumberland, there appeared a Cobbett-style handbill, issued 'by order of the Swing Union', that offered a reward of £1,000 pounds for 'the apprehension of boroughmongers, stockjobbers, tax-eaters, monopolizers, special constables, and the extinguishers of freedom'.[13] Undoubtedly it was Cobbett's sheets that a Somerset machine-breaker had in mind when he informed his judge and jury that he had long been counselled (as well as felt in his own mind) that poverty was 'neither the natural nor necessary condition of the labourer', and that 'if a Government acted with wisdom in the interest of the people ... such a state of things could not exist'.[14] Even Cobbett's doctrines on paper money, by far his most difficult topic, integrated popular experience with sophisticated thinking on economic injustice. 'I canna think where all the money's gone this fair', remarked a labourer at Appleshaw in 1830, 'I used to take back a hand full of notes; I thinks some of the big uns be at the bottom on't.'[15] Rural workers might not have understood the intricacies of currency regulation (few people did, including Cobbett himself inasmuch as he underestimated the capacity of the British economy to withstand a gradual return to payment in specie), but they did know that their interests were not at issue on Threadneedle Street or in the country bank:

> In war times when banks left off paying in cash,
> Then great speculators they made a great dash,
> Some have made their fortunes, in a few years,
> Some rose up from nothing, like mushrooms refin'd,
> And plain honest industry was left far behind.
> Wheat rose to a guinea a bushel, and then,
> Large farmers set up to be fine gentlemen,
> Those who rented large farms could get credit no doubt,
> Banks lent paper money, they wanted it out;
> And farmers who had but one thousand before,
> By credit obtained ten thousand pounds more.
> But small farmers they could no credit obtain,
> If they a large family had to maintain,
> And many of them were turned out of their bread,
> Large farmers they took their farms over their head;
> And this is the way that the small farms are gone,
> And now two or three farms are thrown into one.[16]

Whatever the origins of this text – whether the work of a country Radical or of a professional muse – it serves to show that village culture was engaging in economic debate which probed to the roots of economic injustice, and that Cobbett himself, directly and indirectly, contributed to this process.

By 1830 the villagers of England were agreed that 'we want some alteration',[17] and that 'our friend Cobbett',[18] as one song expressed it, endorsed this quest. The labourers strove, in the words of a Cambridgeshire field worker, 'politically to learn the causes of [our] altered state';[19] or as the labourer-poet John Clare put it upon reading Cobbett's broadsheets, 'I am no politician but I think a reform is wanted.'[20] Not all labourers understood Cobbett's full range of referents, yet at minimum they comprehended his images and metaphors, beginning with such elementary staples as the portrait, suspended in his farmhouse kitchen, of a gagged and bound labourer who bore the melodramatic caption 'free-born Englishman'.[21] At the same time, they endorsed his efforts to recover for popular culture the proverbs and adages that had been appropriated by the élite, such as the inscription above the entrance to a Maidstone workhouse: 'if any shall not work, neither shall he eat'. Rather than refute this wisdom of St Paul, Cobbett installed it as a motto for his lectures against sinecures and the civil list, letting the matter drop only when the inscription was effaced by a coat of whitewash.[22] Cobbett designed many roads to radicalism, but his engagement of examples from labouring life show the extent to which political sensibilities were implicit in ordinary experience and folk memory. Many times he told of his encounter with a Hampshire woman who had been informed by an excise officer that one more dip of her rush in the tallow basin would have qualified her home-made light as an excisable candle. Her raw indignation was itself political. The same applied to one Mr Chalcraft, an elderly cottager near Botley, whose good fortune it was to have some volunteer hops in his garden hedge. Rather than waste this gift of nature he erected a few poles so that he might use the hops in his small brewings. The poles soon brought a visit from the excise officer who asked him when he intended to 'enter' his crop. Chalcraft, as Cobbett related the incident, thought that his questioner was alluding to the time of harvest; accordingly he replied that he would bring in the hops on the next dry day:

> 'Hoot awa, mon', replied the exciseman, 'I mean when ye mean to enter them at our office.' It was some time before Chalcraft clearly understood him, and then he said, 'D—n you and your office and the hops too; for there they shall hang till they are carried away by the wind!' and this they actually did.[23]

Cobbett did not pretend that all labourers rushed instantly from experience to express political thoughts, but he did know that the two moved in tandem, and that the trend in the villages since 1800 had been progress towards a fuller understanding of the root causes of dispossession. This was achieved, as he so often argued, without major adjustments in the labourer's cultural or physical sense of place.

At the time of the Swing revolt, and especially in its immediate aftermath, Cobbett resumed his efforts to achieve a more open and constructive dialogue between the urban and rural reform platforms. The long history of personal antagonisms which plagued the first generation of reformers made that avenue difficult; thus increasingly Cobbett was disposed to collaborate with the new generation, including John Cleave, William

Carpenter and Henry Hetherington. Between late 1829 and 1832, he made frequent appearances and speeches at the Rotunda; and in May and June of 1832, he delivered three lectures at the meeting-house of the National Union of the Working Classes. He also encouraged, in tours and lectures, the maintenance of a hard radical line among the regional political unions which were concentrated in the Midlands and the North, and for the first time in his life he visited northern factories and toured Scotland.[24] More than at any time since 1816–17, with the possible exception of his brief campaign in the cause of Queen Caroline, he sought to pitch his discourse into conceptual territory that would speak to ultra-Radicals, secularists, Owenite co-operators (though he never made overtures towards Owen himself, whose community at New Lanark struck him as too paternal and authoritarian)[25] and even to a select and carefully vetted contingent of middle-class reformers, most notably Thomas Attwood of the Birmingham Political Union. It was a formidable campaign which could have done a great deal to reduce the Whigs to democratic options in 1832, given that in the minds of some leading members of the Whig Cabinet, Cobbett possessed a daunting trump card: the single-handed ability to bring Captain Swing back to life.[26] Cobbett himself did not make this argument, but he did inform the ruling Whigs that the riots were only temporarily halted, and that they would resume if the labourers were displeased with the Reform Bill or its state of progress through Parliament.[27]

But Cobbett had also his liabilities as a national reform leader. Try as he might, he had no essential understanding of the cultural and ideological diversity within the revived artisan radicalism of the 1830s. Secondly, at the same time as he called for a '*common understanding* amongst the people', he continued to profess (including in his six Manchester lectures at the end of 1831) that his political mandate lay in the rural South, despite his sympathy for the political and economic objectives of artisans and industrial workers. It was his purpose to construct a platform that would bring all workers together, but as a prelude to these negotiations he wanted urban reformers to honour the farm workers for inducing the Whigs to table the Reform Bill. As small-minded as this might appear, it was his way of insisting that the village workers not be isolated from the revived radical movement or from the issues to be confronted by the reformed Parliament:

> What, then, was it not the meetings and petitions of the great towns that produced the parliamentary reform? Was it not the political councils and unions, and the meetings ... that turned out Wellington, brought in Grey, and made the Reform Bill? To these questions I answer NO, as loud as I can

> write it. These meetings did good ... but, the great and efficient cause was, the movements of the chopsticks.[28]

Cobbett was asking for something that town-based Radicals could not give, or at least not so unequivocally as to reduce their own pride of place in the reform movement. Heroically, though with dubious prudence, he dared to propose the disenfranchisement of the boroughs, so as to leave only county members:

> For my part, who wish to take from the aristocracy every atom of influence at elections, I should like the thing full as well if there were *none but county members*. It is a most erroneous notion, that the country people are *ignorant* on the subject of political rights, and that they are to be led to the poll like horses. They understand the matter well, they are more stubborn than towns-people in adhering to their rights, and much more difficult to deceive and cajole.[29]

It was not easy for the town worker to applaud the 'people's bill' as the exclusive work of those in '*smock-frocks and nailed shoes*', but Cobbett had seen the farm workers' interests shuffled aside before, and he sensed the same trend in the urban political unions and the NUWC. Everywhere he looked there seemed to be class-based interpretations of reform: farmers and industrialists announced that they would stand by their interests, and Prime Minister Grey assured Parliament that he would not let down the aristocratic order. Thus Cobbett felt obliged to stand by his order – 'the Order of the Chopsticks':[30]

> Will a reform of the Parliament give the labouring man a cow or a pig; will it put bread and cheese into his satchell instead of infernal cold potatoes; will it give him a bottle of beer to carry to the field instead of making him to lie down on his belly to drink out of the brook; will it put upon his back a Sunday coat and send him to church? ... Will parliamentary reform put an end to the harnessing of men and women by a hired overseer to draw carts like beasts of burden; ... [The] enemies of reform jeeringly ask us, whether reform would do these things for us; and I would answer distinctly that IT WOULD DO THEM ALL![31]

This was wishful thinking to excess, but the fact that parliamentary reform was without modern historical precedent meant that not even the Whigs knew precisely what it would entail. Moreover, right up until the Bill's passage in June 1832, Cobbett pressured the ruling class to enfranchise the country workers, if not because they possessed property (the magic word for suffrage) in their labour, then because they would undo the chain of corruption and dependence that beguiled the old regime.[32] If Cobbett seems to have possessed exaggerated notions of the labourers' political virtue, we must remember that he had recently witnessed the backsliding of many urban political unions into the Whig mesh. 'I have observed', he remarked on the eve of the Bill's passage, that when societies of the middle or working classes 'are likely to have political weight, the Thing's people instantly join them, and soon become the leaders of them.'[33] He did not see rural workers as altogether immune from such infiltration, but he did think that their recently manifested resolve to defy the will of the gentry should earn them recognition as leading supporters of popular political independence.

Although the final version of the Reform Act did not allow for any direct exercise of the labourers' political will, Cobbett lent it his conditional support. His only other option was to join the opposition of Henry Hunt, whose position (and here Cobbett's eye might have been all too pragmatic) was manifestly unpopular among rural labourers and small freeholders.[34] Thus for the time being, Cobbett clung to the hope that small farmers would uphold the labourers' interests on election day, much as they had done during the Swing revolt.[35] The final Act, he recognized, granted working people 'only *a part*' of their rights, but it did attain the principle of reform and a foundation from which villagers could continue their struggle for 'freedom and salvation'.[36] It was a position that resembled that of the Suffolk farm worker who interpreted the measure of 1832 as a 'step in the right direction which would lead to our enfranchisement'.[37] Cobbett trusted that the Act would enhance rather than stall rural radicalism; thus he was pleased to find in rural Hampshire a placard reading 'the Reform Bill is only a stepping-stone to our future advantages. Down with the tithes! Down with the Taxes! Down with the Places! And down with the pensions!'[38] Finally, and not the least of his reasons for offering the Act his provisional approval, was his quiet confidence, shared by the Mason brothers, that his own presence in Parliament would enable him to achieve democracy and the cottage charter for English villagers.

On 7 July 1832, in commemoration of the passage of the Reform Act, Cobbett honoured the farm workers by convening a Chopstick Festival at the village of Sutton Scotney in the heart of the hard parishes. Some 7,000 village workers gathered to make merry: Cobbett brought a seventy pound ham as well as a wagon load of mutton, beef and veal; other local reformers contributed bread, plum pudding and hogsheads of beer. Not there were potatoes, which Cobbett ensured did not 'come near the place ... they have done quite enough mischief already'. Arrayed at the head tables, all decked out in frocks and blue ribbons, were the approximately 150 villagers who had signed the petition of Joseph Mason, and who were still at liberty. Despite the long shadow of the transportations and hangings the atmosphere was convivial, with the speeches brief (Cobbett spent most of his time cutting meat) and the songs long. The event, he assured his readers, was 'one of the pleasantest things that ever was seen in this world'. On the following day he travelled to Micheldever, where he visited with labourers and laid a wreath upon the tomb of Henry Cook. After moving on to Sussex he returned to London, where he began preparations to become the first chopstick in the reformed House of Commons.[39]

It is often suggested that the labourers abandoned their protests in the wake of Captain Swing, and that their politics failed to mature beyond wage demands or the cottage diet. Yet this was not the case in the rural South in general or in the hard parishes in particular. During the autumn of 1832, after the passage of the Reform Act, the Duke of Wellington complained to Home Secretary Melbourne of the existence of 'several' political clubs in north Hampshire, which he believed to be engaged in seditious correspondence with one another. According to his informers among the farmers (who were said to be 'a good deal alarmed' by these assemblages) as many as half of all the labourers of Hampshire were in some way involved in the clubs, subscribing a penny a week towards funds which Wellington alleged were intended for the purchase of arms. It was the Duke's further opinion that Cobbett was responsible for founding the unions, and that the members were in regular correspondence with him. As far as he could tell, the members had not yet caused an overt breach of the peace, though he was sorry to note that some members had advised magistrates that the unions 'would stand by them' in their demands for poor relief, and that the club members sought to obstruct employers who attempted to reduce the wage rises negotiated by Swing. It was the recommendation of Wellington, complied with, it appears, that Lord Melbourne dispatch a troop of regular soldiers to supplement the overworked yeomanry cavalry.[40]

Cobbett's involvement in these unions is not extensively documented in his private correspondence or in the *Political Register*, which he kept sanitary in the event that the Whigs decided to launch another prosecution. But the Home Secretary also knew that Cobbett communicated orally with the farm workers, for as he had lamented about Cobbett's indictment of 1831, 'nothing is so difficult to prove as the utterance of words'.[41] Melbourne was certain that the Chopstick Festival was a seditious affair, but no texts from the day were discovered – the songs of the labourers had been sung from memory. Courtesy of Wellington's informers, however, Melbourne had in his hands a document outlining the rules of the Barton Stacey union, which he recognized as modelled upon those of the NUWC, at whose meeting-place in Theobald's Road Cobbett had recently delivered three lectures on the measures that should be adopted by the newly reformed Parliament.[42] Although this apparent liaison with the NUWC might not have emanated directly from Cobbett, it suggests that the rural workers were broadening their platforms to include more contacts with urban reformers as well as a wider range of radical ideologies.[43] There is also the broader message that neither the Special Commissions nor the token of the Reform Act could distract these labourers, who were educated by experience, by Cobbett and by their own dynamic debates and initiatives, from taking charge of their own 'freedom and salvation'.

Cobbett aspired to represent a southern rural constituency, preferably the western division of his native Surrey.[44] But the new Act had done nothing to increase the rural labourer's influence at nomination meetings, much less to overcome the electoral monopolies of the gentry. In many industrial boroughs, however, the £10 franchise ensured a broader-based electorate than in the countryside, and among the first of these to nominate Cobbett was Oldham. Although grateful for the opportunity to enter Parliament, he was all too aware that he was regarded locally as the running-mate of John Fielden, the radical factory owner from Todmorden who had made his own candidacy conditional upon Cobbett's nomination.[45] Although Cobbett campaigned hard to carry the poll in his own right, it was ultimately Fielden's money and influence that secured his endorsement by the artisans and shopkeepers who dominated the borough's electorate.[46] Announcement of Fielden's victory was jubilantly received, according to a Manchester paper, that of the southerner Cobbett politely acknowledged.[47] And no sooner was the final poll reported than Cobbett took a half-step towards circumventing the spirit of his campaign speeches by announcing that the problems of rural workers (meaning principally those of the South) should be the first concern of the new House.[48]

The partnership with Fielden was potentially one of the most formidable radical alliances ever staged at Westminster. Cobbett identified himself as the 'Surrey Ploughboy' MP, and Fielden boasted of being bred and educated at the spinning-jenny.[49] In the construction of a radical consensus, Cobbett could represent the agricultural workers, while Fielden could uphold the platform of industrial and urban ones. Yet in many ways it proved a clumsy partnership. Cobbett clung to his opinions on the uselessness of the very manufactures which were Fielden's livelihood, and which ultimately provided his own ticket to Parliament. Fielden put up with these aspersions, and Cobbett reciprocated with periodic allusions to the superior working conditions in Fielden's mills,[50] yet the fact remains that he still saw agriculture and industry as antagonistic concerns.[51] He even continued to muse that cheaper beer would be a worthier innovation than the power loom, which one must take to include the 1,500 such looms that Fielden worked in his industrial complexes.[52]

Problems also emerged at the grass roots, especially as it became apparent that Cobbett perceived his mandate as that of 'head chopstick' in the battle for the cottage charter, beginning with the malt tax and the game laws.[53] To the disappointment of many of his electors he did not push for the repeal of the Corn Laws, for he feared that without a corresponding reduction in tithes and taxes, the farmers would have a ready excuse to make good their losses out of the rural labourers' wages.[54] In September of 1833, only eight months after taking his seat, Cobbett was called to account for his stewardship by John Knight, secretary of the Oldham Political Association and an active Radical since the mid-1790s. Among the complaints of the Association was Cobbett's apparent ambivalence towards book-learning (but see chapter 4) and his unexplained absenteeism from the House during the crucial divisions which gave rise to the Factory Commission.[55] Knight went as far as to imply that some of Cobbett's 'warmest adherents' in Oldham were now questioning his ability to represent the labouring people of an industrial constituency. There was truth in this, but Cobbett took no heed. 'Take no notice of that nasty conceited fool, Knight', he advised Fielden,[56] preferring to select for publication a more complimentary letter from Manchester that praised him as the champion of all working people, 'whether at the plough or the loom'.[57]

Cobbett's parliamentary career bordered on the unaccountable to his direct electors, but it is to miss the very foundations of his radicalism to describe his parliamentary career as a tribute to his 'lack of fitness to be a political leader'.[58] During his two and a half years in the House of Commons he pursued the radical programme that he had fashioned over the previous thirty years, ranging in his speeches from the malt tax to the decline of living-in and the labourers' right to a living out of the land. Where Cobbett fell down was in his failure to mount an adequate defence of institutions appropriate to what John Foster has identified as the trade union consciousness that prevailed among his Oldham constituents, but the explanation for this failure lies not in Cobbett's supposed appeal to 'the independence of the small producer'.[59] Rather, it was his commitment to the cottage charter, where questions of wages and the length of the working day (issues fundamental to a trade union consciousness, including Fielden's National Regeneration Society)[60] were subordinate to cultural and material requisitions that had few parallels in industrial protest. As he had explained to some northerners even before taking his seat, it was his intention to attend to the southern farm workers first. Thus while lending his full support to Fielden's National Regeneration movement, he concentrated his own parliamentary work on the malt tax, fully aware (as he had informed a Manchester audience in 1831) that the restoration of home-brewing was a much greater issue in the rural South than in the industrial North.[61]

The disjuncture between the cottage charter and the wages and hours platform of industrial workers was substantial, but Cobbett also failed to avail himself of the opportunity afforded by the Tolpuddle Martyrs to forge a new structural link between rural and urban workers. He recognized at once that the high-handedness of the Whigs would rouse 'millions of Englishmen', and that the plight of the Martyrs would provide rural and urban working people with a common platform; he even suggested that this collaboration might mark the beginning of 'the *Revolution*'.[62] But for all this, Cobbett *responded* to the common platform rather than led it. Part of the problem was his location, for the government found it much easier to control him from the inside of Parliament, especially now that he was the recipient of a steady stream of petitions (many on behalf of the Martyrs) which needed presenting to a Whig-dominated assembly that knew how to use parliamentary rules and procedures to delay and frustrate his task.[63] But more importantly, Cobbett had paid little attention over the years to trade union protest, primarily because of its predominantly industrial and handicraft context. The Tolpuddle Martyrs represented the rural and urban labour strategies of tomorrow, while Cobbett personified the culmination of a twenty-five-year struggle of a class to place its leader in Parliament. Having spearheaded the old strategy, and only partly comprehending the new, Cobbett understood his parliamentary and extra-parliamentary role in the terms set out in a letter of electoral congratulation from the workers of Battle: 'We regard it as a happy omen of the restitution of our country's rights, and because we know that it gladdens the heart of the agricultural labourer, who foresees that he will have, as an advocate in the great council of the nation, an able and honest man.'[64] George Loveless could not have written such a letter. Ideological investment in the parliamentary placement of one individual was not the way that the Martyrs or other rural trade unionists envisioned the radical platform. Yet Cobbett was among the first to congratulate the Martyrs' endeavours, for his purposes in Parliament were not only to represent the labourers, but to instil them with 'hope and confidence' to pursue whatever strategies best ensured their political rights. Returning to the old model of leadership that he best understood, he began to plan his autobiography, with special attention to its frontispiece, on which he wanted two portraits of himself: one showing him 'in a smock-frock, driving the rooks from the corn', the other showing him 'standing in the House of Commons, addressing the Speaker'.[65]

Cobbett's brief parliamentary career, as well as his closing political testament, centred around his campaign against the Poor Law Amendment Act. For almost thirty years, beginning with Whitbread's proposals in 1807, he had resisted attempts to reduce the Elizabethan provision, which he upheld as 'the greatest law that ever was passed'.[66] The extent of the threat posed to the Poor Law by the gradual demise of country ideology, which had served for so long as its ideological backbone,[67] was brought home to Cobbett in the Select Vestries Acts of 1817–18, from which time he redoubled his efforts to divide the gentry from the Benthamite quest to apply efficiency ratings and market considerations to the administration of relief. But as late as 1832, even as the Poor Law Commission was conducting its investigations, Cobbett was confident that the old Poor Law was safe: 'the chopsticks will see to that'.[68] This was of a piece with his understanding that the rural revolt was only in abeyance; ironically it was the same belief by the gentry and Whig legislators that convinced them of the need to sanctify a hasty marriage with the Utilitarian reformers and to proceed with revision as soon as possible.[69] Along with Nassau Senior the Whig Cabinet feared that 'sooner or later' the increases in rural wages would be rescinded, and at which point 'the peasantry will rise again – confident, from having been successful; and furious from having been deceived'.[70]

The ostensible ambition of the Poor Law reformers was to restore the independence of labour, something which Cobbett himself had called for since 1800. Yet 'independence' had a variety of objects and meanings. In Cobbett's case it had come to represent the material, cultural and political self-sufficiency of villagers in a class society. The Commissioners and the gentry, whether Whig or Tory in affiliation, gave it no precise definition, or at least no consistent one. They wanted the labourers to be dependent upon the élite for wages, politics and values; and they wanted them to be wholly independent of them in their cottage economy and search for sustenance. In the same breath as employers and legislators resisted a legislated minimum wage on the grounds that wages must be free to find their own level, they defended the restrictive Law of Settlement and maintained their own combinations in local wage-fixing – all the while ignoring the great qualitative stricture of the *Wealth of Nations* (their proclaimed guide on these matters) that the labourer be 'tolerably well-fed, clothed and lodged'.[71] In 1800, as the old moral economy was

39   Cobbett at his seat in the House of Commons. Sketch by Daniel
Maclise. Reproduced by permission of Nuffield College Library.

breaking down, an Essex parson offered an account of the respective thoughts of farmers and labourers in an employment contract. The farmer says to himself,

> I have made an agreement with all my neighbourhood to pay only 7s. a week for labour. If the labourer call this a combination of masters against labour-ers, I do not know that such a combination is contrary to law; and if it should, what evidence can the labourer produce of it. He neither has money nor courage to prosecute, and he knows he never should be employed again in this parish. At the same time there pass in the labourer's mind some reflections similar to the following. Seven shillings a week are but a poor compensation for six days maintenance; but if I refuse those wages for a single day, I must deprive my family of subsistence for a day, and on the day following I must accept the same wages from this master or some other. If I induce the other labourers to refuse to work, the farmers will bring us to justice for unlawful combinations.[72]

Employers understood 'free bargaining' to mean their freedom to apply ceilings to local wage-rates. As was said by labourers later in the century, the phrase was 'a mere *bête noir* to throw at a poor man's head – a sort of charm to be said oracularly when you cannot say anything else in reply to the short and simple annals of the poor'.[73]

The great diffusion of allowance scales from 1795 was less an ex-pression of the old moral economy than a conscious attempt by the gentry to maintain uniform wages and economically dependent workers. Even if the allowance system was in retreat by the 1830s (though there remains considerable debate on the subject),[74] employers valued the dependence and control which it seemed to offer. As a Sussex landholder reported to the 1834 Poor Law Commission, 'we can do little or nothing to prevent pauperism, the farmers will have it; they prefer that the labourers should be slaves'.[75] In their historical ignorance the Commissioners attributed the abuses of the Poor Law to the labouring poor, forgetting who it was in 1795 that opted to reject proposals for a minimum agricultural wage and instead to make dependent paupers of able-bodied labourers.[76] It was not the labourers but rather employers and magistrates who lost sight of the distinction between wages and rates:

> The poor often blame us without any cause,
> For the poor are protected by old English laws,
> The Farmers must make them both healthy and strong,
> By Wages or Rates – 'tis as broad as it's long.[77]

The labourers' point was that it was not as broad as long: parish pay was impersonal, begrudged by rate-payers and laden with the very symbols of dependence that the Poor Law Commissioners claimed to oppose. Accordingly, the cottage charter demanded full wages, and that the poor-rates be applied to their original purpose of providing insurance against sickness, old age and disability. Until employers manifested a disposition to pay a living wage, however, Cobbett and the labourers had no choice but to insist upon the preservation of allowances from the parish. The great shock of the Amendment Act, as Keith Snell has remarked, was that it should seek to end allowances without increasing wages.[78] Edwin Chadwick's glib prediction that the new measure would somehow cause a rise in wages rested upon an ill-informed assumption that employers would abandon their wage-fixing conventions, and at the very moment that the Whig Cabinet (which was in very close dialogue with the Commissioners) was desperately looking for ways to roll back the wage increases achieved by the rural revolt.[79]

Knowing that claims to tradition alone would carry little weight with the Poor Law reformers, Cobbett erected his opposition upon both customary and absolute property rights. The Poor Law, he argued, was 'the Magna Carta of the working people; it is written in their hearts; the writing descends from the heart of the father to that of the son'.[80] More directly for the benefit of the élite, who saw property as an absolute possession, he invoked Blackstone and Locke, perhaps selectively but to the prejudice of neither, in support of his argument that the poor had a legal claim on the rates, and that this claim was a part of their rightful inheritance, originating as it did in recompense for the tithes appropriated by the Crown during the Reformation. Cobbett was able to demonstrate that within the context of rural wage structures, the revised Poor Law prescribed at least poverty, and that this threatened the right to life that Locke had shown to be inalienable by civil authority. If rights in property and civil society were denied – something that the revised Poor Law effectively achieved by imprisoning the poor and separating them from their families – their lot was one of enslavement or of starvation, which either way amounted to a breach of the right to life and liberty.[81]

The Poor Law Amendment Act did not in so many words repeal the Elizabethan statute, Cobbett observed, 'but it does it *in silence*, it does it in fact'.[82] This much was recognized by the labourers, who appealed not only to custom and to the legitimizing power of popular culture, but to their *absolute* right to relief. The labourers of Swallowfield parish in Berkshire were said to view their allowances 'as much their right as the wages they receive', while at Epping in Essex they perceived 'the Parish Fund as their property'. According to Assistant Commissioner Okedon, the rates were sometimes called 'the county allowance', sometimes the 'Government allowance', other times the 'Act of Parliament allowance', but always *our income*.[83] The New Poor Law caused villagers to wonder, in the words of one, if they possessed *'any* rights in this world'.[84] Yet the emotional cries and pleas that fill urban songs on the Amendment Act were much less prevalent in the rural songs treating of the same subject. The latter threaten 'class vengeance' against those who would erect 'Whig Bastilles' or endeavour to put the new measures into full effect, but they stop short of begging for mercy.[85] For one thing the post-Swing mood of the labourers had no patience for special pleading; for another they were confident that the most oppressive features of the Act could be stopped by force of arms. And in some parishes they were during the anti-Poor Law protests of the mid and late 1830s.[86]

The labourers remembered, as Cobbett and Nassau Senior said they would, the efficacy of the Swing protests. But there was nothing new in their determination to exercise their right to life. The ruling class was often reminded of this by Cobbett, who remarked time and again that the villagers of England would not starve, even if it meant taking without leave. Their meals might appear in the shape of pheasants, hares and sheep, but appear they will, and in accordance with the natural principle that 'if they be unable to obtain bread *for work*, they have a right to it without work'.[87] In the labourers' songs of the 1820s and 1830s, landholders were offered precisely this choice. The common sense of some of their own class might have told them as much:

> It is a notorious fact, that cottages not having any ground belonging to them, promote thieving to a great extent; as their inhabitants constantly rob the neighbouring farms and gardens of roots and pulse sufficient for their own consumption; and which they would have no temptation to do, if they had the same articles growing of their own. Hence this evil admits of an easy remedy, namely, allot to each cottager a piece of ground.[88]

This matched James Hawker's explanation of why he helped himself to hog fodder and game: 'poverty is the Mother of Invention', he remarked, 'poverty made me poach'.[89] Just as workers searched in vain for biblical foundations for the separation of husbands and wives within workhouses,[90] so they were unable to locate, 'in the Testament, nor yet in the Bible', any justification for private property in game. 'We always read there', said one agricultural worker, that 'the wild animals is sent for the poor man.'[91] According to another, 'hares have no owner's brand upon them, and country people do not look upon poaching as a crime'.[92] Cobbett advanced this point often, invoking the authority of Blackstone and of popular instinct: 'I must poach *or starve*', he represented the

THE FATAL
ENGLISH POOR LAW BILL,
Or the ways of the World.

COME all you gallant Englishmen
   And listen to my ryhmes,
A word or two I will unfold,
   About these present times;
Enforcing the poor Law Bill,
   Has caused great discontent,
And through the country far and near,
   Some hundreds do relent.

CHORUS.

Go where you will both day and night,
   They are complaining still,
About that awful measure,
   That is called the Workhouse-Bill.

In Norfolk and Suffolk riots have
   Occurred for miles around,
Since passing of the Poor Law Bill,
   In Country and in Town.
If for relief you're forced to go,
   They'll part I do declare,
The father and the mother from,
   The infant children dear.

Near Ipswich town in Suffolk,
   There of late occured a row,
And how this riot did take place,
   I really can't tell how :
But as far as we can understand,
   To wound each bleeding heart,
The children from their parents,
   they did send for miles apart.

There is many a man no work could get,
   And walk about in pain,
Then ventured off to foreign parts
   To Portugal and Spain.
There for Spaniards and for Portuguese,
   In battle lost his life,
And left his family behind,
   His Children and his Wife.

Some early in the morning rise.
   Seeking work for miles he goes,
And how one half the world does live,
   Some thousands never knew.
From morning light till dark at night,
   He far employment roams,
While his tender children and his wife,
   With hunger pine at home.

Some others in a prison pine,
   And others do bewail,
And many a prattling infant says,
   My father is in gaol.
Which makes the tender mother weep,
   And sit and cry her fill
And say he never would be there,
   But for the Poor Law Bill.

Now dont you think it's very hard,
   Poor people's rights to smother,
To send the husband from the wife,
   The children from their mother.
It's done to keep poor people down,
   As you shall understand,
It never was the laws of God,
   Those laws were made by man.

In Bedfordshire and in Kent,
   And down in Norfolk too,
In Northamptonshire & Gloucester-
   shire
   And all the country through,
Near Ipswich town in Suffolk,
   There was the other day,
All through the English Poor Law Bill
   A terrible affray.

40 Ballad on the Poor Law Bill of 1834 and the rural disturbances which attended it. Reproduced by permission of the Syndics of Cambridge University Library (Madden Collection of Ballads).

labourer as saying, which 'means, of course, that he shall poach and that he cannot and will not starve'.[93] Magistrates and landowners were long and eloquent in pressing different arguments, which to the labourers said this:

> We'll transport Poachers, who dare to set snares,
> For we think more of our pheasants and hares,
> Than we do of the starving poor of old England.[94]

From time to time between 1810 and 1830, overt class legislation such as the game laws aroused in Cobbett a professed resolve to see 'every inch of property' transferred from landholders to the labouring poor.[95] In 1819 he suggested that the English rural worker had due cause to turn his hand to revolutionary radicalism, given that 'a society, in which the common labourer ... cannot secure a sufficiency of food and raiment, is a society which ought not to exist; a society contrary to the law of nature; a society whose compact is dissolved'.[96] Revolution, Cobbett argued, was the labourer's right in theory, yet he remained hopeful, right up until 1834, that country ideology could be restored, if not by the voluntary will of landlords and farmers, then by the permanent threat and periodic exercise of physical encouragement from below. It was the Poor Law Amendment Act, approved almost unanimously by the gentry within and without Parliament, that finally convinced him that the Great Reform Act had achieved nothing positive for the labourers, that country ideology and old England were irrecoverable, and that class society had arrived to stay. In July he wrote to his secretary that 'the Lords have read the poor-law Bill a second time. God damn them! But, it may be for good.'[97] To his co-member of Parliament John Fielden he wrote that 'it is revolution all together',[98] and a week before he died in June of 1835, he informed an old and trusted friend that 'before the passing of the Poor-Law Bill, I wished to avoid [a] convulsive termination. I now do not wish it to be avoided.'[99]

It might be tempting to think that Cobbett, now in his last days, felt that he had nothing to lose by recommending a violent redistribution of property. But as late as the Chopstick Festival of 1832 he had still clung to the hope – a distant one he knew – that rural employers might join the labourers in commemorating the Great Reform Act and in helping to make it work for the benefit of the labouring poor. Indeed, his own position on that measure showed more confidence in the electoral sensibility of small farmers than in that of shopkeepers, artisans and industrial workers. While visiting Scotland in 1832, he had written two broadsheets of *Advice for the Chopsticks* in which he proudly reflected upon the 43rd of Elizabeth as a monument to a peculiarly English propensity for fairness and justice, despite these qualities having fallen on hard times among the higher orders. Similarly, during his tour of Ireland in 1834, he wrote ten letters to one of his farm workers, Charles Marshall, in which he described the gruesome poverty of Irish farm workers and peasants. Much of this poverty he attributed to the absence of an English-style Poor Law. It was the Amendment Act that brought a bitter end to Cobbett's trust that the English élite would stop short of corrupting the one statute that set them apart from the élites of other countries. And as he advised Marshall, it also erased the last vertical tether in a horizontal rural society.[100]

Thus it was for ideological reasons that Cobbett committed himself to revolution. For the first time in his life he began to give serious consideration to the revolutionary land plan of the Spenceans. His former ambivalence towards the Spencean platform had rested upon its tolerance of physical force, together with his disagreement with its definitions of property.[101] Formerly, unlike most prominent Spenceans, Cobbett had not recommended the democratic or communitarian control of land. Instead he endorsed its private ownership on the condition that landowners recognize both customary rights and the natural right of everyone to a living out of the soil, which living could take the form of wages, poor relief or the cultivation and possession of the soil, but not exclusively or necessarily the latter.[102] His position now was that landholders had declared absolute ownership of the land; the labouring poor, he argued, should do likewise.

Cobbett's arrival at a definitive theory of permanent class struggle and of revolutionary radicalism came late in his career, and it would be misleading to cast his thirty years of radical endeavour in this context alone. Soon after returning to England in 1800, he had discovered class in the labourer's consciousness and objective experiences, but even this he represented and perceived in terms of a wider cottage charter which embraced many traditional aspirations and ideals of village England. The point was made at the start of this work that Cobbett articulated and personified both radical ideology and cultural traditionalism. Many commentators, as we have noted, understand this as contradiction, or else flee through the back door of 'Tory radicalism' or 'populism'. It might not be too prosaic to suggest that properly to understand Cobbett and his relations with his rural constituency, we must keep that back door locked, and deal with his platform alongside of the referents that he claimed for it: the labourer's own cottage charter.

Heading the charter were the three Bs: bread, bacon and beer.[103] As a youth Cobbett had carried all three to the field;[104] like the labourer John Buckmaster he heralded them as 'the perfection of happiness' in rural life and labour.[105] The labourers liked 'a drop of Good Beer', preferably strong ale 'as brown as a berry', and they wanted to brew it at home with their own untaxed ingredients.[106] Along with Cobbett (whose parliamentary speeches returned again and again to the malt duty) they deplored the innovations of tea and potatoes:

> Tea kettle and potato plot
> What black-arsed things they be,
> Wealth has made these the workman's lot,
> Can such a land be free?[107]

The labourers understood 'freedom' partly to mean the possession of basic material comforts and a self-sufficient cottage economy which enabled them to 'cut and carve for themselves'.[108] Further towards this end, they wanted a pig, access to common land and the recovery of joint-stools, pewter dishes and the fustian coat.

The material provisions of the charter were ridiculed by the ruling élite. In the words of one witness to the 1834 Poor Law Commission, the labourers 'seem to have the idea of nothing beyond bread, bacon and beer'.[109] He was wrong, for the charter also demanded old English hospitality, harvest home, annual holidays, as well as the ideological premises which had sponsored these feasts and traditions. As is apparent in popular rural song, the labourers were reluctant participants in the class struggle; they preferred the times when master and man behaved as 'man and brother', were 'happy in their station' and did 'oft agree at a spree'.[110] But as employers withdrew into a class culture of their own, the labourers responded in kind; they denounced the new-fashioned farmer, honoured the 'labouring' man ahead of the old 'countryman', while moving deeper into the politics of radicalism. The insolence and luxury of the large farmers, said a labourer in the 1840s, 'made men think on things they never would ha' thought on'.[111]

Rural workers did not passively accept a proletarian life. They deemed large farms an act of class robbery, and they rejected every argument in their defence:

> I've heard some farmers say where is the harm,
> To rent one thousand acres in one farm?
> There would be little harm we must allow,
> If there was no one else to live but you.[112]

Out of the ashes of large farms, Cobbett and the labourers hoped, 'small farmers will rise again into life'.[113] They would sometimes claim that three farms had been rolled into one; other times four, six, ten and twenty;[114]

the important thing was not the number of farms engrossed but the new number to be created, as well as the labourers' state of mind upon them:

> Take the larger farms and divide them into ten,
> That we might live as happily as we did then.[115]

The labourer's ideal was to acquire a farm of about 30 acres, and to manage it with minimal dependence on hired labour and the market.[116] And if daily labour had to be the condition of some of their number, they wanted unassuming and unpretentious employers, such as the 'round-frocked' farmers discovered in 1809 by William Stevenson in the weald of Surrey:

> [They are] men who are shy and jealous in their communications ... with much of the ignorance and prejudice of former times, and with all its rigid and inflexible honesty – on whose bare word the utmost reliance may be placed, and who have so little of the *impartial* spirit of commerce, that they prefer selling their grain to an old customer at a lower price, to deserting him and accepting a higher offer from one with whom they have not been in the habit of dealing. The 'round-frocked farmers' (for they pride themselves on frequenting the markets in the dress of their forefathers ...) consider it absolutely necessary for the management of their farms, that they should work like their labourers.[117]

More important than either land or labour was England; the labourers did not want to emigrate, even if it meant forgoing some other aspects of the charter.[118] As Edwin Chadwick (whose own Poor Law Report was a thinly veiled treatise on compulsory emigration) discovered, 'they think the land is not half-cultivated; they often say, "there's no use in going to America, there's America enough at home, if the farmers would but let them cultivate the land"'.[119]

Not wanted by the labourers was a free ride. They wanted to earn a living by the sweat of their brow. When at the Chopstick Festival Cobbett remarked upon the labourer's willingness to work hard, his 7,000-strong audience replied with one voice: 'Yes, sir, we are always willing to work hard, if they will but let us have victuals and drink.'[120] Early rising and long working days, so relentlessly advocated by Cobbett, were not opposed in the charter, providing the labourers had fair treatment and hope for the future. As a class they did not 'seek a *fortune*', as Cobbett put it; nor did they wish to idle away their lives upon the public purse.[121] They wanted only fairer access to nature's provisions, for they saw daily that

> Nature's hand is open wide,
> She has a table spread,

> For all, then why is man denied,
> By man, his daily bread?[122]

This was the great question of the cottage charter as nurtured and represented by Cobbett and the village workers. Parallel to Cobbett's own career, the political content of the charter had taken radical directions since 1800, but this did not alter Cobbett's assessment that 'there never was a working people in the whole world, so easily satisfied'. The chopsticks were 'activated by no *caprices*' or '*imaginary wants*',[123] but when the core of the charter was denied or rescinded, they formed themselves into a class, committed themselves to radical political solutions, and exclaimed: 'a pot of beer for a penny and bread for two pence: Cobbett King'.[124]

EPILOGUE: PLOUGHING THE HOME FIELD

I don't know what period he belonged to, but I had the pleasure of burying him.

The Rev. Hume, rector of Meonstoke, cited in *Hampshire Notes and Queries*, vol. 11 (1898), pp. 81–2.[1]

Not a single person ever speaks, acts, or appears to feel for the poor agricultural labourers. They may be reduced to skin and bone, they may die for want, and their dead bodies may be sold and cut to pieces, and who speaketh in their behalf but this man?

Thomas Brothers, a professed 'Cobbettite', 1833, *PR*, 13 July 1833, p. 96.

> May the poor find relief in good ale and roast beef,
> And assuage every grief with good stuff in each hand.
> May Cobbett, triumphant, soon carry his measures;
> His just propositions will set the 'thing' right;
> May the nation no longer be robb'd of its treasures,
> And the base Whigs and Tories sink out of sight.

Sung at a meeting of the Friends of William Cobbett, 1833, *PR*, 13 July 1833, p. 97.

D URING the last year of his life Cobbett kept a daily diary in which he noted his schedule of lectures on the Poor Law, the days on which he presented petitions to Parliament and the subjects of that week's *Register*. Alongside of these political notations are detailed records of his agricultural activities; the final entry, for example, written in faint hand a week before his death in June 1835, states simply 'Ploughing Home Field'.[1] These homely last words remind us that Cobbett saw nothing extraordinary or quaint about his merger of radical politics with rural culture and the daily routine of farming. Yet upon his death the obituaries of the country's leading newspapers saw fit to pass swiftly over his origins as a 'self-taught peasant' (*The Times*) or 'common agricultural labourer' (*The*

Morning Chronicle) in order to reflect upon his political and journalistic vocations, which they measured according to metropolitan models of culture and politics.[2] And so it is today: Cobbett's rural associations continue to be seen as a curious and inexplicable aside to his political career.

Raymond Williams once observed that the twentieth-century British Left has failed to regard Cobbett as 'a problematic figure'.[3] Over the past several decades it has been conservative scholars who have dominated the study of Cobbett, and the general effect of this monopoly has been the dispersal of Cobbett's radicalism into an abstracted 'populism' or an abiding Toryism. The Left has mounted no challenge to these arguments, doubtless because folk tradition and cottage politics, despite the current surge of work in the 'culture of politics', have become increasingly estranged from the theory and practice of left-wing radicalism. There is also a tendency on the Left to see Cobbett as shallow on political theory, as having yielded too much ground to folk culture and as having removed ideology from politics by reducing the rights of man to a question of bread, bacon and beer. These assessments are misguided and unjust – Cobbett wrote widely and thoughtfully on political theory, he perceived a close relationship between ideological construction and daily experience, and he integrated the three Bs into his search for the economic justice and political democracy that the term 'radicalism' properly denotes. But the Left's difficulty with Cobbett does not end here, for many of its representatives have uncritically applied a Tory imprint to rural England. Richard Johnson, for example, notes that 'since Cobbett almost always had in mind the village labourer or small farmer, his prescriptions have an old-fashioned or "Tory" ring'.[4] But why should this be so? Toryism, like radicalism, is nothing more or less than a political ideology; it carries no preconceived prescriptions about old England or the accidence of rural life. The same can be said for that much-abused phrase 'Tory radicalism', which, if it means anything at all in relation to rural society, might properly describe Michael Sadler's attempt to federate the altar, the throne and the cottage. Such was also the quest of Cobbett during the late 1790s, but the discharge of this ideal by 1805 left him an unqualified Radical who subordinated the Crown and the church to the politics of the cottage. The paternalism which Tory radicalism is thought to feature was likewise discharged by Cobbett as he came to recognize the objective experiences which gave rise to a consciousness of class among rural workers; and whatever symptoms of patriarchy or deference he retained, these did not erode or displace the primacy of class consciousness in his political theories and practices. Cobbett was a class writer who took his final leave of Toryism, including its so-called radical variant, when he shifted away from country ideology to a class-based analysis of rural England. His solutions to the dispossession of the rural poor looked backward and forward, but his uniform purpose was to move rural England towards a new day of political and economic democracy.

In cultural matters, it is true, Cobbett often sought to conserve, but only those traditions and beliefs which the people controlled and which advanced their class interests. The numerous scholars who have attempted to wedge Cobbett into a notional 'populism' have failed to recognize the radical and liberating qualities of many of his cultural prescriptions, particularly his challenge of ruling-class versions of patriotism, Englishness and the supposed backwardness of the English past. The fact that Cobbett deferred to the aspirations of his rural constituency should not be downgraded into an abstract 'populism' but rather elevated into a legitimate and definitive model of popular politics that sought to raise political consciousness within the context of the people's own experiences and testimonies. If 'populism' entails blind subscription to mass opinion within a reform movement, then Cobbett the 'populist' should have gone along with the assumption of urban reformers that country workers (in the words of Francis Place) possessed 'no will of their own', and that Cobbett himself was 'too ignorant' to see that all working people must remain 'imbecile' if not encouraged by leaders with money and influence.[5] Place was sadly mistaken: Cobbett fully recognized the importance of working-class leadership, but not at the price of forgoing his trust in the capacity of individuals and communities to understand their own interests and those of the nation.

Perhaps a legitimate means of measuring the meaning of Cobbett's popular leadership is to pose the counter-factual query of the rural worker's position without him. Merely to contemplate the question calls to mind Marx's observation that a peasantry (and almost certainly he would have included the English rural workers, whose aspirations were peasant-like in the sense that they aspired to cease proletarian employment by owning the land that they farmed) requires economic and political representation from individuals who 'must appear as their master, as an authority over them'.[6] This assumption, far from dead, has been the great contribution of the Left to the stereotype of Hodge as deficient in independent political will. It was an assumption that Cobbett did not share, partly because it neutralized the political sensibilities of his own boyhood, and partly because it did not accord with his subsequent experience in rural communities, where cultural and political leadership was so obviously provided by song-leaders, popular tradition and the likes of Robert and Joseph Mason. According to Marx's view, the representatives of rural popular politics should have been farmers and landlords; but seldom were they. Rural workers assigned and endorsed their own leaders, including Cobbett, who rarely invoked his position as a master or imposed his authority from above. Marx, like Place before him, mistakenly assumed that deference to external authority was a uniform impulse among peasants and rural workers, and that without leadership external to their class, country workers would flounder in a political vacuum, or embrace whatever bourgeois aspirations came their way.

So where does this leave Cobbett as rural leader? We can say that for all his frontal leadership on the urban platform, he led the country workers from the back. The aggressive and uncharitable face that he often showed in metropolitan politics had much to do with the fact that he was not comfortable in that venue; his home and identity lay in the rural South, where he opted to listen and to share in a rural idiom that he valued and understood. Cobbett's practical significance as a rural labour leader lies in the cultural sensitivity with which he represented the cottage charter, and in his heroic struggles to implant that platform in labourer–farmer relations, in the national reform movement and ultimately in parliamentary legislation. In his own day he helped to instil in rural workers a new height of confidence in the national significance of their charter, and he showed them that one of their own number could take charge of their interests in the public press and in the House of Commons. Although no ordinary rural worker could have achieved Cobbett's intercession of high and low politics, no one without a rural labouring heritage could have won the confidence of the country workers themselves. Paradoxically, it was by virtue of his self-education and his temporary removal from the English countryside that he was able to represent the non-literate ploughman, and it was the same special learning that endowed him with the ability (in the words of one worker) to teach 'us to think for ourselves'.[7]

The methods of Cobbett's leadership were appropriate to his day and to his audience, yet this is not to agree with the verdict of The Times in 1835 that 'as a portion of history he is extinct'.[8] It might be argued that in terms of the modern trade union movement, Cobbett's imprint has been negligible, and certainly we must resist any temptation to suggest that he would have collaborated any more effectively with Joseph Arch or George Edwards than he did with Hunt and Burdett. But despite the many detractions that can be made out of Cobbett's reluctance to share leadership on the urban platform, we must remember that he chose to lead the rural labourers as he found them: stationed within their communities, sometimes dubious of outsiders, suspicious of change for change's sake and as too demographically fractured to match the mass political assemblies of the towns. Cobbett did not try to revise these structural characteristics of rural England (hence his cultural conservatism, if we wish to call it that), yet he did create new political networks in the countryside that amounted to a primitive trade union that was centralized in his person and programme. In Regency England, as the fate of the Tolpuddle Martyrs made all too apparent, a more overt or mass-oriented rural trade union movement would not have succeeded, and Cobbett knew it. His leadership was pragmatic, and successful because of it. Indeed, had Cobbett lived until mid-century, Sidney Godolphin Osborne might not have lamented in 1848 (much as had Cobbett himself a half century earlier) that 'the labourer has few to speak for him'.[9] This apparent return of voicelessness to the rural poor attests to the importance of Cobbett's rural representations in their own time, and it also affirms that his style of leadership was not undermined by the appearance of agricultural trade unions from the 1870s. Soon after the foundation of the NALU, Richard Jefferies would confidently proclaim that the country worker possessed no clearly defined 'Cottage Charter' and no 'genuine programme for the future'.[10] Cobbett would not have allowed such comment to pass; he would have stood up to Jefferies's Toryism and disproved his claim that Hodge was incapable of articulating his own rights and aspirations. Thus in the end, Cobbett's greatest legacy is his challenge to the Hodge stereotype that continues to plague much rural history in our own time. Marx, Place and Jefferies – representative of socialism, liberalism and Toryism – held in common a mistrust of the labourer's capacity for independent political thought, which leads us back to the reluctance of either Left or Right to recognize village workers as worthy political agents in need of historical rescue.

Cobbett ploughed the home field both literally and metaphorically. Not only did he hold the plough himself until his last days, he also cultivated his fields in the manner of Voltaire's Candide, attending first to his own class and nation. Many other Radicals were more cosmopolitan and less culturally and occupationally specific, but this is not to say that they attained a higher level of ideological awareness or of class consciousness. Paine and Owen sought to distance themselves from the past and from Cobbett's particular pride in being English; they also went further in anticipating socialism; but there can be no thorough history of radicalism or of rural England, and no genuine political party of labour in the present, that fails to attend to the needs of rural workers.

Rural England today remains home and workplace for tens of thousands of labouring people who have no more in common with their gentrifying middle-class neighbours, or with the practitioners of agribusiness, than Cobbett or the labourers had with the landed merchant or the new-fashioned farmer. So while we might continue to delight in the pastoral images of Cobbett's rural writings, we must not forget their radical political context, and that today's 250,000 farm workers, now relegated to an outpost of the Transport and General Workers, remain among the lowest paid and most ignored members of the British workforce. It is to take a large step towards understanding Cobbett to recognize that his spirit and representations are still necessary to correct an agricultural economy that values the interests of capital over the needs and rights of human labour. The chopsticks, as his first mission reminds us, are the heart, the mind and the hands of rural England.

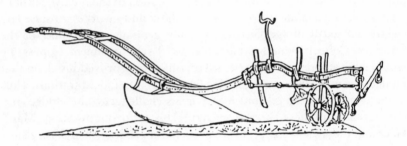

APPENDIX I

POPULAR RURAL SONG

THE lyrical repertoires of Regency villagers were dominated by two main genres of oral and printed verse. First there were the traditional black-letter ballads, often of Tudor and Stuart dating, whose world was dominated by riches and the chivalrous exploits of the nobility. Among the popular heroes of these traditional ballads were Dick Whittington, Robin Hood and the Gallant Poachers, who derived their memorability from their interaction with the élite and from their emancipation from daily labour. The second category of verse was the white-letter broadside which made its appearance at the end of the eighteenth century, and which became the flagship of the pedlar's pack for the next hundred years.[1] If from a literary perspective the white-letter broadsides are inferior to the elegant verse and measured metre of the traditional ballads, the fact remains that they stole market-share from the old ballads, especially after the Napoleonic Wars. The new songs are shorter and more topical; they are more apt to discuss wages and class antagonisms than the amours of Chevy Chase and Barbara Allen. Thus was born in the post-war period a new class of agrarian protest song which was *for* and *about* the country worker. It took its place in the pedlar's pack alongside of chapbooks, traditional ballads, the songs of Hannah More, the tracts of the SDUK and the radical wares of Cobbett's press.[2]

An attempt to ascertain the authorship of popular songs, I would argue, is a fruitless and needless task. At the end of the nineteenth century it was widely believed that folk songs were collectively authored by the village community, and to this day many folklorists refuse to abandon the vision of a group of villagers spontaneously breaking into identical lyrics.[3] The subject of authorship is a non-issue, for as Roger Chartier and Michael Pickering have pointed out, it is the consumption rather than the production of cultural forms that most matters in the analysis of popular thought.[4] A song-maker's creation, in the late Bert Lloyd's words, acquires general currency only when it expresses 'the thoughts and feelings of his community'.[5] The original composer of a song is therefore a drafter of a declaration or edict which a community or class is free to accept, reject or revise. 'The creative folk composer', suggests Hugh Tracey, 'is the mouthpiece for his less articulate countrymen. If they agree with what he expresses, it becomes their own voice also.'[6]

These words reach out to Cobbett's meaning. As with the songs of the rural workers, his texts required traditional signs and symbols to acquire currency in oral and printed culture. The successful broadside, writes Albert Friedman, had 'to be immediately assimilable. On the formal side, it could not vary widely from the norm ... [and] in content, the attitude had to be one which fell in with what was believed or about to be believed.'[7] It was in its content rather than in its formal properties that a song performed ideological experiment. For many village workers, part of the attraction of a song or of a Cobbett tract lay in its normative cultural formulas; its political potential lay in its capacity to rally those traditional symbols, such as fair play, on behalf of experienced injustice.[8] Thus the successful song or political broadside walked a tight-rope between traditional and current referents, catering to the human craving for the traditional and the topical, the poetic and the pragmatic. If the old ballads emphasize the poetic and the traditional, the new songs emphasize the topical and the pragmatic, which points to the structuring of a new relationship between past and present, the traditional and the topical, in rural popular culture. This new orientation was not dismissive of the past, but it did adjust the dynamics between deference and class, the supernatural and the natural, fantasy and experience.

The co-existence of old and new values and ideologies in the pedlar's pack serves as a reminder that we should not assume that popular literature has the capacity to instil cultural and intellectual uniformity in an audience. It can focus the attention of a class or community, and even organize it for concerted response to social and economic problems, but it cannot reduce an audience to an undifferentiated polity. Alan Lomax ventures to say that songs are restricted to matters on which a community is in 'maximal accord',[9] but this fails to account for the co-existence in village culture of songs calling for insurrection against taxes and boroughmongers, and songs calling for a more peaceful and compliant response to change. Popular literature, including Cobbett's texts, should be seen as a discourse that resisted the politics of the dominant culture while embracing some of its values and moral priorities. Thus that which has too often been identified as contradiction in Cobbett – most notably his blend of radicalism and traditionalism – is expressive of popular attempts to reconcile innovative ideologies with traditional cultural forms. Much of Cobbett's success on the rural radical platform can be explained by the fact that unlike Thomas Paine, for example, he explored innovative ideologies without reducing inherited cultural traditions. Popular culture, then, should be understood as an historically rooted, descriptive and normative understanding of the way the world works, and ideology as a statement of the way it should work. It is in its ideological expressions that rural popular culture ventures away from normative description and towards innovative prescription, which it was a major purpose of Cobbett's to transform into the shared meanings of a class.

THE PETITION OF THE HARD PARISHES

(From *Trash*, July 1832)

TO THE
KING'S MOST EXCELLENT MAJESTY

The humble petition of the undersigned persons, belonging to the working and labouring classes of the parishes of Wonston, Barton Stacey, and Bullington, near Winchester, together assembled within their respective parishes,

Showeth,
That, ready and proud to acknowledge your Majesty our lawful Sovereign, we are willing to pay every respect and submission so far as reason and justice dictate, flattering ourselves that this is all your Majesty expects or demands.

That Kings and Governments were instituted for the happiness, welfare, and for the better regulating, civil society; to protect the weak against the strong, the rich against the poor, the poor against the unjust encroachments of the rich, in short, to watch over and protect the welfare and happiness of the people, and this we doubt not will be your Majesty's endeavour, so long as your Majesty sway the royal sceptre.

That, relying on this, and availing ourselves of the liberty the laws of our country afford us, namely, that of 'petitioning the King', we humbly implore your Majesty to cast an eye of pity to the misery and wretchedness that at this moment pervade every part of this country, and of which your Majesty's petitioners have their full share. That many of us have not food sufficient to satisfy our hunger; our drink is chiefly the crystal element; we have not clothes to hide the nakedness of ourselves, our wives, and our children, nor fuel wherewith to warm us; while at the same time our barns are filled with corn, our garners with wool, our pastures abound with cattle, and our land yields us an abundance of wood and coal; all of which displays the wisdom, the kindness, and mercy of a great Creator on the one hand, and the cruelty, the injustice, and the depravity of his creatures on the other. Nearly to this state of misery have your Majesty's humble petitioners long lived, anxiously looking forward for better days; but to our great sorrow and disappointment, we find oppression daily press heavier and heavier on our shoulders, till at length we are driven to the brink of despair. This misery and wretchedness do not proceed from any fault on the part of your Majesty's petitioners, as we use every exertion in our power to subdue these bitter evils; but experience tells us that 'all is vain'. Some of your Majesty's wealthy subjects impute this prevailing depression to an 'over-population', which we positively deny, seeing there is an abundance for the lowest of your Majesty's subjects, if possessed of the ability to purchase. But your Majesty's petitioners more reasonably and justly impute it to a misapplication of the produce of talent and industry; and this proceeds from a misrepresentation in the Commons House of Parliament.

That not one of your Majesty's petitioners has ever been allowed to exercise his right of voting at an election; that right, by the present system, being confined to the rich, in consequence of which, men have been returned to serve in Parliament in whom the people have no confidence; who consult not the people's welfare and happiness, but have entered into unnecessary and unjust wars, to defray the expenses of such wars, and other useless purposes, have laid and are still laying on us, without our consent, an immense weight of taxes, directly contrary to the law of the land, which says, 'that money shall not be taken out of the pockets of the people in the shape of taxes without their consent, or the consent of their representatives'. Such is the language of the supreme law of the land, and is as binding upon every branch of the Government, as the common law is on the subject: and though now we are at the distance of sixteen years from war, the taxes continue but little abated.

That, in consequence of this misrepresentation in the Commons or People's House of Parliament, we have to complain that upwards of £50,000,000 annually are extorted from that part of Great Britain called England, and of which sum the middle and labouring classes pay the greatest part; whilst the Government of the United States of America cost the 12,000,000 of people they govern not so many thousands, in consequence of which the people so governed, live in the greatest state of ease and happiness. We complain that this tax lie most heavy on those articles which are the necessary of the poor man's life; such as malt, hops, tea, sugar, tobacco, soap, candles, &c. &c.: which cause the price of those articles to be twice their real value; that our wages at this time are not more than nine shillings-a-week (at Barton Stacey but eight shillings), out of which we have to pay, one shilling for the rent of our house, and one for fuel, leaving but seven shillings per week, or one shilling per day for the support of a man, his wife, and three children. That at this time the tax on a bushel of malt, or a pound of tea, amount to as much as the labouring man's wages do in two days and a half. We complain that part of the money extorted from us go to pay the interest of a debt, part of which was contracted by the unnecessary wars, and a part of our fathers' fathers' great grandfathers. We complain that another part of the fruit of our labours go to pay grants, pensions, sinecures, &c. &c., wantonly heaped on the heads of the aristocracy and their relations, whose names are known only by the vast sums they receive, and who has never rendered the country any service whatever. We complain that (according to the statement of Sir James Graham), 113 of his late Majesty's Privy Councillors receive amongst them £650,000 per annum, some of whom are members of the Commons House of Parliament, this being contrary to Magna Charta, which says, 'That no person who has an office, or place of profit under the King, or who receives a pension from the Crown, shall be capable of serving as a member of the House of Commons.' We complain that notwithstanding a peace of sixteen years, we have a standing army of nearly 100,000 men, fed and clothed out of the fruit of our labour; part of which force is kept to compel us to pay the dreadful burdens heaped on our shoulders; we complain that, among this force, is twice as many officers as is necessary, such as generals, admirals, colonels, captains, &c., who receive immense salaries, and what chiefly are in some way or other related to the aristocracy; we complain that we never had a voice in the legislature, though, by the law, we are all liable to serve as soldiers, and shed our blood in the defence of our country, in any war the legislature please to engage in; we complain, that that property, commonly called church-property, is applied to very bad and useless purposes, purposes which have no concern whatever with religion; that whilst many poor clergy have scarce enough to maintain the dignity of their calling, others have four, five, six, and seven livings and places of profit; and whilst some of the bishops have revenues amounting to from ten to thirty, thirty-five, and £40,000 annually; that notwithstanding these immense revenues, the bishops, and other rich men in the church, are often calling on us to 'subscribe liberally' towards funds for erecting and enlarging churches and chapels, and for propagating the gospel in foreign parts. As to the uselessness of this church-property, we would cite one instance; that in this parish of Barton Stacey, the great tithes, which in most part are sold from the church, are worth nearly £1,000 per annum, the small tithes, £450 and which belong to the Dean of Winchester. A curate is hired for about £100 per annum, and who does duty twice on every Sabbath day; that the £1,350 between the money collected and the curate's salary has no more concern with religion than the sturdy ox has with the pretty affairs of the bees; nearly half as much as all the labourers in the parish earn, and which is as much loss to the parish as though taken and thrown into the sea; we complain that trial by jury, so highly valued by our ancestors as to be deemed almost sacred, has been, in many cases, abolished from our courts of justice, placing it in the power of magistrates to imprison and otherwise punish us, and who are chiefly members of the aristocracy, officers under the crown, or clergy of the established church, who, notwithstanding live on the fruit of our labour, often insult and haughtily treat us; so that Sir John Pollen, who is the present member for Andover, in the vicinity of which town we live, and a magistrate, did, at a meeting in that town, call us 'poor devils'; and who, he said, 'had hardly a rag to cover them'. We complain, that notwithstanding the misery and half starvation to which we are reduced, the law, under severe imprisonment and heavy fine, forbids us to take for our own use the wild birds and animals that inhabit the woods and fields, or the fish that swim in the water; those being kept not for the service, but for the sports of the rich.

That this unnatural state of things, this misery, this wretchedness, this woe, this degradation, this want, this half-starvation in a land of plenty, proceed from a misrepresentation of that which ought to be the Commons House of Parliament, the members of which are returned by the rich, contrary to the will of the people. That at the election for this county, held at Winchester in August last, one of the members was returned against the will of nineteen-twentieths of the county; a person in whom we have no confidence; who has, in all cases of importance to the poor, voted on the side of oppression, and who was obliged to leave the place of election in disguise for fear of the just-enraged people who had assembled.

Having now laid our sufferings before your Majesty, and the fountain whence they spring, we humbly implore and earnestly pray your Majesty to exercise your royal authority, so far as to cause radical reform in the Commons House of Parliament. Many projects have been made to this effect, even by some of its members, but on a principle calculated to yield us but little or no redress, showing partiality, and which has been proceeded on with such coldness as to denote insincerity on the part of its projector. The mode of reform (sweet word) which your Majesty's humble petitioners would recommend as highly beneficial to the country at large, and to which no honest, fair, and upright man can object, is that of annual Parliaments, universal suffrage, and vote by ballot, but above all we prize the ballot. Till this takes place we, your Majesty's humblest petitioners, can never have the full employment of our hard earned little; not daring to look forward for better days, for the least alleviation of our miseries, or for the enjoyment of those blessings which a merciful God has in profusion thrown round about us.

And your petitioners, as in duty bound, will ever pray.

WONSTON

Enos Diddams
Andrew Diddams
William Snow
Jacob Bay
George Diddams
Henry Wooderson
John Wheeler
John Mills
John Wigmore
Samuel Leach
John Hoar
George Berriman
Thomas Taylor
Edward Wm. Hoar
William Taylor
Richard Pike
Charles Lester
Charles Leach
John Berriman
Joseph Groves
William Ramble
William Lewis
William Ralph
William Norris
William Pearce

William Fisher
Thomas Newman
Joseph Newman
Thomas Wheeler
John Reynolds
James Whichler
George Gamester
Michael Chives
Richard Dollery
Nathaniel Newman
Charles Collis
William Monday
Henry Pitter
John Lewis
Charles Goodfellow
Robert Groves
James Groves, Jun.
Joseph Carter
James Leach
James Taylor
Charles Leach
John Ramble
Charles Marks
William Rudun

Charles Newman
Stephen Newman
John Pearce
James Wits
Thomas Butcher
Thomas Stock
John Newman
George Newman
George Judd
Richard Ventham
Edward Tarrant
Thomas Judd
Charles Diddams
Henry Taylor
Peter Mason
William Rye
George Ball
John Smith
John Hopgood
William Goodall
Thomas Self
Thomas Stub
William Jones
John Tomkins

BULLINGTON

Robert Mason
Thomas Malt
James Pierce
William Gerome

Jacob White
Richard Ventham
Francis Ray
William Goodal

Emmanuel Baverstock
Ambrose Courtney
John Courtney
John Sackley

James Tribbeck
James Ray
George Hatcher
William Perry
Thomas Dudman
James Clifford
Stephen Grist, Jun.
William Scarlet
George Ford
Daniel Rudwic
George Clifford
William Brown
William Dudman

George Goodal
James Taylor
Stephen Maton
John Silcock
Joseph Silcock
Joseph Diddams
John Bastin
John Wheeler
George Wheeler
Peter Wheeler
Richard Withers
Thomas Beaverstock

Joseph Mason
William Sackley
Edmund Sackley
Samuel Sackley
James Maton
Henry Benham
Henry Knoles
Philip Parsons
Charles Anhal
James Tarrant
James Allen
Charles Perry

BARTON STACEY

James Diddams
Charles Blackman
Thomas Tatmage
Henry Hunt
Robert Anthony
Thomas Beryman
John Dore
Charles Stubs
James Ball
John Joyne
Joseph Beryman
William Reynolds
William Mills
John Mackmaster
Nathaniel Panton
George Dazel
John Pane

William Propal
James Wield
George Cannon
Isaac Farmer
James Wheeler
William Garger
Thomas Pitters
Thomas Annal
George Guyatt
Robert Elliott
James Ball
James Antony
John Adams
James Panton
Benjamin Caselman
William Lack
Thos. Becyman, Jun.

Richard Mills
William Roe
Anthony Anthony
Edward Antony
David Cosetman
Robert Hays
Charles Hutchener
James Rolf
Charles Davis
Henry Bugis
Daniel Diddams
Charles Ball
William Pane
John Pane
George Pane
John Guyatt
John Carter

MAY GOD SPEED YOUR PETITION

Mr. Thomas Alexander

Mr. James Prictow

NOTES

1 'COMMON CAUSE': COBBETT AND THE VILLAGE WORKER

1 Karl Marx, letter to the *New-York Daily Tribune*, 22 July 1853; Matthew Arnold, 'The Future of Liberalism', in R. H. Super (ed.), *English Literature and Irish Politics* (Ann Arbor, 1973); G. K. Chesterton, *William Cobbett* (London, n.d., 1926); Michael Foot, *Debts of Honour* (London 1980), *passim; idem*, 'A Radical Spirit', *The Observer*, 4 September 1983; A. J. P. Taylor, 'William Cobbett', in A. J. P. Taylor, *Essays in English History* (London, 1976); Raymond Williams, *Cobbett* (Oxford, 1983); Asa Briggs, *William Cobbett* (London, 1967); E. P. Thompson, *The Making of the English Working Class* (1963, Harmondsworth, 1968), ch. 16; Richard Ingrams (ed.), *Cobbett's Country Book* (Newton Abbot, 1975); *idem*, 'The Pattern John Bull', *The Spectator*, 1 May 1982, pp. 20–1.
2 Karl Schweizer and John Osborne, *Cobbett in his Times* (Leicester, 1990), pp. 7, 105; Richard Johnson, ' "Really Useful Knowledge": Radical Education and Working-Class Culture', in John Clarke, Chas Critcher and Richard Johnson (eds.), *Working-Class Culture* (London, 1979), p. 89; Gertrude Himmelfarb, 'William Cobbett', *The New Criterion*, October 1982, p. 42; Humphrey Phelps, 'The Most English of Englishmen', *Cobbett's New Register* (bulletin of the William Cobbett Society), vol. 7, no. 8 (October 1988), pp. 4–8.
3 G. D. H. and M. Cole, *The Opinions of William Cobbett* (London, 1944), p. 26; John Osborne, *William Cobbett: His Thought and his Times* (New Brunswick, NJ, 1966), p. 87.
4 Osborne, *William Cobbett*, p. 254; John Derry, 'William Cobbett: A Sentimental Radical', in John Derry, *The Radical Tradition: Tom Paine to Lloyd George* (London, 1967), p. 78; Daniel Green, *Great Cobbett: The Noblest Agitator* (London, 1983), p. 5; David Wilson, *Paine and Cobbett: The Transatlantic Connection* (Montreal and Kingston, 1988), p. 185; George Rudé, *Ideology and Popular Protest* (London, 1980), p. 151; Gertrude Himmelfarb, *The Idea of Poverty: England in the Early Industrial Age* (New York, 1983), p. 207.
5 The two leading biographies of Cobbett are G. D. H. Cole, *The Life of William Cobbett*, third edn (London, 1947); George Spater, *William Cobbett: The Poor Man's Friend*, 2 vols. (Cambridge, 1982). For some reflections on the state of Cobbett scholarship see the remarks of the late Raymond Williams in 'The Man who Shifted against the Tide', *New Society*, vol. 60, 29 April 1982; see also Williams's *Cobbett*. A brief but very fine biography is James Sambrook, *William Cobbett* (London, 1973). There is also much of interest in Wilson, *Paine and Cobbett*, and Green, *Great Cobbett*. For early biographies as well as annotated listings of Cobbett's own writings see M. L. Pearl, *William Cobbett*:

A Bibliographical Account of his Life and Times (London, 1953, Westport, Conn., 1971) and Pierce W. Gaines, *William Cobbett and the United States, 1792–1835* (Worcester, Mass., 1971).

6 Spater, *William Cobbett*, II, p. 529. As Malcolm Chase has recently remarked, Cobbett's relationship with the land constituted 'virtually the only consistent element in his long and varied career' ('*The People's Farm': English Radical Agrarianism 1775–1840* (Oxford, 1988), p. 15).

7 *PR*, 9 November 1822, pp. 329–30; 16 February 1822, p. 445; Cobbett to J. P. Cobbett, in *PR*, 22 January 1820, p. 703.

8 *PR*, 29 January 1831, p. 288.

9 Oxford Word and Language Service kindly informs me that Cobbett's use of the term 'chopsticks' is one of the earliest on record, and that later usages appear in J. K. Akerman, *Wiltshire Tales* (1853) and Thomas Hardy, *The Hand of Ethelberta* (1876). 'Chopsticks' also appears in William Howitt, *The Rural Life of England* (1838, Shannon, 1971), pp. 601, 608, and in a broadside song dating from the 1830s: 'Money Makes the Mare to Go: Being a Dialogue between Neighbour Tumbleturf and Neighbour Chopstick' (London: Bassam, printer) JJ: Street Ballads, I.

10 *PR*, 5 November 1831, p. 342; 23 June 1832, p. 743; 16 June 1832, p. 652; 11 February 1832, p. 404.

11 *PR*, 6 April 1822, pp. 50–1.

12 See Place's anonymous and privately printed *Essay on the State of the Country in Respect to the Condition and Conduct of the Husbandry Labourers* (London, 1831), Goldsmiths' 26920: 'Tracts Collected by Francis Place'.

13 G. D. H. Cole, 'Introduction', in *Life and Adventures*, p. 7; idem, *Life of William Cobbett*, p. 4.

14 Himmelfarb, *Idea of Poverty*, p. 216. See also Malcolm Thomis, *Responses to Industrialization: The British Experience 1780–1850* (Newton Abbot, 1976), pp. 26, 39, 129–30.

15 Thompson, *Making of the English Working Class*, p. 820; Olivia Smith, *The Politics of Language* (Oxford, 1984), esp. p. 242.

16 *PR*, 16 June 1832, p. 652.

17 *PR*, 5 May 1821, p. 343.

18 John Belchem, '*Orator*' *Hunt: Henry Hunt and English Working-Class Radicalism* (Oxford, 1985), pp. 133–4.

19 James Obelkevich, *Religion and Rural Society: South Lindsey 1825–1875* (Oxford, 1976), chs. 2, 6, esp. pp. 26–9; Howard Newby, *The Deferential Worker: A Study of Farm Workers in East Anglia* (London, 1977), chs. 1, 7–8.

20 *PR*, 21 May 1831, p. 438.

21 Alan Armstrong, *Farmworkers: A Social and Economic History 1770–1980* (London, 1988), p. 15.

22 K. D. M. Snell, *Annals of the Labouring Poor: Social Change and Agrarian England, 1660–1900* (Cambridge, 1985); Chase, '*The People's Farm*'; Alun Howkins, *Poor Labouring Men: Rural Radicalism in Norfolk 1870–1923* (London, 1985); Barry Reay, *The Last Rising of the Agricultural Labourers: Rural Life and Protest in Nineteenth-Century England* (Oxford, 1990); John Archer, '*By a Flash and a Scare*': Arson, Animal Maiming and Poaching in East Anglia, 1815–1870 (Oxford, 1990); Mick Reed, 'Class and Conflict in Rural England: Some Reflections on a Debate', in M. Reed and R. Wells (eds.), *Class, Conflict and Protest in the English Countryside, 1700–1800* (London, 1990), pp. 1–28; Roger Wells, 'Social Protest, Class, Conflict and Consciousness, in the English Countryside, 1700–1880', in *ibid.*, pp. 121–214. See also the essays in *Rural History*, vol. 1, no. 1 (April 1990).

For a previous example of the use of commentators from outside the labourers' own ranks see David Jones, 'Thomas Campbell Foster and the Rural Labourer: Incendiarism in East Anglia in the 1840s', *Social History*, vol. 1, no. 1 (January 1976), pp. 5–37. The phrase 'cottage charter' is derived from Richard Jefferies, *Hodge and his Masters* (1880, London, 1979), pp. 262–3.

23 *Year's Residence*, para. 16.

24 See the fine essay on Cobbett in W. J. Keith, *The Rural Tradition* (Toronto, 1974) ch. 4, esp. pp. 14–15, 61. Cobbett is discussed in relation to some rural topics in Green, *Great Cobbett*.

25 Richard Heath, 'A Peasant Politician: William Cobbett' (1874), in Richard Heath, *The English Peasant* (1893, East Ardsley, 1978), pp. 245–91.

26 Arnold, 'The Future of Liberalism', p. 136.

27 Leslie Stephen, 'William Cobbett', *New Review*, vol. 9 (1893), p. 488; J. B. Morton, 'William Cobbett', *London Mercury*, vol. 20 (June 1929); G. K. Chesterton, 'Preface', *Cottage Economy* (1822; London, 1926); J. L. and Barbara Hammond, *The Village Labourer* (1911), ed. G. E. Mingay (London, 1978), p. 172; [J. L. Hammond], 'Cobbett's Political Register', *The Edinburgh Review*, vol. 206 (July 1907), pp. 128–48. Edward Thompson similarly upholds Cobbett as 'the greatest tribune of the labourers' (*Making of the English Working Class*, p. 249). For a discussion of the evolution of interpretations of Cobbett's significance see Martin J. Wiener, 'The Changing Image of William Cobbett', *The Journal of British Studies*, vol. 13, no. 2 (May 1974), pp. 135–54.

28 Raymond Williams, *The Country and the City* (London, 1973), pp. 108–13; idem, 'Literature and Rural Society', *The Listener*, 16 November 1967, pp. 630–2; idem, 'Between Country and City', in Simon Pugh (ed.), *Reading Landscape* (Manchester, 1990), pp. 7–18.

29 *The Journals of George Sturt*, 2 vols, ed. E. D. Mackerness (Cambridge, 1967), II, pp. 621–2.

30 H. J. Massingham, *The Wisdom of the Fields* (London, 1945), p. 252. See also pp. 12, 20.

31 Pearl, *Cobbett: A Bibliographical Account*, pp. 105–6.

32 *Rural Rides*, p. 228.

33 *Ibid.*, pp. 321–2.

34 Eric Hobsbawm, 'Peasants and Politics', *Journal of Peasant Studies*, vol. 1, no. 1 (October 1973), pp. 3–22, esp. pp. 7–8. See also Newby, *Deferential Worker*, pp. 50–6.

35 *Rural Rides*, p. 292.

36 *Ibid.*, p. 292.

37 Cobbett to Samuel Clarke, 30 April 1821 (Nuffield).

38 Louis James, for example, remarks that Cobbett 'remains outside any easy classification – even that of popular literature': *Print and the People 1819–1851* (Harmondsworth, 1976), p. 32.

39 For a recent discussion of this see David Vincent, *Literacy and Popular Culture: England 1750–1914* (Cambridge, 1989), p. 245.

40 For a discussion of Cobbett's indebtedness to the eighteenth-century Country platform see Wilson, *Paine and Cobbett*, ch. 6.

41 Isaac Kramnick, *Bolingbroke and his Circle: The Politics of Nostalgia in the Age of Walpole* (Cambridge, Mass., 1968), p. 171.

42 J. G. A. Pocock, *Virtue, Commerce, and Industry: Essays on Political Thought and History* (Cambridge, 1985), p. 297.

43 Donald Macrae, 'Populism as an Ideology', in Ghita Ionescu and Ernest Gellner (eds.), *Populism: Its Meaning and National Characteristics* (London, 1969), p. 161; Peter Wiles, 'A Syndrome, not a Doctrine: Some Elementary Theses on Populism', in *ibid.*, p. 179 n. 4. See also Himmelfarb, *Idea of Poverty*, pp. 228–9; Iain McCalman, *Radical*

Underworld: Prophets, Revolutionaries and Pornographers in London 1795–1840 (Cambridge, 1988), pp. 101–3, 236–7.

44 See, for example, Ionescu and Gellner (eds.), *Populism*; Ernesto Laclau, *Politics and Ideology in Marxist Theory* (London, 1977), ch. 4; Michael Roe, *Kenealy and the Tichborne Case: A Study in Mid-Victorian Populism* (Melbourne, 1974); Rohan McWilliam, 'The Tichborne Claimant and the People: Investigations into Popular Culture, 1867–1886' (PhD thesis, University of Sussex, 1990), esp. ch. 1; Green, *Great Cobbett*, ch. 16.

45 W. D. Rubinstein, 'British Radicalism and the "Dark Side" of Populism', in *Elites and the Wealthy in Modern British Society* (Brighton, 1987), pp. 339–73. I would like to thank Professor Rubinstein for our several discussions on the subject of his essay.

46 *PR*, 26 May 1821, p. 511.

47 J. B. Allcock, '"Populism": A Brief Biography', *Sociology*, vol. 5, no. 3 (September 1971), p. 385 n34.

48 Margaret Canovan, *Populism* (New York, 1981), *passim*; Lawrence Goodwyn, *Democratic Promise: The Populist Movement in America* (New York, 1976), pp. x–xii. See also the essays in Ionescu and Gellner (eds.), *Populism*; Allcock, '"Populism"', pp. 371–87.

49 Canovan, *Populism*, pp. 4, 8–10, 13.

50 See Wiles, 'A Syndrome, not a Doctrine', pp. 154–5; Karel Bicha, 'Prairie Radicals: A Common Pietism', *Journal of Church and State*, vol. 18, no. 1 (Winter 1976), pp. 79–94; Seymour Lipset, *Agrarian Socialism: The Cooperative Commonwealth Federation in Saskatchewan* (1950, New York, 1968); C. B. Macpherson, *Democracy in Alberta* (Toronto, 1953); John Richards, 'Populism: A Qualified Defence', *Studies in Political Economy*, vol. 5 (Spring 1981), pp. 5–27. For an English example of distributionist thought among followers of Cobbett, see *Some Arguments for a Redistribution of Property* (anonymous and undated pamphlet of the Oxford Cobbett Club, *c.* 1930s, Nuffield HB 771A).

51 Thompson, *Making of the English Working Class*, pp. 820–37. See also Conrad Waligorski, 'Radical Traditionalism: William Cobbett in the Industrial Revolution' (PhD thesis, University of Wisconsin, 1973), esp. chs. 1–2.

52 Craig Calhoun, *The Question of Class Struggle: Social Foundations of Popular Radicalism during the Industrial Revolution* (Oxford, 1982), pp. 4, 7–9, 76–7, 99, 103, 171.

53 *Ibid.*, p. 115.

54 *PR*, 14 December 1822, p. 686.

55 *PR*, 14 April 1982, p. 80.

56 Karl Marx, letter to the *New-York Daily Tribune*, 22 July 1853, p. 5.

57 *PR*, 2 June 1832, p. 526; *The Autobiography of Samuel Bamford: Passages in the Life of a Radical* (1838–41), ed. W. H. Chaloner (London, 1967), book I, pp. 18–19; Henry Hunt, *Memoirs of Henry Hunt, Esq.*, 3 vols. (London, 1820), III, pp. 356–7, 218–20; Cobbett, *Paper Against Gold, passim*; Ian Dyck, 'Debts and Liabilities: William Cobbett and Thomas Paine', in Ian Dyck (ed.), *Citizen of the World: Essays on Thomas Paine* (London, 1987), pp. 86–103.

58 John Thelwall, *The Tribune*, 3 vols. (London, 1796), vol. 1, pp. 36–40, vol. 2, pp. 4, 19–20, 28, 38–43, 348–9, 381–3.

2 THE MAKING OF A RADICAL

1 *PR*, 30 August 1834, pp. 529–30.

2 *Life and Adventures*, pp. 20–2, 93.

3 'A Memoir of William Cobbett by James Paul Cobbett' (Nuffield XIV). The introduction to this seventy-page manuscript is dated 1 October 1864. James Paul Cobbett (1803–81)

was the fourth of Cobbett's seven children. William, according to this document, showed from his early teens an interest in public affairs. This is in contradiction of his later claim that 'we neither knew or thought anything about [politics]' in the family home. See *Life and Adventures*, pp. 19–22, 25; *PR*, 21 September 1833, p. 729; Lewis Melville, *The Life and Letters of William Cobbett in England & America*, 2 vols. (London, 1913), I, p. 230; Spater, *William Cobbett*, I, p. 30.

4 *PR*, 28 September 1833, p. 826. On Cobbett's yeoman and soldier-like apparel see Mary Mitford, *Recollections of a Literary Life* (London, 1859, 1883 edn), pp. 200–1.

5 *Woodlands*, para. 32.

6 'Letters of Timothy Tickler, Esq.', *Blackwood's Edinburgh Magazine*, vol. 14, no. 78 (September 1823), p. 329. Italics added.

7 James Grant, in Melville, *Life and Letters*, II, pp. 244–5.

8 William Hazlitt, 'Mr. Cobbett' (1821), in *The Spirit of the Age*, ed. E. D. Mackerness (London, 1969), pp. 244–57.

9 Osborne, *William Cobbett*, p. 18.

10 *Life and Adventures*, p. 27.

11 John J. Buckley, 'The Scarlet and the Blue', in Roy Palmer (ed.), *The Rambling Soldier* (Harmondsworth, 1977), pp. 59–60.

12 *PR*, 12 May 1821, pp. 388–90. The deserters' story is expressed in a song recorded from a Suffolk singer during the 1950s ('Muddley Barracks', in Palmer (ed.), *Rambling Soldier*, p. 94):

> Now I wish that I was home again,
> A-following the bloody old plough, sir.
> Or I wish that I was home again,
> A-milking the bloody old cow, sir.

13 *PR*, 12 May 1821, pp. 388–90. The same can be said for other ploughboy-soldiers: see, for example, Ann Kussmaul, *The Autobiography of Joseph Mayett of Quainton 1783–1839* (Aylesbury, 1986); Alexander Somerville, *The Autobiography of a Working Man* (London, 1848).

14 *Advice*, paras. 44, 311–13; *Year's Residence*, paras. 354–5; *Life and Adventures*, pp. 32–3; Cobbett's *French Grammar* (1824); *PR*, 17 June 1809, p. 913; Spater, *William Cobbett*, I, pp. 17–18.

15 *PR*, 5 October 1805, pp. 523–4; 12 October 1805, pp. 548–9; 17 June 1809, pp. 899–915; *Porcupine's Gazette*, 12 August 1799; Mary Clark, *Peter Porcupine in America: The Career of William Cobbett 1762–1835* (Philadelphia, 1939), p. 8. For the story of Cobbett's attempted exposure of peculating officers, see *Life and Adventures*, pp. 32–7, 30–40. Upon returning to England and obtaining his discharge Cobbett wrote (sometime during the first half of 1792) an anonymous pamphlet entitled *The Soldier's Friend; Or, Considerations on the Late Pretended Augmentation of the Substance of Private Soldiers* (London, 1792). Copies are scarce, but a 1792 edition is at BL 8135 b. 15. On Cobbett and Paine see Dyck, 'Debts and Liabilities', pp. 86–103.

16 On his scheme for a court-martial: *PR*, 17 June 1809, pp. 899–915; Spater, *William Cobbett*, I, pp. 30–6. Prior to his departure to America Cobbett spent six months in France: *Life and Adventures*, p. 39; *PR*, 6 December 1817, pp. 1094–5; 26 March 1831, p. 819.

17 Cobbett to Rachel Smither, 6 July 1794 (Nuffield).

18 See *Porcupine's Works*. For a bibliography of Cobbett's American writings: Gaines, *William Cobbett and the United States*. For accounts of these years: Spater, *William Cobbett*, I, chs. 1–6.

19 *PR*, 29 September 1804, p. 451.

20 Cobbett to [William Gifford], 28 June 1799, in Pierce Gaines, 'Two Letters Written by William Cobbett from America', *The Yale University Library Gazette*, vol. 48, pt I (July 1973), pp. 44–55.

21 Paine and Cobbett never met, but for Paine's remark see his 'Letter to Washington' (1796), in Philip Foner (ed.), *The Complete Works of Thomas Paine*, 2 vols. (London, 1945), II, p. 710n.

22 'To Noah Webster of New-York', *Porcupine's Gazette*, 25 March 1797, in *Porcupine's Works*, V, p. 169. His diplomatic ambitions are implicit in G. D. H. Cole (ed.), *Letters from William Cobbett to Edward Thornton* (London, 1937).

23 'Trial of Republicanism' (June 1799), in *Porcupine's Works*, IX, p. 449. His scurrilous attacks on Paine were largely pilfered from the biography of George Chalmers (pseud. Francis Oldys): see *Porcupine's Works*, IV, pp. 79, 87, V, pp. 159–65; 'Observations &c.', *Political Censor*, no. 4 (May 1796), in *Porcupine's Works*, III, pp. 3–16.

24 'To Joseph Priestley', *The Rush-Light*, no. 5 (30 April 1800), in *Porcupine's Works*, XI, p. 425; *The Rush-Light*, no. 6 (30 August 1800), in *Porcupine's Works*, I, p. 272.

25 See, for example, *Annals of Agriculture*, vol. 19 (1793), pp. 225–42, 255–8; William Strickland, 'Observations on the State of America' (1796), *Communications to the Board of Agriculture*, vol. 2 (1798), pp. 136–66; William Tatham, *Communications Concerning the Agriculture and Commerce of the United States* (London, 1800), p. 52.

26 Cobbett to Edward Thornton, 18 July 1800, in Cole (ed.), *Letters from William Cobbett to Edward Thornton*, p. 111; *PR*, 16 December 1815, pp. 329–31.

27 *PR*, 4 January 1817, p. 17, 20 May 1809, p. 777, 22 February 1823, p. 455, 3 June 1826, p. 586; Cobbett to Edward Thornton (4 September 1800), in Cole (ed.), *Letters of William Cobbett to Edward Thornton*, p. 109; *Year's Residence*, para. 20. On John Reeves, founder of the Association for the Preservation of Liberty and Property against Republicans and Levellers, we have only Cobbett's word (*PR*, 1 May 1830, p. 569); for Windham's reservations see John Cam Hobhouse (Lord Boughton), *Recollections of a Long Life*, 4 vols. (London, 1910), III, p. 138. See also James Sack, *The Grevillites 1801–29: Party Politics and Factionalism in the Age of Pitt and Liverpool* (Chicago, 1979), pp. 59–60.

28 *Prospectus of a New Daily Paper, to be Entitled The Porcupine* (London, 1800), pp. 1–2, 4, 7. Cobbett was delighted with early sales: Cobbett to Messrs Vernon and Hood, 10 December 1800, BM Add. MS 38,730, fol. 55. See *The Porcupine*, 31 October 1800, 5 November 1800, 10 November 1800, 20 November 1800, 3 December 1800, 9 December 1800, 29 December 1800, 4 July 1801, 11 July 1801; *PR*, 1 May 1802, p. 542, 22 May 1802, p. 602; Cobbett to William Windham, 7 October 1801 (BM Add. MS 37,853, fols. 12–13).

29 Spater, *William Cobbett*, I, p. 195.

30 John Chamberlayne, *Magnae Britanniae; or, The Present State of Great Britain* (London, 1755), p. 40.

31 See Robert Malcolmson, *Popular Recreations in English Society, 1700–1850* (London, 1973); Hugh Cunningham, *Leisure in the Industrial Revolution* (London, 1980).

32 Harold Perkin, *The Origins of Modern English Society* (London, 1969), p. 280.

33 Pierce Egan, *Book of Sports* (London, 1832), pp. 2, 11–12, 49–50, 55, 57; Howitt, *Rural Life of England*, pp. 495, 515, 523–7, 531, 541; *The Autobiography of Samuel Bamford: Early Days* (1848–9), ed. W. H. Chaloner (London, 1967), pp. 132–9; George Crabbe, *The Village* (1783), in Geoffrey Grigson (ed.), *Selected Poems of George Crabbe* (London, 1950); J. N. Brewer, *Some Thoughts on the Present State of the English Peasantry* (London, 1807), pp. 32–3; M. K. Ashby, *Joseph Ashby of Tysoe* (1961, London, 1974), pp. 36, 42; Gertrude Jekyll, *Old West Surrey* (London, 1904), p. 244.

34 *The Sporting Magazine*, vol. 30 (September 1807), p. 287, vol. 28 (September 1806), pp. 273–4.

35 Cobbett to Windham, 6 October 1805 (BM Add. MS 37,853, fol. 184).

36 *The Sporting Magazine*, vol. 27 (October 1804), pp. 6–7.

37 Cobbett to Windham, 6 October 1805 (BM Add. MS 37,853, fol. 184).

38 *The Sporting Magazine*, vol. 28 (September 1806), p. 275. See also vol. 33 (October 1808), pp. 14–15. Cobbett was an amateur single-stick player himself, and encouraged his sons to play: see *ibid.*, vol. 30 (August 1807), p. 210; Cobbett to John Hooke Green, 12 January 1807 (Yale), Cobbett to Windham, 6 December 1805 (BM Add. MS 37,853, fol. 191).

39 *The Sporting Magazine*, vol. 27 (October 1805), p. 7.

40 *Hansard's Parliamentary History*, vol. 36 (1802), pp. 829–31.

41 *Ibid.*, pp. 831–41.

42 *Ibid.*, vol. 35 (1800–1), p. 204.

43 There is a large song literature in defence of bull-baits, cock-fights and boxing. On Windham's efforts: 'Bull-Baiting', in John Freeth, *A Touch on the Times* (Birmingham, 1803).

44 *PR*, 5 June 1802, pp. 652–7 (an attack on an anti-bait sermon reviewed in the *British Critic*); *PR*, 27 February 1802, p. 176; 22 May 1802, pp. 603–4; 29 May 1802, pp. 626–8; 29 January 1803, p. 99; 25 January 1803, pp. 287–8; 14 January 1804, pp. 54–5; Cobbett to Windham, 28 July 1805 (BM Add. MS 37,852, fol. 175); Cobbett to Ashbury Dickins, 30 January 1804 (BPL).

45 *PR*, 29 January 1803, p. 99; Cobbett to Windham, 6 December 1805 (BM Add. MS 37,853, fol. 191).

46 'To Noah Webster of New-York', *Porcupine's Gazette*, 25 March 1797, in *Porcupine's Works*, V, pp. 168–9.

47 Hugh Cunningham, 'The Language of Patriotism 1750–1914', *History Workshop*, no. 21 (Autumn 1981), pp. 8–33; *idem*, 'The Language of Patriotism', in Raphael Samuel (ed.), *Patriotism: The Making and Unmaking of the British National Identity*, 3 vols. (London, 1989), I, pp. 57–89. See also Linda Colley, 'Radical Patriotism in Eighteenth-Century England', in *ibid.*, pp. 169–87; *idem*, ' "Whose Nation?" Class and National Consciousness in Britain 1750–1830', *Past and Present*, no. 113 (November 1986); Gerald Newman, *The Rise of English Nationalism: A Cultural History 1740–1830* (New York, 1987), ch. 8.

48 *Loyal and Patriotic Hand-Bills, Songs, Addresses, etc. on the Threatened Invasion of Great Britain* (London, 1803); Frank Klingberg and Siguard Hustuedt (eds.), *The Warning Drum: The British Home Front Faces Napoleon* (Berkeley and Los Angeles, 1944); H. F. B. Wheeler and A. M. Broadley (eds.), *Napoleon and the Invasion of England*, 2 vols. (London, 1908), II, pp. 272–326. For a recent discussion of wartime propaganda see Stella Cottrell, 'The Devil on Two-Sticks: Franco-phobia in 1803', in Samuel (ed.), *Patriotism*, I, pp. 259–74.

49 Klingberg and Hustuedt (eds.), *Warning Drum*, pp. 177–9 (Wilberforce); *Loyal and Patriotic Hand-Bills*, fol. 106 (Sheridan) and fol. 34 (More).

50 'Freedom and Loyalty: With a New Song' (*c.* 1803), in *Loyal and Patriotic Hand-Bills*, fol. 73.

51 *Serious Considerations, Addressed to British Labourers and Mechanics at the Present Crisis* (London, 1803), p. 13; 'Men of England', in Klingberg and Hustuedt (eds.), *Warning Drum*, pp. 208–9.

52 'A Lesson for Labourers', in *Loyal and Patriotic Hand-Bills*, fol. 20.

53 Hannah More to Elizabeth Montagu, 1794, in Wheeler and Broadley (eds.), *Napoleon and the Invasion of England*, I, p. 210.

54 Klingberg and Hustuedt (eds.), *Warning Drum*, pp. 188–9; *The Works of Hannah More*, 11 vols. (London, 1830), II, pp. 75–7.

55 *Considerations* appeared as a pamphlet (BL 9220 b. 17) and as a broadside (*Loyal and Patriotic Hand-Bills*, fol. 107). Cobbett, without noting the author, printed it as a lead article in *PR*, 30 July 1803. For his confession as author: *PR*, 17 June 1809, pp. 916–17; 15 January 1831, p. 157.

56 Green, *Great Cobbett*, pp. 231–6.

57 *PR*, 27 October 1804, p. 617; 10 August 1805, p. 198.

58 *Life and Adventures*, p. 25.

59 *PR*, 27 October 1804, p. 616. On Cobbett's love of military pageantry and honours (much subdued in later years): PR, 23 July 1803, pp. 123–5.

60 Clive Emsley, *British Society and the French Wars 1793–1815* (London, 1979), pp. 53–5, 102–3; *The Carrington Diary*, ed. W. Branch Johnson (London, 1956), p. 161; John Clare, 'The Autobiography, 1793–1824', in *The Prose of John Clare*, ed. J. W. and Anne Tibble (London, 1951), pp. 46–50.

61 'A Good Wish for Old England' (no imprint, *c*. 1803, Madden 4 (I)).

62 *PR*, 23 June 1804, pp. 984–6; 24 September 1803, p. 433.

63 Windham's remarks were subjected to popular criticism in 'The Loyal Volunteers of Great Britain' (1806) Madden 20 (V).

64 *PR*, 23 July 1803, p. 126; 24 September 1803, p. 433; 27 October 1804, pp. 615–16; 1 September 1804, p. 350.

65 *PR*, 21 May 1803, p. 737. Also: *PR*, 1 September 1804, p. 350; 8 September 1804, pp. 376, 380, 384; *Cobbett's Parliamentary Debates* (London, 1804–12); *Cobbett's Parliamentary History of England* (London, 1804–12).

66 William Frend, *Patriotism; or The Love of our Country* (London, 1804), p. 160.

67 Thompson, *Making of the English Working Class*, ch. 13; J. R. Dinwiddy, 'Sir Francis Burdett and Burdettite Radicalism', *History*, vol. 65, no. 213 (February 1980); J. Ann Hone, *For the Cause of Truth: Radicalism in London 1796–1821* (Oxford, 1982), chs. 3–4.

68 *PR*, 8 September 1804, p. 382.

69 *PR*, 1 September 1804, pp. 331–52.

70 *PR*, 6 October 1804, p. 529; 15 September 1804, p. 412; 8 September 1804, p. 380; 21 May 1803, p. 737; Cobbett to John Wright, 31 August 1804 (BM Add. MS 22,906, fol. 20).

71 *PR*, 18 August 1804, p. 236; 12 June 1802, pp. 700–1.

72 *PR*, 30 July 1803, p. 153; 18 June 1803, p. 919.

73 *The Porcupine*, 5 November 1800; 16, 17 December 1800; *PR*, 6 February 1802, p. 94.

74 Cobbett to Windham, 15 August 1804 (BM Add. MS 37,853, fol. 132). On the effect of the war upon raising food prices: Robert Waithman, *War Proved to be the Real Cause of the Present Scarcity* (London, 1801); Walter Stern, 'The Bread Crisis in Britain, 1795–6', *Economica*, 31 (May 1964), p. 183; M. W. Flinn, *An Economic and Social History of Britain since 1700* (London, 1963), p. 103.

75 Cobbett to Windham, 15 August 1804 (BM Add. MS 37,853, fol. 132; *PR*, 18 August 1804, pp. 238–43; 8 September 1804, pp. 370–6; 13 October 1804, pp. 545–54, 559–70; 23 February 1805, pp. 289–309.

76 *PR*, 29 September 1804, p. 457; Dyck, 'Debts and Liabilities', pp. 86–103. Cobbett's early attack on Paine's *Decline and Fall* appears in 'Life of Thomas Paine', *Political Censor*, no. 5 (September 1796), in *Porcupine's Works*, IV, p. 112; III, pp. 3–16. For a fine discussion of Paine's views on finance see Gregory Claeys, *Thomas Paine: Social and Political Thought* (Boston, 1989), pp. 96–101.

77 'Price of Bread and Labour', in 'Rumsey', *PR*, 24 November 1804, pp. 814–15; 13

October 1804, p. 569; 8 December 1804, p. 882; 11 October 1806, pp. 562–3. On wages in early nineteenth-century agriculture: Snell, *Annals of the Labouring Poor*, pp. 37–8; David Davies, *The Case of the Labourers in Husbandry* (1795, Fairfield, 1977); A. L. Bowley, *Wages in the United Kingdom in the Nineteenth Century* (Cambridge, 1900), pp. 24–35; J. E. Thorold Rogers, *A History of Agriculture and Prices in England*, 7 vols. (Oxford, 1902), VII, pp. 493–528; William Hasbach, *A History of the English Agricultural Labourer* (1894, London, 1966), pp. 204–16.

78 The 'memorial' on the cottagers that Cobbett sent to Windham appears not to have survived. The account given here is based on that in *PR*, 26 May 1821, pp. 518–22; 11 September 1830, p. 350; *Trash*, October 1830, p. 86; Anne Cobbett, 'Account of the Family', fol. 121 (Nuffield XV).

79 Michael Turner, *Enclosures in Britain 1750–1830* (London, 1984), esp. pp. 79–80; Snell, *Annals of the Labouring Poor*, esp. pp. 178–84, 194–227; W. G. Hoskins, *The Midland Peasant: The Economic and Social History of a Leicestershire Village* (London, 1957), ch. 6; Hermann Levy, *Large and Small Holdings: A Study of English Agricultural Economics* (1911, London, 1966); Arthur Young's reports in *Annals of Agriculture*, vol. 42 (1804), pp. 319–26, 471–501; *idem*, 'An Inquiry into the Propriety of Applying Wastes to the Better Maintenance and Support of the Poor' (1801), *Annals of Agriculture*, vol. 36 (1801), pp. 497–658; SC of the House of Lords on the Poor Laws, VIII (1830–1), pp. 26–30, 92–5; Third Report of the SC on Emigration, V (1827), pp. 362–5. See Mick Reed, '"Gnawing it Out": A New Look at Economic Relations in Early Nineteenth-Century Rural England', *Rural History*, vol. 1, no. 1 (April 1990), pp. 83–94.

80 *PR*, 19 May 1821, pp. 479–80. The account quoted here reads 1814 instead of 1804, but this is a typographical error: see the other references in n. 78 above.

81 H. T. Dickinson, *Liberty and Property: Political Ideology in Eighteenth-Century Britain* (London, 1977) p. 195.

82 *PR*, 17 March 1821, p. 780.

83 Abstract of Answers and Returns Relative to the Expense and Maintenance of the Poor, VIII (1803–4), printed in May 1804; *PR*, 13 October 1804, p. 610; 26 January 1805, p. 115; 9 February 1805, p. 220; 9 May 1805, p. 372; 20 September 1806, p. 449; 6 December 1806, p. 872; 17 January 1807, pp. 80–1; 20 February 1808, p. 280; 16 July 1808, p. 83.

84 See Himmelfarb, *Idea of Poverty*, pp. 64–73.

85 *Ibid.*, pp. 74–5.

86 For example: *PR*, 12 September 1810, p. 332.

87 *Treatise on Corn*, para. 159; *PR*, 29 September 1804, p. 457; 28 February 1807, p. 336.

88 *PR*, 8 February 1806, pp. 161–2.

89 *Ibid.*, p. 169.

90 *PR*, 8 February 1806, pp. 169–79; 15 February 1805, p. 200; 9 March 1805, p. 372.

91 *PR*, 9 February 1805, pp. 220–2.

92 *PR*, 6 December 1806, pp. 872–3; 8 December 1804, pp. 865–6.

93 *Hansard's Parliamentary Debates*, 1st ser., vol. VIII (19 February 1807), pp. 865, 885–97, 905–10.

94 Cobbett to John Wright, 25 February 1807 (BM Add. MS 31,125, fol. 249).

95 *PR*, 28 February 1807, p. 324. In some parishes the badge was still used to distinguish and humiliate recipients of parish relief: see the Rev. H. B. Dudley, *A Few Observations Respecting the Present State of the Poor* ... (London, 1802), p. 15.

96 John Bohstedt, *Riots and Community Politics in England and Wales 1790–1810* (Cambridge, Mass., 1983), p. 195. For employers' efforts to combine against wages while

leaving the prices subject to the free market, see the response to Arthur Young's questionnaire in *Annals of Agriculture*, vol. 25 (1796).

97 *Hansard's Parliamentary Debates*, 1st ser., vol. VIII (19 February 1807), p. 897; *PR*, 29 August 1807, pp. 328–9; 16 July 1808, pp. 77–8; 21 September 1805, p. 424.

98 J. R. Poynter, *Society and Pauperism* (London, 1969), pp. 214–17; *Hansard's Parliamentary Debates*, 1st ser., vol. IX (24 April 1807), p. 548; *PR*, 29 August 1807, pp. 329–30, 333; 26 September 1807, p. 486.

99 *PR*, 16 July 1808, pp. 73–4.

100 *Ibid.*, p. 78; 8 February 1806, p. 169; 16 July 1808, p. 78.

101 *PR*, 21 October 1809, pp. 577–83. On the Jubilee: *PR*, 10 April 1830, p. 464; *George the Fourth*, paras. 276–81.

102 Smith, *Politics of Language*, pp. 227–33. See also H. T. Dickinson, 'Popular Conservatism and Militant Loyalism 1789–1815', in H. T. Dickinson (ed.), *Britain and the French Revolution* (London, 1989), pp. 103–25.

103 Thompson, *Making of the English Working Class*, pp. 831–2.

104 *Ibid.*, p. 500.

105 Roger Wells, *Insurrection: The British Experience 1795–1803* (Gloucester, 1986), chs. 6–8, 11; Bohstedt, *Riots and Community Politics*, ch. 8.

106 Cobbett to John Wright, 31 March 1809 (BM Add. MS 22,907, fol. 140).

107 For a recent collection of essays on the relationship between the state and the people during the war years see Dickinson (ed.), *Britain and the French Revolution*.

108 On the more generous attitudes towards labour during the eighteenth century see Edgar Furniss, *The Position of the Laborer in a System of Nationalism: A Study in the Labor Theories of the Later English Mercantilists* (Boston, 1920), esp. chs. 22–5; A. W. Coats, 'Changing Attitudes to Labour in the Mid-Eighteenth Century', *Economic History Review*, second ser., vol. 2 (1958), pp. 35–51.

109 *PR*, 1 September 1804, p. 334.

110 *Ibid.*, pp. 331–52.

111 *PR*, 29 April 1815, pp. 518–19. On another occasion he defined Jacobinism as 'the plain and generous and just principles of democracy' (*George the Fourth*, para. 206).

112 *PR*, 18 December 1819, p. 472.

113 *PR*, 21 December 1822, p. 707. For recent work on Paine and the French Revolution see *Bulletin of the Society for the Study of Labour History*, vol. 54, no. 3 (Winter 1989).

114 *PR*, 2 November 1833, pp. 258–9.

115 *PR*, 13 June 1812, pp. 747–52; 20 June 1812, pp. 790–3; 27 June 1820, p. 814; Hone, *For the Cause of Truth*, pp. 225–8; Spater, *William Cobbett*, II, pp. 544–9; McCalman, *Radical Underworld*, pp. 77–85; J. R. Dinwiddy, 'William Cobbett, George Houston and Freethought', *Notes and Queries*, vol. 222 (July–August 1977), pp. 324–8.

116 'Observations on the Emigration of Dr. Priestley' (1794), in *Porcupine's Works*, I, p. 169.

117 *PR*, 20 August 1831, p. 495.

118 Dyck, 'Debts and Liabilities', pp. 86–103.

3 DISCOVERING CLASS: COUNTRYMEN, LABOURERS AND NEW-FASHIONED FARMERS

1 Samuel Jackson Pratt, *Bread; or, The Poor* (London, 1802), 'Preface', pp. 14–15, 21, 41–2, 53; *PR*, 6 February 1802, pp. 92–3. For even more hostile reviews see *The Anti-Jacobin Review* (March 1802), pp. 285–90; *British Critic*, vol. 19 (April 1802), p. 417.

2 *Porcupine's Gazette* (July, September 1798), in *Porcupine's Works*, IX, pp. 45, 251, 254-5.

3 *PR*, 21 July 1810, p. 39; 18 May 1816, pp. 613-14; 22 November 1828, p. 669.

4 For example see James Fitzjames Stephen, 'Cobbett's Political Works', *Saturday Review*, vol. 22, no. 19 (1866), p. 234. For Marx's reference, see his letter to the *New-York Daily Tribune*, 22 July 1853, p. 5.

5 *PR*, 22 May 1813, p. 746; 23 March 1816, pp. 361-5; 28 September 1816, p. 403; 13 January 1827, pp. 135, 144; 26 January 1833, pp. 198-201.

6 Colley, 'Whose Nation?', p. 100.

7 For example: 'The English Character', in Cole and Cole (eds.), *Opinions of William Cobbett*, ch. 3.

8 *PR*, 2 June 1832, pp. 545-6; Cobbett to John Tredwell, 28 March 1832 (Huntington).

9 On the evolution of John Bull's representation see Christopher Hill, 'The English Revolution and Patriotism', in Samuel (ed.), *Patriotism*, I, pp. 165-6; Jeannine Surel, 'John Bull', in *ibid.*, III, pp. 21-2; Newman, *Rise of English Nationalism*, pp. 48, 78, 116, 232-3.

10 For an example see 'Honest John Bull' (n.d., no imprint, *c.* 1810), BL 1876 d. 41, fol. 401:

> Now John is a good natured fellow,
> Industrious, honest, and brave
> Not afraid of his betters when mellow,
> For betters, John knows, he must have;
> There must be fine lords and ladies,
> There must be some little, some great,
> Their wealth the support of our trades,
> Our trade's the support of our state.
>
> The plough and the loom would stand still,
> Were we to be gentlemen all;
> And clodhoppers sadly would fill,
> The senate, the palace, or hall,
> Rights of man make a very fine sound,
> Riches a pleasurable tale.
> Whose labour would then till the ground,
> All would drink but who'd brew the ale.

11 *Protestant 'Reformation'*, para. 211; *PR*, 18 May 1816, pp. 611-28; 21 August 1824, p. 451; *Paper against Gold*, letter III.

12 *Year's Residence*, para. 28; *Trash*, July 1831, pp. 10-12; *Legacy to Labourers*, paras. 1-53. While in America, Cobbett defined a 'countryman' as someone 'who generally lives upon the fruit of his labour, and breathes the sweet air of real independence' (*Porcupine's Works*, X, p. 16).

13 Antonio Gramsci, *Selections from the Prison Notebooks*, eds. Quintin Hoare and Geoffrey Nowell Smith (London, 1971), p. 91.

14 The particular writings alluded to are 'The Class Struggles in France 1848-1850' (1850) and 'The Eighteenth Brumaire of Louis Bonaparte' (1850-2), in Karl Marx and Frederick Engels, *Selected Works* (London, 1968). See also David Mitrany, *Marx against the Peasant* (Chapel Hill, 1951), pp. 15, 24-5.

15 *Rural Rides*, p. 165; *PR*, 11 December 1824, p. 641; 16 December 1826, p. 727. On contemporary debates on the productive and unproductive classes see Patricia Hollis, *The Pauper Press: A Study in Working-Class Radicalism of the 1830s* (Oxford, 1970), pp. 204-5.

16 *PR*, 17 March 1821, pp. 731-2.

17 *PR*, 21 May 1831, p. 439.
18 *Rural Rides*, pp. 308–9.
19 *George the Fourth*, para. 211; *PR*, 5 December 1807, p. 870.
20 Cobbett to [William Gifford], 28 June 1799, in Gaines, 'Two Letters', pp. 47–8. For an example of his public support for commerce see *The Rush-Light*, 30 August 1800, *Porcupine's Works*, I, p. 295.
21 *The War Speeches of William Pitt*, comp. R. Coupland (Oxford, 1915), pp. 239–40 (speech of 1798).
22 *PR*, 20 December 1806, pp. 971–3; 5 December 1807, pp. 868–76; 22 August 1807, p. 263; 28 November 1807, pp. 842–3; 23 January 1808, pp. 106–8; 30 April 1808, p. 677; 14 May 1808, p. 739; 21 May 1808, p. 812; 22 March 1834, p. 708; 7 March 1835, pp. 606–7.
23 *PR*, 23 January 1808, p. 131; 30 April 1808, p. 677. On commerce and national income: Phyllis Deane and W. A. Cole, *British Economic Growth 1688–1959*, second edn (London, 1969), p. 309.
24 *PR*, 28 November 1807, p. 835; 5 December 1807, pp. 872–3, 879–80; *Woodlands*, Preface; and Preface to Cobbett's edition of R. R. Livingstone, *Essay on Sheep* (London, 1811).
25 *PR*, 5 December 1807, p. 872; 28 November 1807, p. 842; 23 November 1811, pp. 652–3; 30 November 1816, pp. 675–9; 14 April 1821, pp. 77–8, 85–92, 101–3; 5 May 1821, p. 249; *Rural Rides*, p. 352
26 For other contemporary schemes to reduce commerce see Poynter, *Society and Pauperism*, pp. 121, 156; Malcolm Thomis, *Responses to Industrialization: The British Experience 1780–1850* (Newton Abbot, 1976), p. 26.
27 Marx's letter to *New-York Daily Tribune*, 22 July 1853, p. 5.
28 *PR*, 7 November 1807, p. 713.
29 *PR* 20 February 1808, pp. 288–303; 5 March 1808, pp. 365–78; 9 April 1808, pp. 568–74; 23 April 1808, pp. 641–8; 30 April 1808, pp. 673–80; 7 May 1808, pp. 705–28; 14 May 1808, pp. 737–49, 768–86; 28 May 1808, pp. 833–62; John Gazley, *The Life of Arthur Young, 1741–1820* (Philadelphia, 1973), pp. 536–40.
30 A copy is in Madden 15. For the history of the song see Claude Simpson, *The British Broadside Ballad and its Music* (New Brunswick, NJ, 1966), pp. 604–6.
31 *PR*, 7 November 1807, p. 713.
32 There are hundreds of copies of this song in broadside collections. Cited here is the text in Roy Palmer (ed.), *The Painful Plough* (Cambridge, 1972), pp. 544–5. The song was listed for sale in the catalogue of the London broadside printer James Catnach in 1832, though a slightly different version than the one cited here (BL: LR 271 a. 2, fol. 105). See J. Catnach, *Catalogue of Songs and Song Book* (London, 1832).
33 Cited here is the version in Madden 5 (II) and BL 1876 d. 41, fol. 45 (London: Catnach, printer). The ballad dates at least as far back as the mid-seventeenth century. Some of the early versions were entitled 'God Speed the Plow, and Bless the Corn-Mow: A Dialogue Between the Husband-Man and Serving-Man', *Roxburgh Ballads*, 8 vols. (Hertford, 1873–90), VI, pp. 521–5; *The Euing Collection of English Broadside Ballads* (Glasgow, 1971), p. 195. For an interpretation of the ballad, see Michael Pickering, 'The Past as a Source of Inspiration: Popular Song and Social Change', in Michael Pickering and Tony Green (eds.), *Everyday Culture and the Vernacular Milieu* (Milton Keynes, 1987), ch. 2.
34 Hyder Rollins (comp.), *An Analytical Index to the Ballad Entries (1557–1709) in the Registers of the Company of Stationers of London* (Chapel Hill, 1924, Hatboro, Penn., 1967), no. 2135. For an early version see *Roxburgh Ballads*, II, pp. 334–8.
35 L. Rider Haggard (ed.), *I Walked by Night* (1935, Oxford, 1982), pp. 104–5.
36 'The Painful Plough' (BL: LR 271 a. 2, fol. 105).

37 *PR*, 28 September 1833, p. 827.

38 'The Jolly Thresherman' (London: Catnach, printer, *c*. 1830s) BL: LR 271 a. 2, v. 5, fol. 203. For other songs with similar themes see 'Generous Gift' (London: Catnach, printer, *c*. 1810s) Firth c. 67; 'The Farmer's Lucky Boy' (no imprint) Bodleian 2806 b. 9.

39 'The Honest Ploughman; or, 90 Years Ago' (London: Fortey, printer). The song was in circulation by the early 1830s: Madden 10 (IV), Madden 22 (VII), JJ: Street Ballads, 28.

40 'Past, Present, Future: Or, The Poor Man's Consolation' (London: Hill, printer) BL: LR 271 a. 2 I (1); another version (Cheltenham: Willey, printer) is at Madden 11 (IV).

41 'The Poor Labourers' (London: Ryle, printer) BL: LR 271 a. 2, v. 1 (2), fol. 120. Printings by Henson of Northampton appear in Madden 19 (IV) and Firth b. 25 (399), c. 16 (300).

42 'A Country Lad Am I' (no imprint, *c*. 1820s) BL: LR 271 a. 2, v. 5, fol. 215.

43 'Advice to Farmers' (London: Catnach, printer) JJ: Street Ballads, 28. The song was listed for sale in the Catnach catalogue of 1832.

44 Ian Dyck, 'Towards the "Cottage Charter": The Expressive Culture of Farm Workers in Nineteenth-Century England', *Rural History*, vol. 1, no. 1 (Spring 1990).

45 *PR*, 5 October 1833, pp. 39–40. See, for example, 'The Farmer's Son' (London: Pitts, printer, *c*. 1810s) Madden VIII (2).

46 The dramatist and composer Charles Dibdin (1745–1814) was instructed by Pitt's government to 'write, sing, publish and give away' war songs (T. Dibdin, 'Memoir of Charles Dibdin', in *Songs of the Late Charles Dibdin* (London, 1841), p. xxviii. Dibdin is said to have composed some 1,300 songs. See Charles Dibdin, *The Professional Life of Mr. Dibdin, Written by Himself, Together with the Words of Six Hundred Songs...*, 4 vols. (London, 1803).

47 Obelkevich, *Religion and Rural Society*, pp. 59–60. On harvest-home songs see Lucy Broadwood and J. A. Fuller-Maitland, *English County Songs* (London, 1893), pp. 81, 143, 148, 151; Fred Kitchen, *Brother to the Ox: The Autobiography of a Farm Labourer* (London, 1951), p. 65; John Buckmaster, *A Village Politician* (1897, Horsham, 1982), p. 20; 'The Autobiography of a Suffolk Farm Labourer', *Suffolk Times and Mercury*, 2 November 1894 – 16 August 1895, pt 2, ch. 2; George Deacon, *John Clare and the Folk Tradition* (London, 1983), pp. 56, 181, 230–3.

48 Flora Thompson, *Lark Rise to Candleford* (1939, Harmondsworth, 1973), p. 238.

49 John Clare, 'The Village Minstrel', in *The Village Minstrel and Other Poems* (London, 1821), stanza xlix.

50 (Preston: Harkness, printer). Broadside versions date from the 1790s, and the song was listed for sale in the Catnach catalogue of 1832. See also the versions (London: Hodges, printer) in Madden 11 (V) and Madden 10 (IV).

51 I am grateful to Michael Yates for this account of his experiences among Sussex singers. See his articles 'Harry Upton: A Singer and his Repertoire', *Traditional Music*, no. 10 (1978); and '"Stand Up Ye Men of Labour": The Socio-Political Songs of Walter Pardon', in *Musical Traditions*, no. 1 (mid-1983).

52 Alexander Somerville, *The Whistler at the Plough* (Manchester, 1852), p. 385.

53 *PR*, 7 January 1832, p. 121. See also *PR*, 25 April 1835, p. 205; 1 February 1834, p. 266.

54 *PR*, 16 December 1815, pp. 329–30.

55 'The New Times' (London: Catnach, printer) BL: LR 279 a. 2, v. 4, fol. 414. See also 'The New-Fashioned Farmer' (London: Pitts, printer, *c*. 1830) Madden 9 (III); 'When My Old Hat Was New' (Preston: Harkness, printer) Madden 18 (III) BL 1871 f. 13, fol. 64.

56 *PR*, 22 December 1832, p. 729; 28 June 1823, p. 784.

57 'What Will Old England Come to?' (London: Catnach, printer, *c*. 1830) Madden 10 (IV); 'A True Picture on the Times' (Norwich: Walker, printer) BL 11661 e. 3, fol. 184, and JJ: Street Ballads, 1.

58 *PR*, 11 November 1815, p. 174.

59 *PR*, 11 November 1815, p. 174; 1 December 1827, pp. 596–7; 11 November 1815, p. 175; 22 September 1821, p. 695; 20 November 1824, p. 452; 'The New Times' (London: Catnach, printer) BL: LR 272 a. 2, v. 4, fol. 414; 'Bad Times among the Farmers' (Sheffield: Crome, printer, 1815) Goldsmiths' 21148; 'Bonny England O!' (Brighton: Phillips, printer) Madden 22 (VII); 'The Truth, the Whole Truth, and Nothing but the Truth' (Portsea: Williams, printer) Madden 22 (VII); 'Country Hirings' (Preston: Harkness, printer) Madden 18 (III), Bodleian 2806 c. 41 (14). See also the evidence of Joseph Stallard, SC on Agriculture, V (1833), p. 493.

60 Similar complaints to those of the Regency songs appear in 'A Call to Gentlemen Farmers, for the Year 1784' (no imprint) Madden 4 (1).

61 'Autobiography of a Suffolk Farm Labourer', pt 1, ch. 2.

62 'The Truth, the Whole Truth, and Nothing but the Truth' (Portsea: Williams, printer) Madden 22 (VII).

63 *PR*, 9 June 1821, p. 681; 13 April 1822, p. 69; 18 January 1812, pp. 84–5; 3 March 1821, p. 594; 6 October 1821, p. 827.

64 Evidence of John Cramp, SC on Agriculture, V (1833), p. 266.

65 *PR*, 19 May 1821, p. 452; March 1821, p. 749.

66 'Country Hiring' (Preston: Harkness, printer) Madden 18 (III), Bodleian 2806 c. 14 (14), BL 1876 d. 41.

67 Mick Reed, 'Indoor Farm Service in 19th-Century Sussex: Some Criticisms of a Critique', *Sussex Archaeological Collections*, no. 123 (1985), pp. 225–41. See also Snell, *Annals of the Labouring Poor*, ch. 2.

68 *Rural Rides*, pp. 228–9.

69 T. Batchelor, *GVAC Bedfordshire* (1808), in William Marshall (ed.), *The Review and Abstract of the County Reports to the Board of Agriculture*, 5 vols. (London, 1817, Newton Abbott, 1969), IV, p. 589. On the labourers' wish to be boarded see Poor Law Report (1834), app. B (1), pt IV, p. 34 (John Drummond's evidence).

70 *PR*, 31 January 1829, p. 137.

71 *PR*, 22 December 1832, p. 726.

72 Poor Law Report (1834), app. B (1), pt IV, p. 466. See also pp. 40, 54, 68, 209, 385; Ann Kussmaul, *Servants in Husbandry in Early Modern England* (Cambridge, 1981), ch. 7; Obelkevich, *Religion and Rural Society*, pp. 66–9, 81–2.

73 Poor Law Report (1834), app. B (1), pt IV, p. 387 (evidence of R. A. Slaney).

74 Travis Crosby, *English Farmers and the Politics of Protection 1815–52* (Hassocks, 1977), chs. 1–3; Donald G. Barnes, *A History of the English Corn Laws 1660–1846* (1930, New York, 1961), ch. 9.

75 *PR*, 28 May 1814, pp. 684–90; 18 June 1814, p. 780.

76 *PR*, 28 May 1814, p. 687. See also *PR*, 25 March 1815, p. 355; 23 March 1822, pp. 755, 758; 28 June 1815, p. 106; 27 March 1811, pp. 753–4. Henry Hunt, who joined Cobbett in the counties to resist the Corn Bill of 1815, believed that Cobbett's *Register* inclined towards protection during the early stages of the Corn Bill lobbies – see Hunt, *Memoirs*, III, pp. 217–18. Hunt was in part responsible for the stiffening of Cobbett's opposition to the Bill.

77 *PR*, 22 October 1814, p. 517; 28 January 1815, p. 106; 4 November 1815, pp. 135–8; 2 December 1815, p. 254; 11 September 1819, pp. 104–5; 19 May 1821, p. 457; *Rural Rides*, pp. 160, 194.

78 *PR*, 12 October 1833, p. 96.

79 John Clare to Marianne Marsh, *c.* January 1832, in *The Letters of John Clare*, ed. Mark Storey (Oxford, 1985), p. 560.

80 John Denson, *A Peasant's Voice to Landowners* (Cambridge, 1830), p. 56; Snell, *Annals of the Labouring Poor*, pp. 37–8; Hunt, *Memoirs*, III, p. 173.

81 *PR*, 7 April 1821, p. 16. On the labourers' desire for the cheap bushel see 'The Labouring Man and his Wife' (London: Disley, printer) BL: LR 271 a. 5, fol. 213, and Madden 14 (VIII); 'The Farmer's Lamentation, but the Poor's Rejoicing because the Wheat is Falling', Firth c. 17 (277); 'The Times' Madden 22 (VIII); 'A New Song on the Times' (London: Pitts, printer) Madden 9 (III).

82 'Autobiography of a Suffolk Farm Labourer', pt III.

83 *The Prose of John Clare*, ed. J. W. and Anne Tibble (1951), pp. 172–3.

84 'Bad Times' (Sheffield: Crome, printer, 1815) Goldsmiths' 21148. 'The Farmer's Son' (London: Pitts, printer, *c.* 1820) Madden VIII (2).

85 *PR*, 17 March 1821, p. 774: 5 May 1821, p. 315.

86 *PR*, 14 May 1814, p. 690; 24 September 1814, pp. 385–9.

87 Hammonds, *Village Labourer*, pp. 192–3; Belchem, *'Orator' Hunt*, pp. 48–9; *Rural Rides*, pp. 296, 313.

88 SC of the House of Commons on the Poor Laws, VI (1817), pp. 87–91; Hunt, *Memoirs*, III, pp. 22–5.

89 *PR*, 3 February 1827, p. 364; 4 June 1831, p. 546.

90 Cobbett to Thomas Law Hodges, 27 October 1833 (NYPL).

91 *PR*, 6 April 1816, p. 427; 17 March 1821, p. 751.

92 To qualify for attendance in Kent, Cobbett gave a false assurance that he held freehold property in the county (*PR*, 10 June 1822, pp. 690–1) and in Wiltshire he was given title to some land (temporarily one assumes) by Henry Hunt (Hunt, *Memoirs*, III, pp. 362–3).

93 *PR*, 11 March 1815, pp. 289–93.

94 *PR*, 29 December 1821, p. 1578.

95 *PR*, 15 February 1823, pp. 428–30, 442–3.

96 *PR*, 2 February 1822, p. 301; 23 February 1822, p. 454; 2 March 1822, pp. 548–9; 6 April 1822, pp. 47–51; 26 October 1822, pp. 218, 234–7; 16 November 1822, pp. 422–3; 21 December 1822, pp. 758–9; 1 April 1826, p. 42; 15 April 1826, pp. 149–59; *Rural Rides*, pp. 50–1; *Trash*, December 1830, pp. 139–40.

97 *PR*, 1 June 1822, pp. 533–4.

98 *PR*, 5 December 1829, pp. 720–1.

99 *PR*, 22 December 1821, pp. 1501–3.

100 *Ibid.*, p. 1510. For examples of the harnessing of paupers to carts as well as other indignities, see SC on Agricultural Labourers' Wages, VI (1824), pp. 20, 27–30, 38–9, 42; SC on Emigration, V (1826–7), pp. 108, 137; SC on the Relief of Able-Bodied Persons from the Poor Rates, IV (1828), pp. 17–18, 21–2, 26–7, 44, 50; SC of the House of Lords on the Poor Laws, VII (1830–1), pp. 18, 44, 171, 212.

101 *PR*, 22 December 1821, pp. 1511–16.

102 *PR*, 19 January 1822, pp. 159–75, 182–4; *The Morning Chronicle*, 11 January 1822; *Sussex Weekly Advertiser*, 17 January 1822.

103 Cobbett to Samuel Clarke, 17 January 1822 (Nuffield). In another letter he boasted of having 'rummaged up that county of Sussex pretty well' (Cobbett to William Palmer, 9 March 1822) (Nuffield XX).

104 *PR*, 24 August 1833, p. 458; 2 March 1822, p. 519; 23 June 1832, p. 754; *Cottage Economy*, para. 6; *Emigrant's Guide*, para. 21; *Advice*, paras. 23, 312.

105 *PR*, 12 April 1834, p. 72.

106 *PR*, 11 January 1817, pp. 40–1; 20 December 1828, p. 777; 16 December 1815, pp. 330–1.

107 *PR*, 11 January 1812, pp. 58–9; 17 May 1834, pp. 392–3; 14 February 1835, p. 391.

108 Manuscript outline for 'Legacy to Lords' in 'Memorandum Book' (Nuffield XXX/315/3); *Legacy to Labourers*, esp. letters I–III.

109 *PR*, 21 December 1816, pp. 774–5.

110 *George the Fourth*, para. 211.
111 *PR*, 16 December 1815, p. 331.
112 *PR*, 22 June 1833, p. 717.
113 *PR*, 11 January 1817, pp. 40–1; 20 December 1828, p. 777; *Protestant 'Reformation'*, para. 153.
114 *Rural Rides*, p. 338.
115 *PR*, 26 May 1821, pp. 525–6.
116 *PR*, 13 January 1827, p. 131.
117 *PR*, 31 August 1822, p. 528.
118 Teodor Shanin, 'Peasantry as a Political Factor', in T. Shanin (ed.), *Peasants and Peasant Societies* (Harmondsworth, 1971), pp. 253–4, 258.
119 Hard questions about class consciousness in early nineteenth-century rural England have not been posed until recently – see the excellent articles by Wells, 'Social Protest', and Reed, 'Class and Conflict'.
120 *PR*, 19 May 1821, p. 452.
121 *PR*, 31 August 1822, p. 528.
122 The suggestion that farmers and labourers possessed the same interests is made in Armstrong, *Farmworkers*, p. 15.
123 See Dyck, 'Towards the "Cottage Charter"', esp. pp. 101–6.
124 Obelkevich, *Religion and Rural Society*, chs. 2, 6, esp. p. 101.

4 THE BATTLE FOR THE PEDLAR'S PACK

1 Thompson, *Making of the English Working Class*, pp. 691, 671.
2 See Hone, *For the Cause of Truth*; Iorwerth Prothero, *Artisans and Politics in Early Nineteenth-Century London* (London, 1979); Belchem, *'Orator' Hunt*; James Epstein, *The Lion of Freedom: Feargus O'Connor and the Chartist Movement 1832–1842* (London, 1982); McCalman, *Radical Underworld*; Chase, *'The People's Farm'*; Stewart Angas Weaver, *John Fielden and the Politics of Popular Radicalism 1832–1847* (Oxford, 1987); Smith, *Politics of Language*.
3 On the Hampden Clubs see *PR*, 27 April 1816, p. 527; 18 January 1817, p. 72; 14 December 1816, pp. 748–9; 4 January 1817, pp. 5–6; *Hundred Days*, letters II, III; McCalman, *Radical Underworld*, pp. 100–1; Hone, *For the Cause of Truth*, pp. 260–3.
4 Belchem, *'Orator' Hunt*, pp. 196, 46–7. For Hunt's account of his work with Cobbett against the 1815 Corn Bill see *Memoirs*, III, pp. 218–25.
5 John Stevenson, 'The Queen Caroline Affair', in John Stevenson (ed.), *London in the Age of Reform* (Oxford, 1977), p. 117. Dr Stevenson's forthcoming study of Cobbett is eagerly awaited. On the Queen Caroline affair see also Thomas W. Laqueur, 'The Queen Caroline Affair: Politics as Art in the Reign of George IV', *Journal of Modern History*, vol. 54 (September 1982); Prothero, *Artisans and Politics*, pp. 133–54. Although the Queen Caroline movement was London-based, Cobbett did much to encourage the distribution of pro-Caroline handbills in the countryside – see *PR*, July–December 1820.
6 *PR*, 10 August 1816, pp. 162–4; 7 December 1816, p. 709; 18 May 1816, pp. 611–12.
7 2 November 1816 is usually cited as the starting-date of the two-penny *Register*; in fact it was 12 October 1816. The October sheets (open letters to Francis Burdett on the subject of parliamentary reform) are scarce, though a broadsheet for 12 October is at BL Colindale.
8 [Board of Agriculture], *The Agricultural State of the Kingdom, in February, March and April, 1816* (London, 1816), pp. 7–8, 25, 40, 42, 86–7, 138, 192, 229, 232, 250–1, 301, 305–6, 316, 335, 356.
9 *PR*, 28 September 1816, pp. 383–90, 403–12.

10 *PR*, 2 November 1816, pp. 545–6, 561.
11 *Hundred Days*, pp. 24, 28; *PR*, 6 December 1817, p. 1097; 22 December 1832, p. 728.
12 *PR*, 21 December 1816, pp. 771–2. On circulation figures for the first broadsheet *Registers* see Pearl, *Cobbett: A Bibliographical Account*, p. 68; *The Times*, 1 January 1818; *PR*, 10 April 1830, pp. 464–5; Spater, *Cobbett*, p. 565 n108.
13 For Cobbett's use of these terms, including with reference to himself, see *PR*, 13 April 1822, p. 70; 7 June 1823, pp. 599–600; 28 February 1835, p. 529; *Mr. Cobbett's Taking Leave of his Countrymen* (5 April 1817), pp. 6–7.
14 *PR*, 26 October 1816, pp. 519–20; *Hundred Days*, p. 27; *PR*, 30 November 1830, pp. 676–7, 689. On rural disturbances in 1816 see A. J. Peacock, *Bread or Blood: A Study of the Agrarian Riots in East Anglia in 1816* (London, 1965).
15 On 'pre-industrial' and 'modern' protests see John Stevenson, 'Food Riots in England 1792–1818', in J. Stevenson and R. Quinault (eds.), *Popular Protest and Public Order* (London, 1974); *idem*, 'Bread or Blood', in G. E. Mingay (ed.), *The Unquiet Countryside* (London, 1989); E. P. Thompson, 'The Moral Economy of the English Crowd in the Eighteenth Century', *Past and Present*, no. 50 (1971); Ian R. Christie, *Stress and Stability in Late Eighteenth-Century Britain* (Oxford, 1984), pp. 150–5; Bohstedt, *Riots and Community Politics*, ch. 9; Rudé, *Ideology and Popular Protest*, ch. 2; Roger Wells, 'Britain's Avoidance of Revolution in the 1790s Revisited', *Bulletin of the Society for the Study of Labour History*, vol. 54, no. 3 (Winter 1989), pp. 32–9.
16 *PR*, 30 November 1816, pp. 675–9, 689, 695–6.
17 'The King against William Cobbett: Trial of William Cobbett for Publishing a Seditious Libel' (1831), in John Macdonell (ed.), *Reports of State Trials*, new ser. (London 1889), II (1823–31), pp. 857–72.
18 *PR*, 2 November 1816, p. 576.
19 Smith, *Politics of Language*, ch. 6.
20 William H. Wickwar, *The Struggle for Freedom of the Press 1819–1832* (London, 1928), p. 52.
21 G. A. Cranfield, *The Press and Society* (London, 1978), pp. 88–94, 109–10. See also Richard Altick, *The English Common Reader: A Social History of the Mass Reading Public* (London, 1957), pp. 324–6; R. K. Webb, *The British Working-Class Reader* (London, 1955, New York, 1971), pp. 49–54; Arthur Aspinall, *Politics and the Press* (London, 1949), pp. 29–31; Hollis, *Pauper Press, passim*.
22 The only difference in the method of propagation between Cobbett's sheets and that of the broadside song or chapbook was that they were not generally advertised by street cries. In the experience of a Wolverhampton magistrate who was attempting to comply with Sidmouth's appeal for due enforcement of the Hawker's and Pedlar's Act, one of Cobbett's vendors was inconveniently silent: 'I detained the man till this morning, intending to have convicted him in the penalty of ten pounds under the Hawker's and Pedlar's Act, but in perusing that Act I do not feel myself justified because he did not proclaim them thro' the streets but only stood with them for sale in the Market Place' (A. B. Haden to Viscount Sidmouth, 23 January 1817) HO 42/158. For Cobbett's instructions to hawkers see *PR*, 28 December 1816, p. 801; 25 January 1817, pp. 97–8, 107; 1 February 1817, p. 129. Many copies of the first broadsheet *Registers* were forwarded to the Home Office by disgruntled magistrates; see HO 42/155–7.
23 Cobbett to Matthew Carey, 4 April 1825 (NYPL, Edward Smith Collection).
24 *An Almanac for the Year 1816 by Francis Moore* (1816), pp. 17–19 (HRO 44M69/K1/15).
25 *PR*, 11 December 1813, p. 751; 6 December 1817, p. 1117.
26 *Moore's Prophecies for 1821* (Newcastle-upon-Tyne: Marshall, printer) JJ: Street Bal-

lads, I. For other radical implications in almanacs see Bernard Capp, *Astrology and the Popular Press: English Almanacs, 1500–1800* (London 1979), pp. 265–6.

27 'A Priest to the Temple, or, The Country Parson' (1652), in F. E. Hutchinson (ed.), *The Works of George Herbert* (Oxford, 1941), ch. 32. The poem was not published until 1652, nineteen years after Herbert's death.

28 Maldwyn Edwards, 'John Wesley', in R. Davis and G. Rupp (eds.), *A History of the Methodist Church in Great Britain* (London, 1965), p. 58. See also Robert Wearmouth, *Methodism and the Common People of the Eighteenth Century* (London, 1945), p. 135.

29 George Ewart Evans, *Ask the Fellows who Cut the Hay* (London, 1956), ch. 6; Keith Thomas, *Religion and the Decline of Magic* (1971, Harmondsworth, 1973), chs. 1, 21; Bob Bushaway, *By Rite: Custom, Ceremony and Community in England 1700–1800* (London, 1982); Charles Phythian-Adams, 'Rural Culture', in G. E. Mingay (ed.), *The Victorian Countryside* (London, 1981), II, ch. 45; Vincent, *Literacy and Popular Culture*, ch. 5; R. W. Malcolmson, *Life and Labour in England, 1700–1780* (London, 1981), ch. 4; John Rule, 'Methodism, Popular Beliefs and Village Culture in Cornwall, 1800–1850', in R. D. Storch (ed.), *Popular Culture and Custom in Nineteenth-Century England* (London, 1982); Obelkevich, *Religion and Rural Society*, ch. 6.

30 Howitt, *Rural Life of England*, p. 113.

31 Many of the radical songs of the 1790s were printed for Thomas Spence: see especially Madden 5 (III), 15. The earliest broadsheet publications by Cobbett that I have located are *Cobbett's Advice* (London, 1800) LUCB, no. 459 (a); and *Important Considerations* (1803), *Loyal and Patriotic Handbills*, fol. 107. Apart from the two-penny *Register* he published numerous petitions and political essays in broadsheet form, such as *Cobbett's Advice to the Chopsticks*, first and second address, 1832. See *PR*, 20 October 1832, pp. 144–7; 27 October 1832, p. 203.

32 Charles Knight, *Passages in a Working Life*, 4 vols. (London, 1864), I, pp. 188, 243. A Kentish correspondent to the Home Office advised that Cobbett was 'worthy of imitation only in his system of propagation' (28 January 1817, HO 42/158).

33 Deacon, *John Clare*, pp. 18, 33, 43, 52–3, 68–9; Margaret Grainger, *John Clare: A Collector of Ballads* (Peterborough, 1964), p. 7, app.; J. W. and Anne Tibble, *John Clare: His Life and Poetry* (London, 1956), p. 130; Clare to Marianne Marsh, *c.* January 1832, in *Letters of John Clare*, ed. Storey, p. 560.

34 Jack Goody, *The Domestication of the Savage Mind* (Cambridge, 1977), p. 27. See also Ruth Finnegan, *Literacy and Orality: Studies in the Technology of Communication* (Oxford, 1988), pp. 165–6; David Cressy, *Literacy and the Social Order: Reading and Writing in Tudor and Stuart England* (Cambridge, 1980), p. 189.

35 *PR*, 23 April 1831, p. 189.

36 'Autobiography of a Suffolk Farm Labourer', pt II, ch. 2. On village song-men see Heath, *English Peasant*, p. 182; Alfred Williams, *Folk-Songs of the Upper Thames* (London, 1923), pp. 20–3.

37 Joseph Spence, 'An Account of the Author', in Stephen Duck, *Poems on Several Occasions* (London, 1736), pp. xii–xiii.

38 Clare, 'Autobiography', pp. 15, 19.

39 Joseph Arch, *The Story of his Life*, ed. The Countess of Warwick (London, 1898), pp. 27, 33–4.

40 *Advice*, para. 44; *PR*, 19 February 1820, p. 26. For a venue of instruction similar to Cobbett's see Kussmaul, *Autobiography of Joseph Mayett*, pp. x, 1.

41 *The Autobiography of John Britton*, 2 vols. (London, 1850), I, p. 59n. Britton (1771–1857) spent his early years as a farm worker and errand boy in Wiltshire.

42 Stephen Duck, 'The Thresher's Labour', in *Poems on Several Occasions* (1736, Monston, 1973); Rayner Unwin, *The Rural Muse: Studies in the Peasant Poetry of England*

(London, 1954), pp. 47–67; Morag Shiach, *Discourse on Popular Culture: Class, Gender and History in Cultural Analysis, 1730 to the Present* (London, 1989), pp. 47–56.

43 Robert Bloomfield, *The Farmer's Boy* (1800), in *The Works of Robert Bloomfield* (London, n.d.), pp. 16, 24–5, 36–7; Unwin, *Rural Muse*, pp. 87–109; *Selections from the Correspondence of Robert Bloomfield*, ed. W. H. Hart (London, 1870), pp. 9–16.

44 Unwin, *Rural Muse*, pp. 105–7; Jonathan Lawson, *Robert Bloomfield* (Boston, 1980), pp. 43–6; Williams, *Country and the City*, pp. 134–6.

45 *PR*, 24 April 1819, pp. 980–1.

46 Dibdin, 'Memoir of Charles Dibdin', p. xxviii. See n. 46, ch. 3.

47 Place Papers, vol. XXXVIII, BM Add. MS 27,825, vol. 1.2, fols 144–5; SC on Education, VII (1835), p. 465 (Place's testimony); *The Autobiography of Francis Place*, ed. Mary Thrale (Cambridge, 1972), p. 15; Douglas Jerrold, 'The Ballad Singer', in *The Heads of the People, or Portraits of the English*, 2 vols. (London 1840–1), I, pp. 288–97.

48 Bert Lloyd argued that 'classic peasant folksong' died a stark and sudden death during the early nineteenth century (A. L. Lloyd, *Folk Song in England* (London, 1967), pp. 41, 218, 299–301, 315, 317), but see Dyck, 'Towards the "Cottage Charter"'; Alun Howkins, 'The Voice of the People: The Social Meaning and Context of Country Song', *Oral History*, vol. 3, no. 1 (Spring 1975); Alun Howkins and Ian Dyck, 'Popular Ballads, Rural Radicalism and William Cobbett', *History Workshp*, no. 23 (Spring 1987); Roy Palmer, *The Sound of History: Songs and Social Comment* (Oxford, 1988), ch. 1. On the activities of broadside song printers in the countryside see Charles Hindley, *The Life and Times of James Catnach* (London, 1878), 'Introduction'; Leslie Shepard, *John Pitts, Ballad Collector of Seven Dials, London 1765–1844* (London, 1969), pp. 46–7; R. S. Thomson, 'The Development of the Broadside Ballad Trade and its Influence upon the Transmission of Folk Songs' (PhD thesis, University of Cambridge, 1974), p. 141.

49 *PR*, 11 December 1813, p. 751; 4 November 1809, p. 644.

50 Dickinson, 'Popular Conservatism and Militant Loyalism', pp. 110–19.

51 See Hannah More, 'A Prefatory Letter', in Ann Yearsley, *Poems on Several Occasions* (London, 1785), pp. iii–xii.

52 Wheeler and Broadley, *Napoleon and the Invasion of England*, I, p. 210; *Memoirs of the Life and Correspondence of Mrs. Hannah More*, 4 vols., ed. William Roberts (London, 1835), I, p. 473; Hannah More to the Bishop of Bath and Wells, 1801, in *The Letters of Hannah More*, ed. R. Brimley Johnson (London, 1925), p. 185; Susan Pederson, 'Hannah More Meets Simple Simon: Tracts, Chapbooks and Popular Culture in Late Eighteenth-Century England', *Journal of British Studies*, vol. 25, no. 1 (January 1986), pp. 85–7; G. H. Spinney, 'Cheap Repository Tracts: Hazard and Marshall Edition', *The Library*, fourth ser., no. 3 (December 1939), p. 299.

53 Cobbett to [John Wright], 28 June 1799, in Gaines, 'Two Letters', p. 54; Cobbett to Hannah More, 20 October 1800 (Illinois). A portion of this letter is printed in Gerald Duff (ed.), *Letters of William Cobbett* (Saltzburg, 1974), p. 15. See also Hannah More to Zachary Macaulay, 8 September 1797, in *Letters of Hannah More to Zachary Macaulay*, ed. Arthur Roberts (New York, 1960), pp. 16–17.

54 See, for example, 'Village Politics, Addressed to all the Mechanics, Journeymen, and Labourers in Great Britain', in *The Works of Hannah More* (London, 1853), II, pp. 221–36; 'Black Giles, the Poacher', in *Works of Hannah More* (London, 1830 edn), II, pp. 181–207; 'The Shepherd of Salisbury Plain', in *ibid.*, I, pp. 251–86. For an excellent discussion of More's discourse see Smith, *Politics of Language*, pp. 90–6.

55 Letter by daughter Anne Cobbett to William, 8 June 1809 (BM Add. MS 22,907, fol. 164). Cobbett acknowledged having read 'a great part of the religious tracts' (*Rural Rides*, p. 45).

56 *PR*, 22 November 1817, p. 1046.

57 Deacon, *John Clare*, p. 33.

58 The two-penny *Register*, he remarked, will do the people 'a great deal more good than Hannah More's *Village Politics*' (*PR*, 22 March 1817, p. 353). More's remark is inscribed in her hand on the reverse side of Cobbett's letter to her of 20 October 1800 (Illinois) – see M. G. Jones, *Hannah More* (New York, 1968), p. 257 n61.

59 *PR*, 31 May 1833, pp. 514, 522.

60 See, for example, Frederick Eden, 'Of the Diet, Dress, Fuel, and Habitation of the Labouring Classes', *Annals of Agriculture*, vol. 28 (1797), pp. 457n–458n.

61 *Mr. Cobbett's Taking Leave of his Countrymen* (5 April 1817), pp. 10–11.

62 'Village Politics', in *Works of Hannah More* (London, 1853 edn), II, p. 236.

63 'The Ploughman's Ditty' (*c.* 1794), in *Works of Hannah More* (London, 1830 edn), II, pp. 75–7.

64 'The Riot...' (London: Marshall, printer, 1795), LUCB, no. 452; Madden 15.

65 *PR*, 11 July 1829, p. 43.

66 *PR*, 20 April 1822, p. 188.

67 *Hundred Days*, p. 16; *Mr. Cobbett's Taking Leave of his Countrymen* (5 April 1817), pp. 10–11.

68 More to William Wilberforce, 31 March 1817 (Duke University); *Life and Correspondence of Mrs. Hannah More*, ed. Roberts, III, p. 133; IV, pp. 4–6, 10–11, 18, 180. See also Webb, *Working-Class Reader*, p. 56.

69 *PR*, 21 July 1821, p. 61.

70 SC on Education, VII (1835), p. 85; More to Zachary Macaulay, 1796, in *Life and Correspondence of Mrs. Hannah More*, ed. Roberts, I, p. 473.

71 *PR*, 29 May 1830, p. 712.

72 Knight, *Passages in a Working Life*, I, p. 188; *PR*, 5 February 1825, pp. 335–9.

73 *PR*, 15 November 1823, p. 437.

74 J. F. C. Harrison, *Learning and Living 1790–1860* (London, 1961), p. 83.

75 *PR*, 26 February 1831, pp. 543–4; 7 April 1832, p. 20.

76 Advertisement in *PR*, 26 January 1833, p. 256; *PR*, 1 March 1834, pp. 524–5.

77 W. Lovett, *The Life and Struggles of William Lovett* (1876, 1967 edn), p. 29.

78 Broadsheet entitled 'Mechanics' Institution' (Birmingham: Hodgetts, printer, 1832) Goldsmiths' 27952–4.

79 *PR*, 21 November 1818, pp. 275–6.

80 *PR*, 7 April 1821, p. 9.

81 As a youth Cobbett had been 'a great reader of the Bible' (*Treatise on Corn*, para. 6) and cited it in his writings more frequently than any other source. He preferred to call his tracts 'sermons': '"tracts" is beneath the thing described' (*PR*, 23 June 1821, p. 361).

82 *Hundred Days*, p. 56.

83 *PR*, 3 August 1822, p. 308.

84 'The Poor Man's Bible' was not published. Manuscript fragments are at Nuffield XXX/307/1. See *PR*, 23 May 1835, p. 457; 7 April 1832, p. 20. Cobbett began publishing his *Monthly Religious Tracts* in early 1821. After the third number he changed their title to *Sermons*.

85 'The Rights of the Poor, and the Punishment of Oppressors', in *Sermons*, no. 4.

86 *Cottage Economy*, paras. 5, 17.

87 Anne Cobbett to John Wright, 2 October 1808, BM Add. MS 22,907, fol. 59; Anne Cobbett to Frederick Reid, 13 July 1812, in Melville, *Life and Letters*, II, p. 72.

88 'Autobiography of a Suffolk Farm Labourer', pt I, ch. 2. See also Somerville, *Whistler*, p. 43; *PR*, 5 June 1824, p. 624; 15 March 1817, p. 327.

89 *Rural Rides*, p. 180; *PR*, 5 October 1822, pp. 52–6.

90 *Legacy to Parsons*, p. 112.

91 *PR*, 8 August 1835, pp. 245–50.

92 *Rural Rides*, p. 187; *PR*, 12 June 1813, pp. 840–1; 21 August 1813, pp. 226–7; 27 January 1820, pp. 717–35, 746.

93 *PR*, 12 June 1813, p. 842.

94 *Rural Rides*, p. 182.

95 *Ibid.*, p. 179.

96 *PR*, 12 October 1833, p. 87.

97 *PR*, 8 March 1828, pp. 302–3.

98 *Cottage Economy*, para. 148. For similar stories see 'The Methodist Parson, Or, The Flitch of Bacon' (BL: LR 271 a. 2, vol. 1 (2), and Madden 23 (VIII); also 'Preaching for Bacon' (BL 1876 d. 41, fol. 458).

99 Cecil Sharp, *English Folk Songs: Some Conclusions* (1907, Belmont, Calif., 1965), p. 114.

100 A. E. Green, 'McCaffery: A Study in the Variation and Function of a Ballad', *Lore and Language*, no. 3 (1970), pp. 4–9; no. 4 (1970), pp. 3–12; no. 5 (1971), pp. 5–11. See also John Ashton, 'Truth in Folk Song: Some Developments and Applications', *Canadian Folk Music Journal*, vol. 5 (1977), pp. 12–17; Howkins, 'The Voice of the People', pp. 61–2.

101 *Cottage Economy*, para. 263; *PR*, 3 November 1821, p. 1073.

102 Buckmaster, *Village Politician*, pp. 39–40, 69–70.

103 See Obelkevich, *Religion and Rural Society*, ch. 5; Howkins, *Poor Labouring Men*, ch. 3.

104 *Cottage Economy*, para. 11; *PR*, 5 February 1825, pp. 347–8; 10 March 1821, p. 689; 15 January 1825, p. 143; 7 December 1833, pp. 579–82; 21 September 1831, p. 731; *Advice*, para. 231.

105 *PR*, 7 June 1834, p. 591.

106 Arthur Young, *A Six Weeks' Tour through the Southern Counties of England and Wales* (London, 1769), p. 216; William Marshall, *Minutes, Experiments, Observations, and General Remarks on Agriculture in the Southern Counties*, 2 vols. (London, 1799), I, pp. 191–2, 383.

107 Kitchen, *Brother to the Ox*, pp. 46–8, 71, 129–30. See also 'Jolly Ploughboy' (BL: LR 271 a. 2, vol. I (1); 'Autobiography of a Suffolk Farm Labourer', pt II, ch. 1.

108 William Stevenson, *GVAC Surrey* (London, 1809), p. 541. See Stuart Macdonald, 'Agricultural Improvement and the Neglected Labourer', *Agricultural History Review*, vol. 31, pt 2 (1983), pp. 81–90.

109 Buckmaster, *Village Politician*, p. 62.

110 *PR*, 28 June 1823, p. 782.

111 *PR*, 28 February 1835, p. 531; *Year's Residence*, paras. 314–17.

112 *PR*, 21 September 1833, p. 735; 28 February 1835, pp. 531–2.

113 Arch, *Story of his Life*, p. 29; Kitchen, *Brother to the Ox*, pp. 46–9; Richard Jefferies, *Toilers of the Field* (1892, Glasgow, 1982), pp. 46, 80.

114 *PR*, 26 December 1831, p. 14; 21 September 1833, p. 730.

115 *PR*, 7 May 1831, p. 308.

116 *PR*, 29 June 1822, p. 820; 27 March 1830, p. 394; 21 January 1832, p. 220; 29 June 1822, p. 820. 'If a cottage is flowery outside,' said Alexander Somerville, 'we may be sure that inside there is neither a want of cleanliness nor a neglect of moral training' (*Whistler*, p. 169).

117 *PR*, 14 December 1816, p. 758. See also *PR*, 14 July 1832, p. 81; 3 January 1825, p. 23; 7 June 1834, p. 590; *Advice*, para. 99; Howitt, *Rural Life of England*, pp. 569–71; Clare, 'Autobiography', pp. 24, 38.

118 *PR*, 4 January 1817, p. 26. See also *PR*, 24 February 1821, pp. 512–13; 7 April 1821, pp. 13–14; 26 April 1828, p. 594; 7 February 1829, pp. 183–4; 30 October 1830, p. 551; 4 October 1835, p. 5.

119 'The Sin of Forbidding Marriage', in *Sermons*, no. 11; *PR*, 14 September 1833, pp. 653–6.

120 *Advice*, para. 99.

121 *Surplus Population: A Comedy in Three Acts*, in *PR*, 28 May 1831, pp. 492–510; *Trash*, June 1831, pp. 265–92.

122 Cobbett to Jesse Oldfield, 25 March 1835 (Cornell); *PR*, 6 June 1835, p. 593.

123 *PR*, 11 June 1831, pp. 650–1.

124 *PR*, 3 January 1835, pp. 20–2; 7 February 1835, p. 358; Edward Lytton Bulwer, *England and the English* (1835, Chicago, 1967 edn), p. 201. One of Cobbett's great purposes in publishing the letters of Sussex emigrants to the United States was to show the humanity and charitable dispositions of rural workers: see *Emigrant's Guide*, letter III.

125 *PR*, 30 November 1816, p. 676; 6 December 1817, p. 1108; 9 November 1822, p. 718; 19 January 1822, p. 138.

126 *PR*, 10 October 1818, p. 242.

127 *PR*, 21 November 1818, p. 269.

128 *PR*, 6 December 1817, pp. 1113–15. Also: *PR*, 21 November 1818, pp. 254–5; 21 December 1822, pp. 719–20; 18 July 1829, p. 71.

129 See Tibble and Tibble (eds.), *Prose of John Clare*, pp. 221–2. For a fine discussion of Clare's agrarian protests see John Barrell, *The Idea of Landscape and the Sense of Place, 1730–1840* (Cambridge, 1972), app.

130 David Williams, *John Frost: A Study in Chartism* (New York, 1969), p. 50.

131 *PR*, 5 February 1825, pp. 348–9.

132 *PR*, 9 May 1835, pp. 322, 340; 6 June 1835, pp. 589–92.

133 John Knight to Cobbett, 10 September 1833 (Rutgers). See also Robert Bloomfield to George Bloomfield, 30 May 1802, in *Correspondence of Robert Bloomfield*, ed. Hart, pp. 25–8. For a brief but insightful discussion of Cobbett's views on education see Johnson, '"Really Useful Knowledge"', pp. 88–90.

134 Frederick Engels, 'Speech at the Graveside of Karl Marx' (1883), in Marx and Engels, *Selected Works*, p. 429.

135 *PR*, 15 November 1823, p. 488. Also: *PR*, 26 November 1825, pp. 542–8.

136 *PR*, 8 June 1816, p. 721; 18 May 1816, p. 614.

137 'The Farmers, Millers, and Bakers' (no imprint, c. 1830s) Firth c. 16 (291).

138 *PR*, 7 May 1831, p. 309; 26 November 1831, p. 557.

5 COTTAGE ECONOMY

1 [Henry Brougham], 'Cottage Economy', *The Edinburgh Review*, vol. 38, no. 75 (February 1823), p. 105. For identification of the author see 'Letters of Timothy Tickler', p. 223.

2 *The Quarterly Review*, vol. 8, no. 16 (December 1812), pp. 319–56; vol. 81 (July 1829), pp. 240–84.

3 For a brief discussion of the genre see Dyck, 'Towards the "Cottage Charter"', pp. 99–100.

4 *PR*, 22 January 1820, pp. 648–9; 7 April 1821, p. 11; *Cottage Economy*, para. 134; *Advice*, para. 327.

5 *PR*, 27 October 1821, p. 1010; *Rural Rides*, pp. 110–11; *Year's Residence*, paras. 86, 185–6, 201. The best sources on Cobbett's farming practices are the family correspondence in the BL and Nuffield College.

6 Osborne, *William Cobbett*, pp. 175–6; Schweizer and Osborne, *Cobbett in his Times*, p. 6. For more discussions of Cobbett's farming, see Green, *Great Cobbett*, ch. 13; A. Julian Pell, 'William Cobbett', *Journal of the Royal Agricultural Society of England*, vol. 63 1902), pp. 1–26. Cobbett and Henry Hunt participated in some agricultural ventures, most notably the importation of the sheep – see Cobbett's letters to Hunt of 28 August 1809, 21 March 1810, 22 November 1813 (Adelphi).

7 *PR*, 26 May 1821, p. 524; 3 November 1821, p. 1036.

8 *PR*, 5 May 1821, p. 336; 26 July 1823, p. 221. Reports on the premiums appeared regularly in *Annals of Agriculture*.

9 Susan Cobbett, 'Additional Notes' (Nuffield XVII/3/2–3).

10 *Rural Rides*, p. 418; *PR*, 29 May 1830, p. 707; 25 May 1822, p. 452; *Year's Residence*, para. 356. See also Marshall, *Review and Abstract*, II, p. 307n.

11 For definitions of a 'peasantry' see Dennis Mills, *Lord and Peasant in Nineteenth-Century Britain* (London, 1980), esp. pp. 43–8; *idem*, 'The Nineteenth-Century Peasantry of Melbourn, Cambridgeshire', in R. M. Smith (ed.), *Land, Kinship and Life-Cycle* (Cambridge, 1984), pp. 481–518; Mick Reed, 'Nineteenth-Century Rural England: A Case for Peasant Studies?', *The Journal of Peasant Studies*, vol. 14, no. 1 (October 1986); *idem*, 'The Peasantry of Nineteenth-Century England: A Neglected Class?', *History Workshop*, no. 18 (Autumn 1984); *idem*, 'Class and Conflict in Rural England', pp. 8–10.

12 'Statement of 1820' (Illinois), reprinted in Duff (ed.), *Letters of William Cobbett*, pp. 52–8; Susan Cobbett's MS notes on land purchases, 1867 (Nuffield XVIII/1/1); Anne Cobbett, 'Account of the Family' (Nuffield XV, fols. 23–4); additional notes by Anne Cobbett (Nuffield XVI/1/5–6) and additional notes by Susan Cobbett (Nuffield XVII/1/2–5; XVII/2/2–3; XVII/5/1; XVII/6/4); Cobbett family correspondence at BL 22,907 (especially Cobbett's letters to John Wright).

13 Bishop's Waltham Vestry Book, 6 October 1816, 18 October 1816, 19 June 1818 (HRO 30 M77A/PC1); *Trash*, October 1830, pp. 88–9; *PR*, 20 December 1828, p. 780; 20 March 1830, pp. 357–8; 15 January 1831, pp. 159–61. On the eventual enclosure of the Chase in 1870 see *The Victoria History of the Counties of England: Hampshire* (London, 1908), III, p. 278.

14 *Journals of the House of Lords*, vol. LIX (1826–7), p. 408; *A Reply to 'An Appeal to the Bond-Land Tenants of the Parish of Droxford', on the Subject of Enclosing the Waltham Chase* (1826) HRO 44 M69/K1/18; *PR*, 29 January 1831, p. 258; *Rural Rides*, p. 481; *Woodlands*, para, 64; *PR*, 31 July 1813, pp. 129–5; 15 January 1831, pp. 159–61; *Trash*, October 1830, p. 86.

15 *Trash*, October 1830, p. 87.

16 *Horse-Hoeing Husbandry*, pp. 315–16, 155.

17 *PR*, 31 July 1813, p. 139.

18 *PR*, 26 May 1821, pp. 516–17, 522–5; 6 November 1824, pp. 349–52; 14 January 1832, pp. 131–3; 25 August 1832, p. 507; 29 January 1831, p. 258.

19 Poor Law Report (1834), app. A, pt I, pp. 27, 170, 186, 379–80, 739; pt III, pp. 41–2; Charles William Stubbs, *The Land and the Labourers* (London, 1891), pp. 13–37, 124; Ashby, *Joseph Ashby*, p. 164; Henry Vavasour, 'Case of a Cottager' (1801), in *Communications to the Board of Agriculture*, vol. 4 (1805), pp. 367–9; Thomas Babington, 'Account of Some Cottagers', in *ibid.*, pp. 392–8.

20 Thomas Thompson, 'Reasons for Giving Lands to Cottagers, to Enable Them to Keep Cows' (1803), *Communications to the Board of Agriculture*, vol. 4 (1805), p. 424.

21 SC of the House of Lords on the Poor Laws, VIII (1830–1), pp. 26–8 (evidence of the Rev. S. Demainbray); *PR*, 14 November 1829, pp. 633–4; 20 December 1828, p. 779.

22 *PR*, 3 December 1831, p. 592; 'A Memoir of William Cobbett by James Paul Cobbett' (1862) Nuffield XIV. See also *PR*, 27 June 1829, p. 819; 17 April 1830, p. 489; 1

December 1821, pp. 1337–9; 12 January 1822, pp. 94–5, 120–1; 10 August 1816, p. 162.

23 *Rural Rides*, pp. 452, 454; Raphael Samuel, 'Village Labour', in R. Samuel (ed.), *Village Life and Labour* (London, 1975), pp. 8–10; C. R. Tubbs, 'The Development of the Smallholding and Cottage Stock-Keeping Economy of the New Forest', *Agricultural History Review*, vol. 13 (1965), pp. 23–39; G. E. Briscoe-Eyre, *The New Forest, its Common Rights and Cottage Stock-Keepers* (Lyndhurst, 1883); Richard Heath, 'Peasant Life in the New Forest' (1892), in *The English Peasant*, pp. 136–41; Winifred Foley, *A Child in the Forest* (London, 1977), pp. 77, 82, 86. See also Chris Fisher, *Custom, Work and Market Capitalism: The Forest of Dean Colliers, 1788–1888* (London, 1981); Howitt, *Rural Life of England*, pt V.

24 E. W. Brayley and John Britton, 'Hampshire', in *The Beauties of England and Wales*, vol. 6 (1805), p. 9. In cash terms during the mid-1790s a fat hog could fetch £20 on the market – see Abraham and William Driver, *GVAC Hampshire* (London, 1794), p. 27.

25 Charles Vancouver, *GVAC Hampshire*, pp. 81, 84, 494; William Gilpin, *Remarks on Forest Scenery*, 2 vols. (1791, Richmond, 1973), II, p. 40. Similar complaints against the cottagers of the Forest of Bere appear in 'Public Report on the Forest of Bere' (1792), in *The Annual Hampshire Repository*, vol. 1 (1797), p. 80. See also J. Middleton, *GVAC Middlesex* (London, 1798), p. 42; Eden, *State of the Poor*, I, pp. xvi–xix; Marshall, *Review and Abstract*, V, pp. 8–9.

26 *PR*, 1 December 1821, pp. 1338–9.

27 *PR*, 14 July 1832, p. 81; 28 July 1832, pp. 199–200, 204, 215; *Rural Rides*, pp. 173, 191, 206, 258, 302–3, 320, 334, 337, 409, 438–9; *PR*, 26 November 1825, p. 531; 1 December 1821, pp. 1338–9; 17 November 1821, pp. 1202–3, 1208–9; 5 January 1822, pp. 1612–13; 27 March 1830, p. 396; 3 December 1831, p. 591; 17 April 1830, p. 489; 29 September 1832, pp. 779–80; *Trash*, July 1830, pp. 11–13; Cobbett to George Woodward, 3 August 1822 (BM Add. MS 31,127, fol. 26).

28 *PR*, 17 April 1830, p. 489; 1 December 1821, pp. 1337–9; 12 January 1822, pp. 94–5; 10 August 1816, p. 162; 27 June 1829, p. 819. For a discussion of these sorts of peasants or 'household producers', see Wells, 'Social Protest, Class, Conflict and Consciousness', pp. 123–5. Wells describes them as 'entrepreneurial', but see Reed, 'Class and Conflict in Rural England', pp. 19–28.

29 Davies, *Case of the Labourers in Husbandry*, app.; the Rev. Arthur Young, *GVAC Sussex*, second edn. (London, 1813), p. 412; *idem*, 'A Tour through Sussex, 1793', in *Annals of Agriculture*, vol. 22, no. 122 (1794); T. L. Richardson, 'The Standard of Living Controversy, 1790–1840 with Special Reference to the Agricultural Labourer in Seven English Counties' (PhD thesis, University of Hull, 1977), p. 190 n5; Somerville, *Whistler*, pp. 142–3.

30 *PR*, 19 May 1821, p. 461; *Rural Rides*, p. 429.

31 Eden, *State of the Poor*, I, pp. vii–ix, 524–33.

32 Stevenson, *GVAC Surrey*, p. 544.

33 Ashby, *Joseph Ashby*, pp. 105–8. See also Edwin Grey, *Cottage Life in a Hertfordshire Village* (St Albans, n.d., *c.* 1935), p. 96. Despite the ovens, some of Cobbett's labourers continued to purchase their bread from the baker (*PR*, 30 November 1816, pp. 684–5).

34 *PR*, 25 October 1828, p. 534; 19 September 1829, p. 354; 20 December 1828, p. 781; 22 April 1826, pp. 243–4; 2 June 1821, pp. 591–2; 18 December 1830, p. 1031; *Cottage Economy*, paras. 113–15, 134, 189–92; Cobbett to Samuel Clarke, 15 September 1821 (Nuffield). On the size of cottage gardens, see the publications of the *Central Society of Education*, vol. 1 (1837), pp. 342–4; vol. 2 (1838), pp. 259–61, 371–4; Davies, *Case of the Labourers in Husbandry*, p. 36; James Phillips Kay, 'Earnings of Agricultural

Labourers in Norfolk and Suffolk', *Journal of the Royal Statistical Society*, vol. 1, no. 7 (July 1838), pp. 179–81.

35 *Cottage Economy*, paras. 81–6; *PR*, 21 April 1821, pp. 191–3; 4 August 1810, p. 140.

36 Arthur Young, *A Farmer's Letters to the People of England*, 2 vols. (London, 1767), I, pp. 200–1; Eden, *State of the Poor*, II, pp. 278, 435; Davies, *Case of the Labourers in Husbandry*, pp. 31–2; *Annals of Agriculture*, vol. 24 (1795), pp. 63, 142, 145, 148, 161, 169, 171, 184–5, 196, 201, 216, 316; Thompson, 'Moral Economy of the English Crowd', p. 82n; *Rural Rides*, p. 508.

37 See, for example, Eden, 'Of the Diet, Dress, Fuel, and Habitations of the Labouring Classes', pp. 449–60; *idem, State of the Poor*, I, pp. vii–viii, 496–9, 525–6, 556–8; Thomas Bernard, 'Extract from an Account of Several Charities at Kendal' (1802), *Reports of the Society for Bettering the Condition of the Poor*, 5 vols. (1797–1808), vol. 3, p. 225n; Russell Garnier, *Annals of the British Peasantry* (London, 1895), pp. 308–9, 318.

38 *PR*, 20 November 1830, pp. 239–42; 20 October 1832, p. 155; 27 March 1830, p. 403; 22 May 1830, pp. 657–8; *Rural Rides*, p. 126.

39 'Cobbett's Advice to the Chopsticks' (1832), in *PR*, 20 October 1832, pp. 130–7; 'Cobbett's Advice (2nd Address) to the Chopsticks', in *PR*, 27 October 1832, pp. 200–2. Both addresses appeared in the *PR* and as broadsheets.

40 *PR*, 22 May 1830, p. 667. See also *Paupers and Pig Killers: The Diary of William Holland, A Somerset Parson 1799–1818* (Harmondsworth, 1986), *passim*; Nathaniel Kent, *Hints to Gentlemen of Landed Property* (London, 1775), pp. 238–40; [Arthur Young], *General Report on Enclosures* (London, 1808), pp. 258–61; SC on Agricultural Labourers' Wages, VI (1824), pp. 31, 45, 55; Davies, *Case of the Labourers in Husbandry*, p. 37; *Annals of Agriculture*, vol. 40 (1803), pp. 53–4; vol. 36 (1801), p. 379; Young, *GVAC Sussex*, p. 457; Arthur Young, 'An Inquiry into the Propriety of Applying Wastes to the Better Maintenance and Support of the Poor' (1801), *Annals of Agriculture*, vol. 36 (1801) p. 635; H. Holland, *GVAC Cheshire* (London, 1808), in Marshall (ed.), *Review and Abstract*, II, p. 110; Eden, *State of the Poor*, II, p. 287; 'The Hard-Earn'd Penny, or the New Roguish Farmers' (no imprint, *c*. 1790s) Madden 5 (III).

41 *PR*, 22 June 1833, p. 727; 13 April 1826, p. 433; 10 November 1832, pp. 350–1; Eden, *State of the Poor*, III, p. cccxli; Davies, *Case of the Labourers in Husbandry*, p. 6; David Durrell, 'Extract from an Account of the Relief Granted the Poor at Mongewell ...' (1800), *Reports of the Society for Bettering the Condition of the Poor* (1797–1808), vol. 3, p. 45.

42 *Cottage Economy*, para. 144; *PR*, 26 March 1825, pp. 808–18; Earl of Winchelsea, 'On the Advantages of Cottagers Renting Land', *Annals of Agriculture*, vol. 26 (1796), pp. 228–45; Sir John Sinclair, 'Observations on the Means of Enabling a Cottager to Keep a Cow ...', *ibid.*, vol. 38 (1801), pp. 231–48; Arthur Young, *GVAC Lincolnshire* (London, 1813), pp. 459–69; *idem*, 'An Inquiry into the Propriety of Applying Wastes ...', pp. 637–8; Nathaniel Kent, *GVAC Norfolk* (London, 1796), section xxvii; William Morton Pitt, *An Address to the Landed Interest, on the Deficiency of Habitations and Fuel, for the Use of the Poor* (London, 1797); J. G. Sherer, *Remarks On the Present State of the Poor* (London, 1796), pp. 34–5. For Malthus's views on cow-keeping see *Annals of Agriculture*, vol. 41 (1804), pp. 211–25.

43 *Cottage Economy*, paras. 154, 156, 158.

44 Walter Rose, *Good Neighbours* (Cambridge, 1945), p. 58.

45 Somerville, *Whistler*, p. 336; *PR*, 20 March 1830, p. 356; James Hawker, *A Victorian Poacher: James Hawker's Journal*, ed. G. Christian (Oxford, 1961), pp. 77–8; Samuel, 'Village Labour', pp. 75–9; John Benson, *The Penny Capitalists: A Study of Nineteenth-Century Working-Class Entrepreneurs* (Dublin, 1983), pp. 19, 22–3, 28–9; SC of the

House of Lords on the Poor Laws, VIII (1830–1), p. 22; the Rev. Dr Glasse, 'Extract from an Account of the Advantage of a Cottager Keeping a Pig' (1797), *Reports of the Society for Bettering the Condition of the Poor* (1797–1808), vol. 1, pp. 158–60; A. L. Merritt, *A Hamlet in Old Hampshire* (London, 1902), pp. 151–2.

46 Joseph Plymley, *GVAC Shropshire* (London, 1803), p. 267; Hunt, *Memoirs*, I, p. 184; Obelkevich, *Religion and Rural Society*, pp. 63–4; Alan Everitt, 'Farm Labourers 1500–1640', in Joan Thirsk (ed.), *The Agrarian History of England and Wales*, IV (Cambridge, 1967), pp. 416–17. The labourers' songs argue for a decline in the number of cottage pigs: see, for example, 'Past, Present and Future' (London: Hill, printer) BL: LR 271 a. 2, vol. I (1), fol. 48; 'Bonny England O!' (Brighton: Phillips, printer) Madden 22 (VII); 'The Honest Ploughman; or 90 Years Ago' (London: Fortey, printer) Madden 10 (V), JJ: Street Ballads, 28. According to the Sussex farmer John Ellman, more labourers kept pigs in 1821 than in 1810 – see Report on the Causes of Agricultural Distress, IX (1821), pp. 53–4).

47 *Rural Rides*, pp. 376, 394–5. There are some fifty references to pig-keeping in the Poor Law Report (1834), app. B (1), pt II (Rural Queries). Of 1,299 rural families examined in Herefordshire, Essex and Norfolk in 1837–8, 493 were found to possess at least one pig; only 73 families had a cow (Publications of the *Central Society of Education*, vol. 1 (1837), pp. 342–4, vol. 2 (1838), p. 259; vol. 3 (1839), p. 371).

48 Thompson, *Lark Rise to Candleford*, pp. 24–7, 279; Jekyll, *Old West Surrey*, p. 243; Kitchen, *Brother to the Ox*, p. 32; Haggard (ed.), *I Walked by Night*, p. 19; George Sturt, *William Smith: Potter and Farmer* (London, 1919, Firle, 1978), p. 213; Grey, *Cottage Life*, p. 116; Thomas Hardy, *Jude the Obscure* (1896, London, 1924 edn), pt I, x–xi; Jennie Kitteringham, 'Country Work Girls in Nineteenth-Century England', in Samuel (ed.), *Village Life and Labour*, pp. 75–9.

49 *PR*, 13 October 1827, p. 140; 22 January 1820, p. 670; *Year's Residence*, paras. 301, 308; John Morgan Cobbett to Nancy Cobbett, 6 June 1817 (Nuffield); Cobbett to Mrs Cobbett, 27 January 1832 (Nuffield); *Cottage Economy*, no. VI. For another learned pig see James Woodforde, *The Diary of a Country Parson* (Oxford, 1978, abridged edn), p. 261.

50 Ashby, *Joseph Ashby*, p. 115.

51 *Treatise on Corn*; *Cottage Economy*, paras. 258–65; *PR*, 17 February 1821, pp. 483–4; 23 August 1828, pp. 310–13; 6 September 1828, pp. 310–13; 17 October 1829, p. 504; 3 December 1831, pp. 587–8. Arthur Young had claimed at the turn of the century that Indian corn could not be grown in England (*Annals of Agriculture*, vol. 38 (1802), p. 430). Cobbett was growing it at Botley by 1808.

52 *PR*, 18 December 1830, p. 1031; 2 April 1831, p. 12; 19 September 1829, pp. 354–5; 26 October, pp. 244–5.

53 *PR*, 14 November 1829, pp. 625–6; 20 December 1828, pp. 778–80.

54 *PR*, 20 December 1828, pp. 778–80; 19 September 1829, pp. 354–5; 17 October 1829, p. 503.

55 *PR*, 22 November 1828, p. 669; Susan Cobbett, 'Additional Notes' (Nuffield XVII/3/3–4).

56 Cobbett received many letters reporting success with the crop: *PR*, August–December 1829, July–December 1831. Detailed comments on his maize appear in Denson, *A Peasant's Voice to Landowners*, letter X; 'L', 'On Maize or Indian Corn – Mr. Cobbett's Work', *The Quarterly Journal of Agriculture*, vol. 2 (1829), pp. 484–517.

57 'The Cobbett Library', *PR*, 15 January 1831, p. 167; undated *PR* MS, BM Add. MS 31,125, fol. 72; *PR*, 19 March 1831, p. 763; 2 July 1831, pp. 50–1; 3 December 1831, pp. 591–8.

58 Enos Diddams to Cobbett, 23 November 1831, in *PR*, 3 December 1831, p. 602.

59 Cobbett to John Cobbett, 3 January 1832 (Nuffield); *Horse-Hoeing Husbandry*; *PR*, 8 December 1821, p. 1390; 19 September 1829, p. 363.

60 On the increase of potato consumption between 1795 and 1800 see *Annals of Agriculture*, vol. 24 (1795), pp. 74, 90, 101, 116, 142, 148, 150, 172, 180, 188, 208, 227, 230–6, 300–5; Eden, *State of the Poor*, II, p. 175, III, p. 704; *The Annual Hampshire Repository*, vol. 2 (1799), p. 183; Arthur Young, *GVAC Suffolk* (London, 1794), p. 600; *idem, GVAC Essex*, 2 vols. (London, 1807), I, p. 382; R. N. Salaman, *History and Social Influence of the Potato* (Cambridge, 1949), chs. 25, 27.

61 *The Times*, 9 December 1982, reported a world-leading per capita consumption of 235 pounds per year.

62 *Cottage Economy*, paras. 78, 107; *Rural Rides*, p. 126; *PR*, 16 October 1813, pp. 485–7.

63 *PR*, 2 October 1813, p. 425.

64 *PR*, 18 October 1828, pp. 510–11.

65 *PR*, 31 May 1823, p. 518. Italics added.

66 J. H. Clapham, *An Economic History of Modern Britain: The Early Railway Age, 1820–1850* (Cambridge, 1939), p. 126.

67 SC on Agriculture, V (1833), p. vii.

68 Somerville, *Autobiography*, p. 98. See also *idem, Whistler*, pp. 142–3.

69 *Rural Rides*, p. 372.

70 William Stevenson, *GVAC Dorset* (1813), in Marshall (ed.), *Review and Abstract*, V, p. 269.

71 *PR*, 11 November 1815, p. 167.

72 Young, *Farmer's Letters*, I, pp. 296–304; John Wesley, *A Letter to a Friend, Concerning Tea* (London, 1825 edn); Davies, *Case of the Labourers in Husbandry*, pp. 37–9; Brewer, *Some Thoughts on the Present State of the English Peasantry*, p. 35.

73 Marshall, *Minutes, Experiments, Observations...*, I, pp. 203, 237–8, 304.

74 J. Bishton, *GVAC Shropshire* (1794), in Marshall (ed.), *Review and Abstract*, II, pp. 181–2.

75 Cobbett's speech at Guildford, 14 December 1822, *PR*, 21 December 1822, pp. 758–9.

76 *PR*, 22 January 1820, p. 697; 27 March 1830, p. 398; 6 April 1816, p. 427; 21 March 1835, p. 723; 24 November 1832, p. 469.

77 'The Sin of Drunkenness, in Kings, Priests and People', *Sermons*, no. 2.

78 *Cottage Economy*, para. 25.

79 *Annals of Agriculture*, vol. 15 (1791), pp. 196–229 (a history of the malt tax by Capel Lofft); Stephen Dowell, *A History of Taxation and Taxes in England*, 4 vols. (1884, New York, 1965), pp. 72–9; Brian Harrison, *Drink and the Victorians: The Temperance Question in England 1815–1872* (London, 1971), p. 72; SC of the House of Lords on the Poor Laws, V (1818), p. 132; *Poor Man's Friend*, pp. 215–16.

80 Report on the Causes of Agricultural Distress, IX (1821), p. 61. For Cobbett this was 'the most valuable part' of all the evidence set before the committee (*PR*, 19 January 1822, p. 161).

81 See, for example, *PR*, 19 January 1822, p. 161; 31 August 1822, p. 518; 21 September 1822, pp. 714–15; 9 March 1822, pp. 602–3; 17 August 1822, p. 426; 19 December 1829, pp. 773–4; 27 November 1830, p. 810; 31 December 1831, pp. 9, 20–1; *Cottage Economy*, paras. 20, 60; *Treatise on Corn*, para. 156.

82 Eden, *State of the Poor*, III, p. 729.

83 SC of the House of Lords on the Poor Laws, VIII (1830–1), p. 63.

84 Davies, *Case of the Labourers in Husbandry*, pp. 18–19, 38, 50, 58–9, 70; Hunt, *Memoirs*, I, p. 228.

85 SC on Agriculture, V (1833), p. 264.

86 Eden, *State of the Poor*, II, p. 280.

87 Poor Law Report (1834), app. B (1), pt III, p. 191.

88 [Board of Agriculture], *Agricultural State of the Kingdom*, p. 95; *PR*, 27 February 1830, p. 286.

89 *PR*, 7 December 1834, p. 803; SC on Agriculture, V (1833), p. 520. See also SC of the House of Lords on Agriculture, V (1837), pp. 78, 165, 226, 306.

90 *Annals of Agriculture*, vol. 20 (1793), p. 412.

91 *PR*, 21 March 1835, p. 718; 7 December 1834, p. 803; 8 December 1832, pp. 581–3; 28 January 1815, p. 107; 11 November 1815, p. 165; 24 August 1833, p. 462; 9 June 1821, p. 694; 5 December 1829, p. 705, 712–15; 19 December 1829, pp. 773–4; *Cottage Economy*, para. 68; *George the Fourth*, para. 504. On the decline of home-brewing see Peter Mathias, *The Brewing Industry in England, 1700–1830* (Cambridge, 1959), p. 377; Peter Clark, *The English Alehouse: A Social History, 1200–1830* (London, 1983), Introduction.

92 M. C. F. Morris, *The British Workman Past and Present* (London, 1928), pp. 13–14; Jefferies, *Hodge and his Masters*, pp. 247–54; Evans, *Ask the Fellows*, pp. 27, 36, 48–9, 55, 61–5; *Journals of George Sturt*, I, pp. 428–9; idem, *Change in the Village* (1912, London, 1956), ch. V; O. A. Merritt-Hawkes, *The Cottage by the Common* (London, 1924), p. 97; J. Alfred Eggar, *Remembrances of Life and Customs in Gilbert White's, Cobbett's and Charles Kingsley's Country* (London, n.d., c. 1870), pp. 76–8.

93 W. H. Hudson, *Afoot in England* (1909, London, 1933), p. 44.

94 *PR*, 4 May 1822, pp. 313–15; *Rural Rides*, p. 205; *PR*, 2 December 1815, pp. 260–1; 9 June 1821, p. 692; 2 March 1822, p. 569. The salt tax was removed in 1825 (Dowell, *History of Taxation*, IV, pp. 3–5).

95 SC on Agricultural Labourers' Wages, VI (1824), p. 55; *PR*, 21 August 1824, pp. 481–2; Brayley and Britton, 'Hampshire', p. 9.

96 Publications of the *Central Society of Education*, vol. 1 (1837), p. 343; J. Plymley, *GVAC Shropshire* (London, 1803), p. 267; *PR*, 21 March 1835, p. 719; 21 April 1821, pp. 194–5; *Cottage Economy*, paras. 203–6; Grey, *Cottage Life*, p. 98; Evans, *Ask the Fellows*, p. 59; Poor Law Report (1834), app. B, pt II, p. 310; Thompson, *Lark Rise to Candleford*, p. 279.

97 *Cottage Economy*, paras. 208–13, 218; *Rural Rides*, pp. 123, 128–9, 136–7, 184; *PR*, 31 May 1823, pp. 542–3; George Rose, *Observations on the Poor Laws* (London, 1805), p. 37n; [Peter Kalm], *Kalm's Account of his Visit to England* (1748), trans. J. Lucas (London, 1892), p. 337; Pamela Horn, *The Rural World: Social Change in the English Countryside 1780–1850* (London, 1980), pp. 59–60; Nigel Agar, 'The Bedfordshire Farm Worker in the Nineteenth Century', *The Publications of the Bedfordshire Historical Record Society*, vol. 60 (1981), pp. 5, 7, 24, 58, 159; Lovett, *Life and Struggles*, p. 12; SC on Agricultural Labourers' Wages, VI (1824), p. 54 (evidence of Thomas Smart); Grey, *Cottage Life*, pp. 68–93; Kitteringham, 'Country Work Girls', pp. 113–27.

98 *Rural Rides*, pp. 137–8; *PR*, 19 July 1823, p. 183; 9 August 1823, pp. 370–5; 23 August 1823, pp. 497–8; 15 September 1827, pp. 720–1; 23 March 1833, pp. 729, 735.

99 *PR*, 31 May 1823, pp. 524–5, 540–1; 29 September, pp. 752–60; 4 June 1825, pp. 608–9; *Cottage Economy*, para. 222; Anne Cobbett's 'Account of the Family' (Nuffield XV), fol. 46; Susan Cobbett's additional notes (Nuffield XVII/3/3).

100 The phrase is Mick Reed's – see '"Gnawing it Out": A New Look at Economic Relations', pp. 83–94.

101 *PR*, 17 March 1821, p. 749; *Year's Residence*, paras. 754–5.

102 'The Poor Labourers' (Northampton: Henson, printer) Madden 19 (IV); 'Swaggering Farmers' (Durham: Walker, printer) JJ: Street Ballads, I; *PR*, 12 April 1823, p. 79.

103 'Autobiography of a Suffolk Farm Labourer', pt III.

6 OLD ENGLAND: NOSTALGIA AND EXPERIENCE

1 Derry, 'William Cobbett', p. 46. See also Osborne, *William Cobbett*, pp. 165–6.
2 Newby, *Deferential Worker*; Max F. Schulz, *Paradise Preserved: Recreations of Eden in Eighteenth- and Nineteenth-Century England* (Cambridge, 1985); Christopher Shaw and Malcolm Chase (eds.), *The Imagined Past: History and Nostalgia* (Manchester, 1989); Alun Howkins, 'The Discovery of Rural England', in Robert Colls and Philip Dodd (eds.), *Englishness: Politics and Culture* (London, 1986); Williams, *Country and the City*; Keith, *Rural Tradition*; Patrick Wright, *On Living in an Old Country* (London, 1985), ch. 1; John Lucas, *England and Englishness: Ideas of Nationhood in English Poetry 1688–1900* (London, 1990); Simon Pugh (ed.), *Reading Landscape* (Manchester, 1990); Raphael Samuel and Paul Thompson, 'Introduction', in Raphael Samuel and Paul Thompson (eds.), *The Myths We Live By* (London, 1990).
3 William Stafford, *Socialism, Radicalism, and Nostalgia: Social Criticism in Britain, 1775–1830* (Cambridge, 1987), ch. 13; Keith, *Rural Tradition*, ch. 4; Gerald Duff, 'William Cobbett's Agrarian Vision of National Reform' (PhD thesis, University of Illinois, 1966), p. 81; Himmelfarb, *Idea of Poverty*, pp. 208, 213; Wiener, 'Changing Image', p. 135.
4 It has been suggested that 'rural myths' compromised a radical consciousness and were to some extent a psychological escape from it: see Martin Wiener, *English Culture and the Decline of the Industrial Spirit* (Cambridge, 1981), pp. 58–60.
5 Williams, 'Literature and Rural Society', pp. 630–2; *idem*, *Country and the City*, pp. 20, 35–6.
6 *Journals of George Sturt*, II, pp. 622–3. See also *idem*, *Change in the Village*, pp. 76–85; Keith, *Rural Tradition*, p. 14.
7 Arch, *Story of his Life*, p. 403, *passim*; 'The Fine Old English Labourer', in [Howard Evans], *Songs for Singing at Agricultural Labourers' Meetings* (Aylesbury, n.d., c. 1874); *A Victorian Poacher: James Hawker's Journal*, p. 76; Haggard (ed.), *I Walked by Night*, p. 90. See also D. Vincent, *Bread, Knowledge and Freedom: A Study of Nineteenth-Century Working Class Autobiography* (London, 1981), pp. 197–8; Michael Winstanley, 'Voices from the Past: Rural Kent at the Close of an Era', in G. E. Mingay (ed.), *The Victorian Countryside* (London, 1981), II, pp. 635–6.
8 Roger Wells, 'The Development of the English Rural Proletariat and Social Protest, 1700–1850', in *The Journal of Peasant Studies*, vol. 6, no. 2 (January 1979), p. 120. Some of the same points that I am making here have been made with reference to John Clare – see Barrell, *Idea of Landscape*, pp. 199–202.
9 See, for example, the anti-Cobbett serial *The Good Old Times; or, The Poor Man's History of England* (London, 1817). It consists mainly of diatribes against Cobbett and lengthy excerpts from Hume's history of England. For discussions of popular efforts to recover control of historical consciousness see Cunningham, 'Patriotism', pp. 9, 15–18; Popular Memory Group, 'Popular Memory: Theory, Politics, Method', in Richard Johnson, *et al.* (eds.), *Making Histories: Studies in History Writing and Politics* (London, 1982), ch. 6.
10 *PR*, 21 January 1815, p. 66; *Advice*, paras. 29, 49–50, 74, 316, 319–20; *Protestant 'Reformation'*, paras. 38–9, 452; *George the Fourth*, paras. 3–4.
11 *Rural Rides*, pp. 316–17; *Protestant 'Reformation'*, paras. 211, 242, 452–4; *Paper against Gold* (1828 edn), p. 28; *PR*, 9 January 1811, pp. 39–40.
12 Raphael Samuel, 'People's History', in R. Samuel (ed.), *People's History and Socialist Theory* (London, 1981), p. xxii.
13 *PR*, 21 August 1824, p. 462; Rev. John Lingard, *A History of England*, 3 vols. (London, 1819). Cobbett drew heavily upon Lingard's work but acknowledged it seldom – see

Rural Rides, pp. 464–7; *Protestant 'Reformation'*, paras. 289–320; Cobbett MSS (Nuffield XIX); *PR*, 30 October 1824, pp. 271–3.

14 *PR*, 21 August 1824, p. 478.

15 *Protestant 'Reformation'*, para. 456. Cobbett's principal source on the Middle Ages was *De Laudibus Legum Angliae* (1468–70) by Sir John Fortescue, Lord Chancellor of Henry VI. See Sir John Fortescue, *The Governance of England* (1468–70), ed. Charles Plummer (Oxford, 1926), chs. 29, 35–6; *Protestant 'Reformation'*, paras. 458–9, 468; *Poor Man's Friend*, para. 55; *PR*, 22 November 1817, pp. 1043–4; *Year's Residence*, paras. 351–2.

16 *PR*, 21 August 1824, p. 463; 17 January 1832, p. 150; *Protestant 'Reformation'*, paras. 37, 120, 332.

17 It is too often assumed that Cobbett's primary golden age was the Middle Ages: see, for example, Charles Kegel, 'Medieval–Modern Contrasts Used for a Social Purpose in the Work of William Cobbett, Robert Southey, A. Welby Pugin, Thomas Carlyle, John Ruskin and William Morris' (PhD thesis, University of Michigan, 1955).

18 *PR*, 21 August 1824, p. 466.

19 *Rural Rides*, p. 125.

20 Derry, 'William Cobbett', p. 56.

21 James E. Thorold Rogers, *The Economic Interpretation of History*, sixth edn (London, 1905), pp. 62–3.

22 Etienne Robo, *Medieval Farnham: Everyday Life in an Episcopal Manor* (Farnham, n.d., c. 1935), pp. 33–7, 38–9.

23 *Rural Rides*, p. 354; *Protestant 'Reformation'*, para. 124.

24 *Protestant 'Reformation'*, paras. 259, 262–80, 294–5, 332, 349; *PR*, 20 September 1834, p. 729; 16 May 1829, pp. 620–1; 9 June 1821, pp. 685–96; 12 February 1825, p. 398; 'The Old Hat, or, The New Hat Growing Old' (Preston: Harkness, printer) BL 1871 f. 13, fol. 64; 'Bonny England O!' (Brighton: Phillips, printer) Madden 22 (VII); 'The Roguish Farmers. A New Song' (no imprint) Firth b. 34 (259).

25 'The Roast Beef of Old England' (Portsea: Williams, printer) Madden 22 (VII). For the earlier version see 'The Roast Beef of *Old England*, A Cantata' (Madden 15; JJ: Street Ballads, VI, fols. 238–9, 241; William Chappell, *Popular Music of Olden Time*, 2 vols. (London, 1855–9), II, p. 636; Simpson, *British Broadside Ballad*, pp. 604–6.

26 See 'A New Song. On the Loss of the Beef of Old England' (no imprint, c. 1800) Madden 5 (II).

27 *PR*, 10 March 1821, pp. 652–3. See also *Paper against Gold* (1828 edn), p. 28; *Legacy to Labourers*, p. 29.

28 *Advice*, para. 74.

29 *PR*, 12 October, p. 71.

30 *PR*, 21 August 1824, pp. 474–5. See also *Cottage Economy*, para. 8.

31 *PR*, 8 March 1828, p. 303.

32 *Jackson's Oxford Journal*, 6 February 1830.

33 [Kalm], *Kalm's Account of his Visit to England*, p. 15.

34 Davies, *Case of the Labourers in Husbandry*, pp. 24–5; Pamela Horn, *A Georgian Parson and his Village: The Life of David Davies* (Abingdon, 1981), p. 30. See also Robert Applegarth, *A Plea for the Poor* (London, 1790), esp. pp. 1–3; Kent, *GVAC Norfolk*, p. 165.

35 *Annals of Agriculture*, vol. 38 (1801), p. 285.

36 *Ibid.*, vol. 25 (1796), p. 609; vol. 34 (1800), p. 561.

37 Young, *Six Weeks' Tour through the Southern Counties*, pp. 222–3.

38 SC of the House of Lords on the Poor Laws, VIII (1830–1), pp. 204–5, 207, 212 (evidence of Lord Stanhope).

39 Young, *Six Weeks' Tour through the Southern Counties*, pp. 222-3; Eden, *State of the Poor*, III, p. 715.

40 *PR*, 19 May 1821, pp. 451-2, 193-5.

41 Thomas Bernard, 'Introductory Letter...' (1805), in *Reports of the Society for Bettering the Condition of the Poor* (1797-1808), vol. 5, pp. 24-7; *PR*, 31 August 1822, pp. 519-20; 19 May 1821, p. 458.

42 *PR*, 13 April 1823, pp. 66, 69-76; 19 May 1821, pp. 452-6, 471.

43 William Marshall, *The Rural Economy of the West of England*, 2 vols. (London, 1805), II, p. 111. The same view is expressed in William James and Jacob Malcolm, *GVAC Surrey* (London, 1794), p. 54n. On bread prices see Levy, *Large and Small Holdings*, p. 9; Thorold Rogers, *History of Agriculture and Prices*, VII, pp. 493-528; Salaman, *Potato*, pp. 492, 496-7; Malcolmson, *Life and Labour*, pp. 37, 145-6. In the opinion of Thorold Rogers, 'the agricultural labourer of the first half of the eighteenth century was better off than he had been at any period since the fifteenth and the first half of the sixteenth' (*Six Centuries of Work and Wages* (London, 1909), p. 480). For the impact of the scarcities see Roger Wells, *Wretched Faces: Famine in Wartime England 1793-1801* (Gloucester, 1988), chs. 17-18. Farm account books covering the last half of the eighteenth century indicate only a very modest rise in wages, if any, during the 1790s – see, for example, 'Farm Account Book' (Shalden Stratten), 1748-1807 (HRO 28 M82/F1).

44 Joanna Innes, 'The Invention of Rural Poverty in Later Eighteenth-Century England' (unpublished paper delivered at the Social History Society Conference, 1990). I am grateful to Joanna for providing me with a copy of her paper and for discussing her work at greater length. She emphasizes that her findings are tentative. See Snell, *Annals of the Labouring Poor*, chs. 1, 3-4, esp. pp. 37-8, 411-17; also G. Boyer, *An Economic History of the English Poor Law, 1750-1850* (Cambridge, 1990), ch. 1, app. A.

45 Young, 'Tour through Sussex, 1793', p. 333.

46 *The Carrington Diary*, pp. 13-14, 19-24, 30-40, 61-7, 113-15, 128-41, 153-4.

47 Thomas Hardy, 'The Dorsetshire Labourer' (1883), in Harold Orel (ed.), *Thomas Hardy's Personal Writings* (London, 1967), pp. 184-5.

48 Report on the Causes of Agricultural Distress, IX (1821), p. 74 (evidence of John Lake, farmer near Sittingbourne, Kent).

49 R. Fraser, *GVAC Devon* (1794), in Marshall (ed.), *Review and Abstract*, V, p. 554.

50 SC of the House of Lords on the Poor Laws, VIII (1830-1), pp. 22-3; Cobbett to T. L. Hodges, 27 October 1833 (NYPL); *Rural Rides*, p. 181.

51 Cobbett's 'Farm Account Book' (Botley), 1808-19 (Nuffield XIII); Cobbett to Mrs Cobbett, 23 December 1829 (Nuffield); William Cobbett Jr in *PR*, 4 July 1835, pp. 15-16; 4 October 1834, p. 4; *Trash*, October 1830, pp. 83-4; *PR*, 18 May 1816, p. 614; 29 July 1809, pp. 111-12; 25 December 1830, p. 1109; 19 October 1833, p. 144. For wage comparisons see Vancouver, *GVAC Hampshire*, pp. 385, 446; Ronald Windle, 'Hampshire Agrarian Society' (PhD thesis, Council for National Academic Awards, 1973), pp. 203, 207-11, 287, ch. 7.

52 Susan Cobbett's 'Additional Notes' (Nuffield XVII/6/4); 'Farm Account Book'; letters between Cobbett and family members, 1806-12 (Nuffield XXIX); *PR*, 29 July 1809, pp. 111-12; *Trash*, October 1830, pp. 83-4; Edward Smith, *William Cobbett: A Biography*, 2 vols. (London, 1879), II, pp. 42-3.

53 Cobbett's 'Farm Account Book' (Botley), B4.

54 Cobbett to Mrs Cobbett, 14 September 1811 (Nuffield).

55 Cobbett to William Cobbett Jr, 1 October 1811 (Nuffield).

56 Cobbett to Frederick Reid, 1 January 1812 (Nuffield); *PR*, 19 February 1820, p. 29; *PR*, 29 July 1809, pp. 97-113; *Cobbett's Oppression!!: Proceedings of the Trial of an Action between William Burgess, A Poor Labouring Man! and William Cobbett, A Patriot and*

Reformer! (London, 1809) Nuffield Cobb. 1809; Cobbett to James Gutsell, 22 May 1834 (Cornell).

57 *PR*, 6 January 1830, p. 812.

58 Cobbett to Mrs Cobbett, 1 January 1812 (Nuffield); *PR*, 29 July 1809, p. 112; 31 July 1813, p. 139; 24 July 1829, p. 112. Benjamin Tilly, one of Cobbett's part-time secretaries, wrote that 'Mr. Cobbett used to offer all beggars some work, they were to be paid as soon as the work was done; but, they almost always took the opportunity of slyly leaving the work and going off!' (Tilly's marginalia on Cobbett's letter to Job Swain, 4 May 1835 (Yale)).

59 Susan Cobbett, 'Additional Notes' (Nuffield XVII/1/3); *Trash*, October 1830, pp. 80–5; Cobbett's 'Farm Account Book' (Botley), A20–5.

60 Cobbett's 'Farm Account Book' (Botley), B1–24.

61 *PR*, 1 December 1827, pp. 578–9; 25 December 1830, pp. 1106–8; 24 February 1829, p. 116; 31 January 1829, pp. 136–7; 18 May 1816, p. 614; *Advice*, para. 294; *Treatise on Corn*, paras. 155, 159; *PR*, 1 December 1827, pp. 588–91, 600–3; 25 December 1830, p. 1170. On the brewing tackle and other utensils at Cobbett's farms see 'Farm Account Book' and *A Catalogue of all the Live and Dead Farming Stock, Household Furniture . . . of Mr. Cobbett, Quitting his Farm at Barn Elm* (London, 1830) Faithfull XXI/8 (Nuffield); Cobbett to Jesse Oldfield, 18 February 1835 (Cornell); 'Cobbett's Diary' (Nuffield XIX); see also the accounts for Normandy farm (Nuffield XIX).

62 *PR*, 3 October 1829, p. 447. A manuscript draft of the advertisement is in the Fitzwilliam Museum. See also *PR*, 18 October 1828, pp. 510–11; 22 May 1830, pp. 667–8; Cobbett to Mrs Cobbett, 10 December 1811 (Nuffield); Cobbett to James Gutsell, 22 May 1834 (Cornell).

63 Cobbett to Miss Boxall, 20 December 1811 (Nuffield XXIX); Cobbett to John Dean, 27 January 1825 (Illinois); *PR*, 14 July 1810, p. 18; *Trash*, October 1830, p. 85.

64 Sir Richard Phillips, *Public Characters of All Nations*, 2 vols. (London, 1823), I, p. 373.

65 Hunt, *Memoirs*, III, pp. 21–5.

66 Somerville, *Whistler*, p. 263. See also *PR*, 4 July 1835, pp. 15–16. On attempts by Cobbett's adversaries to discredit his reputation as an employer see *Treatise on Corn*, paras. 155, 202; *PR*, 19 October 1822, pp. 146–7; 16 January 1830, pp. 85–6.

67 *Year's Residence*, para. 324.

68 Cobbett to Job Swain, 4 May 1835 (Yale).

69 Cobbett to James Gutsell, 17 May 1835 (Yale). When away in London, Cobbett sent instructions by post that his men were to have plenty of bread, bacon and beer: see, for example, Cobbett to John Dean, 27 May 1834 (Lockwood Memorial Library); Cobbett to Ellen Cobbett, n.d., *c.* 1834 (Nuffield XXX/278/1).

70 *PR*, 15 February 1834, p. 411.

71 Duck, 'The Thresher's Labour', pp. 8–10, 13–15.

72 'The Honest Ploughman, or, 90 Years Ago' (London: Fortey, printer) Madden 11 (V).

73 The song was printed in most parts of the country, and there are slight variations from printer to printer. The title also varies: the most common ones were 'The Old Hat', 'My Old Hat', 'The New Hat Growing Old' and 'When this Old Hat was New'. Copies can be found at BL 1871 f. 13, fol. 64; Madden 8 (II); Madden 11 (V); Madden 18 (III); Madden 10 (IV); JJ: Street Ballads, I; Firth c. 16 (293); Bodleian 2806 c. 13 (61). See also Deacon, *John Clare*, pp. 230–1; W. G. Whittaker, *North Countrie Ballads* (London, 1921), pp. 78–9; Joseph Ritson, *A Select Collection of English Songs*, 3 vols. (London, 1813), II, pp. 138–41; *Publications of the Modern Language Association of America*, vol. 38 (March 1923), p. 134; *Roxburgh Ballads*, II, pp. 581–6; Palmer, *Sound of History*, pp. 37–9.

74 'What is the Matter with the Farmers' (London: Pitts, printer) Madden VIII (2); 'The

Farmer's Downfall' (York: Croshaw, printer) Firth c. 16 (278); 'The New Times' (London: Catnach, printer) BL: LR 271 a. 2, vol. 4, fol. 414.

75 'Advice to Farmers' (London: Catnach, printer, c. late 1820s); JJ: Street Ballads, II. Listed for sale in the Catnach catalogue of 1832.

76 Daniel Woolf, in an otherwise excellent essay, states a little too categorically that 'oral cultures have little sense of a relative past', and that oral forms 'ceased to provide an important historical source' after 1800 ('The "Common Voice": History, Folklore and Oral Tradition in Early Modern England', *Past and Present*, no. 120 (August 1988), pp. 31, 52).

77 Michael Ignatieff, 'Primitive Accumulation Revisited', in R. Samuel (ed.), *People's History and Socialist Theory* (1981), p. 130.

78 PR, 19 May 1821, p. 457; 22 December 1821, p. 1516.

79 PR, 5 March 1821, p. 342. See Margaret Spufford, *Small Books and Pleasant Histories: Popular Fiction and its Readership in Seventeenth-Century England* (Cambridge, 1981), ch. 9.

80 PR, 31 December 1831, p. 10; Christopher Hill, 'The Norman Yoke', in John Saville (ed.), *Democracy and the Labour Movement* (London, 1954), p. 59.

81 For a comparison of Cobbett's view of the past with that of Thomas Evans, see McCalman, *Radical Underworld*, pp. 101–3.

82 [Place], *Essay on the State of the Country*, Goldsmith's 26920: 'Tracts Collected by Francis Place'.

83 *The Lion*, vol. 3 no. 12 (20 March 1829), pp. 354–9. I am grateful to Ruth Richardson for this reference.

84 Cobbett to John Barwis, 11 January 1807 (Bodleian).

85 PR, 4 August 1832, p. 265.

86 For Southey's essays see 'Propositions for Ameliorating the Condition of the Poor ...', *The Quarterly Review*, vol. 8, no. 16 (December 1812), pp. 319–56; 'Condition of the English Peasantry', *ibid.*, vol. 41, no. 81 (July 1829), pp. 240–84.

87 PR, 20 August 1831, p. 492.

7 'RURAL WAR': COBBETT AND CAPTAIN SWING

1 PR, 4 December 1830, pp. 871–2; 27 November 1830, p. 810.

2 PR, 19 February 1820, p. 4; 22 December 1821, p. 1501; 14 February 1824, p. 422; 6 March 1824, pp. 610–11; 1 August 1829, pp. 158–9; 15 August 1829, p. 201; 26 September 1829, p. 403; 29 December 1829, p. 815; 15 January 1831, p. 145; *Rural Rides*, p. 261.

3 SC on the Relief of Able-Bodied Persons from the Poor Rates, IV (1828), p. 20. See also PR, 11 July 1829, p. 35; Eric Hobsbawm and George Rudé, *Captain Swing* (New York, 1968), p. 100.

4 PR, 6 March 1830, pp. 289–95; 'The Stone-Breaker' (London: The Religious Tract Society, c. 1830); 'Stones A-Breaking' (BL 1871 f. 13, fol. 78).

5 PR, 6 March 1830, pp. 296–8, 302–3; 7 January 1832, p. 122; letter to the editor of the *Morning Chronicle* by S. Wells, 9 January 1832 (BL Place Collection: Set 21, fol. 234). Many of the witnesses before the 1824 SC on Agricultural Labourers' Wages alluded to the employment of farm workers on road work and other parish projects.

6 PR, 6 March 1830, p. 304; Cobbett's broadside *To the Rate-Payers of Kensington* (February 1830) Fitzwilliam.

7 PR, 27 June 1829, p. 812; 26 September 1829, p. 403.

8 Clapham, *Economic History: Railway Age*, pp. 126–31.

9 Armstrong, *Farmworkers*, pp. 65–6.

10 *PR*, 27 January 1827, pp. 261–2; 3 January 1829, pp. 21–3; 31 January 1829, p. 155; 21 March 1829, pp. 353–4, 372–4; 30 May 1829, pp. 697–701; 6 March 1830, pp. 309–10; 30 June 1832, p. 783; 18 August 1832, pp. 412–16; 7 July 1832, pp. 39–43. On the Dead-Body Bill see *Manchester Lectures, PR*, December 1831, p. 14; Cobbett to Lord Radnor, 25 June 1832 (Nuffield XXX/269/1); Cobbett to Radnor, 26 June 1832 (Nuffield XXX/271/1); Ruth Richardson, *Death, Dissection and the Destitute* (Harmondsworth, 1988).

11 See Bernard Reaney, *The Class Struggle in 19th Century Oxfordshire: The Social and Communal Background to the Otmoor Disturbances of 1830 to 1835* (Oxford, 1971); Hammonds, *Village Labourer*, pp. 27, 35n, 49, 56.

12 *PR*, 11 September 1830, p. 350.

13 *Emigrant's Guide*, para. 3.

14 *Protestant 'Reformation'*, paras. 320, 345, 351–2, 458–9; *Year's Residence*, paras. 20, 321–4, 351–2; *Rural Rides*, pp. 337, 404–5; *George the Fourth*, para. 20; *Poor Man's Friend*, para. 55; *Advice*, paras. 37, 57, 275; *Hundred Days*, pp. 13–16; *PR*, 15 January 1820, p. 597; 17 March 1821, pp. 749, 755–6; 23 August 1817, p. 670; 15 February 1831, pp. 398–9; 14 July 1821, p. 1060. See also Henry Fearon, *Sketches of America* (London, 1818), pp. 69–70, 199, 375–8, 397–8, 437–8. Fearon paid a visit to Cobbett at his Long Island farm.

15 *PR*, 14 November 1829, p. 619.

16 *PR*, 6 June 1829, p. 731; 20 February 1830, p. 239; *Journals of the House of Lords* (1829), p. 530; *England in 1830; Being a Letter to Lord Grey Laying Before Him the Condition of the People as Described by Themselves in their Petitions to Parliament* (London, 1831).

17 Howkins, *Poor Labouring Men*, ch. 2; *PR*, 6 March 1830, p. 618; 14 November 1829, p. 617.

18 *PR*, 20 December 1828, p. 778; 14 November 1829, p. 617; 20 December 1828, p. 778; *Trash*, November 1830, p. 99.

19 Andrew Charlesworth, 'Radicalism, Political Crisis and the Agricultural Labourers' Protests of 1830', in A. Charlesworth (ed.), *Rural Social Change and Conflicts since 1500* (Humberside, 1982), pp. 44–5; idem, 'The Spatial Diffusion of Rural Protest: An Historical and Comparative Perspective of Rural Riots in Nineteenth-Century Britain', *Society and Space*, vol. 1 (1983), pp. 251–63; idem, 'A Comparative Study of the Spread of the Agricultural Disturbances of 1816, 1822 and 1830 in England', *Peasant Studies*, vol. 2, no. 2 (Winter, 1984), p. 108.

20 *PR*, 20 March 1830, pp. 370–1. See, for example, the report to the Home Office from Battle in Sussex: 'there appears to be no bad feeling among the peasantry against the Government, the grievance with them is the low rate of wages' (letter by George Maule, 12 November 1830, HO 42/27).

21 *PR*, 11 December 1830, p. 946.

22 *PR*, 20 February 1830, pp. 245–6.

23 *PR*, 17 April 1830, pp. 495, 502; 1 May 1830, p. 561.

24 *PR*, 3 April 1830, pp. 422–3; 24 April 1830, p. 524; 1 May 1830, p. 557; 27 June 1829, pp. 813–14; *Trash*, December 1830, pp. 125–30.

25 *Trash*, December 1830, pp. 121–2; Melville, *Life and Letters*, II, p. 247.

26 For a collection of petitions addressing some countryman grievances see *England in 1830*.

27 Letter by George Maule, 12 November 1830, HO 40/27. See also *Appeal of the Day-Labourers to the Landowners of England* (London, 1832). For a similar episode in Norfolk: Anne Digby, *Pauper Palaces* (London, 1978), p. 98.

28 *PR*, 6 March 1830, p. 308; 22 May 1830, p. 658.

29 Roger Wells, 'Rural Rebels in Southern England in the 1830s', in Clive Emsley and James Walvin (eds.), *Artisans, Peasants and Proletarians, 1760–1860* (London, 1985), p. 134; *idem*, 'Tolpuddle in the Context of English Agrarian Labour History, 1780–1850', in John Rule (ed.), *British Trade Unionism: The Formative Years* (London, 1988), pp. 114–21. See also n. 19 above.

30 *Eleven Lectures on the French and Belgian Revolutions and English Boroughmongering* (London, 1830). The lectures were delivered in September and October. The Rotunda was rented in 1830 by Richard Carlile. For a fee he made it available to reformers and reform associations.

31 *PR*, 6 March 1830, p. 308; 22 May 1830, p. 658; *Trash*, November 1830, p. 118.

32 *The Morning Chronicle*, 19 November 1830 (BL Place Collection: Set 21).

33 *PR*, 23 October 1824, pp. 239–40.

34 *PR*, 20 February 1834, pp. 241–2.

35 Armstrong, *Farmworkers*, p. 15.

36 *PR*, 6 March 1830, p. 306.

37 *PR*, 25 December 1830, pp. 1105–6, 1113; *Trash*, November 1830, p. 99.

38 *PR*, 22 January 1831, pp. 203–4.

39 Kentish correspondent to *The Morning Chronicle*, 8 November 1830 (BL Place Collection: Set 41, fol. 79).

40 'A Yeoman of Surrey to Henry Brougham', *The Morning Chronicle*, 17 November 1830 (BL Place Collection: Set 21, fol. 87).

41 *The Times*, 15 November 1830.

42 *The Morning Chronicle*, 19 November 1830; *The Times*, 27 November 1830.

43 *PR*, 24 March 1832, p. 791.

44 Hunt, in fact, denounced the rioters (Belchem, '*Orator' Hunt*, pp. 213, 215–16); 'The King against Richard Carlile' (10 January 1831), in John Macdonnell (ed.), *Reports of State Trials*, new ser. (London, 1889), II (1823–31). Carlile was convicted of seditious libel for a passage in his address to the 'Insurgent Agricultural Labourers', *The Prompter*, no. 3 (27 November 1830).

45 'The Poor Labourers' (London: Ryle, printer) BL: LR 271 a. 2, vol. I (2), fol. 120, and Firth b. 25 (399); 'Howls of the Farmers' (BL 11602 gg. 30, fol. 43).

46 'What will Old England Come to?' (Newcastle: Fordyce, printer) Madden 16 (1); Madden 10 (IV). Listed for sale in the Catnach catalogue of 1832.

47 'The Times' (Portsea: Williams, printer) Madden 22 (VII). See also 'The Sporting Farmer' (London: Hodges, printer) JJ: Street Ballads, IV, fol. 17; 'Request of the Poor' (Brighton: Phillips, printer) BL 1876 e. 3, fol. 5.

48 Presentment sheet for William Smith of the parish of Newbury, Isle of Wight (HRO: Quarter Session Rolls, January 1831). The incident occurred in November 1830. I have styled the song into stanzas and added punctuation.

49 Belchem, '*Orator' Hunt*, pp. 212–20; Prothero, *Artisans and Politics*, ch. 14.

50 'A Yeoman of Surrey to Henry Brougham', *The Morning Chronicle*, 17 November 1830 (BL Place Collection: Set 21, fol. 87).

51 Interviewed in SC on Education, VII (1835), pp. 74–5; [Place], *Essay on the State of the Country*. For Cobbett's criticisms of the pamphlet see *PR*, 14 May 1831, pp. 372–3.

52 *A Dialogue on Rick-Burning, Rioting & c.* (London, 1830); *A Word to the White Horse Men* (Oxford, 1830); 'A True Englishman', *Imposture Unmasked; In a Letter to the Labourers & Working People of England* (London, 1831); *The Labourer's Friend* (London, 1830); *Address from the Magistrates to the Inhabitants of Burnham Division* (Maidenhead, 1830); *Machine-Breaking, and the Charges Occasioned by it in the Village of Turvey Down* (Oxford, 1830). Goldsmiths' Library has a rich collection of anti-Swing pamphlets and handbills.

53 *Lectures to the Labouring Classes and their Employers in the County of Sussex, and Elsewhere. Not by a Follower of William Cobbett* (London?: Hatchard, printer, 1831), p. 9.

54 *PR*, 20 October 1832, p. 142.

55 *PR*, 1 December 1830, p. 140; 15 January 1834, p. 882.

56 *PR*, 18 December 1830, p. 1026; 4 June 1831, p. 174; 24 March 1832, p. 787.

57 *The Morning Chronicle*, November 1830 (BL Place Collection: Set 21, fol. 89); *Two Labourers Residing in the County of Sussex* (London, 1830) (handbill in HO 52/10).

58 *PR*, 20 November 1830, pp. 786–7.

59 *The Times*, 25 November 1830.

60 *The Morning Chronicle*, 19 November 1830 (BL Place Collection, Set 21, fol. 86).

61 Report on the Causes of Agricultural Distress, IX (1821), pp. 95–6; SC on Agricultural Labourers' Wages, VI (1824), pp. 42–3, 48–51.

62 Poor Law Report (1834), app. A, pt I, p. 202.

63 *PR*, 23 October 1830, pp. 523–34.

64 Letter to the editor, *The Times*, 13 November 1830.

65 The document was intended for use at Cobbett's trial (Nuffield XI/8/1).

66 *A Short Account of the Life and Death of Swing ... together with the Confession of Thomas Goodman* (London, 1831). Other editions appear in *The Times*, in Sussex newspapers (Goodman 'confessed' at Lewes and Horsham) and in *Confession of Thomas Goodman* (1830), Goldsmiths' 26938. At Nuffield XI and Faithfull MS XXI/9/1 are collections of documents pertaining to the trial. On Cobbett's preparation for the trial, as well as his response to Goodman's 'confessions', see *PR*, 8 January 1831, pp. 81–6; 22 January 1831, pp. 250–2; 19 February 1831, pp. 476–7.

67 Lord Ellenborough's Diary, 26 January 1831, in Arthur Aspinall (ed.), *Three Early Nineteenth-Century Diaries* (London, 1952). According to Lord Ellenborough the King took 'great blame to himself for having been led to propose the pardoning of Goodman' (p. 42).

68 Cole, *Life of William Cobbett*, p. 363.

69 'The King against William Cobbett', *State Trials*, pp. 789–904. There are copies of the indictment at Nuffield XI and XXI. See also *A Full and Accurate Account of the Trial of William Cobbett ...* (London, 1831); *The Mirror of Parliament*, 23 December 1830, pp. 773–5; *The Greville Memoirs: A Journal of the Reign of King George IV and King William IV*, ed. Henry Reeve, 3 vols., fourth edn (London, 1875), II, p. 158. On Cobbett's changed attitudes towards machinery see *PR*, 30 July 1831, pp. 292–3.

70 'The King against William Cobbett', *State Trials*, pp. 802, 855; see also *PR*, 16 November 1833, pp. 398–9.

71 Poor Law Report (1834), app. B, pt V, p. 192.

72 *Ibid.*, p. 268.

73 *Ibid.*, pp. 281, 319, 354, 477, 481, 498, 503, 530; *Extract of a Letter from the Postmaster of Hadleigh to Sir Francis Freeling Bt. dated 6th December 1830* (London, 1830) HO 52/10.

74 Letter by Lord Carnarvon, 5 February 1831, HO 52/13.

75 *PR*, 12 February 1831, p. 405. See also *PR*, 12 July 1834, pp. 72–3; 23 August 1834, p. 463; Cobbett to T. L. Hodges, 27 October 1833 (NYPL).

76 *A Letter to the King* (London, 1830) consisted largely of extracts from Cobbett's petition. It was replied to in *'Nice Pickings': A Countryman's Remarks on Cobbett's Letter to the King* (London, 1830).

77 'The King against William Cobbett', *State Trials*, p. 855.

78 *PR*, 20 November 1830, p. 748.

79 Sidal Howes to Francis Place, 14 January 1831, Place Papers (BM Add. MS 37,950, fols.

108–9). Howes informed Place that he had bought six copies of the SDUK's address on the destruction of machinery, but had managed to give away only two on account that the labourers did not understand the tract's message. See [Henry Gowler], *An Address to the Labourers on the Subject of Destroying Machinery* (London, 1830).

80 *The Morning Chronicle*, 15 April 1831; *Hansard's Parliamentary Debates*, 3rd ser., vol. III (London, 1831), pp. 1327–33; *PR*, 23 April 1831, p. 189.

81 *Trash*, July 1832, p. 274; *PR*, 2 April 1831, pp. 2–3; 15 January 1831, pp. 153–4.

82 *A Report of the Proceedings at the Special Commission, holden at Winchester ...* (Southampton, 1831), p. 38 (HRO).

83 *The Times*, 3 January 1831; *Trash*, July 1832, pp. 268–73; *PR*, 16 June 1832, pp. 654–62; *A Calendar of the Prisoners, in the County Gaol at Winchester, for Trial at the Special Commission* (Southampton, 1830), Winchester Public Library; HRO 14M 50/2; *Sentences of the Prisoners Tried before the Special Commission at Winchester ...* (Southampton, 1830), Goldsmiths' 26447.

84 *Trash*, July 1832, pp. 273–4.

85 *Report of the Proceedings at the Special Commission*, pp. 38, 72; *The Times*, 25 December 1830, 3 January 1831.

86 Interview with Joseph Carter: Somerville, *Whistler*, p. 263.

87 *Ibid.*

88 *Report of the Proceedings at the Special Commission, passim*; *Hampshire Telegraph and Sussex Chronicle*, 3 January 1831; *The Times*, 25 December 1830; Francis Thornhill Baring to his wife, 23 November 1830, in Thomas George Baring (ed.), *Journals and Correspondence of Francis Thornhill Baring, Lord Northbrook*, 2 vols. (Winchester, 1902–5), II, p. 75.

89 *Calendar of the Prisoners, in the County Gaol at Winchester*; *Sentences of the Prisoners*; *Report of the Proceedings at the Special Commission, passim*.

90 Robert Mason to the Rev. D. Cockerton, 3 January 1831. Used extensively in the next few pages are the Baring Papers, which contain the correspondence of the Mason brothers as well as numerous depositions and memoranda pertaining to the revolt. I have attempted to locate the current repository of the papers through the Royal Commission on Historical Manuscripts, the Baring archives in London and the Hampshire Record Office, but without success. The references here are to the documents reprinted in Appendix A of Alice Colson's 'The Revolt of the Hampshire Agricultural Labourers and its Causes, 1812–1831' (MA thesis, University of London, 1937). At the time of Ms Colson's work the papers were in the possession of Lord Northbrook of Alresford.

91 Robert Mason to the Rev. J. Joliffe, 27 January 1831 (Baring Papers).

92 *Ibid.*, *Report of the Proceedings at the Special Commission*, pp. 89–90.

93 Cobbett to Mrs Cobbett, n.d. (*c.* July–August 1831) Nuffield XXX/314/1–2.

94 *Report of the Proceedings at the Special Commission*, p. 90.

95 *The Charge Delivered by the Hon. Robert Vaughan to the Grand Jury ...* (n.p., 1830), pp. 4–5; 'The King against William Cobbett', *State Trials*, pp. 813–15; *Hansard's Parliamentary Debates*, 8 February 1831.

96 For some of Cobbett's earlier comments on the Barings see *PR*, 31 August 1822, p. 71; *Rural Rides*, pp. 44–5, 75, 144, 270–1, 384, 474.

97 Baring (ed.), *Journals and Correspondence of Francis Thornhill Baring*, II, pp. 77–8; Robert Mason to James Ray, 7 February 1831 (Baring Papers).

98 'The Voluntary Declaration of Ruth Cook the Mother of Henry Cook who was executed at Winchester for being concerned in the riots of November last' (Baring Papers); Francis Thornhill Baring to Lady Jane Baring, 23 November 1830, Baring (ed.), *Journals and Correspondence of Francis Thornhill Baring*, II, p. 74.

99 Roach Smith, *Retrospections*, II, pp. 45–6.

100 *PR*, 23 July 1831, pp. 193–205; 30 July 1831, pp. 260–74; 27 August 1831, pp. 530–56; 3 September 1831, pp. 602–10; 17 September 1831, pp. 752–63; 24 September 1831, pp. 790–804; 28 July 1832, pp. 193–209. On the Deacles's participation in the disturbances see the remarks by 'M.H.' in *Hampshire Notes and Queries*, vol. 8 (1896), pp. 97–8; Roach Smith, *Retrospections*, II, p. 245. Cobbett acknowledged his compositions on behalf of the Deacles in his letter to John Cobbett, 14 August 1832 (Nuffield), and in 'Cobbett's Form of Petition', 7 September 1831 (Bodleian).

101 Sir Bingham Baring (Baron Ashburton) to Lady Harriet Baring, 18, 19, 21 November 1830 (HRO 100M70/11M52/F1); *The Times*, 16 July 1831; *Hampshire Chronicle*, 18 July 1831.

102 Place to Cobbett, 21 September 1831, 22 September 1831 (BL Place Collection: Set 21, fols. 185, 211, 213). See also Dudley Miles, *Francis Place: The Life of a Remarkable Radical 1771–1854* (Brighton, 1988), pp. 72–3.

103 *PR*, 10 September 1831, p. 645; 14 May 1831, pp. 376–7.

104 Roach Smith, *Retrospections*, II, p. 44.

105 *PR*, 15 January 1831, p. 160; *The Charge Delivered by the Hon. Robert Vaughan to the Grand Jury*, pp. 4–5; *The Times*, 21 December 1830. On the Bishop of Winchester see Bishop's Waltham Vestry Book, 19 November 1830, 26 November 1830, 31 December 1830 (HRO 30 M77A/PV2).

106 Robert Mason to the Rev. D. Cockerton, 3 January 1831; Robert Mason to the Rev. J. Joliffe, 27 January 1831; Robert Mason to Mary Mason, 6 February 1831; Robert Mason to James Ray, 7 February 1831; Robert Mason to Mary Mason, n.d. (written from New South Wales); Joseph Mason to John Hoar, 30 September 1831 (Baring Papers). See Hobsbawm and Rudé, *Captain Swing*, pp. 268–9. Joseph Mason is here incorrectly referred to as 'James' Mason.

107 *PR*, 2 April 1831, p. 17; 3 December 1831, pp. 598–9; 23 November 1831, pp. 601–2; 14 April 1832, pp. 96–8.

108 Enos Diddams to Cobbett, 6 December 1831, *PR*, 14 April 1831, pp. 97–9.

109 'A True Englishman', *Imposture Unmasked*, p. 3 (BL T. 1394). See also *PR*, 25 June 1831, pp. 744–5.

110 *PR*, 29 October 1831, pp. 288–301; Cobbett to John Cobbett, 27 October 1831 (Nuffield).

111 *PR*, 11 December 1830, p. 944. See also W. H. Hudson, *A Shepherd's Life* (1910, London, 1944), pp. 179–80.

112 *PR*, 24 September 1831, p. 779; 22 January 1831, p. 204.

113 Cobbett to Mrs Cobbett, n.d. (*c.* July–August 1831) Nuffield XXX/314/1–2.

114 Robert Mason, written upon the execution of Henry Cook, and communicated in his letter to the Rev. J. Joliffe, 27 January 1831 (Baring Papers).

115 *PR*, 3 August 1833, p. 285.

116 Cobbett to Mrs Cobbett, n.d. (*c.* July–August 1831) Nuffield XXX/314/1–2; *PR*, 4 August 1832, p. 271; 28 January 1832, p. 288. Wage-rates in the 'hard parishes' were elevated from 9s. or 10s. a week to 12s. – see Roach Smith, *Retrospections*, p. 247. See also Barton Stacey Vestry Minute Book, 1831–57 (HRO 60M70/PV1; Micheldever Vestry Minutes, 1826–86 (HRO 7M80A/PV1).

117 *PR*, 2 April 1831, p. 11; 13 July 1833, p. 74; 10 September 1831, p. 653. See also Bethanie Afton, '"The Motive which has Operated on the Minds of my People": 1830, The Propensity of the Hampshire Parishes to Riot', *Proceedings of the Hampshire Field Club and Archaeological Society*, no. 44 (1988), pp. 115–16.

118 *PR*, 14 May 1831, p. 380.

119 Poor Law Report (1834), app. A, pt I, pp. 196, 199A, 201A, 202, 203A–4A.

120 SC of the House of Lords on the State of Agriculture, VIII (1836), p. 119.

121 Poor Law Report (1834), app. B, pt V, p. 510.
122 *Ibid.*, pt III, p. 332.
123 Bishop's Waltham Vestry Book (HRO 30M77A/PV2), entries for 14, 19, 26 November 1830, 31 December 1830.
124 Poor Law Report (1834), app. A, pt I, p. 206.
125 *PR*, 24 March 1832, p. 789.
126 *PR*, 12 February 1831, pp. 402–6; *The Times*, 30 November 1830; *Hansard's Parliamentary Debates*, 8 February 1831; G. E. Mingay, '"Rural War": The Life and Times of Captain Swing,' in G. E. Mingay (ed.), *The Unquiet Countryside* (London, 1989), pp. 45–6.
127 *The Morning Chronicle*, 14 December 1832. See *PR*, 14 January 1832, p. 132.
128 Montagu Gore, *Allotments of Land* (London, 1831); *A Plain Statement of the Case of the Labourer* (London, 1831); *The Life and History of Swing, the Kent Rick-Burner* (London, n.d., 1830–1); *The Arbour Colloquy* (London, 1830); Joseph Marriage, *Letters on the Distressed State of the Agricultural Labourer* (Chelmsford, 1831). See also *The Labourer's Friend: Selections from the Publications of the Labourer's Friend Society* (London, 1835); D. C. Barnett, 'Allotments and the Problem of Rural Poverty, 1780–1840', in E. L. Jones and G. E. Mingay (eds.), *Land, Labour and Population in the Industrial Revolution* (London, 1967); Hasbach, *Agricultural Labourer*, pp. 235–41; Horn, *Rural World*, pp. 142–4.
129 *PR*, 9 November 1833, p. 372; 3 December 1831, p. 635; 24 November 1832, p. 459.
130 *PR*, 22 January 1831, p. 203; 14 December 1833, p. 687.
131 Quoted part is from W. A. Armstrong, 'The Position of the Labourer in Rural Society', in G. E. Mingay (ed.), *The Agrarian History of England and Wales*, VI (Cambridge, 1989), p. 833.
132 Hobsbawm and Rudé, *Captain Swing*, p. 292.

8 TOWARDS REVOLUTION: THE REFORM BILL, THE POOR LAW AND THE COTTAGE CHARTER

1 George Eliot, *Felix Holt, the Radical* (1866, Philadelphia, n.d.), pp. 4, 51.
2 *Rural Rides*, p. 292.
3 *A Memoir of Thomas Bewick*, ed. Ian Bain (London, 1975), p. 32.
4 Ashby, *Joseph Ashby*, p. 7.
5 [Lucy Broadwood], 'Songs Noted in Sussex and Surrey since 1892', *Journal of the Folk-Song Society*, vol. 1, no. 4 (1902), pp. 139–40; Henry Burstow, *Reminiscences of Horsham* (Horsham, 1911).
6 'Autobiography of a Suffolk Farm Labourer', pt 2, ch. 1.
7 Joanna Innes, 'The Invention of Rural Poverty in Later Eighteenth-Century England', p. 2. Again, I am grateful to Joanna for providing me with a copy of her unpublished paper.
8 See the old but very fine study by Furniss, *Position of the Laborer*, esp. ch. 7. For insightful analyses and counterpoints see Coats, 'Changing Attitudes to Labour', pp. 35–51; *idem*, 'The Classical Economists and the Labourer', in E. L. Jones and G. E. Mingay (eds.), *Land, Labour and Population in the Industrial Revolution* (London, 1967), pp. 100–30. On Young, compare *Farmer's Letters, A Six Weeks' Tour through the Southern Counties*, and *The Farmer's Tour through the East of England*, 4 vols. (London, 1771) with his later writings in the *Annals of Agriculture*, the county surveys of the Board of Agriculture, and especially 'An Inquiry into the Propriety of Applying Wastes'.
9 Frederick Law Olsted, *Walks and Talks of an American Farmer in England* (1852, Ann Arbor, 1967), pp. 238–9; Poor Law Report (1834), app. B, pt V, p. 245.

10 Armstrong, *Farmworkers*, esp. p. 250. The continuance of the Hodge stereotype in the present is implicitly explored in Renée Danziger, *Political Powerlessness: Agricultural Workers in Post-War England* (Manchester, 1988), esp. ch. 6.

11 *PR*, 17 March 1821, p. 754. See also *PR*, 1 August 1829, p. 148; 23 February 1828, p. 230.

12 *PR*, 9 January 1819, pp. 474–81; 11 August 1827, p. 402; 7 September 1816, p. 316; 16 November 1816, pp. 614, 618; 11 July 1829, p. 37; *Trash*, November 1830, pp. 116–17; Edmund Burke, 'Thoughts and Details on Scarcity' (1795), in *Annals of Agriculture*, vol. 36 (1801); Poynter, *Society and Pauperism*, p. xiv. For other examples of political statements by Swing rioters see Wells, 'Social Protest, Class, Conflict and Consciousness', pp. 184–7.

13 *The Morning Chronicle*: *PR*, 6 November 1830, p. 669.

14 'An Appeal to the Justice of his Judges and his Country from an Agricultural Labourer on his Trial at Salisbury for Machine Breaking', *The Morning Chronicle*, 6 January 1831 (BL Place Collection: Set 21, fol. 241).

15 *The Hampshire Chronicle*, 15 March 1830.

16 'On the Times, Corn Bills, Paper Money and Trade' (Whitehaven: Wilson, printer, 1815) Goldsmiths' 21149. For similar commentaries see 'The Poor Man's Lamentation' (BL 1871 f. 13, fol. 81); 'Past, Present and Future' (BL: LR 271 a. 2, vol. I (1); 'The Good Old Days of Adam and Eve' (BL 1876 e. 3, fol. 161) and also LUCB, vol. IV, nos. 486, 493, 515, 525, 537(1), 539, 603.

17 'The Sporting Farmer' (London: Hodges, printer) JJ: Street Ballads, IV, fol. 17.

18 'A True Picture of the Times' (Portsea: Williams, printer) Madden 22 (VII).

19 Denson, *Peasant's Voice to Landowners*, p. 47.

20 Clare, 'Autobiography', p. 221.

21 *PR*, 21 August 1830, p. 355.

22 *Trash*, May 1832, pp. 235–8. The quotation was inexact: 2 Thessalonians iii, v. 10 reads 'If any would not work, neither should he eat.'

23 *PR*, 19 December 1892, p. 776.

24 *PR*, 23 January 1830, pp. 104–5; 9 June 1832, pp. 602–6; *Tour in Scotland: And in the Four Northern Counties of England* (London, 1833).

25 *PR*, 18 December 1819, pp. 453–4; 17 November 1832, pp. 387–92; 17 November 1827, p. 499; 24 November 1827, pp. 537–49; 14 December 1833, pp. 652–3; *Hundred Days*, p. 39; *Rural Rides*, p. 351.

26 This is frequently implied in the proceedings at Cobbett's trial: see 'The King against William Cobbett', *State Trials*, pp. 789–904.

27 *PR*, 26 March 1831, p. 820; 25 June 1831, p. 743; 9 July 1831, p. 214; 29 October 1831, p. 266; 23 April 1831, pp. 188–90.

28 *PR*, 13 July 1833, p. 70.

29 *PR*, 21 May, 1831, p. 458. See also *PR*, 16 July 1832, p. 652.

30 *The Ballot*, 5 June 1831; *PR*, 5 November 1831, p. 342; 26 October 1831, p. 342; 22 December 1832, p. 713.

31 *PR*, 2 April 1831, pp. 4–5.

32 *PR*, 28 April 1821, pp. 227–31; 17 March 1821, pp. 715–16; 30 October 1830, pp. 558–9; 5 November 1831, p. 330.

33 *PR*, 21 April 1832, pp. 140–1.

34 *PR*, 21 May 1831, p. 438; *The Taunton Courier*, 11 May 1831; *The Ballot*, 15 May 1831; Belchem, *'Orator' Hunt*, pp. 221, 225, 269.

35 *PR*, 20 June 1829, p. 799; 27 February 1830, p. 272; 19 March 1831, p. 713; 20 August 1831, p. 484; 21 May 1831, p. 438; 3 September 1831, pp. 582–3; 5 November 1831,

p. 359; 12 October 1833, p. 110. With regard to the £10 franchise, Cobbett represented the rural workers as saying:

I have no possession but my *labour*; no enemy will take that from me; you, the rich, possess all the land and all its products; you make what laws you please without my participation or assent; you punish me at your pleasure; you say that my want of property excludes me from the right of having a share in the making of the laws; you say that the property I have is *nothing worth*; what ground, then, do you call on me to risk my life [in defence of the country]?

(*PR*, 5 November 1831, p. 330)

36 *PR*, 16 June 1832, p. 644.

37 'Autobiography of a Suffolk Farm Labourer', pt III. On the political atmosphere in the countryside during the deliberations on the Reform Bill see Buckmaster, *Village Politician*, p. 53.

38 Discussed by the Rev. Robert Wright: *PR*, 3 August 1833, p. 300.

39 *PR*, 23 June 1832, pp. 754–7; 30 June 1832, pp. 791–2; 14 July 1832, pp. 65–86; Cobbett to Mrs Cobbett, 8 July 1832 (Nuffield); Cobbett to Mr Palmer, n.d. (*c*. July 1832) Nuffield XXX/279/1.

40 *Lord Melbourne's Papers*, ed. Lloyd Sanders (London, 1889), pp. 147–52.

41 *Ibid.*, p. 126.

42 *Ibid.*, pp. 149–50. The Home Secretary believed the rules to have been drawn up by 'those persons in London who designate themselves the National Political Union, and who hold their meetings at a house in Theobald's Road'. The National Political Union was the title of Francis Place's organization which met principally at the Crown and Anchor and assorted outdoor venues; the premises in Theobald's Road were the main meeting-place of the National (Political) Union of the Working Classes, founded in April 1831. Melbourne was alluding to the latter. On the activities of the NUWC see Prothero, *Artisans and Politics*, pp. 290–9.

   Although much work remains to be done on post-Swing political activity, Roger Wells is making some important contributions in this way. He has shown, for example, that the Tolpuddle Union was created in part by the initiative of sectors of the Grand National Consolidated Trade Union, and that rural unionism in Dorset revived, partly through advice and propaganda received from London, during the summer of 1838. See his essays 'Social Protest, Class, Conflict and Consciousness', esp. pp. 184–7; 'Tolpuddle', esp. pp. 121–3; and essay on southern Chartism in *Rural History*, vol. 2 no. 1 (April 1991).

43 The Duke of Wellington reported that he had heard 'a good deal of the circulation of "Cobbett" and the "Poor Man's Guardian"' in this district (*Melbourne's Papers*, ed. Sanders, p. 150). The *Guardian*'s Henry Hetherington opposed the Reform Bill from the start.

44 *PR*, 25 August 1832, p. 459; 21 July 1832, pp. 143–4. For a thinly veiled appeal for a nomination in Hampshire or Surrey, see *PR*, 10 September 1831, pp. 648–58.

45 Weaver, *John Fielden*, pp. 49, 53, 69; *PR*, 23 January 1830, pp. 104–5; 2 June 1832, pp. 560–2. Fielden did not specify that Cobbett's nomination be for Oldham. See the letter to Cobbett by the Oldham Radical William Fitton: *PR*, 21 July 1832, pp. 129–31.

46 *List of the Voters in the Borough of Oldham, Royton, Crompton and Chatterton* (Manchester, 1832) Institute of Historial Research. See Weaver, *John Fielden*, ch. 2; John Foster, *Class Struggle and the Industrial Revolution* (London, 1974), ch. 3, esp. pp. 131–40; D. S. Gadian, 'Class Consciousness in Oldham and Other North-West Industrial Towns 1830–1850', *Historical Journal*, vol. 21, no. 1 (1978), pp. 161–72. On radical support for Cobbett among what John Foster calls the 'Jacobin core', including John Knight and William Fitton see *PR*, 21 July 1832, pp. 130–3; Foster, *Class Struggle*, pp. 131–40, 151–2, 287 n90.

47　*The Manchester Times and Gazette*, 15 December 1832; *PR*, 2 June 1832, pp. 560–2.
48　*PR*, 22 December 1832, p. 725. For Cobbett's pledges see *PR*, 10 September 1831, pp. 641–6; 27 September 1832, pp. 708–9.
49　*PR*, 22 December 1832, p. 713; 30 March 1833, p. 794.
50　Cobbett referred to Fielden as the 'greatest' of all manufacturers in the Kingdom: *PR*, 21 July 1832, p. 133.
51　For the benefit of his industrial constituents he occasionally let up on this theme. See, for example, *PR*, 21 July 1832, pp. 135–6.
52　Weaver, *John Fielden*, p. 20; *PR*, 30 March 1833, pp. 793–4.
53　*PR*, 9 March 1833, p. 582; 1 June 1833, p. 517; Manchester lecture IV (*PR*, 4 February 1832, p. 371); Manchester lecture V (*PR*, 11 February 1832, pp. 417–21). Cobbett's best parliamentary performances were his speeches against the malt tax: see *PR*, 22 March 1834, pp. 707–29; 14 March 1835, pp. 642–98; 21 March 1835, pp. 706–25.
54　*PR*, 29 March 1834, pp. 769–70, 800–3; 29 November 1834, p. 528; 8 August 1829, pp. 170–1; 1 December 1832, p. 579; 19 January 1833, p. 156.
55　John Knight to William Cobbett, 10 September 1833 (Rutgers). On Knight see Foster, *Class Struggle*, pp. 43, 63, 101, 152.
56　Cobbett to John Fielden, 28 September 1833 (Rutgers).
57　*PR*, 10 January 1835, pp. 68–70.
58　Osborne, *William Cobbett*, p. 249. See also Schweizer and Osborne, *Cobbett in his Times*, ch. 9. Gladstone described Cobbett as a 'contemptible antagonist' in Parliament (John Morley, *The Life of William Ewart Gladstone*, 3 vols. (London, 1903), I, p. 114).
59　Foster, *Class Struggle*, ch. 4, esp. p. 42.
60　*PR*, 7 December 1833, pp. 624–34; 11 January 1834, pp. 95–114. For the prospectus of the Society see *PR*, 14 December 1832, pp. 652–9. The Society and Fielden's role in it receive excellent treatment in Weaver, *John Fielden*, ch. 3.
61　Manchester lecture IV, in *PR*, 4 February 1832, p. 371.
62　*PR*, 29 March 1834, p. 52; Cobbett to John Fielden, 24 April 1834 (Rutgers).
63　*PR*, 29 March 1834, pp. 796–7; 5 April 1834, pp. 47–52; 12 April 1834, p. 81; 19 April 1834, pp. 167–8; 26 April 1834, pp. 198–9; 10 May 1834, p. 341; 17 January 1835, p. 133; 21 February 1835, pp. 463–4; 4 April 1835, pp. 54–5; Cobbett to John Halliwell, 19 April 1835 (John Rylands Library); Cobbett to James Gutsell, 17 May 1835 (Yale). See also Joyce Marlow, *The Tolpuddle Martyrs* (1971, St Albans, 1974), pp. 111–14.
64　Of all the congratulatory addresses that Cobbett received, this one pleased him the most: *PR*, 29 December 1832, p. 802; 12 January 1833, pp. 82–3; 22 December 1832, p. 708.
65　*PR*, 29 December 1832, p. 803; 12 February 1834, pp. 409–10.
66　*PR*, 21 January 1832, p. 203; 11 September 1830, p. 333.
67　For an excellent discussion and interpretation of country ideology and the Poor Law see Peter Mandler, 'The Making of the New Poor Law *Redivivus*', *Past and Present*, no. 117 (November 1987).
68　*PR*, 23 February 1828, p. 233; 11 February 1832, pp. 401–3; 21 April 1832, p. 143; 21 January 1832, p. 222; 6 April 1833, p. 23. He also believed that a reformed Parliament would promptly dismiss the Commission (*PR*, 16 June 1832, p. 676; *Legacy to Labourers*, p. 7).
69　The effect of the rural disturbances upon the Whig Cabinet and the Poor Law Commissioners is well discussed in Peter Dunkley, 'Whigs and Paupers: The Reform of the English Poor Laws 1830–1834', *Journal of British Studies*, vol. 20, no. 2 (Spring 1981); *idem, The Crisis of the Old Poor Law in England 1795–1834* (New York, 1982), esp. chs. 4–5. J. P. D. Dunbabin, *Rural Discontent in Nineteenth-Century Britain* (London, 1974), wrongly suggests that the rural revolt had virtually no influence on the central government (pp. 299–300).

70 Nassau Senior, 'Remarks on Emigration with a Draft of a Bill' (1831), in S. Leon Levy, *Nassau W. Senior 1790–1864* (New York, 1970), p. 70.
71 Adam Smith, *The Wealth of Nations* (1776, Harmondsworth, 1970), pp. 177, 181.
72 The Rev. North, reporting to *Annals of Agriculture*, vol. 25 (1800), p. 466.
73 Stubbs, *The Land and the Labourers*, pp. 24–5.
74 See Mark Blaug, 'The Myth of the Old Poor Law and the Making of the New', *Journal of Economic History*, vol. 23 (1963); D. A. Baugh, 'The Cost of Poor Relief in South-East England, 1790–1834', *Economic History Review*, second ser., vol. 28, no. 1 (1975); J. Huzel, 'The Labourer and the Poor Law 1750–1850', in G. E. Mingay (ed.), *Agrarian History of England and Wales* (Cambridge, 1989), VI, pp. 755–810; Michael Rose, 'The Poor Law and the Historians: Changing Attitudes to Relief in Nineteenth-Century England', in Malcolm Chase (ed.), *The New Poor Law* (Middlesbrough, 1985); Snell, *Annals of the Labouring Poor*, ch. 3.
75 Poor Law Report (1834), app. A, pt I, p. 610. On magisterial recognition of the illegality of the allowances see BL Place Collection, Set 41, fol. 318; *The Philanthropist*, vol. 2, no. 112 (1830); G. Scrope, *A Letter to the Magistrates of the South of England . . .* (London, 1831), pp. 3–14.
76 On rural resistance to proposals for a legislated minimum wage see *Annals of Agriculture*, vol. 25 (1796), pp. 144, 258, 494, 626; *A Temperate Discussion of the Causes which have Led to the Current High Price of Bread . . .* (London, 1800); Hammonds, *Village Labourer*, pp. 48–9, 86–8, 91–5, 108, 134, 170. Lord Melbourne, for example, wrote simply of the 'great errors' which had been committed in the 'paying of wages of labour out of the poor rate', proceeding to a recommendation that they be curtailed: *Melbourne's Papers*, ed. Sanders, p. 127.
77 'The Farmer's Rent Day' (Newcastle: Marshall, printer) Madden 16 (I).
78 Snell, *Annals of the Labouring Poor*, pp. 124–31.
79 Dunkley, 'Whigs and Paupers', pp. 124–49; *idem, Crisis of the Old Poor Law*, chs. 4–5.
80 *PR*, 21 January 1832, p. 210.
81 *Protestant 'Reformation'*, paras. 19–20, 337, 471; *PR*, 2 November 1816, p. 560; 24 February 1821, pp. 504–6; 13 July 1822, p. 83; *Legacy to Labourers*, letters III–IV, esp. pp. 45–7, 62–7, 72, 117–18, 122–3; *Poor Man's Friend*, nos. I–IV; *PR*, 29 October 1827, pp. 193–231 (no. V of *Poor Man's Friend*). For critical comment on Cobbett's attitude towards the Poor Law see Himmelfarb, *Idea of Poverty*, pp. 210–13.
82 *PR*, 21 June 1834, p. 705. Also: *Legacy to Labourers*, pp. 121–2.
83 Poor Law Report (1834), app. A, pt III, p. 44; app. B (1), pt III, pp. 174, 305.
84 'Autobiography of a Suffolk Farm Labourer', pt III, ch. IV.
85 'The Little Farm, or the Weary Ploughman' (London: Paul, printer) Firth b. 34, c. 164; 'A Terror to the Rent Day' (Manchester: Kiernan, printer) Bodleian 2806 c. 17 (421); 'Request of the Poor' (Brighton: Phillips, printer) BL 1876 d. 41, fol. 521; 'Revolt of the Workhouse' (Portsea: Williams, printer); 'Poor Law Bill' (Cambridge: Talbot, printer) LUCB, vol. VI, no. 579 (1); 'The Old and New Poor Law: Who Gains? and Who Loses?' (London, 1835) BL: T. 2125; William Gaspey, *Poor Law Melodies* (London, 1842), esp. nos. 1–4.
86 John Knott, *Popular Opposition to the 1834 Poor Law* (Beckenham, 1986), chs. 3–5; Nicholas Edsall, *The Anti-Poor Law Movement 1834–44* (Manchester, 1971), ch. 2; John Lowerson, 'The Aftermath of Swing: Anti-Poor Law Movements and Rural Trades' Unions in the South East of England', in A. Charlesworth (ed.), *Rural Social Change and Conflicts since 1500* (Humberside, 1982), pp. 55–83; Roger Wells, 'Resistance to the New Poor Law in the Rural South', in Chase (ed.), *The New Poor Law*, pp. 15–53; Digby, *Pauper Palaces*, ch. 12.
87 *PR*, 1 August 1829, p. 148; 23 February 1828, p. 230; 22 December 1821, p. 1502.

88 Middleton, *GVAC Middlesex*, p. 47n.

89 Hawker, *Victorian Poacher*, p. 77.

90 Somerville, *Whistler*, p. 353; Haggard (ed.), *I Walked by Night*, p. 105.

91 Bill H., *The Autobiography of a Working Man*, ed. Eleanor Eden (London, 1862), p. 29.

92 'Autobiography of a Suffolk Farm Labourer', pt III, ch. V.

93 *PR*, 2 January 1830, pp. 1–2; 6 April 1822, pp. 6–7; *Legacy to Labourers*, p. 11.

94 'The Working Poor of Old England' (no imprint) BL: LR 271 a. 2, vol. 5, fol. 240.

95 *PR*, 29 May 1823, p. 799.

96 *PR*, 11 September 1819, p. 115. Also: *PR*, 28 August 1819, p. 46; 'Old Merry England' (no imprint, *c.* 1830s) BL 1876 d. 41, fol. 189. See also 'The Peasant's Home in the Isle of Wight' (Portsea: Williams, printer) Madden 22 (VII); 'Hard Times and No Beer' (London: Catnach, printer) Madden 11 (V).

97 Cobbett to [James] Gutsell, 22 July 1835 (Illinois).

98 Cobbett to John Fielden, 30 April 1834 (Rutgers).

99 Cobbett to John Oldfield, 6 June 1835 (Cornell). See also *Legacy to Labourers*, pp. 124, 140.

100 *Cobbett's Advice to the Chopsticks* (first and second addresses), *PR*, 20 October 1832, pp. 147–59; 27 October 1832, pp. 200–3; Cobbett to John Dean, 16 October 1834 (Rutgers). The letters to Charles Marshall appear in *PR*, 27 September–29 November 1834.

101 *PR*, 14 December 1816, pp. 748–54. See also *Hundred Days*, pp. 78, 99–100, 106.

102 *PR*, 24 November 1832, p. 462; 9 August 1834, p. 351; 18 October 1834, pp. 135–6; 28 February 1835, pp. 513, 517. See Chase, '*The People's Farm*', pp. 180–2.

103 'The Times in Hertfordshire' (London: Taylor, printer) Madden 13 (VII).

104 *Life and Adventures*, p. 93.

105 Buckmaster, *Village Politician*, p. 23.

106 'I Likes a Drop of Good Beer' (BL: LR 271 a. 2, vol. 5); 'Harvest Home' (BL: LR 271 a. 2, vol. 6); 'The Merry Haymakers' (Madden 5 (II)).

107 'Old Merry England' (BL 1876 d. 41, fol. 189).

108 *PR*, 7 April 1832, pp. 5–6; Poor Law Report (1834), app. B (1), pt II, pp. 492, 494.

109 Poor Law Report (1834), app. B (1), pt II, p. 413.

110 'A New Song on the Times' (London: Pitts, printer) Madden 8 (II); 'The Sporting Farmer' (London: Pitts, printer) Madden 22 (VII); 'The Kingdom's Complaint' (London: Pitts, printer) BL 11661 dd. 20, fol. 27.

111 Somerville, *Whistler*, p. 42.

112 Anderson, 'Bad Times' (Goldsmiths' 21148).

113 *PR*, 17 March 1821, p. 757.

114 *PR*, 12 April 1823, p. 79; 26 May 1821, p. 508; 11 October 1834, p. 79; 16 December 1815, p. 330; 25 June 1831, p. 775.

115 'The Farmer's Son' (London: Pitts, printer) Madden 8 (II). See also 'Swaggering Farmers' (Durham: Walker, printer) BL: LR 271 a. 2, vol. 3; JJ: Street Ballads, XII, fols. 85–7; 'The Poor Labourers' (London: Ryle, printer) BL: LR 271 a. 2, vol. I (2), fol. 120; Firth b. 25 (399).

116 'A Farmer's Son and Daughter, 1751' (London: Pitts, printer) JJ: Street Ballads, VI; 'The New-Fashioned Farmer' (London: Catnach, printer) Madden 20 (V); 'The Farmer' (London: Pitts, printer) BL 11621 i. 12, fol. 82.

117 Stevenson, *GVAC Surrey*, pp. 88–90.

118 'The Labourer's Worthy of his Hire' (London: Disley, printer) Firth c. 22 (109).

119 Poor Law Report (1834), app. A, pt III, p. 14. See also *PR*, 9 April 1831, pp. 72–3.

120 *PR*, 14 July 1832, p. 76.

121 *PR*, 16 June 1821, p. 731; 8 January 1831, p. 66.

122 'Why is Man Denied by Man his Daily Bread' (Whitehaven: Wilson, printer, *c.* 1835) Madden 17 (II).
123 *PR*, 6 October 1832, p. 24; March 1832, p. 790.
124 *PR*, 25 October 1817, p. 906.

EPILOGUE: PLOUGHING THE HOME FIELD

1 Cobbett's Diary (Nuffield XIX).
2 *The Times*, 27 June 1835; *The Morning Chronicle*, 19 June 1835.
3 Williams, 'The Man who Shifted against the Tide'.
4 Richard Johnson, '"Really Useful Knowledge"', p. 89.
5 [Place], *Essay on the State of the Country*, p. 2; Place Papers, BM Add. MS 27,809, fol. 17.
6 Marx, 'The Eighteenth Brumaire of Louis Bonaparte', p. 171.
7 Letter to the editor of the *Brighton Patriot*, quoted in *PR*, 15 August 1835, p. 339.
8 *The Times*, 27 June 1835.
9 Sidney Godolphin Osborne, 'To the Editor of the *Wiltshire Independent*', 10 June 1848, in *The Letters of S.G.O.*, 2 vols. (London, n.d., *c.* 1888), I, p. 161.
10 Jefferies, *Hodge and his Masters*, pp. 262–3.

APPENDIX I POPULAR RURAL SONG

1 On the history of the broadside ballad see Leslie Shepard, *The Broadside Ballad: A Study in Origins and Meaning* (London, 1962); Victor Neuburg, *Popular Literature: A History and Guide* (Harmondsworth, 1977); Gordon Hall Gerould, *The Ballad of Tradition* (Oxford, 1957).
2 See Dyck, 'Towards the "Cottage Charter"'; Thomson, 'Broadside Ballad Trade', esp. p. 204.
3 On the debate see Francis Gummere, 'The Ballad and Communal Poetry' (1896), in MacEdward Leach and Tristram Coffin (eds.), *The Critics and the Ballad* (Carbondale, Ill., 1961), pp. 20–9; Louise Pound, *Poetic Origins and the Ballad* (1921, New York, 1962), ch. 1; D. K. Wilgus, *Anglo-American Folksong Scholarship since 1898* (New Brunswick, NJ, 1959), *passim*; Thomson, 'Broadside Ballad Trade', p. 16.
4 Roger Chartier, 'Culture as Appropriation: Popular Cultural Uses in Early Modern France', in Steven Kaplan (ed.), *Understanding Popular Culture: Europe from the Middle Ages to the Nineteenth Century* (New York, 1984), p. 234; Michael Pickering, *Village Song and Culture* (London, 1982), p. 65.
5 Lloyd, *Folk Song in England*, p. 65.
6 Hugh Tracey, 'The State of Folk Music in Bantu Africa', *Journal of the International Folk Music Council*, vol. 6 (1954), p. 34.
7 Albert Friedman, *The Ballad Revival* (Chicago, 1961), pp. 60–1.
8 See Clifford Geertz, 'Ideology as a Cultural System', in David Apter (ed.), *Ideology and Discontent* (New York, 1964), pp. 63–4.
9 Alan Lomax and John Halifax, 'Folk Song Texts as Cultural Indicators', in Alan Lomax (ed.), *Folk Song and Culture* (Washington, 1968), p. 275.

BIBLIOGRAPHY

A Manuscript sources
   I   Cobbett papers
   II Other papers
B Printed primary sources
   I   Cobbett's writings
   II Anti-Cobbett
   III Collections of ballads and broadsides
   IV Government reports
   V Periodicals, newspapers, parliamentary proceedings
   VI Other
C Secondary sources
   I   Cobbett studies, bibliographies and published correspondence
   II Other
   III Unpublished theses

A MANUSCRIPT SOURCES

I Cobbett papers

The largest collections of Cobbett correspondence and manuscripts are held at Nuffield College and the British Library. Smaller holdings consulted in this study, principally letters, are held at the following institutions:

Adelphi University	Huntington Library
Bodleian Library	Lockwood Memorial Library
Boston Public Library	New York Public Library
Cornell University	Public Record Office (Kew)
Duke University	Rutgers University
East Sussex Record Office	John Rylands University Library
Farnham Museum	University of Illinois
Fitzwilliam Museum	University of London
	Yale University

II Other papers

Baring Papers: Hampshire Record Office
Barton Stacey Vestry Books: Hampshire Record Office
Bishop's Waltham Vestry Books: Hampshire Record Office
Correspondence of Hannah More: Duke University
Droxford Vestry Books: Hampshire Record Office
'Farm Account Book', Shalden Stratten: Hampshire Record Office
Faithfull MSS: Nuffield College
Hampshire Quarter Session Order Books and Rolls: Hampshire Record Office
Home Office Papers: Public Record Office (Kew)
    40/3–31: Disturbances, 1816–33
    41/4–11: Disturbances, entry books, 1818–34
    52/4–18: Municipal and Provincial, 1824–32
Micheldever Vestry Books: Hampshire Record Office
Place Papers: British Museum Additional Manuscripts
Titchfield Vestry Books: Hampshire Record Office

B PRINTED PRIMARY SOURCES

Place of publication is London unless otherwise stated.

I Cobbett's writings (including newspapers, journals and edited works)

Advice to Young Men and (Incidentally) to Young Women (1830).
Cobbett's Advice (1800).
Cobbett's Advice to the Chopsticks, two broadsides (1832).
Cobbett's Collective Commentaries (1822).
Cobbett's Evening Post (1820).
Cobbett's Manchester Lectures, in Support of his Fourteen Reform Propositions ... (1832).
Cobbett's Parliamentary Debates (1804–12).
Cobbett's Parliamentary History of England (1804–12).
Cobbett's Sermons ... (1821–2).
Cottage Economy: Containing Information Relating to the Brewing of Beer, Making of Bread, Keeping of Cows ... (1822).
Eleven Lectures on the French and Belgian Revolutions ... (1830).
The Emigrant's Guide; in Ten Letters ... (1829).
The English Gardener; or, A Treatise on the Situation, Soil, Enclosing and Laying-Out, of Kitchen Gardens ... (1828).
Essay on Sheep ..., by R. R. Livingstone, edition by Cobbett (London, 1811).
French Grammar, Or, Plain Instruction for the Learning of French (1824).
A Grammar of the English Language ... (New York, 1818).
A History of the Last Hundred Days of English Freedom, ed. J. L. Hammond (1921), reprints from the *Political Register* of 1817.
A History of the Protestant 'Reformation' in England and Ireland ... (1824–7).

History of the Regency and Reign of King George the Fourth ... (1830–4).

Horse-Hoeing Husbandry: Cobbett's edition of Jethro Tull's *Horse-Hoeing Husbandry* ... (1731, 1822).

Important Considerations for the People of this Kingdom ... (1803).

'The King against William Cobbett: Trial of William Cobbett for Publishing a Seditious Libel' (1831), *Reports of State Trials*, ed. J. Macdonell, new ser. (1889), II (1823–31).

Legacy to Labourers; Or, What is the Right which Lords, Baronets and Squires have to the Lands of England? (1834).

Legacy to Parsons; Or, Have the Clergy of the Established Church an Equitable Right to the Tithes ... ? (1835).

A Letter to the King (1830).

The Life and Adventures of Peter Porcupine, ed. G. D. H. Cole (1796, 1927).

Mr. Cobbett's Taking Leave of his Countrymen (1817).

Norfolk Yeoman's Gazette (Norwich, 1823).

Paper Against Gold and Glory Against Prosperity ... (1815, 1828).

Political Censor (Philadelphia, 1796–7).

Political Register: variously titled *Cobbett's Political Register*, *Cobbett's Annual Register*, *Cobbett's Weekly Political Register*, *Cobbett's Weekly Register*, 89 vols. (1802–35).

Poor Man's Friend, Or, A Defence of the Rights of Those who do the Work ... (1826–7).

The Porcupine (1800).

Porcupine's Gazette (Philadelphia, 1797–9).

Porcupine's Works; Containing Various Writings and Selections ..., 12 vols. (1801).

Prospectus of a New Daily Paper, to be Entitled The Porcupine (1800).

Rural Rides in the Counties of Surrey, Kent, Sussex, Hampshire ..., ed. G. Woodcock (1830, Harmondsworth, 1967).

The Rush-Light (London and New York, 1800).

The Soldier's Friend; Or, Considerations on the Late Pretended Augmentation of the Substance of Private Soldiers (1792).

Tour in Scotland: And in the Four Northern Counties of England ... (1833).

A Treatise on Cobbett's Corn ... (1828).

Treatise on the Culture and Management of Fruit Trees ... by William Forsyth, edition by Cobbett (Philadelphia, 1803).

Two-Penny Trash; Or, Politics for the Poor (1830–2).

The Woodlands; Or, A Treatise on the Preparation of the Ground for Planting ... (1828).

A Year's Residence in the United States of America ... (New York, 1818–19).

II Anti-Cobbett

Address to the Men of Hampshire, Intended as a Postscript to Cobbett's Weekly Political Register (Winchester, 1817).

Anti-Cobbett, or, Weekly Patriotic Register (1817).

Brunswick Weekly Political Register, in Direct Opposition to William Cobbett's Work (Norwich, 1817).

Calm Appeal to the Friends of Freedom and Reform, on the Double Dealings of Mr. Cobbett ... (Norwich, 1817).

Cameleon; or, the Cobbett of 1802, contrasted with the Cobbett of 1807 ... (1807).

Cobbett's Genuine Two-Penny Trash (1831).

Cobbett's Gridiron: Written to Warn Farmers of their Danger ... (1822).

Cobbett's Imposture Unmasked: In a Letter to the Labourers and Working-People of England ... (1831).

Cobbett and the Learned Languages ... (1807).

Cobbett's Oppression!!: Proceedings of the Trial of an Action between William Burgess, A Poor Labouring Man! and William Cobbett, A Patriot and Reformer! (1809).

'Cobbett's *Political Register*', *Edinburgh Review*, vol. 10, no. 20 (July 1807).

Cobbett's Ten Cardinal Virtues (Manchester, 1832).

Collection of Addresses, Squibs, Songs &c. ... *Shewing the Changeable Opinions of Mr. Cobbett* ... (Preston, 1826).

The Good Old Times; or, The Poor Man's History of England (1817).

Lectures to the Labouring Classes and their Employers in the County of Sussex, and Elsewhere. Not by a Follower of William Cobbett (1831).

Letter to William Cobbett (Birmingham, n.d., c. 1819).

'*Nice Pickings*': *A Countryman's Remarks on Cobbett's Letter to the King* (1830).

Remarks on Cobbett's History of the Protestant Reformation (n.d., c. 1825).

Rich and Poor. A Letter from William Cobbett to the Ploughboys and Labourers of Hampshire (1826).

Speech of the Member for Odium (1833).

'A True Englishman', *Imposture Unmasked; In a Letter to the Labourers & Working People of England* (1831).

True History of the Protestant 'Reformation' ... *in reply to William Cobbett* (1825).

III Collections of ballads and broadsides

1. W. A. Barrett's collection of ballads (English Folk Dance and Song Society).
2. Ballad sheets collected by Lucy Broadwood (English Folk Dance and Song Society).
3. British Library collections
   Collection of broadsides and ballads (1770–1830): 1876 e. 20.
   Collection of ballads printed on single sheets (1750–1840): 1871 f. 13.
   Collection of ballads. Collected by Thomas Bell, 1780–1820: 11621 i. 12.
   Collection of English ballads and chapbooks (1733–1832): 12331 ee. 40.
   Collection of ballads (1800–50): 1875 b. 19.

Collection of ballads ... collected by S. Baring-Gould: LR 271 a. 2.; LR 31 b. 19.

Collection of ballads, songs ... : 11661 dd. 20.

Collection of songs (1807–60): 1876 d. 41.

Collection of tracts, broadsides and newspapers cuttings, chiefly political (1807–23): Cup. 1248 a. 16.

Collection of ballads (1820–75): 1876 e. 3.

Collection of ballads (1820–42): 11602 g. 28.

Collection of single-sheet poems, songs ... (1743–1820): 1880 b. 29.

Collection of broadsides, printed between 1800 and 1840: N. Tab. 2017/13.

Broadsides collected by Miss Sophia Banks: LR 301 h. 3–11.

Collection of ballads and other broadside sheets, c. 1665–1835: 1875 d. 16.

Collection of songs and poems, many of them relating to current political events (1733–1875): 1871 f. 16.

Collection of ballads and prose broadsides chiefly printed in London by J. Pitts (1790–1825): 1875 d. 5.

Loyal and Patriotic Hand-Bills, Songs, Addresses, etc. on the Threatened Invasion of Great Britain (1803): 650 a. 12.

4. Douce collection of broadsides (Bodleian).
5. C. H. Firth collection of ballads (Bodleian).
6. G. B. Gardiner collection of songs (English Folk Dance and Song Society).
7. John Johnson collection of printed ephemera (Bodleian).
8. London Library broadside collection (London Library).
9. London University collection of broadsides (University of London).
10. Sir Frederic Madden's collection of ballads (Cambridge University Library).

IV Government reports

Abstract of Returns made by the Overseers of the Poor, IX, 1787.

First and Second Reports on the High Price of Provisions, IX, 1795.

First, Second and Third Reports on the Present High Price of Provisions, II, 1800–1.

Abstract of Answers and Returns Relative to the Expense and Maintenance of the Poor, VIII, 1803–4.

Report from the Lords' Committee Respecting Grain and the Corn Laws, V, 1814–15.

SC of the House of Commons on the Poor Laws, VI, 1817.

SC of the House of Lords on the Poor Laws, V, 1818.

SC on the Poor Laws, V, 1818.

SC on the Poor Laws, II, 1819.

SC on Petitions Complaining of Agricultural Distress, II (1820).

Report on the Causes of Agricultural Distress, IX, 1821.

SC on the Petitions Complaining of the Distressed State of Agriculture, I, 1822.

SC on Agricultural Labourers' Wages, VI, 1824.

Abstract of Returns on Labourers' Wages, XIX, 1825.

SC on Emigration from the United Kingdom, VI, 1826.

First, Second and Third Reports from the SC on Emigration, V, 1826–7.
SC on the Relief of Able-Bodied Persons from the Poor Rates, IV, 1828.
SC of the House of Lords on the Poor Laws, VIII (1830–1).
SC on Agriculture, V, 1833.
SC on the Sale of Beer, XV, 1833.
Poor Law Report, XXVII–XXXVIII, 1834.
SC on Education, VII, 1835.
First Annual Report of the Poor Law Commissioners, XXXV, 1835.
SC on the Causes of Agricultural Distress, VIII, 1836.
SC of the House of Lords on the State of Agriculture, VIII, 1836.
SC of the House of Lords on Agriculture, V, 1837.
SC on the Labouring Poor (Allotments of Land), VII, 1843.
Report on the Employment of Women and Children in Agriculture, XII, 1843.
Return of all Inclosure Awards, LXXVIII, 1904.

V Periodicals, newspapers, parliamentary proceedings

Annals of Agriculture
Annual Hampshire Repository
Anti-Jacobin Review
Athenaeum
Ballot
Brighton Chronicle
Brighton Guardian
Brighton Patriot
British Critic
Central Society of Education: First, Second and Third Publications
Communications to the Board of Agriculture
Edinburgh Review
Farmer's Journal
Farmer's Magazine
Gentleman's Magazine
Hampshire Chronicle
Hampshire Notes and Queries
Hampshire Telegraph and Sussex Chronicle
Hansard's Parliamentary Debates
Hansard's Parliamentary History
Jackson's Oxford Journal
Journal of the English Folk Dance and Song Society
Journal of the Folk-Song Society
Journal of the Royal Agricultural Society
Journal of the Royal Statistical Society
Journals of the House of Commons
Journals of the House of Lords
Kent Herald

Labourer's Friend
Lion
Manchester and Salford Advertiser
Manchester Times and Gazette
Mirror of Parliament
Morning Chronicle
Morning Post
Philanthropist
Francis Place Newspaper Collection, British Library
Poor Man's Guardian
Prompter
Quarterly Journal of Agriculture
Quarterly Review
Reports of the Society for Bettering the Condition of the Poor
Reports of State Trials
Sporting Magazine
Sussex Weekly Advertiser
Taunton Courier
Times (London)
Tribune (John Thelwall)

VI Other

Allen, W., *A Plan for Diminishing the Poor's Rate in Agricultural Districts* ...
    (1833).
Anderson, E., *Bad Times among the Farmers* (1815).
Anon., *An Address to the Labourers on the Subject of Destroying Machinery*
    (1830)
    Address from the Magistrates to the Inhabitants of Burnham Division (Maid-
    enhead, 1830).
    An Address to the Men of Hawkhurst (1830).
    'Advantage to a Cottager from Keeping a Pig', in *The Labourer's Friend:
    Selections from the Publications of the Labourer's Friend Society* (1835).
    Appeal of the Day-Labourers to the Landowners of England (1832).
    The Arbour Colloquy (1830).
    John Bull's Petition for Cheap Beer (Newcastle, 1822).
    *A Calendar of the Prisoners, in the County Gaol at Winchester, for Trial at the
    Special Commission* (Southampton, 1830).
    The Cottager's Own Book (1830).
    A Dialogue on Rick-Burning, Rioting &c. (1830).
    Dorchester Labourers (1834).
    *England in 1830; Being a Letter to Lord Grey Laying Before Him the Condition
    of the People as Described by Themselves in their Petitions to Parliament*
    (1831).
    A Full and Accurate Account of the Trial of William Cobbett ... (1831).

Hints Respecting the Distresses of the Poor (1795).

The Labourer's Friend: Selections from the Publications of the Labourer's Friend Society (1835).

The Life and History of Swing, the Kent Rick-Burner (n.d., 1830–1).

List of the Voters in the Borough of Oldham, Royton, Crompton and Chatterton (Manchester, 1832).

Machine-Breaking, and the Charges Occasioned by it in the Village of Turvey Down (Oxford, 1830).

Malt. Let the Poor Man Make his Own Malt (1836).

The Old and the New Poor Law: Who Gains and Who Loses? (1835).

A Plain Statement of the Case of the Labourer (1831).

The Poor Man's Friend (Brighton, 1826).

A Reply to 'An Appeal to the Bond-Land Tenants of the Parish of Droxford', on the Subject of Inclosing the Waltham Chase (1826).

A Report of the Proceedings at the Special Commission, holden at Winchester, December 20, 1830, and Eight Following Days ... (Southampton, 1831).

Sentences of the Prisoners Tried before the Special Commission at Winchester ... (Southampton, 1830).

A Serious Caution to the Poor (1792).

Serious Considerations, Addressed to British Labourers and Mechanics at the Present Crisis (1803).

A Short Account of the Life and Death of Swing ... together with the Confession of Thomas Goodman (1831).

Some Arguments for a Redistribution of Property (n.d., Oxford Cobbett Club, c. 1935).

A Temperate Discussion of the Causes which have Led to the Current High Price of Bread ... (1800).

Two Labourers Residing in the County of Sussex (1830).

A Word to the White Horse Men (Oxford, 1830).

Applegarth, R., *A Plea for the Poor* (1790).

Arber, E., *A Transcript of the Registers of the Company of Stationers of London, 1554–1640,* 5 vols. (1875–94).

Arch, J., *The Story of his Life*, ed. The Countess of Warwick (1898).

Arnold, M., 'The Future of Liberalism', in R. H. Super (ed.), *English Literature and Irish Politics* (Ann Arbor, 1973).

Ashby, M. K., *Joseph Ashby of Tysoe* (1961, 1974).

Babington, T., 'Account of Some Cottagers', *Communications to the Board of Agriculture*, vol. 4 (1805).

Baker, A. O., *Considerations on the Present State of the Peasantry of England* ... (Winchester, 1830).

Bamford, S., *The Autobiography of Samuel Bamford: Early Days* (1848–9), ed. W. H. Chaloner (1967).

The Autobiography of Samuel Bamford: Passages in the Life of a Radical (1839–41), ed. W. H. Chaloner (1967).

Baring, T. G. (ed.), *Journals and Correspondence of Francis Thornhill Baring, Lord Northbrook*, 2 vols. (Winchester, 1902–5).

Baring-Gould, S., *A Garland of Country Song* (1895).

Barrett, W. A., *English Folk-Songs* (n.d., *c.* 1891).

Barton, J., *An Enquiry into the Causes of the Progressive Depreciation of Agricultural Labour in Modern Times* ... (1820).

Observations on the Circumstances which Influence the Condition of the Labouring Classes of Society (1817).

Batchelor, T., *General View of the Agriculture of the County of Bedfordshire* (1808).

Bate, H. B., *A Few Observations Respecting* ... *the State of the Poor* (1802).

Beddoes, T., *A Letter to the Right Hon. W. Pitt on the Means of Relieving the Present Scarcity* ... (1796).

Bernard, T., 'Account of a Cottage and Garden near Tadcaster' (1797), *Communications to the Board of Agriculture*, vol. 2 (1802).

'Extract from an Account of Several Charities at Kendal' (1802), *Reports of the Society for Bettering the Condition of the Poor* (1797–1808), vol. 3.

'Introductory Letter ...' (1805), *Reports of the Society for Bettering the Condition of the Poor* (1797–1808), vol. 5.

Bewick, T., *A Memoir of Thomas Bewick*, ed. I. Bain (1975).

Bloomfield, R., 'The Farmer's Boy' (1800), in *The Works of Robert Bloomfield* (n.d.).

Selections from the Correspondence of Robert Bloomfield, ed. W. H. Hart (1870).

[Board of Agriculture], *The Agricultural State of the Kingdom, in February, March and April, 1816* (1816).

Boys, J., *General View of the Agriculture of the County of Kent* (1796).

Brayley, E. W., and Britton, J., 'Hampshire', *The Beauties of England and Wales*, vol. 6 (1805).

Brereton, C. D., *Observations on the Administration of Poor Laws in Agricultural Districts*, second edn (Norwich, 1824).

Brewer, J. N., *Some Thoughts on the Present State of the English Peasantry* (1807).

Briscoe-Eyre, G. E., *The New Forest, its Common Rights and Cottage Stock-Keepers* (Lyndhurst, 1883).

A Transcript of the Registers of the Worshipful Company of Stationers, 1640–1708, 3 vols. (1913–14).

Britton, J., *The Autobiography of John Britton*, 2 vols. (1850).

[Broadwood, J.], *Old English Songs as Now Sung by the Peasantry of the Weald of Surrey and Sussex* (1843).

Broadwood, L., 'Introduction', *Journal of the Folk-Song Society*, vol. 1, no. 4 (1902).

(ed.), *English Traditional Songs and Carols* (1908).

[Broadwood, L.] 'Songs Noted in Sussex and Surrey since 1892', *Journal of the Folk-Song Society*, vol. 1, no. 4 (1902).

Broadwood, L., and Fuller-Maitland, J. A., *English County Songs* (1893).

[Brougham, H.], 'Cottage Economy', *Edinburgh Review*, vol. 38, no. 75 (February 1823).

Brown, R., *General View of the Agriculture of the West Riding* (1799).

Brown, T., *General View of the Agriculture of the County of Derby* (1794).

Buckmaster, J., *A Village Politician* (1897, Horsham, 1982).

Bulwer, E. L., *England and the English* (1835, Chicago, 1967).

Burke, E., 'Thoughts and Details on Scarcity' (1795), *Annals of Agriculture*, vol. 36 (1801).

Burstow, H., *Reminiscences of Horsham* (Horsham, 1911).

Byng, Hon. J., *The Torrington Diaries*, ed. C. B. Andrews, 4 vols. (1934–6).

Caird, J., *English Agriculture in 1850–51* (1852).

[Carrington, J.], *The Carrington Diary*, ed. W. B. Johnson (1956).

Catnach, J., *Catalogue of Songs and Song Book* (1832).

Chamberlayne, J., *Magnae Britanniae; or, The Present State of Great Britain* (1755).

Chappell, W., *Popular Music of Olden Time*, 2 vols. (1855–9).

Clare, J., 'The Autobiography, 1793–1824', in *The Prose of John Clare*, eds. J. W. and A. Tibble (1951).

    The Letters of John Clare, ed. M. Storey (Oxford, 1985).

    The Prose of John Clare, ed. J. W. and A. Tibble (1951).

    Selected Poems of John Clare, ed. J. Reeves (1954).

    The Shepherd's Calendar (1827), eds. E. Robinson and G. Summerfield (1964).

    Sketches in the Life of John Clare, Written by Himself (1821), ed. E. Blunden (1931).

    The Village Minstrel and Other Poems (1821).

Claridge, J., *General View of the Agriculture of the County of Dorset* (1793).

Clayden, A., *The Revolt of the Field* (1874).

'Clergyman', *An Earnest Address to the Labouring Classes Occasioned by the Late Disturbances* (1830).

Colquhoun, P., *Treatise on Indigence* (1806).

Crabbe, G., *The Village* (1783).

Curwen, J. C., *Hints on the Economy of Feeding Stock ... and Bettering the Condition of the Poor* (1808).

Davies, D., *The Case of the Labourers in Husbandry* (1795, Fairfield, 1977).

Denson, J., 'Information Communicated by our Old Correspondent, Mr. Denson', *The Labourer's Friend* (1835).

    A Peasant's Voice to Landowners (Cambridge, 1830).

Dibdin, C., *The Professional Life of Mr. Dibdin, Written by Himself. Together with the Words of Six Hundred Songs ...*, 4 vols. (1803).

Dibdin, T., 'Memoir of Charles Dibdin', in *Songs of the Late Charles Dibdin* (1841).

Dixon, J. H., *Ballads and Songs of the Peasantry of England*, ed. R. Bell (n.d., *c.* 1845).

Driver, A., and W., *General View of the Agriculture of the County of Hampshire* (1794).

Duck, S., 'The Thresher's Labour', in *Poems on Several Occasions* (1736, Monston, 1973).

Dudley, H. B., *A Few Observations Respecting the Present State of the Poor ...* (1802).

Duppa, B. F., *The Causes of the Present Condition of the Labouring Classes in the South of England* (1831).

Durrell, D., 'Extract from an Account of the Relief Granted the Poor at Mongewell ...', *Reports of the Society for Bettering the Condition of the Poor* (1797–1808), vol. 3.

Duthy, J., *The Different Effects of Peace and War on the Price of Bread-Corn ...* (Winchester, 1801).

Dyer, G., *The Complaints of the Poor People of England* (1793).

Eden, F. M., 'Of the Diet, Dress, Fuel, and Habitation of the Labouring Classes', *Annals of Agriculture*, vol. 28 (1797).

The State of the Poor, 3 vols. (1797).

Egan, P., *Book of Sports* (1832).

Eggar, J. A., *Remembrances of Life and Customs in Gilbert White's, Cobbett's and Charles Kingsley's Country* (n.d., c. 1870).

Eliot, G., *Felix Holt, the Radical* (1866, Philadelphia, n.d.).

The Euing Collection of English Broadside Ballads (Glasgow, 1971).

Evans, H., *Songs for Singing at Agricultural Labourers' Meetings* (Aylesbury, n.d., c. 1874).

Evershed, H., 'Farm Labourers and Cow Plots', *The Fortnightly Review*, vol. 14 (1873).

Fearon, H., *Sketches of America* (1818).

Foley, W., *A Child in the Forest* (1977).

Fortescue, J., *The Governance of England* (1468–70), ed. C. Plummer (Oxford, 1926).

Fowler, J., *Echoes of Old Country Life* (1892).

Fraser, R., *General View of the Agriculture of the County of Devon* (1794).

Freeth, J., *The Political Songster* (Birmingham, 1790).

A Touch on the Times (Birmingham, 1803).

Frend, W., *The Effect of Paper Money on the Price of Provisions* (1801).

Patriotism; or, The Love of our Country (1804).

Gardiner, G. B., *Folk-Songs from Hampshire* (1909).

Gaspey, W., *Poor Law Melodies* (1842).

Gilpin, W., *Remarks on Forest Scenery*, 2 vols. (1791, Richmond, 1973).

Glasse, G. H., 'Extract from an Account of the Advantage of a Cottager Keeping a Pig', *Reports of the Society for Bettering the Condition of the Poor* (1797–1808), vol. 1.

[Goodman, T.], *Cobbett's Lecture. Confession of T. Goodman* (1830).

Confession of Thomas Goodman (1830).

Gore, M., *Allotments of Land* (1831).

[Gowler, H.], *An Address to the Labourers on the Subject of Destroying Machinery* (1830).

Gramsci, A., *Selections from the Prison Notebooks*, eds. Q. Hoare and G. N. Smith (1971).

The Greville Memoirs: A Journal of the Reign of King George IV and King William IV, ed. H. Reeve, 3 vols., fourth edn (1875).

Grey, E., *Cottage Life in a Hertfordshire Village* (St Albans, n.d., c. 1935).

Grey, J., *Two Letters on the State of the Agricultural Interests, and the Condition of the Labouring Poor* (1831).

H., B., *The Autobiography of a Working Man*, ed. E. Eden (1862).

Haggard, L. R. (ed.), *I Walked by Night* (1935, Oxford, 1982).

Hanway, J., *Letters on the Importance of the . . . Labouring Part of our Fellow Men* (1767).

Hardy, T., 'The Dorsetshire Labourer' (1883), in H. Orel (ed.), *Thomas Hardy's Personal Writings* (1967).

Jude the Obscure (1896, 1924 edn).

Hawker, J., *A Victorian Poacher: James Hawker's Journal*, ed. G. Christian (Oxford, 1961).

Heath, R., *The English Peasant* (1893, East Ardsley, 1978).

Heggs, P., 'The Labourer's Own Statement', in *The Labourer's Friend* (1835).

Herbert, G., 'A Priest to the Temple, or, The Country Parson' (1652), in F. E. Hutchinson (ed.), *The Works of George Herbert* (Oxford, 1941).

Hill, G. (ed.), *Wiltshire Folk Songs and Carols* (1904, reprint, 1975).

Hobhouse, J. C., *Recollections of a Long Life*, 4 vols. (1910).

Holland, H., *General View of the Agriculture of the County of Cheshire* (1808).

Holland, W., *Paupers and Pig Killers: The Diary of William Holland, A Somerset Parson 1799–1818* (Harmondsworth, 1986).

Hone, W., *The Every-Day Book and Table Book*, 3 vols. (1826–7).

Howitt, W., *The Rural Life of England* (1838, Shannon, 1971).

Howlett, J., 'The Different Quantity, and Expense of Agricultural Labour, in Different Years' (1792), *Annals of Agriculture*, vol. 18 (1792).

Hudson, W. H., *Afoot in England* (1909, 1933).

A Shepherd's Life (1910, 1944).

Hume, D., *The History of Great Britain* (1754, Harmondsworth, 1970).

Hunt, H., *Memoirs of Henry Hunt, Esq.*, 3 vols. (1820).

James, W., and Malcolm, J., *General View of the Agriculture of the County of Surrey* (1794).

Jefferies, R., *Hodge and his Masters* (1880, 1979).

Toilers of the Field (1892, Glasgow, 1982).

Jekyll, G., *Old West Surrey* (1904).

Jerrold, D., 'The Ballad Singer', in *The Heads of the People, or Portraits of the English*, 2 vols. (1840–1).

Jones, M. G., *Hannah More* (New York, 1968).

[Kalm, P.], *Kalm's Account of his Visit to England* (1748), trans. J. Lucas (1892).

Kay, J. P., 'Earnings of Agricultural Labourers in Norfolk and Suffolk', *Journal of the Royal Statistical Society*, vol. 1, no. 7 (July 1838).

Kent, N., *General View of the Agriculture of the County of Norfolk* (1796). *Hints to Gentlemen of Landed Property* (1775).

Kidson, F., *Traditional Tunes* (Oxford, 1891). (ed.), *Collection of English Folk-Songs* (n.d., *c.* 1926). *et al.* (eds.), *English Peasant Songs* (1929).

Kitchen, F., *Brother to the Ox: The Autobiography of a Farm Labourer* (1951).

Klingberg, F., and Hustuedt, S. (eds.), *The Warning Drum: The British Home Front Faces Napoleon* (Berkeley and Los Angeles, 1944).

Knight, C., *Passages in a Working Life*, 4 vols. (1864). *The Working Man's Companion. The Results of Machinery ...* (1831).

Kussmaul, A., *The Autobiography of Joseph Mayett of Quainton 1783–1839* (Aylesbury, 1986).

Liardet, F., 'State of the Peasantry in the County of Kent', *Central Society of Education*: Third Publication (1839, 1969).

Lingard, Rev. J., *A History of England*, 3 vols. (1819).

Lovett, W., *The Life and Struggles of William Lovett* (1876, 1967 edn).

Macqueen, T. P., *The State of the Nation at the Close of 1830* (1831). *Thoughts and Suggestions on the Present State of the Country* (1830).

Malthus, T. R., *A Letter to Samuel Whitbread, Esq. M.P. on his Proposed Bill for the Amendment of the Poor Laws* (1807).

Marriage, J., *Letters on the Distressed State of the Agricultural Labourer* (Chelmsford, 1831).

Marshall, W., *Minutes, Experiments, Observations, and General Remarks on Agriculture in the Southern Counties*, 2 vols. (1799). *The Rural Economy of the Southern Counties*, 2 vols. (1798). *The Rural Economy of the West of England*, 2 vols. (1805). (ed.), *The Review and Abstract of the County Reports to the Board of Agriculture*, 5 vols. (1817, Newton Abbot, 1969).

Martin, C. W., *An Address to the Labourers of Egerton in Kent* (1835).

Lord Melbourne's Papers, ed. L. Sanders (1889).

Merritt, A. L., *A Hamlet in Old Hampshire* (1902).

Merritt-Hawkes, O. A., *The Cottage by the Common* (1924).

Middleton, J., *General View of the Agriculture of the County of Middlesex* (1813).

Misson, M., *Memoirs and Observations in his Travels over England* (1719).

Mitford, M., *Recollections of a Literary Life* (1859, 1883).

[Molesworth, J. E. N.], *The Rick-Burners: A Tale for the Times* (Canterbury, 1830).

Moore, F., *An Almanac of the Year 1816 by Francis Moore* (1816).

Moore's Prophecies for 1821 (Newcastle, 1821).

More, H., *The Letters of Hannah More*, ed. R. B. Johnson (1925).

Letters of Hannah More to Zachary Macaulay, ed. A. Roberts (New York, 1960).

Memoirs of the Life and Correspondence of Mrs. Hannah More, ed. W. Roberts, 4 vols. (1835).

'A Prefatory Letter', in A. Yearsley, *Poems on Several Occasions* (1785).

The Works of Hannah More, 11 vols. (1830).

Morris, M. C. F., *The British Workman Past and Present* (1928).

Olsted, F. L., *Walks and Talks of an American Farmer in England* (1852, Ann Arbor, 1967).

Osborne, S. G. O., *The Letters of S.G.O.*, 2 vols. (n.d., c. 1888).

Paine, T., 'Letter to Washington' (1796), in P. Foner (ed.), *The Complete Works of Thomas Paine*, 2 vols. (London, 1945), II.

Rights of Man, ed. H. Collins (1791–2, Harmondsworth, 1969).

Palmer, R. (ed.), *The Painful Plough* (Cambridge, 1972).

(ed.), *The Rambling Soldier* (Harmondsworth, 1977).

Phillips, Sir R., *Public Characters of All Nations*, 2 vols. (1823).

Pitt, W., *The War Speeches of William Pitt*, comp. R. Coupland (Oxford, 1915).

Pitt, W. M., *An Address to the Landed Interest, on the Deficiency of Habitations and Fuel, for the Use of the Poor* (1797).

Place, F., *The Autobiography of Francis Place*, ed. M. Thrale (Cambridge, 1972).

[Place, F.], *Essay on the State of the Country in Respect to the Condition and Conduct of the Husbandry Labourers* (1831).

Plymley, J., *General View of the Agriculture of the County of Shropshire* (1803).

Postans, T., *A Letter to Sir Thomas Baring on the Causes which have Produced the Present State of the Agricultural Labouring Poor* (1831).

Powys, L., *Somerset Essays* (1937).

Pratt, S. J., *Bread; or, The Poor* (1802).

Richardson, E., *National Agricultural Labourers' and Rural Workers' Union Song Book* (Norwich, n.d., c. 1875).

Ritson, J., *A Select Collection of English Songs*, 3 vols. (London, 1813).

Roach, T., 'The Riots of 1830', *Hampshire Notes and Queries*, vol. 8 (1896).

Roach Smith, C., *Retrospections, Social and Archaeological*, 3 vols. (1883–91).

Rollins, H. E. (comp.), *An Analytical Index to the Ballad Entries (1557–1709) in the Registers of the Company of Stationers of London* (Chapel Hill, 1924, Hatboro, Penn., 1967).

Rose, G., *Observations on the Poor Laws* (1805).

Rose, W., *Good Neighbours* (Cambridge, 1945).

Roxburgh Ballads, 8 vols. (Hertford, 1873–90).

Rudge, T., *General View of the Agriculture of the County of Gloucester* (1807).

Ruggles, T., 'On the Police and Situation of the Poor', *Annals of Agriculture*, vol. 11 (1789) – vol. 20 (1793). Serialized periodically.

Salisbury, W., *The Cottager's Agricultural Companion ...* (1822).

Scrope, G. P., *A Letter to the Magistrates of the South of England ...* (1831).

Sherer, G., *Remarks on the Present State of the Poor* (1796).

Sinclair, Sir J., 'Observations on the Means of Enabling a Cottager to Keep a Cow
...', *Annals of Agriculture*, vol. 38 (1801).

Smith, A., *The Wealth of Nations* (1776, Harmondsworth, 1970).

Somerville, A., *The Autobiography of a Working Man* (1848).

The Whistler at the Plough (Manchester, 1852).

Southey, R., 'Propositions for Ameliorating the Condition of the Poor ...', *Quarterly Review*, vol. 8, no. 16 (December 1812).

[Southey, R.], 'Condition of the English Peasantry', *Quarterly Review*, vol. 41, no. 81 (July 1829).

Spence, J., 'An Account of the Author', in S. Duck, *Poems on Several Occasions* (1736, Monston, 1973).

Spence, W., *Britain Independent of Commerce* (1808).

Stevenson, W., *General View of the Agriculture of the County of Surrey* (1809).

Strickland, W., 'Observations on the State of America' (1796), *Communications to the Board of Agriculture*, vol. 2 (1798).

Strutt, J., *The Sports and Pastimes of the People* (1801).

Stubbs, C. W., *The Land and the Labourers* (1891).

Sturt, G., *Change in the Village* (1912, 1956).

The Journals of George Sturt, 2 vols., ed. E. D. Mackerness (Cambridge, 1967).

William Smith: Potter and Farmer (1919, Firle, 1978).

[Suffolk Farm Labourer], 'The Autobiography of a Suffolk Farm Labourer', *Suffolk Times and Mercury*, 2 November 1894–16 August 1895. Serialized at irregular intervals.

Sumner, H., *The Besom-Maker and Other Country Folk-Songs* (1888).

Tatham, W., *Communications Concerning the Agriculture and Commerce of the United States* (1800).

Thompson, F., *Lark Rise to Candleford* (1939, Harmondsworth, 1973).

Thompson, T., 'Reasons for Giving Lands to Cottagers, to Enable Them to Keep Cows' (1803), *Communications to the Board of Agriculture*, vol. 4 (1805).

'Tickler, T.', 'Letters of Timothy Tickler, Esq.', *Blackwood's Edinburgh Magazine*, vol. 14, no. 78 (September 1823).

Vancouver, C., *General View of the Agriculture of the County of Devon* (1813).

General View of the Agriculture of the County of Essex (1795).

General View of the Agriculture of the County of Hampshire (1810).

Vancouver, J., *An Enquiry into the Causes and Production of Poverty ...* (1796).

Vaughan, R., *The Charge Delivered by the Hon. Robert Vaughan to the Grand Jury ...* (n.p., 1830).

Vavasour, H., 'Case of a Cottager' (1801), *Communications to the Board of Agriculture*, vol. 4 (1805).

Wade, J., *Extraordinary Black-Book* (1831).

Waithman, R., *War Proved to be the Real Cause of the Present Scarcity* (1801).

Wakefield, E. G., *Swing Unmasked* (n.d., c. 1831).

Warde, G., 'An Idea for the Relief of the Poor', *Annals of Agriculture*, vol. 24 (1795).

Watson, J., 'Reminiscences of James Watson' (1854), in D. Vincent (ed.), *Testaments of Radicalism* (1977).

Wesley, J., *A Letter to a Friend, Concerning Tea* (1825 edn).

Weyland, J., *Observations on Mr. Whitbread's Bill* (1808).

Whitbread, S., *Substance of a Speech on the Poor Laws* (1807).

Whittaker, W. G., *North Countrie Ballads* (1921).

Williams, A., *Folk-Songs of the Upper Thames* (1923).

Winchelsea, Earl of, 'On the Advantages of Cottagers Renting Land', *Annals of Agriculture*, vol. 26 (1796).

Windham, W., *The Diary of the Right Hon. William Windham* (1966).

Woodforde, J., *The Diary of a Country Parson* (Oxford, 1978, abridged edn).

Yearsley, A., *Poems on Several Occasions* (1785).

Young, A., *The Autobiography of Arthur Young*, ed. M. Betham-Edwards (1898).
A Farmer's Letters to the People of England, 2 vols. (1767).
The Farmer's Tour through the East of England, 4 vols. (1771).
General View of the Agriculture of the County of Essex, 2 vols. (1807).
General View of the Agriculture of the County of Lincolnshire (1813).
General View of the Agriculture of the County of Norfolk (1804).
General View of the Agriculture of the County of Suffolk (1794).
'An Inquiry into the Propriety of Applying Wastes to the Better Maintenance and Support of the Poor' (1801), *Annals of Agriculture*, vol. 36 (1801).
A Six Weeks' Tour through the Southern Counties of England and Wales (1769).

[Young, A.], *General Report on Enclosures* (1808).

Young, Rev. A., *General View of the Agriculture of the County of Sussex*, second edn (1813).
'A Tour through Sussex, 1793', *Annals of Agriculture*, vol. 22, no. 122 (1794).

C SECONDARY SOURCES

Place of publication is London unless otherwise stated.

I Cobbett studies, bibliographies and published correspondence

Briggs, A., *William Cobbett* (1967).

Carlile, E. I., *William Cobbett: A Study of his Life as Shown by his Writings* (1904).

Chesterton, G. K., *William Cobbett* (n.d., 1926).

Clark, M., *Peter Porcupine in America: The Career of William Cobbett 1762–1835* (Philadelphia, 1939).

Cole, G. D. H., 'Introduction', *Life and Adventures of Peter Porcupine* (1927).
The Life of William Cobbett, third edn (1947).
(ed.), *Letters from William Cobbett to Edward Thornton* (1937).

Cole, G. D. H., and Cole, M., *The Opinions of William Cobbett* (1944).

Derry, J., 'William Cobbett: A Sentimental Radical', in J. Derry, *The Radical Tradition: Tom Paine to Lloyd George* (London, 1967).

Duff, G. (ed.), *Letters of William Cobbett* (Saltzburg, 1974).

Egerton, H., 'A Scarce Book', *The National Review*, vol. 5 (1885).

Foot, M., 'A Radical Spirit', *The Observer*, 4 September 1983.

Gaines, P. W., 'Two Letters Written by William Cobbett from America', *The Yale University Library Gazette*, vol. 48, pt 1 (July 1973).

William Cobbett and the United States, 1792–1835 (Worcester, Mass., 1971).

Gaskell, C. M., 'William Cobbett', *The Nineteenth Century*, vol. 19 (February 1886).

Green, D., *Great Cobbett: The Noblest Agitator* (1983).

[Hammond, J. L.], 'Cobbett's Political Register', *The Edinburgh Review*, vol. 206 (July 1907).

Hazlitt, W., 'Mr. Cobbett' (1821), in *The Spirit of the Age*, ed. E. D. Mackerness (1969).

Heath, R., 'A Peasant Politician: William Cobbett' (1874), in R. Heath, *The English Peasant* (1893, East Ardsley, 1978).

Himmelfarb, G., 'William Cobbett', in G. Himmelfarb, *The Idea of Poverty: England in the Early Industrial Age* (1984).

'William Cobbett', *The New Criterion*, October 1982.

Ingrams, R. (ed.), *Cobbett's Country Book* (Newton Abbot, 1975).

'The Pattern John Bull', *The Spectator*, 1 May 1982.

Kebbel, T. E., 'Cobbett', *Cornhill Magazine*, vol. 39 (April 1879).

Keith, W. J., 'William Cobbett', in W. J. Keith, *The Rural Tradition* (Toronto, 1974).

L, 'On Maize or Indian Corn – Mr. Cobbett's Work', *The Quarterly Review of Agriculture*, vol. 2 (1829).

Lemrow, L., 'William Cobbett's Journalism for the Lower Orders', *Victorian Periodicals Review*, vol. 15 (Spring 1982).

Marx, K., letter to *The New-York Daily Tribune*, 22 July 1853.

Massingham, H. J., *The Wisdom of the Fields* (1945).

Melville, L., *The Life and Letters of William Cobbett in England & America*, 2 vols. (1913).

Morton, J. B., 'William Cobbett', *London Mercury*, vol. 20 (June 1929).

Osborne, J., *William Cobbett: His Thought and his Times* (New Brunswick, NJ, 1966).

Pearl, M. L., *William Cobbett: A Bibliographical Account of his Life and Times* (1953, Westport, Conn., 1971).

Pell, A. J., 'William Cobbett', *Journal of the Royal Agricultural Society of England*, vol. 63 (1902).

Phelps, H., 'The Most English of Englishmen', *Cobbett's New Register*, vol. 7, no. 8 (October 1988).

Reitzel, W. (ed.), *The Progress of a Ploughboy to a Seat in Parliament* (1933).

Rogers, J. E. T., 'William Cobbett', in J. E. T. Rogers, *Historical Gleanings* (1869).

Sambrook, J., *William Cobbett* (1973).

Schweizer, K., and Klein, R., 'The Progress of William Cobbett', *Durham University Journal*, vol. 81, no. 2 (June 1989).

Schweizer, K., and Osborne, J., *Cobbett in his Times* (Leicester, 1990).

Smith, E., *William Cobbett: A Biography*, 2 vols. (1879).

Spater, G., *William Cobbett: The Poor Man's Friend*, 2 vols. (Cambridge, 1982).

Stafford, W., '*Rural Rides*, William Cobbett, 1830', in W. Stafford, *Socialism, Radicalism, and Nostalgia: Social Criticism in Britain, 1775–1830* (Cambridge, 1987).

Stebbing, W., 'William Cobbett', *The Edinburgh Review*, vol. 149 (April 1879).

Stephen, J. F., 'Cobbett's Political Works', *Saturday Review*, vol. 22, no. 19 (1866).

Stephen, L., 'William Cobbett', *New Review*, vol. 9 (1893).

Sturt, G., 'Seventy Years Ago', *Longman's Magazine*, vol. 45 (February 1905).

Taylor, A. J. P., 'William Cobbett', in A. J. P. Taylor, *Essays in English History* (1976).

Thompson, E. P., 'William Cobbett', in E. P. Thompson, *The Making of the English Working Class* (1963, Harmondsworth, 1968).

Wiener, M., 'The Changing Image of William Cobbett', *The Journal of British Studies*, vol. 13, no. 2 (May 1974).

Williams, R., *Cobbett* (Oxford, 1983).

'The Man who Shifted against the Tide', *New Society*, vol. 60, 29 April 1982.

Wilson D., *Paine and Cobbett: The Transatlantic Connection* (Montreal and Kingston, 1988).

II Other

Afton, B., ' "The Motive which has Operated on the Minds of my People": 1830, The Propensity of Hampshire Parishes to Riot', *Proceedings of the Hampshire Field Club and Archaeological Society*, no. 44 (1988).

Agar, N., 'The Bedfordshire Farm Worker in the Nineteenth Century', *The Publications of the Bedfordshire Historical Record Society*, vol. 60 (1981).

Allcock, J. B., ' "Populism": A Brief Biography', *Sociology*, vol. 5, no. 3 (September 1971).

Altick, R., *The English Common Reader: A Social History of the Mass Reading Public* (1957).

Archer, J., '*By a Flash and a Scare*': *Arson, Animal Maiming and Poaching in East Anglia, 1815–1870* (Oxford, 1990).

Armstrong, A., *Farmworkers: A Social and Economic History 1770–1980* (1988).

'The Position of the Labourer in Rural Society', in G. E. Mingay (ed.), *The Agrarian History of England and Wales*, VI (Cambridge, 1989).

Ashton, J., *Modern Street Ballads* (1968).

'Truth in Folk Song: Some Developments and Applications', *Canadian Folk Music Journal*, vol. 5 (1977).

Aspinall, A., *Politics and the Press* (1949).

(ed.), *Three Early Nineteenth-Century Diaries* (1952).

Barnes, D. G., *A History of the English Corn Laws 1660–1846* (1930, New York, 1961).

Barnett, D. C., 'Allotments and the Problem of Rural Poverty, 1780–1840', in E. L. Jones and G. E. Mingay (eds.), *Land, Labour, and Population in the Industrial Revolution* (1967).

Barrell, J., *The Idea of Landscape and the Sense of Place, 1730–1840* (Cambridge, 1972).

Baugh, D. A., 'The Cost of Poor Relief in South-East England, 1790–1834', *Economic History Review*, second ser., vol. 28, no. 1 (1975).

Belchem, J., *'Orator' Hunt: Henry Hunt and English Working-Class Radicalism* (Oxford, 1985).

'Republicanism, Popular Constitutionalism and the Radical Platform in Early Nineteenth-Century England', *Social History*, vol. 6, no. 1 (January 1981).

Benson, J., *The Penny Capitalists: A Study of Nineteenth-Century Working-Class Entrepreneurs* (Dublin, 1983).

Bicha, K., 'Prairie Radicals: A Common Pietism', *Journal of Church and State*, vol. 18, no. 1 (Winter 1976).

Blaug, M., 'The Myth of the Old Poor Law and the Making of the New', *Journal of Economic History*, vol. 23 (1963).

Bohstedt, J., *Riots and Community Politics in England and Wales 1790–1810* (Cambridge, Mass., 1983).

Bowley, A. L., *Wages in the United Kingdom in the Nineteenth Century* (Cambridge, 1900).

Boyer, G., *An Economic History of the English Poor Law, 1750–1850* (Cambridge, 1990).

Brock, M., *The Great Reform Act* (1973).

Brundage, A., *The Making of the New Poor Law* (1978).

Buchan, D., *The Ballad and the Folk* (1972).

Bushaway, B., *By Rite: Custom, Ceremony and Community in England 1700–1800* (1982).

Calhoun, C., *The Question of Class Struggle: Social Foundations of Popular Radicalism during the Industrial Revolution* (Oxford, 1982).

Canovan, M., *Populism* (New York, 1981).

Capp, B., *Astrology and the Popular Press: English Almanacs, 1500–1800* (1979).

Carter, I., *Farm Life in North-East Scotland, 1840–1914: The Poor Man's Country* (Edinburgh, 1979).

Chambers, J. D., and Mingay, G. E., *The Agricultural Revolution, 1750–1880* (1966).

Charlesworth, A., 'A Comparative Study of the Spread of the Agricultural Disturbances of 1816, 1822 and 1830 in England', *Peasant Studies*, vol. 2, no. 2 (Winter 1984).

'Radicalism, Political Crisis and the Agricultural Labourers' Protests of 1830', in

A. Charlesworth (ed.), *Rural Social Change and Conflicts since 1500* (Humberside, 1982).

'The Spatial Diffusion of Rural Protest: An Historical and Contemporary Perspective of Rural Riots in Nineteenth-Century Britain', *Society and Space*, vol. 1 (1983).

Chartier, R., 'Culture as Appropriation: Popular Cultural Uses in Early Modern France', in S. Kaplan (ed.), *Understanding Popular Culture: Europe from the Middle Ages to the Nineteenth Century* (New York, 1984).

Chase, M., *'The People's Farm': English Radical Agrarianism 1775–1840* (Oxford, 1988).

(ed.), *The New Poor Law* (Middlesbrough, 1985).

Christie, I., *Stress and Stability in Late Eighteenth-Century Britain* (Oxford, 1984).

Claeys, G., *Thomas Paine: Social and Political Thought* (Boston, 1989).

Clapham, J. H., *An Economic History of Modern Britain: The Early Railway Age, 1820–1850* (Cambridge, 1939).

Clark, P., *The English Alehouse: A Social History, 1200–1830* (1983).

Coats, A. W., 'Changing Attitudes to Labour in the Mid-Eighteenth Century', *Economic History Review*, second ser., vol. 2 (1958).

'The Classical Economists and the Labourer', in E. L. Jones and G. E. Mingay (eds.), *Land, Labour, and Population in the Industrial Revolution* (1967).

Colley, L., 'Radical Patriotism in Eighteenth-Century England', in R. Samuel (ed.), *Patriotism: The Making and Unmaking of the British National Identity*, 3 vols. (1989), I.

'"Whose Nation?", Class and National Consciousness in Britain, 1750–1830', *Past and Present*, no. 113 (November 1986).

Collins, E. J. T., 'Dietary Change and Cereal Consumption in Britain in the Nineteenth Century', *Agricultural History Review*, vol. 23 (1975).

Cottrell, S., 'The Devil on Two-Sticks: Franco-phobia in 1803', in R. Samuel (ed.), *Patriotism: The Making and Unmaking of the British National Identity*, 3 vols. (1989), I.

Cranfield, G. A., *The Press and Society* (1978).

Cressy, D., *Literacy and the Social Order: Reading and Writing in Tudor and Stuart England* (Cambridge, 1980).

Crosby, T., *English Farmers and the Politics of Protection 1815–52* (Hassocks, 1977).

Cunningham, H., 'The Language of Patriotism 1750–1914', *History Workshop*, no. 21 (Autumn 1981).

Leisure in the Industrial Revolution (1980).

Danziger, R., *Political Powerlessness: Agricultural Workers in Post-War England* (Manchester, 1988).

Deacon, G., *John Clare and the Folk Tradition* (1983).

Deane, P., and Cole, W. A., *British Economic Growth 1688–1959*, second edn (1969).

Dean-Smith, M., *A Guide to English Folk-Song Collections, 1822–1952* (Liverpool, 1954).

An Index of English Songs Contributed to the Journal of the Folk-Song Society 1899–1931 and its Continuation The Journal of the English Folk Dance and Song Society to 1950 (1951).

Dickinson, H. T., *Liberty and Property: Political Ideology in Eighteenth-Century Britain* (1977).

'Popular Conservatism and Militant Loyalism 1789–1815', in H. T. Dickinson (ed.), *Britain and the French Revolution* (1989).

Digby, A., *Pauper Palaces* (1978).

Dinwiddy, J. R., 'Sir Francis Burdett and Burdettite Radicalism', *History*, vol. 65, no. 213 (February 1980).

'William Cobbett, George Houston and Freethought', *Notes and Queries*, vol. 222 (July–August 1977).

Dowell, S., *A History of Taxation and Taxes in England*, 4 vols. (1884, New York, 1965).

Dunbabin, J. P. D., *Rural Discontent in Nineteenth-Century Britain* (1974).

Dunkley, P., *The Crisis of the Old Poor Law in England 1795–1834* (New York, 1982).

'Whigs and Paupers: The Reform of the English Poor Laws 1830–1834', *Journal of British Studies*, vol. 20, no. 2 (Spring 1981).

Dyck, I., 'Debts and Liabilities: William Cobbett and Thomas Paine', in I. Dyck (ed.), *Citizen of the World: Essays on Thomas Paine* (1987).

'Towards the "Cottage Charter": The Expressive Culture of Farm Workers in Nineteenth-Century England', *Rural History*, vol. 1, no. 1 (April 1990).

Dyck, I., and Howkins, A., 'Popular Ballads, Rural Radicalism and William Cobbett', *History Workshop*, no. 23 (Spring 1987).

Edsall, N., *The Anti-Poor Law Movement 1834–44* (Manchester, 1971).

Edwards, M., 'John Wesley', in R. Davis and G. Rupp (eds.), *A History of the Methodist Church in Great Britain* (1965).

Elbourne, R., *Music and Tradition in Early Industrial Lancashire* (Woodbridge, 1980).

Emsley, C., *British Society and the French Wars 1793–1815* (1979).

Engels, F., 'Speech at the Graveside of Karl Marx' (1883), in K. Marx and F. Engels, *Selected Works* (1968).

Epstein, J., *The Lion of Freedom: Feargus O'Connor and the Chartist Movement 1832–1842* (1982).

'Understanding the Cap of Liberty: Symbolic Practice and Social Conflict in Early Nineteenth-Century England', *Past and Present*, no. 122 (February 1989).

Evans, G. E., *Ask the Fellows who Cut the Hay* (1956).

Everitt, A., 'Farm Labourers 1500–1640', in J. Thirsk (ed.), *The Agrarian History of England and Wales*, IV (Cambridge, 1967).

Finnegan, R., *Literacy and Orality: Studies in the Technology of Communication* (Oxford, 1988).

Fisher, C., *Custom, Work and Market Capitalism: The Forest of Dean Colliers, 1788–1888* (1981).

Flinn, M. W., *An Economic and Social History of Britain since 1700* (1963).

Foot, M., *Debts of Honour* (1980).

Foster, J., *Class Struggle and the Industrial Revolution* (1974).

Friedman, A., *The Ballad Revival* (Chicago, 1961).

Furniss, E., *The Position of the Laborer in a System of Nationalism: A Study in the Labor Theories of the Later English Mercantilists* (Boston, 1920).

Gadian, D. S., 'Class Consciousness in Oldham and Other North-West Industrial Towns 1830–1850', *Historical Journal*, vol. 21. no. 1 (1978).

Garnier, R., *Annals of the British Peasantry* (1895).

Gazley, J., *The Life of Arthur Young, 1741–1820* (Philadelphia, 1973).

Geertz, C., 'Ideology as a Cultural System', in D. Apter (ed.), *Ideology and Discontent* (New York, 1964).

Gerould, G. H., *The Ballad of Tradition* (Oxford, 1957).

Gilboy, E. W., 'The Cost of Living and Real Wages in Eighteenth-Century England', *Review of Economic Statistics*, vol. 18 (1936).

Goodwyn, L., *Democratic Promise: The Populist Movement in America* (New York, 1976).

Goody, J., *The Domestication of the Savage Mind* (Cambridge, 1977).

Grainger, M., *John Clare: A Collector of Ballads* (Peterborough, 1964).

Green, A. E., 'McCaffery: A Study in the Variation and Function of a Ballad', *Lore and Language*, no. 3 (1970); no. 4 (1970); no. 5 (1971).

Gummere, F., 'The Ballad and Communal Poetry' (1896), in M. Leach and T. Coffin (eds.), *The Critics and the Ballad* (Carbondale, Ill., 1962).

Hammond, J. L., and B., *The Village Labourer* (1911), ed. G. E. Mingay (1978).

Harker, D., *Fakesong: The Manufacture of British 'Folksong', 1700 to the Present Day* (Milton Keynes, 1985).

Harrison, B., *Drink and the Victorians: The Temperance Question in England 1815–1872* (1971).

Harrison, J. F. C., *Learning and Living 1790–1860* (1961).

The Second Coming: Popular Millenarianism, 1780–1950 (1979).

Hasbach, W., *A History of the English Agricultural Labourer* (1894, 1966).

Hawker, T., 'The Devonshire Farm Labourer Now and Eighty Years Ago', *Report and Transactions of the Devonshire Association*, vol. 14 (July 1882).

Heaney, M., *A Checklist of Dates Assigned to Printers in Wehse's Schwankleid und Flugblatt in Grossbritannien* (1984).

Hill, C., 'The English Revolution and Patriotism', in R. Samuel (ed.), *Patriotism: The Making and Unmaking of the British National Identity*, 3 vols. (1989), I.

'The Norman Yoke', in J. Saville (ed.), *Democracy and the Labour Movement* (1954).

Himmelfarb, G., *The Idea of Poverty: England in the Early Industrial Age* (New York, 1983).

Hindley, C., *The Life and Times of James Catnach* (1878).

Hobsbawm, E., 'Peasants and Politics', *Journal of Peasant Studies*, vol. 1, no. 1 (October 1973).

Hobsbawm, E., and Rudé, G., *Captain Swing* (New York, 1968).

Holderness, B. A., 'The Victorian Farmer', in G. E. Mingay (ed.), *The Victorian Countryside* (1981), I.

Hollis, P., *The Pauper Press: A Study in Working-Class Radicalism of the 1830s* (Oxford, 1970).

Hone, J. A., *For the Cause of Truth: Radicalism in London 1796–1821* (Oxford, 1982).

Horn, P., *A Georgian Parson and his Village: The Life of David Davies* (Abingdon, 1981).

The Rural World: Social Change in the English Countryside 1780–1850 (1980).

Hoskins, W. G., *The Midland Peasant: The Economic and Social History of a Leicestershire Village* (1957).

Howkins, A., 'The Discovery of Rural England', in R. Colls and P. Dodd (eds.), *Englishness: Politics and Culture* (1986).

Poor Labouring Men: Rural Radicalism in Norfolk 1870–1923 (1985).

'The Voice of the People: The Social Meaning and Context of Country Song', *Oral History*, vol. 3, no. 1 (Spring 1975).

Howkins, A., and Dyck, I., 'Popular Ballads, Rural Radicalism and William Cobbett', *History Workshop*, no. 23 (Spring 1987).

Huzel, J., 'The Labourer and the Poor Law 1750–1850', in G. E. Mingay (ed.), *Agrarian History of England and Wales*, VI (Cambridge, 1989).

Ignatieff, M., 'Primitive Accumulation Revisted', in R. Samuel (ed.), *People's History and Socialist Theory* (1981).

James, L., *Print and the People 1819–1851* (Harmondsworth, 1976).

John, A. H., 'Farming in Wartime: 1793–1815', in E. L. Jones and G. E. Mingay (eds.), *Land, Labour and Population in the Industrial Revolution* (1967).

Johnson, R., '"Really Useful Knowledge": Radical Education and Working-Class Culture', in J. Clarke, C. Critcher and R. Johnson (eds.), *Working-Class Culture* (1979).

Jones, D., 'Thomas Campbell Foster and the Rural Labourer: Incendiarism in East Anglia in the 1840s', *Social History*, vol. 1, no. 1 (January 1976).

Joyce, P., *Visions of the People: Industrial England and the Question of Class, 1848–1914* (Cambridge, 1980).

Keith, W. J., *The Rural Tradition* (Toronto, 1974).

Kerr, B., 'The Dorset Agricultural Labourer 1750–1850', *Proceedings of the Dorset Natural History and Archaeological Society*, vol. 89 (April 1963).

Kitteringham, J., 'Country Work Girls in Nineteenth-Century England', in R. Samuel (ed.), *Village Life and Labour* (1975).

Knott, J., *Popular Opposition to the 1834 Poor Law* (Beckenham, 1986).

Kramnick, I., *Bolingbroke and his Circle: The Politics of Nostalgia in the Age of Walpole* (Cambridge, Mass., 1968).

Kussmaul, A., *A General View of the Rural Economy of England, 1538–1840* (Cambridge, 1990).

Servants in Husbandry in Early Modern England (Cambridge, 1981).

Laclau, E., *Politics and Ideology in Marxist Theory* (1977).

Laqueur, T. W., 'The Queen Caroline Affair: Politics as Art in the Reign of George IV', *Journal of Modern History*, vol. 54 (September 1982).

Lawson, J., *Robert Bloomfield* (Boston, 1980).

Levy, H., *Large and Small Holdings: A Study of English Agricultural Economics* (1911, 1966).

Levy, S. L., *Nassau W. Senior 1790–1864* (New York, 1970).

Lipset, S., *Agrarian Socialism: The Cooperative Commonwealth Federation in Saskatchewan* (1950, New York, 1968).

Little, H. J., 'The Agricultural Labourer', *Journal of the Royal Agricultural Society*, second ser., vol. 14 (1878).

Lloyd, A. L., *Folk Song in England* (1967).

Lomax, A., and Halifax, J., 'Folk Song Texts as Cultural Indicators', in A. Lomax (ed.), *Folk Song and Culture* (Washington, 1968).

Lowerson, J., 'The Aftermath of Swing: Anti-Poor Law Movements and Rural Trades' Unions in the South East of England', in A. Charlesworth (ed.), *Rural Social Change and Conflicts since 1500* (Humberside, 1982).

Lucas, J., *England and Englishness: Ideas of Nationhood in English Poetry 1688–1900* (1990).

McCalman, I., *Radical Underworld: Prophets, Revolutionaries and Pornographers in London 1795–1840* (Cambridge, 1988).

Macdonald, S., 'Agricultural Improvement and the Neglected Labourer', *Agricultural History Review*, vol. 31, pt 2 (1983).

Macpherson, C. B., *Democracy in Alberta* (Toronto, 1953).

Macrae, D., 'Populism as an Ideology', in G. Ionescu and E. Gellner (eds.), *Populism: Its Meaning and National Characteristics* (1969).

Malcolmson, R., *Life and Labour in England, 1700–1780* (1981).

Popular Recreations in English Society, 1700–1850 (1973).

Mandler, P., 'The Making of the New Poor Law *Redivivus*', *Past and Present*, no. 117 (November 1987).

Marlow, J., *The Tolpuddle Martyrs* (1971, St Albans, 1974).

Martin, J. M., 'Village Traders and the Emergence of a Proletariat in South Warwickshire, 1750–1851', in *Agricultural History Review*, vol. 32 (1984).

Marx, K., 'The Class Struggles in France 1848–1850' (1850), in K. Marx and F. Engels, *Selected Works* (1968).

'The Eighteenth Brumaire of Louis Bonaparte' (1850–2), in K. Marx and F. Engels, *Selected Works* (1968).

Mathias, P., *The Brewing Industry in England, 1700–1830* (Cambridge, 1959).

Miles, D., *Francis Place: The Life of a Remarkable Radical 1771–1854* (Brighton, 1988).

Mills, D., *Lord and Peasant in Nineteenth-Century Britain* (1980).

'The Nineteenth-Century Peasantry of Melbourn, Cambridgeshire', in R. M. Smith (ed.), *Land, Kinship and Life-Cycle* (Cambridge, 1984).

'Peasants and Conflict in Nineteenth-Century Rural England: A Comment on Two Recent Articles', *Journal of Peasant Studies*, vol. 15, no. 3 (1988).

'The Quality of Life in Melbourn, Cambridgeshire, in the Period 1800–1850', *International Review of Social History*, vol. 23 (1978).

Mingay, G. E., '"Rural War": The Life and Times of Captain Swing', in G. E. Mingay (ed.), *The Unquiet Countryside* (1989).

Mitrany, D., *Marx against the Peasant* (Chapel Hill, 1951).

Morley, J., *The Life of William Ewart Gladstone*, 3 vols. (1903).

Muskett, P., 'The East Anglian Riots of 1822', *Agricultural History Review*, vol. 32, pt 1 (1984).

Neuburg, V., *Popular Literature: A History and Guide* (Harmondsworth, 1977).

Newby, H., *The Deferential Worker: A Study of Farm Workers in East Anglia* (1977).

Newman, G., *The Rise of English Nationalism: A Cultural History 1740–1830* (New York, 1987).

Obelkevich, J., *Religion and Rural Society: South Lindsey 1825–1875* (Oxford, 1976).

Palmer, R., *The Sound of History: Songs and Social Comment* (Oxford, 1988).

Peacock, A. J., *Bread or Blood: A Study of the Agrarian Riots in East Anglia in 1816* (1965).

'Village Radicalism in East Anglia 1800–50', in J. P. D. Dunbabin, *Rural Discontent in Nineteenth-Century Britain* (1974).

Pederson, S., 'Hannah More Meets Simple Simon: Tracts, Chapbooks and Popular Culture in Late Eighteenth-Century England', *Journal of British Studies*, vol. 25, no. 1 (January 1986).

Perkin, H., *The Origins of Modern English Society* (1969).

Phythian-Adams, C., 'Rural Culture', in G. E. Mingay (ed.), *The Victorian Countryside* (1981), II.

Pickering, M., 'The Past as a Source of Inspiration: Popular Song and Social Change', in M. Pickering and T. Green (eds.), *Everyday Culture and the Vernacular Milieu* (Milton Keynes, 1987).

Village Song and Culture (1982).

Pocock, J. G. A., *Virtue, Commerce, and Industry: Essays on Political Thought and History* (Cambridge, 1985).

Popular Memory Group, 'Popular Memory: Theory, Politics, Method', in R. Johnson *et al.* (eds.), *Making Histories: Studies in History Writing and Politics* (1982).

Pound, L., *Poetic Origins and the Ballad* (1921, New York, 1962).

Poynter, J. R., *Society and Pauperism* (1969).

Prothero, I., *Artisans and Politics in Early Nineteenth-Century London* (1979).

Pugh, S. (ed.), *Reading Landscape* (Manchester, 1990).

Rashid, S., 'The Scarcity of 1800: A Contemporary Account', *Agricultural History Review*, vol. 28 (1980).

Reaney, B., *The Class Struggle in 19th Century Oxfordshire: The Social and Communal Background to the Otmoor Disturbances of 1830 to 1835* (Oxford, 1971).

Reay, B., 'The Last Rising of the Agricultural Labourers: The Battle in Bossenden Wood, 1838', *History Workshop*, no. 26 (Autumn 1988).

The Last Rising of the Agricultural Labourers: Rural Life and Protest in Nineteenth-Century England (Oxford, 1990).

Reed, M., 'Class and Conflict in Rural England: Some Reflections on a Debate', in M. Reed and R. Wells (eds.), *Class, Conflict and Protest in the English Countryside, 1700–1880* (1990).

'"Gnawing it Out": A New Look at Economic Relations in Nineteenth-Century Rural England', *Rural History*, vol. 1, no. 1 (April 1990).

'Indoor Farm Service in 19th-Century Sussex: Some Criticisms of a Critique', *Sussex Archaeological Collections*, no. 123 (1985).

'Nineteenth-Century Rural England: A Case for Peasant Studies?', *The Journal of Peasant Studies*, vol. 14, no. 1 (October 1986).

'The Peasantry of Nineteenth-Century England: A Neglected Class?', *History Workshop*, no. 18 (Autumn 1984).

Richards, J., 'Populism: A Qualified Defence', *Studies in Political Economy*, vol. 5 (Spring 1981).

Richardson, R., *Death, Dissection and the Destitute* (Harmondsworth, 1988).

Richardson, T. L., 'The Agricultural Labourers' Riots in Kent in 1830', *Cantium*, vol. 6 (Winter 1974).

'The Agricultural Labourer's Standard of Living in Kent 1790–1840', in D. Oddy and D. Miller (eds.), *The Making of the Modern British Diet* (1976).

Robo, E., *Mediaeval Farnham: Everyday Life in an Episcopal Manor* (Farnham, n.d., c. 1935).

Roe, M., *Kenealy and the Tichborne Case: A Study in Mid-Victorian Populism* (Melbourne, 1974).

Rogers, J. E. T., *The Economic Interpretation of History*, sixth edn (1905).

A History of Agriculture and Prices in England, 7 vols. (Oxford, 1902).

Six Centuries of Work and Wages (1909).

Rose, M., 'The Poor Law and the Historians: Changing Attitudes to Relief in Nineteenth-Century England', in M. Chase (ed.), *The New Poor Law* (Middlesbrough, 1985).

Rubinstein, W. D., 'British Radicalism and the "Dark Side" of Populism', in *Elites and the Wealthy in Modern British Society* (Brighton, 1987).

Rudé, G., *Ideology and Popular Protest* (1980).

Rule, J. G., 'Methodism, Popular Beliefs and Village Culture in Cornwall, 1800–

1850', in R. D. Storch (ed.), *Popular Culture and Custom in Nineteenth-Century England* (1982).

Sack, J., *The Grevillites 1801–29: Party Politics and Factionalism in the Age of Pitt and Liverpool* (Chicago, 1979).

Salaman, R., *History and Social Influence of the Potato* (Cambridge, 1949).

Samuel R., 'People's History', in R. Samuel (ed.), *People's History and Socialist Theory* (1981).

'Village Labour', in R. Samuel (ed.), *Village Life and Labour* (1975).

(ed.), *Patriotism: The Making and Unmaking of the British National Identity*, 3 vols. (1989).

Samuel, R., and Thompson, P. (eds.), *The Myths We Live By* (1990).

Schulz, M. F., *Paradise Preserved: Recreations of Eden in Eighteenth- and Nineteenth-Century England* (Cambridge, 1985).

Shanin, T., 'Peasantry as a Political Factor', in T. Shanin (ed.), *Peasants and Peasant Societies* (Harmondsworth, 1971).

Sharp, C., *English Folk Songs: Some Conclusions* (1907, Belmont, Calif., 1965).

Shaw, C., and Chase, M. (eds.), *The Imagined Past: History and Nostalgia* (Manchester, 1989).

Shepard, L., *The Broadside Ballad: A Study in Origins and Meaning* (1962).

The History of Street Literature (Newton Abbot, 1973).

John Pitts, Ballad Collector of Seven Dials, London 1765–1844 (1969).

Shiach, M., *Discourse on Popular Culture: Class, Gender and History in Cultural Analysis, 1730 to the Present* (1989).

Simpson, C. M., *The British Broadside Ballad and its Music* (New Brunswick, NJ, 1966).

Singleton, F., 'Captain Swing in East Anglia', *Bulletin of the Society for the Study of Labour History*, no. 8 (Spring 1964).

Smith, O., *The Politics of Language* (Oxford, 1984).

Snell, K. D. M., *Annals of the Labouring Poor: Social Change and Agrarian England, 1660–1900* (Cambridge, 1985).

Spinney, G. H., 'Cheap Repository Tracts: Hazard and Marshall Edition', *The Library*, fourth ser., no. 3 (December 1939).

Spufford, M., *Small Books and Pleasant Histories: Popular Fiction and its Readership in Seventeenth-Century England* (Cambridge, 1981).

Stafford, W., *Socialism, Radicalism, and Nostalgia: Social Criticism in Britain, 1775–1830* (Cambridge, 1987).

Stern, W., 'The Bread Crisis in Britain, 1795–6', *Economica*, vol. 31 (May 1964).

Stevenson, J., 'Bread or Blood', in G. E. Mingay (ed.), *The Unquiet Countryside* (1989).

'Food Riots in England 1792–1818', in J. Stevenson and R. Quinault (eds.), *Popular Protest and Public Order* (1974).

'The Queen Caroline Affair', in J. Stevenson (ed.), *London in the Age of Reform* (Oxford, 1977).

Surel, J., 'John Bull', in R. Samuel (ed.), *Patriotism: The Making and Unmaking of British National Identity*, 3 vols. (1989), III.

Thomas, K., *Religion and the Decline of Magic* (1971, Harmondsworth, 1973).

Thomis, M., *Responses to Industrialization: The British Experience 1780–1850* (Newton Abbot, 1976).

Thompson, D., *Change and Tradition in Rural England* (1980).

Thompson, E. P., 'The Crime of Anonymity', in D. Hay, P. Linebaugh and E. P. Thompson (eds.), *Albion's Fatal Tree* (1975).

The Making of the English Working Class (1963, Harmondsworth, 1968).

'The Moral Economy of the English Crowd in the Eighteenth Century', *Past and Present*, no. 50 (1971).

Thompson, F. M. L., *English Landed Society in the Nineteenth Century* (1963).

Tibble, J. W., and A., *John Clare: His Life and Poetry* (1956).

Tracey, H., 'The State of Folk Music in Bantu Africa', *Journal of the International Folk Music Council*, vol. 6 (1954).

Tubbs, C. R., 'The Development of the Smallholding and Cottage Stock-Keeping Economy of the New Forest', *Agricultural History Review*, vol. 13 (1965).

Turner, M., *Enclosures in Britain 1750–1830* (1984).

Unwin, R., *The Rural Muse: Studies in the Peasant Poetry of England* (1954).

Vicinus, M., *The Industrial Muse* (1974).

Vincent, D., *Bread, Knowledge and Freedom: A Study of Nineteenth-Century Working Class Autobiography* (1981).

'The Decline of the Oral Tradition in Popular Culture', in R. D. Storch (ed.), *Popular Culture and Custom in Nineteenth-Century England* (1982).

Literacy and Popular Culture: England, 1750–1914 (Cambridge, 1989).

'Reading in the Working-Class Home', in J. K. Walton and J. Walvin (eds.), *Leisure in Britain 1780–1939* (Manchester, 1983).

Wearmouth, R., *Methodism and the Common People of the Eighteenth Century* (1945).

Weaver, S. A., *John Fielden and the Politics of Radicalism 1832–1847* (Oxford, 1987).

Webb, R. K., *The British Working-Class Reader 1790–1848* (1955, New York, 1971).

Wells, R., 'Britain's Avoidance of Revolution in the 1790s Revisited', *Bulletin of the Society for the Study of Labour History*, vol. 54, no. 3 (Winter 1989).

'The Development of the English Rural Proletariat and Social Protest, 1700–1850', *The Journal of Peasant Studies*, vol. 6, no. 2 (January 1979).

Insurrection: The British Experience 1795–1803 (Gloucester, 1986).

'Resistance to the New Poor Law in the Rural South', in M. Chase (ed.), *The New Poor Law* (Middlesbrough, 1985).

'Rural Rebels in Southern England in the 1830s', in C. Emsley and J. Walvin (eds.), *Artisans, Peasants and Proletarians, 1760–1860* (1985).

'Social Protest, Class, Conflict and Consciousness, in the English Countryside,

1700–1880', in M. Reed and R. Wells (eds.), *Class, Conflict and Protest in the English Countryside, 1700–1880* (1990).

'Tolpuddle in the Context of English Agrarian Labour History, 1780–1850', in J. Rule (ed.), *British Trade Unionism: The Formative Years* (1988).

Wretched Faces: Famine in Wartime England 1793–1801 (Gloucester, 1988).

Wheeler, H. F. B., and Broadley, A. M. (eds.), *Napoleon and the Invasion of England*, 2 vols. (1908).

Wickwar, W. H., *The Struggle for the Freedom of the Press 1819–1832* (1928).

Wiener, M., *English Culture and the Decline of the Industrial Spirit* (Cambridge, 1981).

Wiles, P., 'A Syndrome, not a Doctrine: Some Elementary Theses on Populism', in G. Ionescu and E. Gellner (eds.), *Populism: Its Meaning and National Characteristics* (1969).

Wilgus, D. K., *Anglo-American Folksong Scholarship since 1898* (New Brunswick, NJ, 1959).

Williams, D., *John Frost: A Study in Chartism* (New York, 1969).

Williams, R., 'Between Country and City', in S. Pugh (ed.), *Reading Landscape* (Manchester, 1990).

The Country and the City (1973).

'Literature and Rural Society', *The Listener*, 16 November 1967.

Winstanley, M., 'Voices from the Past: Rural Kent at the Close of an Era', in G. E. Mingay (ed.), *The Victorian Countryside* (1981), II.

Woolf, D., 'The "Common Voice": History, Folklore and Oral Tradition in Early Modern England', *Past and Present*, no. 120 (August 1988).

Wright, P., *On Living in an Old Country* (1985).

Yates, M., 'Harry Upton: A Singer and his Repertoire', *Traditional Music*, no. 10 (1978).

'"Stand Up Ye Men of Labour": The Socio-Political Songs of Walter Pardon', *Musical Traditions*, no. 1 (mid-1983).

III Unpublished theses

Amos, S. W., 'Social Discontent and Agrarian Disturbances in Essex, 1795–1850' (MA thesis, University of Durham, 1971).

Birch, M. F., 'From Desperation to Conciliation: Agricultural Depression and County Politics, 1816–31' (PhD thesis, University of Cambridge, 1980).

Colson, A., 'The Revolt of the Hampshire Agricultural Labourers and its Causes, 1812–1831' (MA thesis, University of London, 1937).

Duff, G., 'William Cobbett's Agrarian Vision of National Reform' (PhD thesis, University of Illinois, 1966).

Dutt, M., 'The Agricultural Labourers' Revolt of 1830 in Kent, Surrey, and Sussex' (PhD thesis, University of London, 1967).

Kegel, C, 'Medieval–Modern Contrasts Used for a Social Purpose in the Work of William Cobbett, Robert Southey, A. Welby Pugin, Thomas Carlyle, John Ruskin and William Morris' (PhD thesis, University of Michigan, 1955).

McWilliam, R., 'The Tichborne Claimant and the People: Investigations into Popular Culture, 1867–1886' (PhD thesis, University of Sussex, 1990).

Miller, C. M., 'Farming, Farm Work, and Farm Workers in Victorian Gloucestershire' (PhD thesis, University of Bristol, 1980).

Richardson, T. L., 'The Standard of Living Controversy, 1790–1840, with Special Reference to the Agricultural Labourer in Seven English Counties' (PhD thesis, University of Hull, 1977).

Thomson, R. S., 'The Development of the Broadside Ballad Trade and its Influence upon the Transmission of Folk Songs' (PhD thesis, University of Cambridge, 1974).

Waligorski, C., 'Radical Traditionalism: William Cobbett in the Industrial Revolution' (PhD thesis, University of Wisconsin, 1973).

Windle, R., 'Hampshire Agrarian Society' (PhD thesis, Council for National Academic Awards, 1973).

INDEX

agricultural improvement, 19, 64, 68; C's views on, 108–9, 112, 137–8
agricultural meetings, 65–75, 81
agricultural protection, C opposes, 65–7
agricultural societies, 56, 109
agricultural workers: character of, 102–6; skills and importance of, 79–80, 101–2, 105–6; stereotype of, 6, 14, 15, 84, 96–87, 102, 104–5, 108, 190–2, 215–17, 267 n10
agriculture, importance of, 48–9, 51–3, 191–2, 199–200
Alberta, 11
allotments, 67, 124, 153, 181, 185–7
allowance system (Speenhamland), 36, 38, 138, 203–5
All-the-Talents, Ministry of, 34–5, 36, 39
almanacs, 82–3
Andover, 8, 9
anti-Cobbett tracts, 92, 94, 127, 140–1, 166, 256 n9; and Captain Swing, 168–71, 183, 185
anti-Jacobinism, v, 2, 7, 15, 16, 19, 20, 23, 28, 31, 92; C abandons, 31, 35, 41–2, 44; C defines, 41–2, 44, 237 n11
anti-Semitism, 10
Arch, Joseph, 75, 86, 100, 126, 216
Archer, John, 6
aristocracy, landed, C's attitude towards, 71–3
Armstrong, W. A., 74, 153, 161; quoted, 189, 191
Arnold, Matthew, 2, 6
Ashby, Elizabeth, 190
Ashby, Hannah, 113
Ashby, Joseph, 113, 116
Association for the Preservation of Liberty and Property against Republicans and Levellers, 26, 88, 233 n27
Attwood, Thomas, 5, 195
Australia, 182–3
autobiographies, working-class, 83–4, 86–7

bacon, 66, 106, 112, 114–16, 122, 127, 139, 145, 153, 188, 209–10; supposed attraction of Methodist preachers to, 97–9
Bagshot (Surrey), 97
bailiffs, farm, 62, 64, 166
Baker, Rev. Richard, 96
Ball, John, 13
ballot, 168
ballot system (military), 27
Bamford, Samuel, 13, 78
Baring, Bingham, 176–81
Baring, Francis Thornhill, 175, 177
Baring, Sir Thomas, 175–6, 177–82
barley, 51, 121, 140
Barn Elm farm, 139–42, 189
Barton Stacey (Hants), 174, 176, 198, 222
Battle (Suss.), 159, 167–8, 173, 184–5, 201, 261 n20
Bedfordshire, 156
beer, 92, 106, 114, 120–5, 130–1, 137, 142–3, 145, 166–7, 197, 200, 209–10, 212, 254 n80
bees, 30, 124, 156
Belchem, John, 5, 77
Belgian Revolution (1830), 160, 168, 171
Belloc, Hilaire, 127
Benenden (Kent), 97, 139
Benett, John, 67, 169, 177, 185
Berkshire, 32, 135, 205
Berlin, Isaiah, 10
Bewick, Thomas, 190
Bible, 82, 96–7, 102–3, 182, 194, 206, 247 n81
Birmingham Political Union, 195
birth control, 103
Bishop's Waltham (Hants), 110, 185
Blackstone, William, 205, 206
Bloomfield, Robert, 87–8
Blythe, Ronald, 126
Board of Agriculture, 78
Bohstedt, John, 40

Bolingbroke, Henry St John, 41
Bonaparte, Napoleon, 28–9, 89, 94
book-learning, 9, 86–9, 92, 94–5, 100–6
boroughmongers, 13, 33, 47, 192
Botley (Hants), 21, 22, 33, 34, 38–9, 49, 78, 96, 110, 113, 123, 139–45, 175, 194, 253 n51
bread, 29–30, 34, 92, 98, 106, 113–14, 119, 122, 127, 131, 145, 153, 166, 183, 209–10
'Bread or Blood' riots (1816), 106, 152
Brede (Suss.), 167, 169
brewing, 39, 66, 120–4, 139–43, 145, 194, 201, 209–10, 254 n80, 255 n91, 259 n61
Briggs, Asa, 2
Brighton, 174–5
British Columbia, 11
Britton, John, 87
broadsheet *Register*, 77–9, 81–3, 84–6, 87–106, 114, 244 n22
broadsides, 9, 25; C uses broadside format, 25, 78–9, 81–2, 84–6, 88–9, 92, 95–6, 208, 219–21, 245 n31
Brougham, Henry, 81, 101, 105, 107, 169
Buckinghamshire, 156
Buckmaster, John, 100, 101, 209–10
bull-baiting, 20, 21, 22, 105, 234 nn43–4
Bullington (Hants), 171, 174, 182, 184, 222
Bulwer, Edward Lytton, 104, 191
Burdett, Sir Francis, 4, 28, 32, 41–2, 76, 216, 243 n6
Burgess, Jesse, 141
Burgoyne, Montagu, 121
Burke, Edmund, 18, 32, 39, 90, 192
Burstow, Henry, 190

Calhoun, Craig, 11, 12
Cambridgeshire, 15, 185
Canada, 11
Canning, George, 19
capitalism, C seeks to modify and reduce, 49–50, 67–75, 109, 111, 113, 116–24, 138–51, 156
Captain Swing revolt, 4, 67, 71, 74, 81, 152–89, 192, 194–8
Carlile, Richard, 4, 150; and Captain Swing, 162, 262 n30, 262 n44
Carnarvon, Lord Henry George Herbert, 169, 171, 189
Caroline, Queen, 5, 10, 42, 77, 195, 243 n5
Carpenter, William, 194–5
Carrington, John, 137
Carter, Jimmy, 10
Carter, Joseph, 142, 175

Cartwright, John, 4, 13, 42
Catholic Association, 128
Catholic Emancipation, 128–30
Catnach, James, 239 n32
Cato Street Conspiracy, 5
Chadwick, Edwin, 205, 211
Chamberlayne, John, 20
chapbooks, 9, 27, 82, 84, 126–7, 147, 219, 244 n22
Charlesworth, Andrew, 157, 160
Chase, Malcolm, xv, 6, 229 n6
Cheap Repository Tract Society, 89, 94
Chesterton, G. K., 2, 6, 11, 127, 130
chopstick festival, 197–8, 208, 211
chopsticks, 3, 4, 5, 13, 39, 79, 96, 157, 183, 196, 212, 229 n9
Christianity, C's view of, 43–4, 96–7, 104, 128–30
Church of England, C's attitude towards, 96, 128–30
Clapham, J. H., 119, 153
Clare, John, 66, 85, 86, 91, 104, 193, 249 n129, 256 n8
class consciousness: C at first resists, 45–6, 47–8; C discovers and develops, 3, 5, 6, 11, 12, 23, 90, 104, 138, 156–7, 160, 191, 196, 202, 206–12; emerges among labourers and farmers, 52–75; absent in cheap *Register*, 79–81; in C's historiography, 127; and Captain Swing, 164–6, 177, 182; and Poor Law, 209; *see also* countryman consciousness
Cleave, John, 194
clergy: C and, 42, 96–9; and Captain Swing, 176, 182
Cobbett, James Paul (C's third son), 16, 231–2 n3
Cobbett, John Morgan (C's second son), 116, 183
Cobbett, Nancy (C's wife), 16, 91, 100, 184
Cobbett, William: boyhood, v, 14, 147; appearance, 14–15, 16, 68, 232 n3; as ploughboy, 14, 15, 121; early reading, 232 n3; in army, v, 2, 7, 15, 16, 23, 27, 232 n15, 86; as anti-Jacobin, v, 3, 17, 18, 19, 20, 25; returns to England and is discharged from army (1791), 17, 232 n16; and United States, v, 1, 17–20, 23, 29, 31–2, 42, 46, 77, 90, 92, 116–17, 156; arrives again in England (1800), v, 1, 3, 18–19; in Newgate (1810–12), 77, 139–40; as farmer, 12, 38, 39, 62, 67–9, 101, 108–10, 113, 139–45; as employer, 139–46, 259 nn66, 69; opposes enclosure, 111, 116–17, 124; flees to America (1817), 77, 92; turns to

radicalism, 19–43; pitches discourse to popular audience, 76–106; launches cheap *Register*, 78–9, 81, 84–6; as writer, 78–86, 94, 100; and country cottage, 107–24; veneration for old England, 125–51; and Captain Swing, 152–89; 1831 trial, 169–70, 184–9; in Parliament, 199–203; as reformer and representative of cottage charter, 190–212

COBBETT'S WRITINGS: *Address to Journeymen and Labourers*, 78–9, 82, 89; *Advice to the Chopsticks*, 208; *Advice to Young Men*, 1; autobiography (unpublished), 143–4, 201–2; *Cottage Economy*, 1, 107–24; *Eleven Lectures on the French and Belgian Revolutions*, 262 n30; *Emigrant's Guide*, 156, 249 n124; *French Grammar*, 9; *Grammer of the English Language*, 7, 104–6; *Important Considerations*, 25, 26, 27, 235 n55, 89; *Letter to the King*, 170–1; *Letter to the Luddites*, 81; *Life and Adventures*, 18, 19; *Manchester Lectures*, 195; *Political Register*, 1, 4, 19, 20, 28, 29, 67, 70, 78–9, 81–2, 89, 97, 103, 105, 115, 122, 166, 169–71, 181, 186, 190, 198, 213; 'Poor Man's Bible' (unpublished), 96, 247 n84; *Porcupine*, 19, 233 n28; *Porcupine's Works*, 1; *Protestant 'Reformation'*, 128–35, 177; *Rural Rides*, 1; *Sermons*, 96, 247 n81, 84; *Soldier's Friend*, 232 n15; *Surplus Population*, 103–4; *Treatise on Corn*, 108, 115–18, 183, 253 n51, 253 n56; two-penny *Register*, 78–9, 81–8, 91, 105, 169–71, 243 n7, 244 n12, 247 n58; *Two-Penny Trash*, 94, 169–71, 174, 181, 188; *Year's Residence*, 9

Cobbett Jr, William, 146

Cobbett's Corn, 108, 115–18, 183, 253 n51, 253 n56

Coke, Thomas (Coke of Norfolk), 3, 62, 68, 73, 108–9, 111, 121

Cole, G. D. H., 4, 169

Colley, Linda, 46

commerce, 10, 13, 18; C's contempt for, 18, 49–53, 60, 150, 239 n26

common land, 20, 30–1, 39, 109–12, 156, 185, 210

common rights, 20, 30–1, 39, 111–12

conservatism, C's form of, 2, 3, 17–19, 22–3, 24, 35, 39–40, 44, 125–6, 147, 150–1, 209, 214–15

consolation, as function of folk song, 92

Cook, Henry, 152, 176, 177–81, 184, 197

Cook, John, 177–8, 184

Cook, Ruth, 177–8, 184

Cooper, James, 181

Co-operative Commonwealth Federation (CCF), 11

Corn Bill (1815), C opposes, 66–8, 241 n76

Corn Laws, 65–8, 200

cottage, dispossession of, 14, 29–31, 130–7, 147–51

cottage agriculture, 30–2, 39, 108–24

cottage charter, 6, 12, 13, 145, 153, 157, 186, 197, 200–5, 209–12, 216–17; Richard Jefferies's use of phrase, 230 n22

cottage industry, 49, 108, 122–4, 140

cottagers, 30, 110–13

country gentlemen, 10, 13, 21–3, 33, 41; and sports, 20–1

countryman, C as, 5, 7, 25, 28, 40, 46, 47–51, 156

countryman consciousness, 46–8, 50–69, 72–4, 120, 126, 157, 191, 202, 208–11, 215, 238 n12, 269 n67; *see also* class consciousness

Country platform, 5, 6, 9, 10, 13, 17, 18, 20–3, 24, 28, 30; early mandate of *Political Register*, 28–9; gradually abandoned, 32, 33, 39, 41

Country Tories, 10, 22, 23, 24, 32, 37, 39–40

Cowherd, James, 140, 143

cow-keeping, 30, 33, 36, 39, 112, 115, 156, 168

Cumberland, 192

Cunningham, Hugh, 23

Davies, David, 120, 135

Deacle, Mr and Mrs (Hampshire farmers), 178, 181

Dead-Body Bill, 153–4, 168

Dean, John, 143

deference, 71–3, 98, 161, 214

deism, C's attitude towards, 42, 87

Denman, Sir Thomas, 169, 170, 177

Devon, 139

Dibdin, Charles, 58, 88, 240 n46

Dickens, Charles, 40

Dickinson, H. T., 32, 89

Diddams, Enos, 175, 178

diet, 27, 107–24

'distillery question', 51

Dorset, 115, 136

Drake, Francis, 25

Duck, Stephen, 86–7, 145

Eastbourne (Suss.), 168

Eden, quests for, 125–8
Eden, Sir F. M., 113, 119, 121, 136–7
Edinburgh Review, 107–8, 114, 123
education, 9, 86, 200, 249 n133; C's
    attitude towards, 100–6; C defines,
    100–1; and Samuel Whitbread, 35–8
effeminacy, 46–7, 119–20; C opposes,
    20–2, 27, 28
Egan, Pierce, 21
Egremont, Lord George O'Brien
    Wyndham, 69
Eliot, George, 190
Elizabeth, Queen, 20, 131–2
Ellenborough, Lord Edward Law, 68
Ellman, John, 120, 137, 253 n46
Ellman Jr, John, 69, 137
emigration, 156, 159, 211
enclosure: C supports, 19; C opposes,
    30–1, 109–10, 112–13, 145, 149,
    155–6, 168, 186–7; C quarrels with
    Arthur Young over, 51, 87
enfranchisement of rural workers, C calls
    for, 68, 124, 168, 195–7, 199, 268 n35
Engels, Frederick, 106
Englishness, 22–3, 28–9, 41, 42–3, 45–7,
    125–8, 215
Essex, 121, 205
Evangelicals, 3, 21, 22, 23; C's contempt
    for, 22, 23, 46
Evans, George Ewart, 84

Fabianism, 11
factories, 4–5, 81, 195, 199–200
Factory Commission, 200
fair play, 22, 23, 40, 46, 82, 120, 140
farmer, C as, 12, 38, 39, 62, 67–9, 101,
    108–10, 113, 116, 120, 122, 139–46,
    251 n33, 253 n51, 259 nn66, 69
farmers: C's attitudes towards large, 111,
    116, 117, 124; C and labourers like
    small, 64–5, 69, 72, 110, 116, 123–4,
    139, 157, 186–7, 193, 208–12; prosper
    in wartime, 19, 39, 56–65, 137–8; reject
    radicalism, 39; C associates with at
    Botley, 39–40; C defends new-fashioned
    ones, 45; and class consciousness, 51,
    53–9, 137, 145, 210–12; conflict with
    labourers, 53–5, 61–2; avoid work, 53,
    56, 59; benevolent ones, 53, 55, 210;
    promote class society, 39, 51, 137–8,
    160; C quarrels with Arthur Young
    over, 51; and luxuries, 62–3, 64–6, 109,
    137–8; and improvements, 108–9; resist
    living-in, 64–5; and agricultural
    meetings, 65–75; suffer from post-war
    prices, 65–6; relationship with urban
    middle class, 65–8; and popular

literature, 82–4, 88–9; songs of, 56–8;
    and Captain Swing, 152–89; and
    Reform Bill, 194–208; in United States,
    18
Farmer's Journal, 116
farm servants, 7, 64–5, 139–43
Farnham (Surr.), 119, 130–1, 136, 142,
    181; C's boyhood at, v, 14–15, 18, 19,
    20, 30, 32; C praises 'Bourners', 111; C
    speaks at, 69
Federalist faction (US), 18
feudal dues, C's view of, 129–31
Fielden, John, 4, 199–201, 208, 268 n45,
    269 n50, 269 n60
finances, C begins to study, 9, 10, 11, 30,
    42
fires, 155, 159, 162, 166, 168–9, 177,
    185–6
Firle (Suss.), 96
Fitton, William, 268 nn45–6
Fleming, Willis, 121
Foot, Michael, 2
forest workers, 112–13, 251 n23, 251 n25
Fortescue, Sir John, 257 n15
Foster, John, 200, 268 n46
France: C's attitude towards, 17, 19, 44,
    89, 131–2, 159, 160, 168; and invasion
    threat of British Isles, 24–7, 41–2, 51–2
freeborn Englishmen, 24, 194
French Revolutionary Wars, 17, 139
Frend, William, 28
Frost, John, 104
fuel, 31, 111–13, 140, 168
funding system, 13, 30, 33

game laws, 71, 168, 186, 200, 206–8
gardens, 30, 39, 102, 109–15, 119, 122,
    140–2, 185–6, 206
Gibbon, Edward, 127, 135
Gifford, William, 88
Gilpin, William, 112
Gladstone, William, 40, 269 n58
Gloucestershire, 115, 121, 169
golden age theory, 10, 126–51
Goldsmith, Oliver, 41
Goodman, Thomas, 168–9, 172–3, 263
    nn66–7
Goody, Jack, 85–6
Goudhurst (Kent), 97
grammar: C and French, 9; C's study of, 7,
    17, 86–7, 104–6
Gramsci, Antonio, 47
Green, A. E., 98
Grenville, Lord William Wyndham, 34–5,
    36
Grey, Lord Charles, 195, 196

Halévy, Elie, 100

Hamilton, Alexander, 18
Hammond, J. L. and B., 6
Hampden Clubs, 76
Hampshire, 21, 29–31, 32, 33, 35, 112, 117, 160; and Captain Swing, 162–6, 169–89; and Reform Bill, 194, 198–201
Hampshire Special Commission, 174, 176, 178, 180-1
Hansard's Parliamentary Debates, 1, 37
'hard parishes', 171, 174–89, 197–9, 222–7
Hardy, Thomas (novelist), 116, 138, 229 n9
Harrison, J. F. C., xv
harvest home, 58–60, 63, 137; songs at, 58–9, 210, 240 n47
Hawker, James, 126, 206
Hazlitt, William, 6, 15, 87
Heath, Richard, 6
Herbert, George, 83
Hetherington, Henry, 195, 268 n43
Highclere (Hants), 169
Hill, Christopher, 127, 147
Hill, Sir Richard, 22
Himmelfarb, Gertrude, 4
historical consciousness, popular, 126–8
history, C's sense of, 125–51
Hobsbawm, Eric, 8, 189
'Hodge', stereotype of, 6, 14–15, 84, 86–7, 102, 104–5, 108, 190–2, 215–17, 267 n10
Hodges, Thomas Law, 139
Honiton (Devon), 35
Horton Heath (Hants), 30–2, 37
household producers, 31, 109–10, 112–13, 124
Howitt, William, 84, 119, 146–7, 191, 229 n9
Howkins, Alun, xv, 6, 156
Howlett, Rev. John, 136
Hudson, W. H., 122
Hume, David, 127, 128, 130, 135, 256 n9
humour, C and, 98–9
Hunt, Henry, 4, 5, 13, 66, 77, 87, 117, 142, 143, 150, 162, 183, 197, 216, 241 n76, 242 n92, 243 n4, 262 n44
husbandman, C's and labourers' use of word, 52–4, 239 n33
Huskisson, William, 19

Ignatieff, Michael, 147
Indian corn, 108, 115–18, 183, 253 n51, 253 n56
industrial manufactures, 48, 49, 81, 123, 150–1, 169, 198–200
industrial workers, 4–5, 49, 81–2, 84, 94–5, 160–1, 195, 198–201

Ingrams, Richard, 2
Innes, Joanna, xv, 136, 191, 258 n44, 266 n8
internationalism, 42–3, 46
invasion threat, 20, 24, 25, 26, 27–9
Ireland, 209
Isle of Thanet, 112, 121
Isle of Wight, 115
Ives, James, 102

Jackson's Oxford Journal, 135
'Jack the Giant-Killer', 84
James, Louis, 230 n38
Jefferies, Richard, 122, 217, 230 n23
Jefferson, Thomas, 18
Jenkinson, Robert (Lord Liverpool), 19
John Bull, 46, 89, 238 nn9–10
Johnson, Richard, 214
Johnson, Samuel, 10, 12, 23, 28, 41
Jones, David, 6

Keats, John, 7
Keith, W. J., 230 n24
Kensington, C farms at, 109
Kent, 115, 117, 121, 123, 152, 156, 160, 166–9, 181
'King of the Norfolk Poachers', 126
Kitchen, Fred, 101
Knatchbull, Sir Edward, 181
Knight, Charles, 84–5, 95, 200, 268 n46
Kramnick, Isaac, 9

Labourer's Friend Society, 185–6
labour theory of value, 12, 48–9, 50, 162
Lancashire, 103, 160–1
landlords, 13, 64–5, 71–3, 138, 156
Leicestershire, 169
Leveridge, Richard, 131, 133
Lewes (Suss.), 70–1
Lincolnshire, 115
Lingard, Dr John, 128, 256 n13
literacy, 5, 82–8; C's attitude towards, 100–6
living-in, 7, 64–5, 66, 71, 139, 145, 149, 186
Lloyd, A. L., 219–20, 246 n48
Lloyd George, David, 10, 40
local attachments, 8, 9, 190–4
Locke, John, 205
Lomax, Alan, 220
London, 33, 47, 77, 88, 157–61, 165, 194–201
Loveless, George, 201
Lovell, David, 179
Lovett, William, 95
Luddites, 4, 50, 81, 169

machinery, 81, 94, 199–200; *see also* threshing machines

Macrae, Donald, 10
McWilliam, Rohan, xv
Maidstone (Kent), 194
magic, 82–4
malt duty, 71, 120–2, 135, 186, 200,
209–10, 269 n53
Malthus, Thomas, 32, 37, 94, 102–4
Manchester, 199–201
manliness, 20–2, 27, 28, 46–7, 119–20
Marshall, Charles, 209
Marshall, William, 101, 120, 136
Marx, Karl, 2, 5, 13, 46, 47, 50, 73, 106,
147, 215–17
Mason, Joseph, 171, 174, 176, 182–9,
197, 216
Mason, Mrs, 171, 182, 183, 184
Mason, Robert, 171, 176, 177, 182–9,
197, 216
Massingham, H. J., 6
Mechanics' Institutes, 94–5
medieval England, C's attitude towards,
128–30, 257 nn15, 17
Melbourne, Lord, and Captain Swing,
198–9, 268 n42, 270 n76
merchants, C's and labourer's view of, 19,
41, 50, 52
Methodism, 46; C's hostility towards,
96–100, 123
Micheldever (Hants), 171, 175, 177, 184,
198
middleman, 81
Middlesex platform, 28, 41
Mills, Dennis, 109
monarchy, C's view of, 42
monasteries, 128–30
Moore's Almanac, 82–3, 95, 98
Moore's Prophecies, 83
moral economy, 81, 138, 202–3
More, Hannah: C approves of M's
writings, 24–5, 39, 90; C disapproves
of, 89–94, 166, 219, 247 n58
Morning Chronicle, 185, 213–14
Morton, J. B., 6

'nation', idea of, 38, 44–6, 127
National Agricultural Labourers' Union,
75, 217
national debt, 13, 30, 33, 81, 171; and
labourers' understanding of, 192–4
National Regeneration Society, 200–1
National Union of the Working Classes,
105, 195–6, 198–9, 268 n42
New Brunswick, C there as soldier, v, 15
Newby, Howard, 5
New Forest cottagers, 111–12
Newgate prison, C there (1810–12), 77
New South Wales, 182–3

Norfolk, 169, 171
Normany farm (Ash, Surr.), 139–42, 189
'Norman Yoke', 130, 147
Northamptonshire, 185
Northiam (Suss.), 167
Northington (Hants), 176, 179
Norwich, agricultural meeting at (1821),
68
nostalgia, 125–51

Obelkevich, James, 5
O'Connell, Daniel, 128
'Old Corruption', 7–8, 28, 33, 87–8; see
also pensions; sinecures
Old England, 6, 13, 32, 125–51, 156, 161,
185; see also historical consciousness;
history; nostalgia
Oldham, C represents in House of
Commons, 199–202
Oldham electors, 105
Oldham Political Association, 200
Old Sarum, 7
oral culture, 9, 27, 53, 77, 83–6, 95–100,
105–6, 130–3, 137, 147, 194; C as
story-teller, 97–8, 115–16, 260 n76
Orkney Islands, 123
Osborne, Sidney Godolphin, 217
Otmoor enclosure, 155
ovens, 113, 251 nn33, 140
Overton (Hants), 166, 175
Owen, Robert, 4, 147, 195, 217
Owenite co-operation, 11, 124, 195
Owslebury (Hants), 190

Paine, Thomas, 13, 17, 18, 19, 77, 84,
147, 217, 221, 233 n21; C favours P's
economic and political thought, 42–4; C
retrieves P's bones, 42–4; P's works: Age
of Reason, 42, Decline and Fall of the
English System of Finance, 30, 235 n76,
233 n23, 237 n113; Rights of Man, 18,
19
paper money, 10, 13, 30, 33; labourers'
view of, 193
parish carts, 69, 152–3, 159, 166–8, 181,
189, 196, 242 n100
parish overseers, 69, 128, 150, 153, 159,
169
Parker, Martin, 145
Parliament, C's career in, 199–203
parliamentary debates, C studies, 28
parliamentary reform, 10–13, 32–3; C
moves towards, 41–2, 78–81, 87; C
advances the movement towards, 96,
150, 167–72, 193–200; and Captain
Swing, 175, 182–3; petition of hard
parishes, 186, 222–7

paternalism, 36, 39, 140, 150–1, 195
patriotism: C's approach to, 17, 19, 20, 23, 24, 26–7, 28–9, 38, 41–2, 46–7, 88–90; and tract writers, 94, 131, 215
pauperism, 20, 32, 33, 35, 38–9; drives C towards radicalism, 32–3, 39; C observes and laments, 69–73, 114, 130–2, 145, 152–3, 166–9, 202–5
peasant: concept of, 5, 6, 7, 10, 13, 47, 74, 79, 107, 109–10, 113, 123–4, 150–1, 215, 250 n11, 250 n28; *see also* household producers
peasant poets, 84–90
Peel, Robert, 120
Pennsylvania, 18
Penny Magazine (SDUK), 95
pensions, 33, 41, 71, 81; and labourers' understanding of, 192–4, 197, 222–7
'people's history', 129–30
Perkin, Harold, 21
Peron, Juan, 10
Peterloo Massacre, 5, 77
Philadelphia, 17
Phillips, Sir Richard, 143
Physiocrats, 49
Pickering, Michael, 219
pigs, 30, 111–12, 115–16, 119, 122, 140, 147, 156, 210, 251 n24, 253 nn46–7, 253 n49
Pitt, William (the Younger), 1, 10, 17–19, 23–4, 27–30; C approves of, 25–6; introduces 'taxing and pauperizing system', 33, 35, 39, 40–2, 49; and Poor Law reform, 33–4, 88; P's 'system', 13, 19, 23–4, 33, 40
Place, Francis, 4, 76, 88–9, 150, 164–6, 171, 181, 215, 217, 229 n12, 264 n79, 268 n42
placemen, 9, 28, 197
plough, importance of, 51–2, 53–6
plum pudding, 135, 137, 197
poaching, 108, 165, 206, 208
Pocock, J. G. A., 10
Poland, 42–3
Poor Law, 20, 32–3; and Whitbread's proposals of reform, 36–9; pauper badge, 37; directs and shapes C's radicalism, 37–9, 78, 94, 114, 122, 130, 139, 150, 152–4, 159; abuse of, 166–7, 185–6, 269 n69, 270 n76, 270 n81; C opposes Amendment Act, 202–6, 208–9
poor-rates: C thinks proof of idleness, 19; C identifies abuses in allowance system, 24, 25, 32, 68–9, 130–1, 137–9, 159, 166–8, 204–5
Pope, Alexander, 10, 17, 23, 28, 41
populism, 9. 10, 11, 12, 42, 192, 209, 214–15

Porcupine, Peter (C's pseudonym in US), v, 18, 90
Portsmouth, 15
potatoes, 66, 98, 106, 107, 112, 115, 118–20, 143, 145, 153–4, 161–3, 166, 181, 196, 197, 210, 254 n60; and Captain Swing, 166–7, 176, 192
poultry, 30–1
Powell, Enoch, 10
Pratt, Samuel Jackson, 44
'pre-industrial' protest, 81, 92, 157–8, 160, 244 n15
Preston, 9
prices, C studies long-term movements in, 29–30
Priestley, Joseph, 42
Primitive Methodists, 100
primogeniture, 72
printed culture, 27, 83–6, 88–9, 91–2, 94–8, 100–6, 131–5, 244 n22
producers, C's definitions of, 12, 48–50, 53, 238 n15
progress, C's and labourers' idea of, 147, 150–1
proletarians, 7, 10, 72, 98, 108–9, 111–13, 190, 210
property rights, 205–9
Protestant Reformation, C's view of, 128–30, 205
psalm-singing, 96
public houses, 82, 88, 97, 120–1, 142–3, 169–71

Quarterly Review, 107

racism, 10, 35
radicalism, C moves towards, 19–45, 214–15; among farm workers, 5, 6, 83–6; defined, 39–40, 214–15
readership, C's, 82, 85–6, 169–71, 244 n22, 245 n32
Reay, Barry, 6
Reed, Mick, xv, 6, 31, 64, 74, 109
Reeves, John, 19, 26, 233 n27
Reform Bill, 1, 195–200, 208, 268 n37
religious tracts, 91–2, 94–100, 104–6, 123, 153, 246 n55; C composes his own, 95
Republican faction (US), 18
republicanism: C's view of, 17, 19, 42; and Robert Bloomfield, 87
revolution, 168, 175–6, 184; C predicts, 201, 208–9
Richardson, Ruth, xv, 260 n83
Ringmer (Suss.), 166
roast beef, 20, 51–2, 92, 131–5, 137, 183, 213, 257 n25
Robin Goodfellow, 83

Robin Hood stories, 82, 219
Roebuck, John, 105
Rogers, J. E. Thorold, 130
Roman Catholicism, C's attitude towards, 128–30
Romantics, interpretation of C by, 7
Rose, Walter, 115
Rotunda, 160, 262 n30, 195; *see also* urban platform
Rousseau, Jean-Jacques, 42–3
Royal Jubilee, 39
Royle, Edward, xv
Rubinstein, W. D., 10, 231 n45
Rudé, George, 189
rural imagery, C's inability to escape, 81
rural writer, C as, 6–7, 126–7, 145–6
Russell, Lord John, 128
Rye (Suss.), 184

Sadler, Michael, 214
Salisbury, 69
salt, 122, 255 n94
Saskatchewan, 11
Saxon constitution, 130
scarcity, 19, 29–30, 32, 78, 90, 94, 110, 114, 137
Scotland, C and, 114, 195, 208
Scott, Sir Walter, 62, 130
Select Vestries Acts (1817–18), 202
self-help, 108, 109
Senior, Nassau, 202
Settlement Acts, 130, 202
Sharp, Cecil, 98
sheep, 30; C imports, 108, 250 n6
Shelley, Percy B., 7
Sheridan, Richard, 24
shopkeepers, C opposes, 109, 114–15, 122
Shropshire, 120
Sidmouth, Lord (Henry Addington), 77, 244 n22
Sinclair, Sir John, 119
sinecures, 9, 13, 28, 33, 71, 81, 171, 192–4; and labourers' understanding of, 222–7
single-stick, C patronizes, 21, 22, 105, 234 n38
slave trade, 35
smallholders, 5, 10, 11, 72, 109–10, 197
Smart, Thomas, 122
Smith, Adam, 202
Smith, Olivia, 4–5, 39
Smith, William, 164
Snell, K. D. M., xv, 6, 66, 137, 205
Social Credit, 11
Society of Arts, 123
Society for the Diffusion of Useful Knowledge, 36, 94–5, 105, 219, 264 n79

Somerville, Alexander, 119, 126, 142, 248 n116
song, 9, 56–65, 67, 72–4, 82, 84–6, 90–4, 98, 147, 153, 190, 193, 198, 206–7, 244 n22, 244 n31, 246 n48; anti-Cobbett songs, 88–9, 94; and the Captain Swing revolt, 162–5, 171, 186–7, 197; and the English past, 126, 131–5, 147–50, 219–21; farmers' songs, 88–9; labourers and psalm-singing, 96; loyalist, 88–9; and radical thought, 9
song-leaders, 86
Southampton, 18, 25
Southey, Robert, 7, 62, 87, 88, 107, 150–1
spade husbandry, 115
Spa Fields, 5, 77
Spater, George, xv, 19
Special Commissions (1831), 174, 176–7, 182–3, 199
Spence, William, author of *Britain Independent of Commerce* (1808), 49–50
Spenceans, 76, 124; C's sympathy with, 209
Sporting Magazine, 21, 22
sports, 20–4, 29, 46, 234 n38
stamp laws, 78, 82, 85
Stationers' Company, 53
Stephen, Leslie, 6
Stevenson, John, 77, 243 n5
Stevenson, William, 101, 211
stock-jobbers, 9, 41, 47, 192
Stoke Charity (Hants), 171, 175
story-teller, C as, 97–8, 115–16, 130–1, 194
straw-plait, C promotes, 123–4
Sturt, George, 6, 126
Suffolk, 169, 190, 197
Sunday coat, 31, 106, 131, 147, 196, 210
superstitions, 83–4, 90, 91, 95, 98, 100, 112
Surrey, 68, 157, 165, 169, 199, 211; *see also* Farnham
Sussex, 32, 69–73, 103–4, 112, 114, 117, 130, 156, 160, 166–9, 184–5, 192, 198–9, 201
Sussex farmers, C quarrels with, 69–71, 137, 242 n103
Sutton Scotney (Hants), 171, 175–6, 197
Swift, Jonathan, 10, 17, 23, 28

Tawney, R. H., 127
taxes, 28, 30, 33, 41–2, 68, 81, 114–15, 120–2, 159, 171, 194, 197, 200, 209–11, 222–7
Taylor, A. J. P., 2
Taylor, Sir Herbert, 174–5

tea, 66, 107, 113, 119–22, 139, 142, 153–4, 210
Thelwall, John, 13
Thompson, Dorothy, xv
Thompson, Edward, xv, 2, 3, 4, 11, 12, 40, 76, 100, 230 n27
Thompson, Flora: and harvest home, 58; and pigs, 115; and beer, 122
threshing machines, 159, 162, 165, 166, 168–9, 175–6, 264 n79
Tichborne case, 10
Tilly, Benjamin, 259 n58
Times (London), 116, 123, 168, 213–14, 216
tithes, 68–9, 72, 159, 171, 177, 197, 200, 205, 222–7
Tolpuddle Martyrs, 201, 217, 268 n42
Tooke, John Horne, 42
Tory Radicalism, deficiences of phrase as relates to C, 2, 3, 35, 39–40, 125–6, 147, 150–1, 209, 214–15; *see also* conservatism
town worker, 5, 49, 81–2, 84, 94–5, 160–1, 195–201, 208
trade unionism, C's understanding of, 4, 12, 100, 189, 198–201, 216–18, 268 n42
tradition, C's use of, 11, 12, 27, 100, 106, 116, 132–3, 161, 205, 219–21
transportation, 176–7, 180, 182–5
Treason and Seditious Practices Acts, 1, 28
Trevor, Arthur, 186–7
Trimmer, Sarah, 91
Tull, Jethro, 108, 111
Tunbridge Wells (Kent), 112
Tuscany, 123
Tyler, Wat, 13

United States, 17, 18, 90; C's attitude towards, 17, 19–20, 23, 29; C resides in, 17, 18, 42, 77, 92, 116–17; condition of farmers in, 18, 31–2; enlists its support for English radicalism, 46, 156; labourers' view of, 211
urban platform, 28, 32, 40, 77, 81, 150, 157, 200–1; and Captain Swing, 160–5, 183, 194–200, 216–17
Utilitarianism, 5, 36, 76; and Poor Law reform, 202

Vancouver, Charles, 112
Vaughan, Sir John, 177
Vice Society, 88
Vincent, David, 230 n39
Virgil, 126
volunteers, 27, 28

wages, C's concern about, 29–30, 34–5,
37, 62, 64, 81, 198, 236 n7, 236–7 n96; and cottage charter, 200–1; effects of Captain Swing revolt on, 184–5, 202, 205; labourers' real wages, 66, 135–8, 153, 258 n14
Walpole, Robert, 10
Waltham Chase, 110–11, 250 nn13, 185
Warwickshire, 185
Waterloo, Battle of, 77, 79
Watson, James, 76
Wealth of Nations, 202
Weaver, S. A., 269 n60
Wellington, Duke of, 164–5, 189, 195, 198, 268 n43
Wells, Roger, xv, 6, 40, 74, 126, 160, 268 n42
Wesley, John, 83, 97, 98, 119; C's similarities to, 100; *see also* Methodism
Wesleyans, 99–100; *see also* Methodism
Westminster election (1804), 28, 32
Whigs, 3, 10, 183, 185; C cautiously supports in 1806, 35–8; develops mistrust of, 94–5; as educators, 84–5, 94–5, 101, 105, 107–8, 113; and historiography, 127–8; opposed to the beer of old England, 120; and Reform Bill, 195–9; and Tolpuddle Martyrs, 201
Whitbread, Samuel, 36–8, 202
Wilberforce, William, 22, 24, 35–6, 94
Wiles, Peter, 10
William IV, King, 173
Williams, Raymond, 2, 6, 7, 126, 214
Wilson, David, 228 n5, 230 n40
Wiltshire, 32, 62, 112, 113, 122, 169
Winchester, 176–7, 181, 184
Winchester Cathedral, 130–1
Windham, William, 19, 21, 22, 23; and volunteers, 27; as C's patron and mentor, 19, 20, 32, 33; supports popular sports, 20–2; C moves away from, 33, 36, 37, 150
Winstanley, Gerrard, 13
witches, 100, 106
women, 8, 12, 62, 114–16, 122
Wonston (Hants), 171, 174, 222
Wordsworth, William, 7, 130
workhouses, 168, 194, 206
working-class improvers, 17, 126–7

Wright, Rev. Robert, 184
Wykeham, William of, 130–1

Yates, Michael, 240 n51

Yeo, Eileen, xv
Yeo, Stephen, xv
Young, Arthur, 50–1, 101, 119, 191,
    236–7 n96, 253 n51, 266 n8

DATE DUE